Selected Letters of
Cotton Mather

Selected Letters of Cotton Mather

COMPILED WITH COMMENTARY BY

KENNETH SILVERMAN

LOUISIANA STATE UNIVERSITY PRESS

Baton Rouge

For Willa and Ethan

ISBN 0-8071-0920-7
Library of Congress Catalog Card Number 78-142338
Copyright © 1971 by Louisiana State University Press
All rights reserved
Manufactured in the United States of America
Printed by Vail-Ballou Press, Inc.

90144

IT WAS AN observation long since made by a renowned Ancient, That our Lord Jesus Christ gave the most sensible and pathetic manifestations of His love to the youngest of His disciples. . . . since 'tis especially by printing of sermons that I labor to give the most provocation to the Devil, 'twill be no more surprise to me if I find the Devil assaying by the printing of slanders to take his revenges on me.

—"The Young Man's Glory," in *Addresses to Old Men, and Young Men, and Little Children* (1690)

YOU ARE conformed unto your Saviour in your watchful endeavors to do good, and be fruitful in every good work. But your conformity unto Him yet lacks one thing; that is, after all, to be despised and rejected of men, and patiently to bear the contempt, and malice, and abuses of an untoward generation. . . . 'Tis an excellent thing to come to nothing. If you hear the hopes of disaffected men, to see you come to nothing, hear it with as much of satisfaction as they can hope it. Embrace *exinanitions*; embrace *annihilations*.

—*Bonifacius. An Essay upon the Good* (1710)

OF ALL THE arts that are understood and professed among the children of men: Yea, of those arts in the mysteries whereof some have bidden a rich price to be instructed, there will be none found comparable to this holy skill of sacrificing. I will call upon you, in the ancient language, Oh, Come and taste, and see how gracious the Lord will be unto the Sacrificer. And be it known unto you, nothing so comfortable, nothing so profitable, as the Heavenly skill of Sacrificing. All our enjoyments themselves, none of them all so valuable as the skill of Sacrificing all.

—*The Sacrificer* (1714)

HIS OWN kindred had those among them who maltreated Him and called Him all that was bad. I find by travellers, the Jews to this day make this their great offense against Him. *He went about doing of Good;* yet a great part of mankind conspired for to treat Him as an evil doer. Tho' He could not challenge all men living to tax Him with the least ill thing, yet He was *numbered with transgressors;* He was crucified between *two robbers;* from whence Hierocles, almost three hundred years after, published and fomented a tradition that He was a highwayman, the head of a desperate crew of *banditti.* Thus a Generation of Vipers, the most remarkable set of the Seed of the Serpent that had been in any generation, stung the *Holy, Harmless, Undefiled* JESUS!

—*The Right Way to Shake off a Viper.*
An Essay upon a Case too commonly calling for Consideration;
What shall Good Men do, when they are Evil spoken of? (1720)

Contents

Introduction

THE SURVIVING LETTERS of Cotton Mather represent the largest extant correspondence of any American Puritan figure. This selection of his letters is the product of a search which covered fifteen states and twenty-one different countries and located 569 of Mather's letters. Judging from scattered evidence in his diary, his complete correspondence amounted to some eight thousand letters. No doubt many of the missing letters would prove informative and amusing. But apparently nothing has survived of his extensive correspondence with theologians in Holland and with acquaintances in the West Indies. Nor have we the letters he wrote to Joseph Addison, Daniel Defoe, and Sir Isaac Newton, nor his communications during the witchcraft trials with Samuel Sewall and with Henry Selyns, the Dutch Calvinist minister in New Amsterdam. Still, what remains is an unusually rich harvest. Mather wrote literally around the world, and his letters swarm with the names of the leading and lesser figures, and all the great events, of his day. They touch on virtually every aspect of colonial American life in an important phase of its development and delineate the life and habits of colonial New England's most famous family.

Mather's curiosity about his world was ravenous, and among the delights of his correspondence is its variety of subjects. If any one feature can be said to dominate his letters it is his way of seeing and understanding himself, his tendency, accentuated toward the end of his life, to make sense of his experience in terms of a pattern. The attempt to divine a pattern in one's life was common among Puritans. For all its insistence on the mystical experience of grace, on man's being made new by Christ suddenly or gradually entering his heart, Puritan life and faith was highly formalized. Where Puritanism abandoned a dozen Catholic ceremonies, it invented a dozen rituals. Such Puritan saving arts as meditation, affliction, preparation, and sermonizing became subject to rules and methods which were explained, often with great inventiveness and subtlety, in scores of lectures and manuals. Each step toward the fervid, transcendent experience of grace became, for many Puritans, some routinized, conventionalized performance. It was the number and the degree of formalism of such performances that determined each minister's, each congregation's, and each individual's place within the very broad spectrum of Puritan philosophy. But for every Puritan, whether ultra-orthodox or ultra-liberal, prayer took some form, sermons fell handily into some outline, vocation took shape from some ideal pattern.

The reader of these letters will see that Cotton Mather often explained his life to himself in the terms of one such pattern. That pattern—illustrated by the quotations above—increasingly determined his thinking about himself and his errand in the world, and it arranged the forms of argument in many of his four hundred books and treatises. As he undertook his duties as heir to the prestigious Mather line (in a Boston whose growth as a political center consisted largely, he believed, in casting that line off), the pattern seemed clearer and clearer to him and became subject to conscious appraisal and action. That pattern was the Imitation of Christ. Mather's letters, works, and diaries repeatedly express his conviction that this pattern inspired, explained, and justified his life. With a persistency that must at first strike a modern reader as implausible or tiresome and leave him wary or amused, Mather saw his life as an effort to imitate his Saviour by Doing Good.

To Mather, the concept of Doing Good was no vague sense of compassion or easy hope for human improvement. Its meaning was specific and unique to his own personality and to the state of Protestantism in his time. In the largest sense, Doing Good meant seeing to it that God's Word prevailed among men on earth. It meant to him that he must exhaust his energies to insure the worldwide triumph of the Reformation. To that end he often, but of course not always, directed his correspondence. Through his letters he studied the progress of the Reformation at home, helped to solve church controversies, kept himself posted on the bloody persecutions of Protestants in Europe, and spread God's Word by dispatching his many works to India, Germany, France, Scotland. Through his letters he often lent intellectual and financial support to such enterprises as the Frederician University in Germany or the Danish missions in Malabar and saw to it that Harvard had an orthodox faculty, that the American churches were supplied with orthodox ministers, that the Indians were converted to Puritanism and not to Anglicanism. Through his letters he courted the favor of governors, councillors, representatives, and judges, of anyone influential, so as to redirect their power into forwarding the Reformation. Mather's unctuous tone with the high and mighty, his daily bowing and flattery to provincial bigwigs were—in his own mind at least—in the service of God. He did not consider politics an end, but always a means for Doing Good. As he saw it, power and influence enabled him to publish and distribute his pious works, to station the orthodox in places of authority, to obtain more money for converting the Indians.

At first glance this Doing Good to people who want to be left alone and making them stand in line while doing it seems authoritarianism in disguise. But Mather, unlike some of his American Puritan predecessors, had a notably ecumenical view of Protestantism and a theology deeply colored by the teachings of August Hermann Francke that might be described as Frederician. Although grounded in a passionate piety, Mather's was a benevolent, social-minded Protestantism that would identify the terms of communion with the terms of salvation and would devise a church franchise broad enough to admit nearly all Protestants, except such heretics as Arians. He sometimes preached at even Baptist services.

In a narrower but equally operative sense, Doing Good for Mather meant doing good to God's creature, man. Innumerable times, his letters indicate, his staggering energy issued in specific acts of kindness: money for the poor, firewood for the sick, consolation for the grief-stricken, care for the orphaned, letters of recommendation or encouragement for the young, visits to the languishing, uplift for the degraded. His whole life, as he presents it, consisted in finding objects for his compassion. In this realm, Doing Good meant championing the smallpox inoculation, which he was convinced would save millions of people from a devouring scourge. Each day of his adult life he entered into his diary some new proposal for Doing Good or some new person to whom good might be done—some new scientific project, financial scheme, or scholarship; some widow, friend, or invalid. Behind his single-minded pursuit of Doing Good, he leads us to believe, lay human love and reverence for life.

Yet in this pursuit lay a sinister trap as well—one that Mather fell into. As Benjamin Franklin combined self-interest with social welfare and became a millionaire, Mather combined Doing Good with Reformation and became, in his own eyes, a saint. He identified his prestige with his piety; his personal reputation and acts of goodness became for him interchangeable with the success of the Reformation. His fame and God's triumph became one. He was the preacher of God's Truth; so, by a sinister logic, to defy or blast him was to defy or blast that Truth. Good reviews of his books signified to him the success of the Reformation; bad reviews meant the Reformation was failing. If his advances to some governor were flattered, Mather believed that through him Christ was succeeding; if his advances were rebuked, he believed that Christ had been spurned. He saw those who attacked him personally as the Devil in disguise. Especially after 1710, he felt himself single-handedly to be holding all of New England, indeed the whole world, together, its only bulwark against a takeover by the Roman Church and Satan. At moments when he saw himself battling for the very survival of Protestantism, he confused imitating Christ with being Christ.

Doing Good made up only half the pattern. What Mather regarded as the bickerings and corruptions of eighteenth-century Boston completed it. Like Christ, he came to feel, his task in life was to Do Good to God's whole creation—and to be hounded in return. He made sense out of his experience in the formula—Do Good, and be crucified for it. At the end of his life he reflected that for all his Christlike acts he could number many enemies and few friends, and he decided that the Reformation was doomed unless Christ interceded directly through a Second Coming. He felt that at every turn his efforts, like his Saviour's, had been denied, thwarted, reviled. He desired to Do Good through his writings; yet his largest and most important works remained unpublished. He tried to Do Good to his wife and children; yet his wife Lydia turned into a lunatic, and his son became the scandal of Boston. He opened his library and dinner table to pious visitors from Scotland; they refused to take communion with him. He tried to instruct his flock; it swarmed from him. He tried to prevent smallpox; a bomb was thrown through his window. And like Jesus, he believed, he accepted his crucifixion with meekness and turned on his enemies a sunny forgiveness. A modern reader may find nothing in Mather's personality more annoying than this magnanimous grinning-and-bearing, the constant forgiving of enemies, the glorying in defeats, and the blessing of tormentors—all of which is so close to pride, yet perhaps not pride.

The question of whether it was pride or not must occupy any biographer of Mather and any historian of colonial New England. How accurate was Mather's view of his own life? Was he merely enacting to a grotesque extreme the sense of moment-to-moment peril bequeathed to Puritans through memories of Laudian persecution at home, drums and kettles beaten at ministers' windows, threats of jail? Or was he the victim of real malice and real persecution for his acts of real good? Was he, as Perry Miller believed, "neurotic," or a godly remnant in a sick society? Was he paranoid or pursued?

A well-founded answer to this question—one of the most far-reaching in American cultural history—must await the enviably tireless, and possibly only hypothetical, writer who in undertaking Mather's definitive biography sits down to read what Mather wrote and to understand what currents played into his thought through his myriad public and personal connections with the eighteenth-century world, internationally and in its every aspect. Yet Mather's letters allow for a few generalizations.

Traditionally Mather looms as a fascistic superprig bloated with the kind of self-regard that results from filiopiety. The unctuous pomposity that has made him obnoxious to history often resulted from his courting the powers and influences of the eighteenth century in the hope of using them to advance God's Word. The complementary private self-degradation and dustbiting that make "this mean hand" almost his favorite phrase were Puritan rituals, conventionalized evidence of humility. Formulas of self-loathing abound in the writings of eminent Scottish Presbyterians, of such American Puritans as Edward Taylor, or of such English Puritans as Richard Baxter. Pompous in the manner of the times and masochistic by tradition, Mather was also, however, very devious. The reader will discover, for instance, that Mather himself wrote a letter recommending one of his works and signed it "an unknown friend"; at other times he took credit for someone else's work.

One of the chief biographical revelations offered by Mather's correspondence is of his many weaknesses. In some instances his view of himself as a hounded Christ seems a simple rationalization of his own failings. Wanting to be, and to be known as, a writer, he had a writer's horror that his best work would never see the light, and he often demeaned himself to get his works published. His need for patrons to finance the publication of his works, quite as much as his desire to spread God's Word, often explains why he courted favor with men of influence. Moreover, as he knew very frustratingly, his practical judgment was extremely poor. He often mistook people's intentions: at first he favored the Dudleys and thought of King James II as a protector of Protestantism. He mismanaged his personal finances until he reduced his family to beggaring poverty. He was also in many ways intellectually timid. He sometimes allowed others to dictate his behavior and then felt he was being forced to act as he did. His deep conservatism and filiopiety often led him to defer, against his better judgment, to the elder or the celebrated. During the witchcraft trials, which he opposed, he lacked the courage to turn against such eminences as his own father, William Stoughton, and John Richards, defenders of the trials.

Yet on Mather's behalf it could be said that what often corrupted his simplicity and often lured his high purposes into devious means were the worldly and unscrupulous men—Randolph, Dudley, Elisha Cooke, the powerful bankers and merchants—coming to rule the public life of Boston in the train of the no longer effective Puritan ministry. Mather very often became the dupe of such men. In rebuilding a city on the hill that few people any longer cared to inhabit, he often had to fight fire with fire and to assume some of the vices of eighteenth-century Boston. As his letters reveal, and many other sources confirm, the quality of political life in the city had become degraded. Few people other than Mather were shocked anymore by the daily interception of letters, the stealing and forging of documents, the thriving slave trade, the treason, the bribery, the betrayal of confidences. And except for its political writers and for some notable painters, Boston between Mather's death in 1728 and Emerson's *Nature* in 1836 was culturally stagnant. That long dearth, it is worth remembering, was produced by the society Mather operated in and detested. His attack on dead-heartedness, venality, gossiping, narrowness, and the lack of cultural aspiration, charity, and love—his unwelcome reminder of the buried reality of spiritual strivings—made him less highly regarded in Boston than in such foreign capitals as Glasgow, Rotterdam, and London. For all his pathetic confusion of himself with the Messiah, Mather does seem at many points in his career to be merely the victim of the outrage and condescension that greets the possibility that "business as usual" may not be part of the order of things. Mather's letters thus betray him as being neither paranoid nor pursued, but rather as a human being with differing moods, acting from different motives—a more complex personality than the Christ he took himself to be or the dictator he often seemed to others. His letters show him by turns peevish, loving, dishonest, devout, spiteful, witty, unctuous, self-sacrificing, petty, ambitious, courtly, and brilliant—by and large a charitable and holy man tainted with an overreaching pride, fearful of antagonizing his elders, and temperamentally unsuited for the worldly affairs in which he felt he must play a part.

The importance of Mather's correspondence rests not only, of course, in its expression of his view of himself. The letters also clarify his role in the unfolding of colonial American culture. That role has often been summed up by the phrase "from piety to moralism" or by calling him a "transitional" figure. Those who use these tags are guiltily aware that they tell us less about Mather than about our ignorance of him. His letters show that what he failed to bring forward from the Puritan past was not the older piety but its complement, the enormously rich and complex intellectual tradition which had explained and sustained it. Mather put Puritanism into a new context. The older Puritanism had been preoccupied with resolving the intellectual and social tensions within Calvinist-Augustinian thought. It devoted what it considered its best energies to thorny questions of church organization, baptism, free will, grace—questions which occupied Jonathan Edwards in 1740 as fully as they had occupied Edward Taylor in 1700 or John Cotton in 1640 or John Calvin a century earlier. The idiom and terminology of Puritan thought remained virtually unchanged for a century and a half; its exponents continued to stare at the same problems. The continuity of tone, the artistic intensity, and the communal solidarity of Puritanism were products of this constant return to a few intellectually challenging questions of immense social consequence. But Mather saw Puritanism not merely as a faith that had to demonstrate its plausibility and intellectual soundness. It would also have to devote its best energies to fighting its way in the marketplace and to being implemented at the seats of power in the world. Mather was the ward boss of Puritanism. The wonderfully dense intellectual and theological problems of Puritanism interested him less than did its evangelical possibilities. Where the older Puritans shared the underdog psychology of an embattled minority, he led from strength, assuming that American Puritanism was a nonpareil for good works and social usefulness.

To say this in another way, Cotton Mather obsessively wanted to put America on the cultural map. He desired to restore American Puritanism to the mainstream of European culture from which it had departed in its separation from Catholicism. He wanted to claim for and to include in Puritanism the best that was being thought and said in the world, while always preserving the purity of Puritan worship and the chaste strength of its piety. He desired to be not a provincial, but a part of international Protestantism—to speak not in the homely voice of Anne Bradstreet or in the Parthian terms of William Bradford's "little band," but in the self-assured, cultivated tone of the Enlightenment virtuoso. His incurable punning, his literary elegances, his displays of "quality," his scientific inquisitiveness, his efforts to keep in touch with the best minds of his time, and, not least, his prodigious correspondence identify him as The Eighteenth-Century Gentleman. It is a tribute to his extraordinary vigor that he single-handedly made up the cultural lag separating America from Europe and kept himself abreast of the instant developments in European thought and culture. Whatever else one may say of him, he was an amazingly literate and learned man, the one man of his time in America not dwarfed beside the virtuosi of the continent.

Perhaps we do Mather most justice by thinking of him as the first native American writer. No special praise is intended. His acute consciousness of the unique difficulties of writing in the New World and his wish to keep up and compete with the best in far-away Europe give his writing the sort of provincial vulgarity and disproportion that mark much American culture after his time. To put America on the map culturally meant to him doing something enormous, something gluttonously big. His gargantuan "Libri Elephantini," as he called his larger works, and the indecent number of them, inaugurate in America a line of overreaching, too-opulent works that stretches from failures like the bombastic epics of the Connecticut Wits to successes like *Moby Dick* to the latest state university system and urban culture palace. The gaudy novelty and elephantine scale of Mather's works, like the later Niagaran or Californian excesses of American culture, are rooted in a single desire to overcome a sense of cultural inferiority at one mighty blow. In his need to tell the Old World that he existed, Cotton Mather, for better or worse, was one of us.

THE TEXT

This edition contains, in whole or part, about four-fifths of Mather's 569 extant letters. I have purposely omitted three kinds: (1) lengthy newsletters in which Mather by and large merely copied out for his correspondent various dispatches from the *Boston News-Letter;* (2) formal epistles which he designed for publication in newspapers and broadsides (a list of these appears in Thomas Holmes's bibliography of Mather's works); (3) very brief notes, except when of special interest—notes to the languishing, accompaniments to gifts, brief letters of introduction or recommendation. I have also omitted portions of the letters included in this volume. These omissions are restricted, for the most part, to florid salutations and closes, passages that only repeat—usually in the same words—matter from other letters, and very lengthy quotations from other writers. I have, however, included whatever crossouts or marginalia seemed significant. All of the omissions, of course, are indicated by ellipses or by summaries in brackets. Occasionally Mather omitted such short closings as "Your obedient servant," especially in draft letters. In such cases I have allowed the omission to stand without further comment.

The headnote to each letter indicates Mather's correspondent and the date Mather wrote to him. Only a few times have I entered the place, for this was almost invariably Boston. Mather rarely travelled and less than half a dozen of his letters are posted outside the city. I have modernized Mather's dating, which he set arbitrarily sometimes in the New Style and sometimes in the Old. (Sometimes March appears as "I m"—i.e. the first month—and sometimes as "March.") Where the name of his correspondent or the date does not appear on the letter, I have enclosed them in brackets. I have pursued such cases as far as I was able, but in a few I have taken calculated guesses. The bracketed dates or correspondents represent my best efforts, but it would not surprise me to learn that in a few I have erred.

The present edition represents a compromise between a text according to contemporary American conventions and a text which preserves Mather's own stylistic and rhetorical practices. My aim has been to preserve the content of his letters. In many individual cases, however, I have construed "content" widely enough to include, for example, capital letters that indicate Mather's veneration for titles or his wish to advertise his "quality." On the whole I have modernized his spelling so that "cypher" becomes "cipher" and "small-pox" becomes "smallpox": "chirurgeon," however, remains "chirurgeon." In such individual instances I have consulted my judgment of the specific case rather than some overall design. Specific judgments have also guided me in transcribing Mather's punctuation. He often wrote fragmentary sentences, some of which I have retained to preserve a grammatical emphasis; others I have attached to the stem sentence where I felt that no emphasis was intended. Where his syntax became bollixed to the point of incomprehensibility I have allowed it to stand, for his tangled syntax invariably reveals him trying to write a highfaluting sentence to impress someone mighty. He used colons, semicolons, dashes, and a variety of horizontal squiggles interchangeably. These I have regularized according to contemporary grammatical practices. Only in two or three letters did Mather employ the typographical flourishes of his published works. Where such ornaments appeared in the letters I have tried to duplicate them as well as can be done in modern print. Luckily, the problems in transcribing Mather's actual language are very few because he wrote a very legible late-Secretary hand and his letters are immaculately preserved.

Of course, by modernizing in this way something is lost, namely those nuances of rhythm, sound, and appearance that subtly affect meaning. Some loss, I am a little relieved to think, is incurred simply by setting Mather's handwriting into type since the writing itself is rhetorical. Calligraphic neatness suggests special respect for a correspondent or the hope of getting something out of him, while scrawls and blots suggest despondency, feeble health, or a correspondent who can be taken for granted. Thus in the fullest sense the meaning of the letters resides in the holographs and nowhere else.

To repeat, my aim has been to produce a text that will show us something about Cotton Mather, about whom we know little. I am aware that the "something" has been influenced by my own sensitivity to Mather, but with virtually none of his works in print it seemed important to make him, in every sense, available. While I trust that my transcriptions represent a word-for-word recounting of Mather's letters, I share the Puritans' disdain for the sin they called "scrupulosity." I have treated Mather with a fairly rough respect—far more respectful than rough, however—as a figure of great importance still capable of pleasing the general reader and, at every turn, intriguing the scholar. Some readers will regret the absence of footnotes in the text, but because in Mather everything needs to be footnoted, this volume might easily have quadrupled in size. Aside from practical considerations I also share some discomfort with J. D. Salinger over what he called "the aesthetic evil of a footnote." I have incorporated the information that is essential to understanding Mather's correspondence into the historical and analytic essays which tie the letters together. What has been lost in fulness of explication will, I hope, be won in readability and a larger sense of perspective. Given Mather's interests, however, nothing fully explains his correspondence but the whole history of the Christian world in the eighteenth century. Correspondents not fully identified in the introductory essays are sketched in the glossary at the rear of the volume.

SOURCES

These essays have been mined from many articles and books about Cotton Mather and his times. The following list includes only the more useful as a general indication of my sources and a guide to further reading. The fullest, but very inadequate, listings of Mather's manuscripts are found in *American Literary Manuscripts* (Austin, Tex., 1960); *American Book-Prices Current* (New York, 1894——); Charles Andrews and Frances Davenport, *Guide to the Manuscript Materials for the History of the United States to 1783* (Washington, D.C., 1908); Bernard Crick and Miriam Alman, *A Guide to Manuscripts Relating to America in Great Britain and Ireland* (London, 1961); Thomas J. Holmes, *Cotton Mather: A Bibliography of His Works,* 3 vols. (Cambridge, Mass., 1940; a superb and vastly informative bibliography); *The National Union Catalog of Manuscript Collections* (Hamden, Conn., 1959——). For general background material on Mather's age I have most often consulted the *Boston News-Letter,* 1704–1776 (Micro Research Corporation, for the American Antiquarian Society);

J. Hastings, ed., *Encyclopedia of Religion and Ethics*, 12 vols. (New York, n.d.); Everett Kimball, *The Public Life of Joseph Dudley* (New York, 1911); Perry Miller, *The New England Mind: From Colony to Province* (Cambridge, Mass., 1953); J. G. Palfrey, *A Compendious History of New England* (Boston, 1872); Howard Peckham, *The Colonial Wars 1689–1762* (Chicago, 1964); Josiah Quincy, *The History of Harvard University*, 2 vols. (Cambridge, Mass., 1840); William Warren Sweet, *Religion in Colonial America* (New York, 1942); and the papers of Cotton Mather's contemporaries as reprinted in the publications of the American Antiquarian Society, the Colonial Society of Massachusetts, and the Massachusetts Historical Society.

Unfortunately, none of the extant biographies of Mather are in the slightest way adequate. Of only limited usefulness are Abijah P. Marvin, *The Life and Times of Cotton Mather* (Boston, 1892) and Barrett Wendell, *Cotton Mather: The Puritan Priest* (New York, 1891). Of greater usefulness have been *The Diary of Cotton Mather*, ed. Worthington Chauncey Ford, 2 vols. (repr. New York, n.d.) and *The Diary of Samuel Sewall*, 3 vols. (Boston, 1878–82). To identify Mather's correspondents, both in the introductory essays and in the glossary, I have most often consulted such standard guides as *Burke's Peerage*, *The Dictionary of American Biography*, *The Dictionary of National Biography*, *The New England Historical and Genealogical Register*, and *Sibley's Harvard Graduates*.

For more specialized material I have found the following helpful. On English booksellers of the time: Henry Plomer, *A Dictionary of Printers and Booksellers who were at work in England, Scotland, and Ireland from 1668 to 1725* (Oxford, 1922). On Mather's scientific interests: Otho T. Beall and Richard H. Shryock, *Cotton Mather: First Significant Figure in American Medicine* (Baltimore, 1954); George Lyman Kittredge, "Cotton Mather's Scientific Communications to the Royal Society," *Proceedings of the American Antiquarian Society*, XXVI (1916), 18–57; *The Philosophical Transactions of the Royal Society* (London, 1666———); Dorothy Stimson, *Scientists and Amateurs: A History of the Royal Society* (New York, 1948). On Mather's relations with Scotland: Niel Caplan, "Some Unpublished Letters of Benjamin Colman 1717–1725,"

Proceedings of the Massachusetts Historical Society, LXXVII (1965), 101–42; Thomas M'Crie, ed., *The Correspondence of the Rev. Robert Wodrow*, 3 vols. (Edinburgh, 1842); Hew Scott, ed., *Fasti Ecclesiae Scoticanae*, 8 vols. (Edinburgh, 1915–28). On Arianism: Julius H. Tuttle, "William Whiston and Cotton Mather," *Publications of the Colonial Society of Massachusetts*, XIII (1912), 197–205. On other members of Mather's family: Thomas J. Holmes, "Samuel Mather of Witney, 1674–1733," *Publications of the Colonial Society of Massachusetts*, XXVI (1926), 312–22, and the same author's *The Minor Mathers: A List of their Works* (Cambridge, Mass., 1940). On missionary activity of the times: L. W. Cowie, *Henry Newman: An American in London* (London, 1956); William Kellaway, *The New England Company 1649–1776* (New York, 1962); *Two Hundred Years: The History of the S.P.C.K.* (London, 1898). On the Winthrop family: Richard L. Bushman, *From Puritan to Yankee: Character and the Social Order in Connecticut, 1690–1765* (Cambridge, Mass., 1967).

My search for Mather's letters uncovered a huge amount of other unpublished materials by him both in the United States and abroad—memorials, notes, treatises, marginalia, and so on. Much of this deserves publication, especially the sermons, scores of which seem to be extant. Like Emerson, Thoreau, and many later New England writers, Mather wrote very directly out of his immediate experience. All of his sermons, published or unpublished, take their occasion from his life: in debt he preached on debtors; observing his wife's breakdown he preached on insanity. No comprehensive biography of Mather can be undertaken without these sermons.

Acknowledgments

MY DEEPEST THANKS to the following institutions for preserving and allowing me to publish Cotton Mather's letters, and for many services along the way: the American Antiquarian Society in Worcester, Mass.; the Bodleian Library in Oxford, England; the Boston Public Library; the British Museum in London, with permission of the Trustees of the British Museum; the Duxbury Rural and Historical Society in Duxbury, Mass.; the Guildhall Library in London; the Harvard College Library in Cambridge, Mass., by permission of the Harvard College Library; the Historical Society of Pennsylvania in Philadelphia; the Henry E. Huntington Library in San Marino, Cal.; the Library of Congress in Washington, D.C.; the Maine Historical Society (Fogg Collection) in Portland; the Massachusetts State Archives and the Massachusetts Historical Society in Boston; the McGill University Library (collection of Mrs. J. B. Learmont) in Montreal; the New England Historic Genealogical Society in Boston; the National Library of Scotland in Edinburgh, with permission of the Trustees of the National Library of Scotland; the New-York Historical Society in New York City; the Royal Society in London (letters marked "RS" copyright the Royal Society); the private library of William H. Scheide in Princeton, N.J.; the Southern Historical Collection (New England Papers), University of North Carolina Library in Chapel Hill; the Tracy W. McGregor Library in the University of Virginia Library in Charlottesville.

My thanks also go to the Arts and Sciences Research Fund of New York University for a grant which subsidized the research. To be able to also thank the friends who have helped me is a special, and very personal, pleasure. Of my colleagues at New York University, Warren Herendeen did many intricate services for me at the Royal Society in London, and John Mulder again helped patiently with Mather's Latin. It is the nature of my friends Harold Turner, Everett Emerson, Mason I. Lowance, A. W. Plumstead, Leo Lemay, and Jack Zipes—students of American literature—that their very friendship is encouragement. But only my wife Sharon can keep up with both *"Libri Elephantini"* and the hockey scores.

K. S.

New York City
June 1969

Abbreviations

The abbreviation at the upper left corner of each letter reveals any previous publication(s) of the letter and, to the right of the slant line, the present location of the manuscript. Thus, U/MHS indicates an unpublished letter at the Massachusetts Historical Society.

AAS: American Antiquarian Society (Worcester, Mass.)
Bodleian: Bodleian Library (Oxford)
BPL: Boston Public Library (Boston)
Brit Mus: British Museum (London)
Calef: Robert Calef, *More Wonders of the Invisible World* (London, 1700), reprinted in George L. Burr, *Narratives of the Witchcraft Cases 1648–1706* (New York, 1914).
DI and DII: *Diary of Cotton Mather*, ed. Worthington Chauncey Ford, *Collections of the Massachusetts Historical Society*, 7th Ser., VII and VIII.
Duxbury: Duxbury Rural and Historical Society (Duxbury, Mass.)
Ford: John W. Ford, ed., *Some Correspondence between the Governors and Treasurer of the New England Company in London and the Commissioners of the United Colonies in America* (London, 1896).
IV Coll 8: *The Mather Papers, Collections of the Massachusetts Historical Society*, 4th Ser., VIII.
Guildhall: Guildhall Library (London)
HCL: Harvard College Library (Cambridge, Mass.)
Hinckley: *The Hinckley Papers, Collections of the Massachusetts Historical Society*, 4th Ser., V.
HM: *Historical Magazine*, VI (September, 1869)
Holmes: Thomas J. Holmes, *Cotton Mather: A Bibliography of His Works*, 3 vols. (Cambridge, Mass., 1940).
HSP: Historical Society of Pennsylvania (Philadelphia)
Hunt: Henry E. Huntington Library (San Marino, Calif.)
Hutchinson: *Hutchinson Papers, Collections of the Massachusetts Historical Society*, 3d Ser., I.

LC: Library of Congress (Washington, D.C.)

Levin: David Levin, ed., *What Happened in Salem?* (New York, 1960).

M: Abijah Marvin, *The Life and Times of Cotton Mather* (Boston, 1892).

Maine: Fogg Collection (clerical), Maine Historical Society (Portland, Maine).

Mass Arch: Massachusetts State Archives (Boston)

MHS: Massachusetts Historical Society (Boston)

MUL: McGill University Library, collection of Mrs. J. B. Learmont (Montreal).

Murdock: Kenneth B. Murdock, ed., *Selections from Cotton Mather* (New York, 1926).

NEHGR: *New-England Historical and Genealogical Register*, XXIV

NEHGS: New England Historic Genealogical Society (Boston)

NLS: National Library of Scotland (Edinburgh)

NYHS: New-York Historical Society (New York)

I Coll 3:   *Collections of the Massachusetts Historical Society*, Ist Ser., III.

PCSM: *Publications of the Colonial Society of Massachusetts*

Proceedings: *Proceedings of the Massachusetts Historical Society*

Quincy: Josiah Quincy, *The History of Harvard University* (Cambridge, Mass., 1840).

Report: *Ninth Report of the Historical Manuscripts Commission* (London, 1884).

RS: The Royal Society (London)

Scheide: Scheide Library, Princeton University (Princeton)

SHC: Southern Historical Collection, University of North Carolina Library (Chapel Hill).

TLHSQ: *Transactions of the Literary and Historical Society of Quebec*, II.

U: Unpublished

Upham: C. W. Upham, *Salem Witchcraft* (Boston, 1867)

UVL: University of Virginia Library (Charlottesville, Va.)

WI, II, and III: Thomas M'Crie, ed., *The Correspondence of the Rev. Robert Wodrow*, 3 vols. (Edinburgh, 1842).

*:   Manuscript unlocated, letter reproduced from printed or other source.

Selected Letters of
Cotton Mather

CHAPTER ONE

1678[?]–1699

Harvard; relations with John Cotton; the Andros government; marriage to Abigail Philips; Increase Mather's charter agency; the Glorious Revolution; the new Massachusetts charter; King William's War; the Salem witchcraft
trials; death of John Cotton.

I

COTTON MATHER's extant correspondence begins with the
letters he wrote during his adolescent years to his uncle JOHN
COTTON (1639–1698), son of the great New England theologian.
A voluminous correspondent himself, Cotton reputedly wrote twice
as many letters as any other man in New England. Some letters
from uncle to nephew in 1677 speak of still earlier letters, and what
survives clearly represents only part of what must have been a
frequent exchange.

Mather's sometimes chiding tone in these letters speaks for and
at his uncle's shady career. In May, 1664, Cotton was excommuni-
cated from his father's church for unspecified immoral conduct.
Soon after, he moved to Martha's Vineyard, where he learned
Indian languages, preached to the natives in their own tongue, and
helped John Eliot to prepare his Indian Bible. In September, 1666,
he accepted a pastoral call from the church at Plymouth, where
Mather later wrote to him. Mather's advice to his uncle is leavened
with respect, however, and with a playfulness that reveals his fondness for Cotton and Cotton's family, whom he occasionally visited
in Plymouth. In 1677 Cotton wrote to Increase Mather asking that
his nephew be allowed to come to Plymouth and tutor his sons
in writing and ciphering. But illnesses brought on by pious bouts
of fasting and prayer (and, as noted in one letter, the muddy con-

3

dition of the Boston docks) apparently kept Cotton Mather at home. He did stay at Plymouth in August, 1678, studying diligently and trying to restore his health by drinking each morning from the celebrated mineral spring.

Mather's early letters to his uncle tell us much of what he thought about himself as an adolescent. He sometimes compares himself to an actor on stage, and indeed his learned, multilingual prose is a performance, an effort to strike the right pose by a brilliant youth from whom much is expected and who demands much of himself. The sometimes tangled syntax and the reference to young "mutes" look ahead to the tongue-tied prose he produced whenever he wrote to someone he wanted to impress, and seem related to his stammering, which he feared might make him unfit for the ministry. In March, 1681, he dreamed of being speechless; even in adulthood he worried that his youthful speech difficulties would recur. Perhaps his logorrhea was a mighty attempt to overcome this fear of speechlessness. Genial, ambitious, clever, inwardly fearful, the young Mather was also something of a prig who regarded Harvard, which he entered in 1674, as "a place of much temptation."

His innermost life, however, Cotton Mather kept to himself. The forced elegances of his early letters betray nothing of the extraordinary events he was at the same time recording in the privacy of his diary. His tormented fasts and prayers at last led him to see visions and hear voices. After a particularly zealous fast in February, 1685, he spoke to an angel sent by Jesus in answer to his prayers. It assured him that his fate was "to find full expression for what in him was best," and it described "the books this youth should write and publish, not only in America, but in Europe." Wary of becoming prideful, however, he wrestled with rather conventionalized anxieties about his unworthiness for salvation and fought down his "ambitious affectation of pre-eminencies, far above what could belong to my own age or worth." As commonly happened among Puritans, he paid for his "macerating exercises" of fasting and prayer by "splenetic maladies" and by the pains in his jaw and head that would plague him throughout his life.

4

But the reward, Cotton Mather hoped—and nothing is more clear to a reader of his early letters and diaries than that he hoped it—was to become the greatest man in America. And, indeed, his prospects were hopeful. In February, 1681, he became an assistant to his famous father at the prestigious North Church. In August of that year he received his master's degree from Harvard. A few months later, the congregation at New Haven applied to him to become their pastor. But he refused them, claiming that the North Church, having voted for his settlement with them, would turn against his father if he moved. On January 8, 1683, the North Church voted him its pastor, even though he was not to be ordained for another two years.

While making his mark in Boston, Cotton Mather kept in touch with affairs in the world, about which his curiosity was intense. In answer to John Cotton's specific request for news of England, he sent his uncle detailed accounts of the end of King Charles's reign, especially the persecution of Dissenters and the threats against the Massachusetts charter. The events are well-known: the king appointed Edward Randolph as collector of customs for Massachusetts and sent him to New England to watch for signs of treason, to enforce the crown's sway, and to halt evasions of the navigation laws by Boston merchants. Randolph reported back to the Lords of Trade; as a result, in October, 1681, Charles wrote to Massachusetts threatening the charter and demanding that the colony send agents within three months to defend it. For this mission the General Court delegated Joseph Dudley and JOHN RICHARDS (1641?–1694), a prosperous Boston merchant and member of Mather's church who had married into the Connecticut Winthrops, Mather's close and lifelong friends. Richards held numerous offices in Massachusetts—Speaker of the House of Deputies, judge of the Supreme Court—and later served as one of the judges at Salem. Mather's letter to him is addressed to London during Richards' agency which, despite his political experience, failed utterly, largely because the General Court specifically forbade its agents to act upon any measure implying some infringement of the old charter. The king demanded that the agents be granted the power to negotiate, but the court still refused. Then the London Board of Trade directed the attorney general to issue a *quo warranto*. Randolph—the "insolent Tobias" as Mather calls him—returned to Boston to exact full submission from the governor and the assembly in exchange for the king's promise not to vacate the charter. Still the colony would not yield.

Like the rest of New England, Mather followed these events closely and grimly awaited an end to Puritan rule in Massachusetts, his fears compounded by renewed persecutions of Dissenters in England, Scotland, and the continent.

The turbulence abroad did not prevent Mather from ordering some books from the English bookseller RICHARD CHISWELL (fl. 1660–1680) in what is the earliest extant example of his remarkable foreign correspondence. Barely out of his teens, Mather had begun building the magnificent private library that was the one worldly possession he cherished. "As the Bodleian Library at Oxford is the glory of that university, if not of all Europe," wrote John Dunton in 1701, "so I may say Mr. Mather's library is the glory of New-England, if not of all America."

To John Cotton

U/BPL   [1678?]

Honored Sir,

You know I suppose how if a few of the eldest are *vocales*, then the rest either *semi-vocales* or mutes. Behold! how I make a virtue of necessity. Time and business have formerly forbad me to do that which at present it but just [as much?], *ut canis [ad nilum?]*.

It may be, Sir, you'll wonder at my brevity with a *quantum mutatus ab illo. Ille ego qui quondam*. I who once used to send by every opportunity a whole cartload of news, etc.—and spin out like [Tranlissus?] now to furl my sails, and come just like Cato on the stage, [ere?] only to go off again.

But, Sir, be pleased to know, I am now at Cambridge, and since it is so, what should the chief errand of this epistle be? and the burden of each line, exit of each sentence in it, but what the martyr once—pray, pray, pray, never more need than now. If residing in a place of much temptation, if being debarred the special opportunities of seek-

6

ing and seeing the face of God, which have once been enjoyed, if an inconstant frame of spirit, a deceitful heart, or in a word, a condition full of wants, *mutato nomine*, be named a need of prayer, then I have great cause to bespeak such a boon.

To John Cotton

M; IV Coll 8/BPL   [c. November, 1678]

I should fling a *proh pudor* upon my delays of doing you that service that duty does as much oblige as you desire, but that I am made brazen-faced by excuses sufficient to bear me out.

I wonder what you impute my non-transmission of those things of yours which are in my hands to. I know your candor will not charge me with idleness, your courtesy will not implead me for forgetfulness, and most of all, [your very?] reason will not accuse me of unwillingness to serve you in what I may, even *usque ad aras* and if possible, there too. But if I am of age to speak for myself, sickness, which had the first part in hindrance, was succeeded by uncertainty of conveyance, and that again seconded by other avocations. How frequently and unweariedly I have been engaged in seeking Plymouth boat, if nothing else yet my old shoes will testify, who in this time, when Boston is become another *Lutetia* (q. *Luto sata*) do proclaim that they wanted a pair of galoshes when traveling near the dock-head. I would be more frequent in letters testimonial of my gratitude, if I could but either fling salt on the tail of time, or get the wind and tide to be favorable to my designs, which possibly may in a sense be before the Greek calends.

Never was it such a time in Boston. Boston burying-places never filled so fast. It is easy to tell the time wherein we did not use to have the bells tolling for burials on a Sabbath-day morning by sunrise, to have 7 buried on a Sabbath-day night after meeting, to have coffins crossing each other as they have been carried in the street, to have I know not how many corpses following each other close at the heels, to have 38 die in one week—6, 7, 8, or 9 in a day. Yet thus hath it lately been, and thus is it at this day. Above 340 have died of the smallpox in Boston since it first assaulted the place. To attempt a bill of mortality, and number the very spires of grass in a burying place, seem to have a parity of difficulty and in accomplishment. At first the gradual mercy

7

of God to my father's family was observable and remarkable. First, my brother Nathaniel gently smitten, and I more gently than he, and my sister Sarah yet more gently than I. But the order is broken on my sister Maria, who on the same month and day of the month that my father was visited with the same disease twenty-one years ago, was taken very ill, the symptoms grievous and our fears great. Sometimes light-headed, but her father prayed down mercy for her and her pox having turned a day or two ago, she is now so *inter spemque metumque locata*, that *spes* bears down the scales. So that of my father's septenary of children, four have been visited. God fit and prepare for the three strokes that are yet behind.

Sir, let us not want the help of your prayers for all of us, especially for him who is not more your nephew than desirous to be your servant,

To John Cotton

U/NYHS   January 19, 1682

Worthily respected Uncle,

[Regrets having no remarkable foreign news to report.]

As to what concerns New England in Old England. The King hath sent a pretty favorable letter, wherein yet he says, He don't so accept our excuse for our not sending agents, but that he expects we should within three months (I think) yet do it, or incur the blot and guilt of disloyalty. That which made exceeding well for a moderate letter sent to us from His Majesty, was, that the states of Holland sent over to England a somewhat rugged embassade who declared their expectations that the King should now manifest himself, whether he would join cordially in the Protestant League, or be a friend to the French King's interest. This put the Court into a huge perplexity; and coming just at the time when the New England business was under debate, it did so divert them that they had not leisure to take rigid notice of us.

In all other respects so far as I can learn, things continue in *statu quo prius*. Randolph is come with his family and has hired Mr. Hez: Usher's house, where the ministers were wont to meet. *Heu! Domus Antiqua* etc. . . .   Your,

1678[?]-1699

TO JOHN COTTON

U/HCL   March 28, 1682

Honored Sir!

Your last was very welcome for it brought me nothing but good news. The increase of Christ's Church among you must increase the joy of every well-principled heart that knows it. Really! the report of one soul's being brought to renounce idols and draw near to God in Christ, is—to say no more, worth hearing. Happy New England! where our glorious Master has not yet broke up house!

But will you not wonder that I could find nothing but good news in your affectionate lines, when some of the first of them are, I have tasted deeply of the cup of affliction this winter! Nay, but I don't recall the word. For you as well as David will say—It is good for me that I have been afflicted! Surely! you have many a time given yourself and yours and all your concerns, into the hands of God in Christ Jesus! What? And will you not stand to His managements? Or will you imagine any other, but that, as not a sparrow in your field, no, nor a hair on your head, falls to the ground without a concernment of His ever-watchful providence about the same, so, He that has performed all things for you, has disposed of them ten thousand times better than if you had carved for yourself. Oh! for such gallant and lofty attainments as to love no creature with a distinct love from the love of God, and to have no will distinct from the will of God! But— *facilè omnes cum Valemus recta Consilia agrotis dam* [us?].

Nay, I do but pour water in the sea when one of my low and dirty spirit goes to revive in you the noble inclinations, wherein doubtless you abound. Only then, in the upshot, I can hear of no ill befallen you, for, say to the righteous, It shall be well with him! And, our light afflictions work more glory.

[Reports having been ill himself during the winter; again regrets having no news to report.] Except I should say that London has lately been forced to part with their liberties so far, as to admit sheriffs not of their own, but the courts' choosing—and what shall we poor shrubs expect when the stately cedars crack! . . . Our church did about two months ago pass a unanimous vote, desiring a day might speedily be appointed for the ordination of that same sorry soul who, I suppose, will no ways comply with the mentioned address. But who, I am sure,

9

does both need and crave your daily prayers. For I need not tell you—my paper will scarce give me room to tell you—'Tis, Your,

[To John Cotton]

U/BPL draft   [April, 1682]

Worthily esteemed Sir,

I have received your lines, etc., and do count that you have honored me in what notice you take of me. Had not sundry engagements and the unexpected departure of the vessel hurried me, I think I should by this opportunity been very large (so large as to be even troublesome) in my return.

This of public notice: France's persecution; Holland's inundation; England's every way perplexed condition; aye, and the universal combustions of Europe, you have been, I doubt not, as fully and as early acquainted with as we. Only methinks 'twill kindle sympathy to observe what is well known, that the persecuted people of God have no place on earth to betake themselves unto. Heaven help them! And now my pen is running, let me add that as the Lord's people in England are very apprehensive, so we in New England are not altogether unapprehensive—but—

As for what is of a more private concern. Either *dè* the happy reconciliation of O. and N.C. consummated on 7d instant, or as to the state of C., or lastly as to Mr. D's M.SS., I doubt not but my father has written what is knowable. . . .

To John Richards

IV Coll 8/*   November 13, 1682

Worshipful Sir!

Although to give you the interruption of a rude epistle, *Quum tot sustineas, et tanta Negotia,* may have a hand in producing almost as bad an effect as the applause of the spectators did upon that gallant actor whom the people stifled to death with the multitude of roses which they threw upon him, yet many considerations encourage me and embolden me—some even enforce me, and compel me—to do what in this literary address I do, for, not to mention the kindness which on a late occasion I received by some weeks' entertainment in the house that laments the absence of you as its master and owner, and for which, I think, somewhat of acknowledgment may well be made unto yourself; and, not to insist on the relation that God has given me to bear unto the particular church which may look upon itself as happy in having your worship a member of it, I shall only call to mind that when a person of great worth in a Grecian city was entertained with the various presents of innumerable persons, one among the rest, having nothing else, took up a palm-full of water from the street and signified as much respect as he could with the offer of that, and this too, not without good acceptance. And truly, Sir! may my handfull of water prove like Solomon's cold waters to a thirsty soul, as good news from a far country are called by his inspired pen; I shall count it one of the best services to which my ink can be put. When any are engaged in action for us we think we have commission enough to cry, courage! Cheer up! But, excellent Sir! you are employed in a concern wherein the thoughts of this whole land are called to be upon you! And therein it is not improbable that you meet with mountains of difficulty; that you are involved in wonderful intricacies and labyrinths; that you have a field for the exercise of the wisdom of an Angel of God, and of more grace than one man is wont to have. Yet now, be strong, O Zerubbabel, saith the Lord; for I am with you, saith the Lord of Hosts. It was a Moses-like and a Paul-like act of self-denial in you to forego all the inviting enjoyments of a pleasant home, to venture over the perilous Atlantic ocean, and to appear at a Court which I shall not attempt to put right epithets upon, on the behalf of a sinful and unworthy land. [Assures Richards, with effusive flattery, that ultimately his agency is for "Lord Jesus Christ Himself."]

. . . within two or three days before the day wherein I write this, diverse strange and sudden deaths have fallen out. Mrs. Brattle died at an hour's warning, and was this day buried. A man at Concord was found dead in his field. Of a couple of men overtaken in drink, at Boston, one was on the Saturday, at night, rolling a barrel of cider down a cellar; he falling, the barrel ran over him and bruised him to death immediately. Another, after he had been spending a great part of the Sabbath (yesterday) in drinking at a private house, returned in the night towards his vessel, which lay near one of our wharfs; but his drink was so strong as to throw him over the wharf, and there the poor wretch was miserably drowned. [Affairs in New Hampshire.] . . . the insolent Tobias, R. (there are three or four names equally applicable to that canine initial letter!) was born to do mischief, tho' the poor man has been of later months very, very pitifully of it by straits and discomposures in his family. (His wife in particular now lies near death, if she be not already as before we are aware, we are prone to wish her husband.) And he that makes disturbances in a greater family is but retaliated by such a punishment. . . .

Worshipful Sir! Your humble servant,

To Richard Chiswell

U/Bodleian (MS Rawl. lett.   November 27, 1683
        108, fol. 87r)

Sir,

[Sends along ten pounds as part of his debt to Chiswell.]

Sir! I thank you for the trouble you have been at from time to time to gratify me; and my thoughts are not only to uphold still my correspondence with you, and to request that you will transmit me what I find in the catalogue of books printed, to suit me (tho' I am willing first to discharge all my past obligations), but also to make an agreement with you concerning an impression of some discourses which have my father for their author, and which myself with some of my acquaintances would be at the charges of publishing, if providence favor that design (only this also is not yet so ripe, but that it must be reserved for the matter of another letter).

All that I shall at present add is that the Alsop's *Anti-Sozzo* which I had from you was by some mistake such a defective one, as to be without several sheets; and therefore I desire you would supply the want of that, with a complete one. If the fifth volume of Cane's *Weekly Pacquet of Advice from Rome* be extant, I crave that likewise. If the second part of Dr. Owen, concerning *Evangelical Churches*, have seen the light, I would see that too. Starkey's *Pyrotechny Triumphing* bears an extravagant price, but I am urged by a near friend to procure it for him. Send it, and you shall not be unpaid.

I have met with *The Weekly Memorials for the Ingeniose*; as far as August 7, 1682, I have already; be pleased to let me have what of them have come out since. . . .   Your friend and servant,

To John Cotton

U/AAS   December 20, 1683

Honored Sir,

[Opening paragraph blotted] . . . persecutions of the Dissenters do increase in England and to a marvellous height, and many persons of all ranks are forced to fly. A gentleman, a Deacon of Dr. Annesley's church, that is arrived here last week, told me that there are warrants out for every Non-conformist minister in the city of London. Two or three religious noblemen are said to have absconded in Scotland lately; in London, the common-council having an instrument sent them by the King for them to sign their resignation to His pleasure, retracted their old vote of compliance and refused to do what was required in the matter of submission; upon which His Majesty has entered judgment against the charter, and appointed instead of the mayor, a *Custos Civitatis,* and instead of the aldermen, a number of picked justices, to supply their place.

[Tells of the banishment of Jesuits from Hungary and from all Turkish dominions.]

At Piscataqua, just now the Governor's Council have passed an act, that all above sixteen years old shall not be debarred the Blessed Sacrament and that all children shall be christened; and this after the liturgy-way, if it be desired by the parents; and half a year's imprisonment, without all bond or bail, is the penalty of transgressing the said act—

Here's enough to bespeak and quicken your prayers. . . .

II

COTTON MATHER's entry into adult life coincided with revolutionary events in Massachusetts. On October 23, 1684, the colony's charter was vacated. Six months later news reached Boston of the death of Charles II and the succession of James II. Misjudging, like many others, James's intentions, Mather speculated that James would work toward liberty for Dissenters. On the contrary, while promising to preserve the standing forms of civil and church government in Massachusetts, James hoped to establish

Catholicism. When news of Argyll's capture and death and of Monmouth's uprising reached Boston in September, 1685, Mather wrote that because of the "calamities and confusions in the English nation" he had wakened an hour earlier than his wont in order to sigh, pray, and sing psalms. (Mather often reviled himself for late rising; characteristically, the sin for which he most often indicted himself was sloth.) The revocation of the Edict of Nantes in October, 1685, ended the hope of toleration for Dissenters in France and sanctioned new severities against the Huguenots. Mather regarded their persecution as "perhaps the horriblest that ever was in the world" (*Wonders of the Invisible World*). He tried to welcome and comfort the persecuted Dissenters who came to New England by way of the West Indies.

Mather's letters in this period record the establishment of the new provincial government in Massachusetts—and local efforts to thwart it. In May, 1686, Randolph once again landed in New England, aboard the royal frigate *Rose*, with a commission establishing a council under the presidency of Joseph Dudley, a central figure in Mather's life during the next decade. Temporarily it was the end of charter government in New England. The new governor, Sir Edmund Andros, arrived in December to preside over the Dominion of New England, which by 1688 included New York and New Jersey. As Mather explains in his letter to John Cotton in January, 1687, Andros tried to use one of the three Boston churches for Anglican worship. The protests of Increase Mather forced him to use the Town House instead. But, to both Mathers' disgust, many otherwise orthodox Bostonians attended the services out of curiosity, and in March, 1687, Andros succeeded in holding a Good Friday service at the South Meeting House, which for a while was used for both Anglican and Congregational worship.

Mather's private life was equally eventful. On May 13, 1685, he was ordained by his father. Inwardly he prayed, meditated, and wholly devoted himself to God and his own flock. Having spent several weeks visiting the Cottons in Plymouth (from where he writes to Increase), he sent his "Plymouth family" gifts, including some almanacs. He had made his entry into print by producing an almanac himself. Having begun to write and publish actively,

14

he also began to accumulate detractors. Some people in Boston, he wrote in May, 1686, "have a very low and mean opinion of me, and perhaps an undue prejudice against me." In his letter to John Cotton in December, 1685, he only alluded to what was probably the most significant personal event in his life, his search for a wife. Throughout the winter of 1685 he had prayed for God to lead him toward a proper match, but he felt obstructed by some unnamed "follies which might have an influence to deprive me of the bless- ing. . . ." During a pastoral visit on February 12, 1686 (his birthday), he met the widow Abigail Philips of Charlestown. He married her before Major Richards on May 4, only ten days be- fore the arrival of Randolph. The apparently well-attended wed- ding flattered his sense of station, for it was graced, he wrote, "with many circumstances of respect and honor, above most that have ever been in these parts of the world." He and his bride settled into Increase Mather's house, where Cotton had spent part of his boyhood. The surviving documents offer little more information about the marriage than Mather's offhand notice in his diary that Abigail made "an extremely desirable companion."

To Increase Mather

Proceedings XLV/MHS   Plymouth July 27, 1685

My most honored Father,
    It were a failure in my duty towards you, if I should not give you an account of what are the present circumstances of that part of your estate which is now at Plymouth, your son, I mean, and daughter. We had a very comfortable passage hitherward, expecting to land here that night after we set out from Boston, till in the evening the wind turned against us, and we were forced to cast anchor, and spend all the night upon the sea, not getting to shore till almost noon the next day. Our passage was attended with much sickness on my part, but more on my poor sister's, tho' we are now with our fresh air, and kind entertainment here, very much recruited, hoping to return home- ward the beginning of the next week. I meet already with some encouragement to think that my journey hither will be very much for my health, which is a thing that I am extremely ambitious of, not so

much for my own sake, *being thro' the rich grace of a Redeemer who hath shown somewhat of His glory to me, almost prone to err with my desires to be dissolved and be with Him,* as for the sake of being further serviceable to yourself and the Church of God. . . .

Your obedient son,

To John Cotton

U/AAS   September 25, 1685

But now, My ever-honored Uncle,

Now some people will hang their harps upon the willows. The great God hath given them the Wine of Astonishment to drink. The news which was so fresh at your departure hence, was a grievous abuse put upon the silly doves. First a vessel comes in from England, which lying at the Isle of Wight and at Falmouth, received certain intelligence that the Duke of Monmouth is utterly routed, taken a prisoner, and on the 15th of July beheaded on Towerhill, undergoing his death with much magnanimity, refusing to make any answers to what was asked him on the scaffold, saying, That he came there not to speak, but to die. He never had much above ten thousand men, most unarmed; had once beaten the King's forces, but the second time, thro' the ill management of the Lord Gray, he was over-powered, tho' he himself, 'tis said, fought in his own person with incredible valor till he lost the day. 'Tis suspected that Gray was treacherous, for he and one or two more be reserved for discoverers of all that had any hand, and so much as a little finger, in the conspiracy. And what use is now made of this attempt to ruin all Protestants, is obvious to any considerate person, nor is it to be thought on without bleeding lamentations.

But since, there comes in another vessel from Scotland which brings hither some of Argyle's men to be sold for slaves; and these inform us that the Earl landed in a place where he never could get much above a thousand men, the forces of the kingdom being raised against him before he came on shore and intercepting all passages, so that they who had promised him their assistance, failed him. He had a little brush or two with his enemies, once over-night, but their hearts were so taken from them, that before morning they every one went to shift for himself. Argyle was taken in the disguise of a grazier [cattle farmer], and on the last of June he was beheaded at Edinburgh. Some that are come over were present at his execution. We have here a copy of his speech, which doth abundantly justify and augment the opinion that we had of him. I am sorry I cannot get a copy of it to send unto you, but in due time expect it. His death had this odd circumstance in it, that after his head was off, he rose up on his feet, and had like to have gone off the scaffold, if they had not prevented it.

[Mentions five hundred people slain at Taunton, England.]

You know what to think of these things, and you are no doubt so much of a Protestant as to make this use of the hideous calamities which these things will occasion to all Protestants, that you will quicken the importunate groaning prayers of your own people, and those that are in the neighbor-towns, with due privacy and discretion. I lift up prayers. He that does not now arise and call upon God, and cry mightily, is one of those sleepy sinners who make the times perilous. But you need not me for your monitor. [Asks to be remembered to his aunt and cousins.]   Your observant kinsman,

To John Cotton

U/MUL   December 28, 1685

Reverend Sir, and much honored Uncle,

Many are the thanks which myself, with my relations, have to return to our good friends at Plymouth for their many kindnesses to us. Thank Mrs. Clark for her fowls, and tell her that my prayers for her are that she may be gathered among the chickens under the saving wings of the Lord Jesus. My little sister would write her acknowledgments to her cousin and namesake for her pullet, but she has not yet so plucked it as to get a quill from it wherewith to do her duty.

I send you a few almanacs, for which you shall pay me in country-pay, I mean, with acceptance and love. God make the next year as peaceable and plentiful to us as this hath been, and obtain from us such another thanksgiving as our late free-will-offering in that kind, than which never any was better attended in New England.

[Declares that he has no news to report.]

One thing I find to my own joy unspeakable. Since my beginning in a course of catechising-visitations, I find that there are more serious young people far away than I could have imagined. O let Divine Mercy increase the number of them. But no greater joy could I easily have, than that my cousin, my sister, my child (what shall I call

17

her?) your daughter Eliza, walked in the Truth. Present my hearty love to her, and tell her that I wish this sentence of her Lord's were dwelling in her mind as if written by the point of a diamond there, *I love them that love me, and they that seek me early shall find me.* I have a notion of a match some time or other to propound unto her, a match (for she is old enough to be [illegible] married long ago) unto the Lord of Lords, the perfection of beauty, the joy of the whole Heaven, the immortal King, who is altogether lovely! But my time at present is strangely devoured. Let not my good mother be forgotten in my salutations; tell her that I have sent her a piece of honey-comb; it came from the upper Canaan that flows with milk and honey; and I wish that she would suck out every drop of the vast sweetness which [is] in it; it is this, *Our light afflictions here, which are but for a moment, work for us a far more exceeding and eternal weight of glory.*

I have now a jog to leave off my scribble. I began with thanks to other people, I end with some to *you.* I thank you for the blessings which you bestow upon a poor, and yet painful, laborious, and yet dis- consolate kinsman. Continue them; they are very grateful, and I hope will not be altogether thrown away upon, Sir, Your

To John Cotton

U/AAS   February 5, 1686

Reverend Sir,

In answer to your Athenian inquiries, these lines shall tell you that the last vessel from England brings us these accounts:

Concerning France: that the persecution is grown horribly violent and bloody there. This one instance of popish cruelty lately given will show the rest. About forty persons (of some quality, as 'tis said) having privately shipped themselves to escape out of the kingdom, were pursued and overtaken by some of the King's frigates, who im- mediately set the vessel on fire, consuming it and the poor people in it. But, which are worse tidings far away, we are certified that in last September the number of French Protestants which had turned Roman Catholics since the beginning of this persecution, is amounted to five-hundred eighty-three thousand, and some odd scores.

Concerning home: that multitudes of the rebels are executed (one Alsop, of Taunton, in particular condemned to die). A woman that lived in Wapping, whom some of our people that knew her are so vain as to reckon a devout religious person, was burnt to death for concealing some obnoxious folks. But in one town (as this ship received intelligence when it lay at the Cows [seaport near Southampton]) a company of the rebels not yet seized, being assaulted by the King's forces, made a sturdy resistance till the whole town came to their assistance, and wickedly beat His Majesty's soldiers out of the town. What this may occasion we can't yet understand.

Concerning ourselves: that the Rose-frigate was ready to set out and Randolph, having a commission for himself to be vice-president, Mr. J.D. to be president, and eighteen more to be a council, was gone so far as Canterbury in much state towards shipping himself therein.

These are the chief things which with my service to my mother, and respects to my cousins, I have to gratify you with this information about. I am   Still yours, as formerly,

To John Cotton

U/AAS   [January, 1687]

Reverend Sir,

I thank you for the kind notice you continue to take of your careless kinsman. Instead of a letter I do here enclose a little printed pamphlet which I entreat your acceptance of. I enclose also a few written sheets which I recommend unto the perusal of my cousin Roland, as a specimen of the method which I could wish his theological studies might proceed in, desiring that they may be safely in convenient time returned unto me again.

I have no great affection for the writing of news. But we are daily expecting to have one of our meeting-houses demanded by the Governor, who is very much dis[tressed?] (they say) by our late untowardness when he requested a meeting-house at his first arrival. He [a few words blotted] content unto many people, if not unto all, by his [blotted] and prudent government. The College particularly he expresses a very obliging kindness unto.

The Parliament that was to sit in November is prorogued unto February. The Turk is amazingly going down the wind.

[Few words blotted] in England, 'tis said, may have their liberty and [pr?]otection from the King's Broad-seal if they will ask it; but they generally are unwilling to ask it.

Present all my service and love to my Plymouth-mother, and my cousins.   I am, Yours,

III

THE behavior of Andros and Randolph aggravated the resentment Massachusetts felt as a result of losing its charter. Among other repressive and high-handed acts, Randolph arrested Increase Mather for publishing an anonymous pamphlet against him. In the hope of retaining the charter and of having Randolph recalled, Increase slipped away to England. On the night of April 3, 1688, he fled his house in a wig and white cloak, tailed by one of Randolph's men. His sons Samuel and Cotton and some friends helped him to get a boat to Plymouth, "like those," Increase wrote in his autobiography, "that let Paul down at a window in a basket." While Increase stood becalmed at Plymouth aboard the *President*, his son Cotton prayed, sang and humbled himself in his study until his father-in-law came with the good news that a single wind had sped Increase to London and had retarded his pursuers. A few days later Cotton dreamed that he was left alone and had to preach a sermon for which he was not prepared. His sense of inadequacy for taking over his father's many, prestigious chores is implied also in his letter to Increase at London in May, 1690, urging his return. The nineteenth century historian John Gorham Palfrey suggested that Increase lengthened his stay in England because of the flattering attention he received, and because he knew that a cold reception awaited him at home. In fact, Increase's friends did advise him to remain in England because the people of Massachusetts were, as his son would find out, ungrateful.

When Bostonians learned, on April 4, 1689, that William of Orange had landed in England from Holland, many decided to rebel. Two weeks later they dismantled the royal frigate in the harbor and imprisoned Andros. (He was returned for trial to England in February, 1690, but the new king received him favorably and later appointed him governor of Virginia and Maryland.) A temporary government was formed while Massachusetts waited to see what sort of charter its agent could obtain from William and Mary. The Glorious Revolution—Mather called it a "Happy Revolution"—made William seem a savior who had rescued

Protestantism from Louis XIV and the pope. Massachusetts responded with praise for his tolerance and with proofs of loyalty that eventually included waging war in his name.

How far Cotton Mather took up with the radicals during the "Happy Revolution" is uncertain. His son Samuel claimed that when the news of William's arrival in England reached Boston, Mather was sought out for counsel, that he tried to calm the impassioned mob and urged them to let Parliament decide Randolph's fate. Samuel implied that by advising against insurrection, Mather humanely saved Andros, Randolph, and others from execution. But Robert Calef claimed that when the people called for the old government to resume under the old charter, Mather argued against such a move as a slight to his father, who was seeking in London a complete restoration of charter privileges. Calef also attributed to Mather the Assembly's plan—which enraged many people in Boston—of having the old officers resume their places only with an explicit declaration that this did not mean a restoration of charter privileges.

Mather's letters at this time unfortunately do not show whether he was a humane moderate aghast at the prospect of rolling heads, or merely a loyal subject and son afraid of challenging the crown and offending his father. But they do make clear in detail his feelings about the new charter. Several problems stood in the way of drafting a charter satisfactory both to the king and to New England. For one, the Plymouth colony, which had never had a charter, feared becoming annexed by New York, a move by which its trade would become reduced, its militia taken away, and its significance, Cotton Mather wrote, "squeezed into an atom." Plymouth authorized Increase Mather to say that if it could not be granted a separate charter, it desired to be united to Boston. In his letter to THOMAS HINCKLEY (c. 1618–1706), governor of Plymouth, Mather blames the near defeat of this hope on the Plymouth agent in London, Ichabod Wiswall. Wiswall felt slighted at court, complained at length about the better treatment accorded the representatives from Massachusetts, and desired a separate charter for Plymouth or no charter at all. A more serious obstacle, as Mather explains in his letter to John Cotton in September, 1691, concerned the authority for appointing a new governor. In April, 1691, the king declared it for the good of New England to have its governor appointed by himself; but he would allow Increase Mather and the other agents to nominate the governor. After the king left for Holland, an order was drawn up; but it stated merely that the king wanted to appoint the governor himself, in the manner of Barbados, whose assemblies existed by the grace of the crown. Increase protested the loss of his power of nomination, and appealed in writing to the king, but got no reply. The attorney general prepared a draft charter that was accepted by the king, naming Sir William Phips as governor.

The terms and implications of the new charter are well known. It created a new province that embraced the old colony, Plymouth, Nantucket, Martha's Vineyard, plus Maine and Nova Scotia and the country in between them as far north as the St. Lawrence. This gave Massachusetts a huge, exposed frontier bound to bring it into collision with France, to whom Nova Scotia belonged. Under the new charter the governor could call, prorogue, or dissolve any assembly at will. The councillors were to be chosen not by the freemen but by the General Court or Assembly. The king could repeal laws made in Massachusetts and appoint its governor. On the other hand, the structure of the legislature favored popular rights: the court, not the governor, imposed and levied taxes, and the council controlled the governor's salary. Although the total effect of the charter was to subject Massachusetts to the crown as never before, the new arrangements delighted Mather. They allowed him to capitalize on his connections. Quite bluntly he noted in his diary that "instead of my being made a sacrifice to wicked rulers, all the Councillors of the province are of my father's nomination." More important, he enthusiastically approved of the new governor, Sir William Phips, a man he himself baptized in March, 1690.

One consequence of the Glorious Revolution was the involvement of Massachusetts in a war that would prove ruinous to its political and financial stability. The fanatically anti-French William declared war on France in the summer of 1689, after only three months of his reign. Some historians regard King William's War (also called the War of the League of Augsburg) as the beginning of a new Hundred Years War, ending at Waterloo in 1815. To eliminate France from the New World became for New Englanders a test of loyalty to William, a victory over popery, and a dream of safety. The price was a series of wars against New France lasting seventy years.

Mather's letters over the next few years abound with references to the fighting. In April, 1690, an intercolonial defense council met in New York to mount a joint attack on Montreal under Major-general Fitz-John Winthrop, son of the governor of Connecticut. In May of that year, Phips took Port Royal and forced the inhabitants to swear allegiance to the English crown. But the later expeditions did not succeed as well. The attack on Montreal in August failed dismally: Phips estimated that Massachusetts lost two hundred men there; other estimates run as high as a thousand. In October, Massachusetts raised two thousand men and thirty-four ships for an attack on Quebec under Phips. Mather delivered an exhortation to the departing troops. But Phips proved fumbling, and the expedition turned out to be fruitless and expensive. To pay for it Massachusetts issued paper money for the first time and levied heavy taxes. For these financial measures Mather would himself later pay a terrible cost.

Such diverse historians as John Palfrey and Perry Miller have seen Massachusetts' willingness to conquer Canada for the crown as simply an expedient designed to curry favor with William. But for Cotton Mather the war was not simply a proof of loyalty, but a means, valuable in itself, of extirpating French Catholicism from the American continent. Since in his mind the war was a crusade, he felt free to meddle in its conduct. His letter to John Cotton in October, 1690, records the appearance of an unlicensed newspaper entitled *Public Occurrences*, which insinuated that Massachusetts should drop its alliance with the Maquas (Mohawks) as being indecently barbarous and probably traitorous. Mather's denial of having had any direct hand in the writing is rather ambiguously expressed and leaves one fairly certain that he had. At the same time, perhaps to preserve the purity of the crusade, he undertook a reformation of the New England churches. Together with some Cambridge ministers he called on the churches to catalogue their faults for ministers and communicants to reflect upon. The call went out to many churches, but few responded. Mather prepared his own church with a fast, and printed a declaration of the sixteen evils rampant in it, which he sent to John Richards.

To John Cotton

U/UVL   April 11, 1688

Reverend and dear Sir,

Last Saturday was with us a day of many fears and of many prayers. Before the Sabbath, our good God answered the latter and removed the former. The wind came about so far easterly on the sudden, that the vessels which were hastening after the ship of our hope, were forced into Nantasket, while that ship very happily being got a little beyond the point, bore away, till about six p.m., when with the joyful acclamations of all the ship's company our friend was received aboard, and so he is now gone, not without fresh testimony of God's presence with him. Praises, many praises do we now owe, unto the Keeper of Israel.

The designs laid against my father were very many and malicious. His pursuers (who are now exposed unto all manner of derision) had a particular intent to seize and search his papers, and this the rather because they had got a notion (how or why, I cannot imagine) that he had certain Plymouth papers with him. But blessed be the Lord, who has not given him as a prey to their teeth. A vessel is within a day or two bound for London, by which I shall send your letter. The public service my father is upon, in carrying our address of thanks to the King, makes it be an *equal* thing, as his other circumstances make it a *needful* thing, for us to do somewhat about supporting his personal expenses. [Mentions the Queen's pregnancy and the animosity between the Pope and the French King.]   Sir, entirely yours,

To Governor Hinckley

Hinckley/BPL   [Probably April] 26, 1690

Sir,

You find here enclosed some letters from my father to yourself. By his letters to me, I perceive that about the middle of last November,

God had so blessed his applications as that when all other means of restoration to our ancient liberties failed us, he had obtained of the King, an order to the Judges Holt and Pollexfen, and the Attorney and Solicitor-General, to draw up a new charter for us, which was done, but just as this vessel came away, and waited for the Broad-seal.

Governor Sclater of New York had Plymouth put into his commission, but purely thro' my father's industry and discretion, he procured the dropping of it. Our friends at Whitehall assured him, that if he had petitioned for a charter to be bestowed upon Plymouth by itself, there had none been obtained for you, nor for us neither; wherefore he procured Plymouth to be inserted into our grant. But when Mr. Wiswal understood it, he came and told my father, *Your colony would all curse him for it*; at which the Solicitor-General being extremely moved, presently dashed it out. So that you are now again like to be annexed unto the government of New York; and if you find yourselves thereby plunged into manifold miseries, you have none to thank for it but one of your own. The only hope, if there be any, left for you, is for you immediately to petition the King and Queen, that you may yet become a province united unto a colony, which you may find it more advantageous for you to belong unto. But it is not for me to be your adviser; I pray the wonderful Counsellor to direct you. . . .

Sir, Your most humble servant,

To Increase Mather

DI/AAS
May 17, 1690

Sir,

'Tis not a little trouble unto me to find your so speedy and sudden an inclination in you, to such a dishonorable thing as *Your not returning to New England*—where you have such measures of respect and esteem, as no person in this part of America ever had before you, and where the slights which you have thought cast upon you are but so *imaginary*.

[Mentions the return of other agents.]

This distressed, enfeebled, ruined country have hitherto designed nothing but your honor; they celebrate you as *their deliverer*, and have all along resolved not only the repayment of our debts, which our affairs in your hands have made, but also such a requital of all your pains for us, as would have been proper when you should have arrived here, in the way of receiving it. Perhaps our delays have been imprudent and ungrateful things; but place them in a true light and you will see that they have been purely necessary. Nor have we forborne to give you and our friends with you, those assurances which you ought rather to complain for the miscarrying, than the not-sending of.

But have you indeed come to resolutions of seeing New England no more? I am sorry for the country, the College, your own church, all which languishes for want of you. I am sorry for your family, which cannot but be exposed unto miserable inconveniences in transportation. I am sorry for myself, who am left alone in the midst of more cares, fears, anxieties, than, I believe, any one person in these territories, and who have just now been within a few minutes of death by a very dangerous fever, the relics whereof are yet upon me. But I am sorry for my dear father too, who is *entered into temptation,* and will find snares in his resolutions. May the God of Heaven direct you, and prevent every step which may not be for the honor of His blessed name!

I confess that I write with a most ill-boding jealousy that I shall never see you again in this evil world; and it overwhelms me into tears which cannot be dried up, unless by this consideration, That you will shortly find among the spirits of just men made perfect,

Your son,

To James Brown

Report/UVL   June 30, 1690

Reverend Sir,

I am well assured that you will be glad always to hear from New England, a country where you have met with many afflictions, and some refreshments. We have (like you) passed thro' various and very difficult revolutions within this year and half; but we are in our ancient form of government, for the full settlement whereof we are humbly waiting on the blessing of God unto the endeavors of my father, who has now been these two years at London, applying himself to the service of these distressed colonies.

In this form, we have newly made an expedition against Nova Scotia, and old Scotland will not complain of it that we have brought that country under the English government. But we are now also

26

forming an expedition against Canada, which has been the seminary
of our troubles from the Indians, and would place our hope in God
for the success.

We rejoice exceedingly to hear of the progress which the Reformation has had in your kingdom; and I have strong persuasions, it never
will revert. [Mentions sending along "a few little books."] If any of
your booksellers might see cause to reprint any of them (especially
my dear brother's life) I shall rejoice that I may be serviceable to the
souls of men in a land which I never saw. And I should be willing
that the churches of God among you, may see how much of their
spirit is in this corner of America. [Asks him to forward some packets.]

Your sincere servant,

To John Cotton

U/UVL   October 17, 1690
                                                  Die ob Fratris mortem et
                                                  memorabili, et miserabili

Reverend Sir,

[Commends his cousin Roland Cotton for accepting a pastorate at
Sandwich.]

The late sheet of *Public Occurrences* has been the occasion of
much discourse, it seems, about the country; and some that might as
well have been spared. People had and have a notion that I was the
author of it; but as it happened well, the publisher had not one line
of it from me, only as accidentally meeting him in the high-way, on
his request, I showed him how to contract and express the report
of the expedition at Casco and the east. However, the government,
knowing that my name was tossed about it, and knowing nevertheless
that there was but one publisher who picked up here and there what
he inserted, they emitted a very severe proclamation against the poor
pamphlet, the first line whereof thunders against *some*, that had published that scandalous thing. This accident gave a mighty assistance
to the calumnies of the people against poor me, who have deserved
so very ill of the country. The reason why I sent you not one of the
papers, was because I did myself at first agree in my opinion with
such as disliked the two passages of the Maquas and the monster
Louis; but I have since changed my mind. I now find, there is not a
word said of the Maquas but what we ought to say *to* them, or else

we bring guilt upon ourselves. As for the French tyrant, nothing is mentioned of him but as a remote report, and yet we had the thing in print long ago; and he is permitting the wickedest libels in the world to be published of our King William; and for us to talk (as his good subjects here do) of being afraid of offending him, when we are taking from him the best country he has in America, is methinks a pretty jest. But let it go as it will; they that had a mind to make me odious, have attained their end, with as much injustice as could well have been used; and a few such tricks will render me uncapable of serving either God or man in New England. [Goes on to praise the *Public Occurrences* as "noble, useful, and laudable."]

No less your servant than your kinsman,

To John Cotton

DI/AAS   September 14, 1691

Reverend Sir,

The short and long, and the truth, of our intelligence from England, is that the King the last day he was at Whitehall, declared it his pleasure and purpose that New England should have charter privileges restored. Nevertheless (said he) 'I think it will be for the welfare of that people, if I send over a general, or a governor, to unite the territory and inspect the militia of it. However (added he) I will not send any person, but one that shall be acceptable to that people, and recommended by their agents here.' This notwithstanding, the clerk of the Council made a false entry of the King's order, as if we were to be settled like Barbados etc., at which our Tories there grew mighty brisk. But before the month was out, they grew down in the mouth. The clerk's forgery was discovered, and, by order, our charter was finished (tho' not yet sealed) by which our colony, unto which the eastern parts are added, have power to choose Deputy Governor and Assistants, and all general officers, on the last Wednesday of every May. Only the King reserves to himself the liberty of sending a general for all the United Colonies, who nevertheless will have no power to do anything in our colony without the concurrence of our own magistrates; nor can any laws be made, or taxes levied, without a General Court. There are several additional privileges in this charter which make it better than our old one; and our friends in England express much satisfaction in it. This is now like to be our settlement;

but I suppose Plymouth, *which is so wonderfully sottish as to take no care of itself, is like to be thrown in as a province, which the Governor may have particular instructions about.* [Stoughton will be the first Deputy Governor.]   Your kinsman and servant,

[To John Cotton]

U/SHC   December 8, 1691

Reverend Sir,

[Mentions sending along some books.] The story of my father's having sent for his family, is false. If we have certain advice of Andros's return to New England, you will find half a dozen, or half a score, of the most considerable persons in the country (who are yet nameless) immediately to strike into England; and they will not go, except I accompany them. There will be no other way to save all; and that way (for certain causes that must not be mentioned) will certainly save all. The gentlemen will not fly, as our fools call it, but go where our Tories would be loath to have them go. The danger of things coming to this pass has made it necessary for me to speak aforehand of my inclinations; for I shall not stir without the advice of the church I belong to; others may go, with less antecedent preparations.

But this day we have advice that the King was returned into England, which gives us cause to hope that our adversaries are still clogged. God clog them a little further, and all will be well.

Remember me to yours, and pray continually for,

To John Richards

IV Coll 8/MHS   February 13, 1692
                                             the first day in my thirtieth year

My dear Major,

You are doubtless, as well as I, convinced that it is a time for churches to do some remarkable thing in the matter of returning unto God; and perhaps you have lately read what I have writ upon that article.

I now send you a recognition of the duties to which our covenant has obliged us, and of the evils wherein we are most in danger to forget our covenant.

The voting of such recognitions, in such terms as are here laid before you, does most effectually obtain the ends of a renewed covenant; and yet it is a thing so agreeable to the sense of even the weakest Christian, that I cannot imagine where those persons that have needlessly scrupled renewal of covenant, can here find any objections.

The vast benefits of our voting such an instrument (when it has undergone any alterations that shall be found necessary) in our church, are too considerable to be in this place reckoned up. I'll now only say, I believe God would make it an occasion of much blessing to us, and a medicine for such cures among us, as would fit us for every blessing.

If the church pass this vote, I would use my cares that every communicant should have a copy of it, for his constant monitor in a holy conversation.

I put it first into your hands because my value for your person and judgment (which I have in print everlastingly signalized unto the world) will cause me either to proceed or desist in the design which lies much upon my heart. And I desire you to use the more exact thoughts upon it because if I have your countenance, I am sure I shall have the immediate concurrence of *all this people* to do a thing that would be as great a compliance with the loud calls of God, as any that I am capable of devising; and *I think also that I am somewhat awake.* [Says he will call on the Major.]

Your approved servant,

IV

WHEN Increase Mather arrived from England with the new governor, Sir William Phips, Cotton Mather pointedly preached a sermon against the persecution of conscientious Dissenters and the hanging of Quakers. The sermons "ran the hazard of much reproach," he wrote in his diary, and made him "the only minister living in the land that have testified against the suppression of heresy by persecution." His hatred of persecution grew from his own genuinely charitable and humane disposition, incensed by his anger at the persecution of Dissenters abroad, and justified by eighteenth-century theories of benevolence. His convictions were now tested by the outbreak of the persecution for witchcraft at Salem.

Some of Mather's letters concerning the witchcraft appeared in print in the nineteenth century. But the holographs of these have either vanished or, more likely, have become the possessions of private collectors. Several of the following letters are thus reproduced from printed sources or from copies. Their importance demands their inclusion here despite some reservations about their accuracy. They are doubly valuable because Mather's *Diary* offers only a single summary, not a day-by-day account, of his part in the proceedings, and because during the trials he wrote to the men chiefly concerned in them. JOHN FOSTER (d. 1711), an important merchant in Mather's congregation, was a member of the council at the time of the trials; John Richards was one of the judges; STEPHEN SEWALL (1657–1725), brother of the diarist, was the clerk; and WILLIAM STOUGHTON (c. 1631–1701) was appointed by Phips to preside over the tribunal as chief justice.

It is Mather's part in the trials that, more than anything else, identifies him in the popular mind and, by extension, still symbolizes Puritanism. The identification rests on the defense of the proceedings which Mather wrote (*The Wonders of the Invisible World*), on Robert Calef's singling out of Mather for special abuse, and on a simpleminded marrying of the most prominent man of his time to the most notorious incident of his time. Actually, Mather had very little to do directly with the trials; his suspicions of them were momentous; he did not want to defend them; and he played Poe to Calef's Griswold. His health, broken by his grave fasts and bouts of prayer, prevented his attendance at the trials until the very end. Throughout the summer of the witchcraft proceedings he stayed at home, preoccupied with a sense of his approaching death. In actuality he did no more than fast, pray, and offer to put an end to the possession of six of the witches by praying with them in his house. Although the trials began on June 2, 1692, he was too ill to attend until August 19, when he travelled to Salem to attend and speak at the executions. Yet people reviled him, he wrote, "as if I had been the doer of all the hard things."

As Mather's letters make clear, common sense, respect for the law, and sheer self-preservation made him oppose the Salem trials.

By common sense he distrusted the use of "specter evidence"—the testimony of a witness that someone had appeared to him in spectral form and done mischief. And it was on spectral evidence that William Stoughton, the chief justice, rested his case, theorizing that the devil could not assume the shape of an innocent person. In opposing spectral evidence, Mather thus opposed the basic legal principle of the trial. "I was always afraid," he wrote in his diary, "of proceeding to convict and condemn any person as a confederate with afflicting demons upon so feeble an evidence as a spectral representation." Such evidence not only was feeble, but also violated the common law notion that an act must be seen by two witnesses. Mather had a more personal reason to distrust spectral evidence, as he mentions in his letter to John Foster. Beginning to accumulate enemies, he anticipated being accused by them of witchcraft himself. That in fact happened. In the winter of 1693 a young girl in Boston said that she saw Mather's image before her, threatening and molesting her. Dreading the ruin of his good name, he prayed for the girl and managed to depossess her.

While Mather both feared and distrusted the witchcraft trials, he never, of course, doubted the reality of witchcraft. Few men have ever dealt more intimately with the invisible world than Cotton Mather. He did believe that witches were living in Massachusetts, and he connected their arrival with a previous influx of fortune-telling books to New England. Although he distrusted specter evidence he proposed other kinds of evidence—for instance, the ability of the accused to read aloud from the works of the Puritan theologian John Cotton. (During a witchcraft case in Boston in 1687, some possessed children proved unable to do so, but they could read easily from the Anglican *Book of Common Prayer.* Mather's concern for his stammering perhaps subtly announces itself again here.) The reality of witchcraft came home to him when on March 28, 1693, Abigail bore him a son who died the next month. An autopsy revealed that the infant's intestines were closed. Mather charged its death to witches since a few weeks before her delivery, Abigail had been frightened on Mather's porch by a specter which "caused her bowels to turn within her." As he hinted in his letter to John Cotton, but brooded over in his diary, the invisible world also manifested itself to him as he communed directly with Heaven. Angels, throughout the witchcraft period, came to him as he fasted and prayed. They told him that he would publish many books, that French Catholicism would be defeated, and that his father would be called again to England. These visionary experiences—"particular faiths" he called them—would later set him up for tragic disappointments. He speaks of them in his diary with secrecy and a privileged wonder, unwilling to divulge them to others.

Mather's belief in the efficacy of witches, however, had little to do with his emergence as the chief defender of the trials. His letters indicate that he was simply caught between his cautious, conservative attitude toward the proceedings and his desire not to offend the judges, eminences in Massachusetts who were members of his own church and whose public prominence and greater age awed him. His own father, after all, had persuaded the authorities in London to appoint William Stoughton lieutenant governor in the new administration: besides, Stoughton was a great bene-factor to Harvard. And it was Governor Phips himself who asked Mather to write in defense of the trials. Phips needed a plausible account of them because the chaos at Salem had created misgivings in London about his leadership. Mather's letter to Stephen Sewall, the court clerk, requesting transcripts in order to write his defense (*Wonders of the Invisible World*), sounds very much as if he were trying to convince himself that he was doing the right thing. His doubt registers itself in the notably ambiguous first sentence of the published work: "I live by neighbors that force me to produce these undeserved lines." The halfheartedness of Mather's defense did not go unnoticed. When his father's *Cases of Conscience* appeared, shortly after *Wonders*, Cotton was accused of contradicting his parent's views. Cotton Mather's letters to the judges abound with deferentially expressed cautions against hasty action. But however much he disliked the judgments, he reverenced the judges. The burden of his message to them was "But You Know Better," and his own judgment was emasculated by class and family loyalty.

Mather suffered for his part in the trials immediately. Returning from Salem in September, 1693, he found one of his neighbors,

Margaret Rule, under the spell of evil spirits. He forbade her to accuse any neighbors (including, no doubt, himself), and spent three days praying and fasting for her. After exorcising the spirits he wrote up his success in "Another Brand Pluckt out of the Burning." The manuscript somehow came to ROBERT CALEF (1648–1719), a Boston cloth merchant, who accused Mather of trying to incite a fresh witchcraft delusion in Boston. Calef included Mather's account in his own *More Wonders of the Invisible World*. He made it known around Boston that Mather's motives were unsavory and that his exorcism amounted to lewdly peeping at and perhaps sexually molesting a young girl. Mather denounced Calef from his pulpit and at last had him arrested for libel, but dropped the charge after Calef gave him a rather ambiguous explanation. Unable to publish *More Wonders* in Boston, Calef published it in London in 1700. He claimed in the book that he never said the things Mather accused him of saying. The story about Margaret Rule's breast lying uncovered while Mather exorcised her, he implied, came from Mather himself during a dinner with Sir William Phips. Increase Mather had a copy of *More Wonders* burned in the Harvard Yard. The mention of Calef's name could provoke Cotton Mather's wrath years later.

The witchcraft proceedings, threatening as they were to Mather's reputation, occupied only the foreground of his activities in the early 1690's. By the end of the summer of 1693 he had begun working on his mammoth *Biblia Americana*. Originally he planned to write one illustration each day on some portion of Scripture, for seven years. He ended up working on the book, and agonizing over the failure to find a publisher, for the rest of his life. (It remains in six folio volumes at the Massachusetts Historical Society.) In the same year he also began to plan the *Magnalia*, meanwhile preaching and performing his pastoral duties. He suffered through the death of some of his children, thirteen of whom died during his lifetime. To read Mather's diary on these occasions is to understand the Puritans' morbidity; the mortality rate of children in Massachusetts then must have been unbearably high. Like other communal crises, the witchcraft epidemic led Mather to seek ways of strengthening the church. He wrote his *Companion for Communicants* and broached a plan for public affirmation of the covenant and a more liberal treatment of baptism. He would make the day on which the church renewed its covenant the day for people to sue for baptism, which he now looked upon as a seal not of faith but of the possibility of salvation. (In July, 1692, he received to communion one Jane Deuce, who had a long record of drunkenness.) To liberalize the baptismal practices in his own church and bring it into "a posture more agreeable unto the advice of our Synod in the year 1662," as he wrote in his diary, he prepared a paper on baptism and gave it to his church members. Most of them consented to his changes; among those he had to persuade, however, was John Richards, to whom he wrote on the matter in December, 1692.

To John Richards

IV Coll 8; Levin/MHS   May 31, 1692
(not in Mather's hand)

Honorable Sir,

I could not have asked you as I now do to excuse me from waiting upon you, with the utmost of my little skill and care to assist the noble service whereto you are called of God this week, the service of encountering the wicked spirits in the high places of our air, and of detecting and confounding of their confederates, were it not that I am languishing under such an overthrow of my health as makes it very dubious that my company may prove more troublesome than serviceable; the least excess of travel, or diet, or anything that may discompose me, would at this time threaten perhaps my life itself, as my friends advise me; and yet I hope before you can get far into that mysterious affair which is now before you, I may with God's blessing recover so far as to attend your desires, which to me always are commands. In the meantime, least I should be guilty of any sinful omission in declining what no good man amongst us can decline, even to do the best I can for the strengthening of your honorable hands in that work of God, whereto (I thank Him) He hath so well fitted you, as well as called you, I thought it my duty briefly to offer you my poor thoughts on this astonishing occasion.

I. I am not without very lively hopes that our good God will prosper you in that undertaking which He hath put you now upon. His people have been fasting and praying before Him for your direction; and yourselves are persons whose exemplary devotion disposeth you to such a dependance on the wonderful Counselor, for His counsel in an affair thus full of wonder, as He doth usually answer with the most favorable assistances. You will easily pardon me that I do not back my thoughts with confirming histories; it is not a sudden letter that will admit them, and it would be too like ostentation to produce them; nevertheless, I cannot for once forbear minding of the famous accidents at Mohra in Swedeland, where a fast was kept among the people of God because of a stupendous witchcraft, much like ours, making havoc of the kingdom, was immediately [followed] with a remarkable smile of God upon the endeavors of the judges to discover and extirpate the authors of that execrable witchcraft. Wherefore be encouraged.

II. And yet I must humbly beg you that in the management of the affair in your most worthy hands, you do not lay more stress upon pure specter testimony than it will bear. When you are satisfied or have good, plain, legal evidence that the demons which molest our poor neighbors do indeed represent such and such people to the sufferers, tho' this be a presumption, yet I suppose you will not reckon it a conviction that the people so represented are witches to be immediately exterminated. It is very certain that the devils have sometimes represented the shapes of persons not only innocent, but also very virtuous, tho' I believe that the just God then ordinarily provides a way for the speedy vindication of the persons thus abused. Moreover, I do suspect that persons who have too much indulged themselves in malignant, envious, malicious ebullitions of their souls, may unhappily expose themselves to the judgment of being represented by devils, of whom they never had any vision, and with whom they have much less written any covenant. I would say this: if upon the bare supposal of a poor creature's being represented by a specter, too great a progress be made by the authority in ruining a poor neighbor so represented, it may be that a door may be thereby opened for the devils to obtain from the courts in the invisible world a license to proceed unto most hideous desolations upon the repute and repose of such as have yet been kept from the great transgression. If mankind have thus far once consented unto the credit of diabolical representations, the door is opened! Perhaps there are wise and good men that may be ready to style him that shall advance this caution, a witch advocate; but in the winding up, this caution will certainly be wished for.

III. Tho' 'tis probable that the devils may (tho' not often, yet sometimes) make most bloody invasions upon our exterior concerns, without any witchcrafts of our fellow creatures to empower them, and I do expect that as when our Lord was coming in His human nature among us, there was a more sensible annoyance of the destroyer upon our human nature than at other times, thus it will be just before our Lord's coming again in His human nature, when He will also dispossess the devils of their aerial region to make a New Heaven for His raised there. Nevertheless there is cause enough to think that it is a horrible witchcraft which hath given rise to the troubles wherewith Salem Village is at this day harassed; and the indefatigable pains that are used for the tracing this witchcraft are to be thankfully accepted, and applauded among all this people of God.

IV. Albeit the business of this witchcraft be very much transacted upon the stage of imagination, yet we know that, as in treason there is an imagining which is a capital crime, and here also the business thus managed in imagination yet may not be called imaginary. The effects are dreadfully real. Our dear neighbors are most really tormented, really murdered, and really acquainted with hidden things, which are afterwards proved plainly to have been realities. I say, then, as that man is justly executed for an assassinate, who in the sight of men shall with a sword in his hand stab his neighbor into the heart, so suppose a long train laid unto a barrel of gunpowder under the floor where a neighbor is, and suppose a man with a match perhaps in his mouth, out of sight, set fire unto the further end of the train, tho' never so far off. This man also is to be treated as equally a malefactor. Our neighbors at Salem Village are blown up, after a sort, with an infernal gunpowder; the train is laid in the laws of the kingdom of darkness limited by God himself. Now the question is, who gives fire to this train? and by what acts is the match applied? Find out the persons that have done this thing, and be their acts in doing it either mental, or oral, or manual, or what the devil will, I say *abeant quo digni sunt.*

V. To determine a matter so much in the dark as to know the guilty employers of the devils in this work of darkness, this is a work, this is a labor. Now first a credible confession of the guilty wretches is one of the most hopeful ways of coming at them, and I say a credible confession because even confession itself sometimes is not credible. But a person of a sagacity many times thirty furlongs less than yours, will easily perceive what confession may be credible, and what may be the result of only a delirious brain, or a discontented heart. All the difficulty is how to obtain this confession. For this I am far from urging the un-English method of torture, but instead thereof I propound these three things: first, who can tell but when the witches come upon their trials, they may be so forsaken, as to confess all. The Almighty God having heard the appeals of our cries to Heaven, may so thunder-strike their souls, as to make them show their deeds. Moreover, the devils themselves who aim at the entrapping of their own miserable clients, may treacherously depart from them in their examinations, which throws them into such toiling vexations that they'll discover all. Besides, when you come solemnly in God's name to exhibit yourselves as His viceregents, and when you come to form a most awful type of the Last Judgment, whereat the devils of all things tremble most, even they also may be smitten with such terrors as may contribute a little to their departure from the miscreants whom they have entangled. An unexpected confession, is that whereunto witches are very often driven. Secondly, I am ready to think that there is usually some expression or behavior whereto the devils do constantly oblige the witches, as a kind of sacrament, upon their least failure wherein the witches presently lose the thus forfeited assistances of the devils, and all comes out. Please then to observe, if you can find any one constant scheme of discourse or action, whereto the suspected seem religiously devoted, and (which may easily be done by the common policies of conversation) cause them to transgress that, a confession will probably then come on apace. Thirdly, whatever hath a tendency to put the witches into confusion is likely to bring them unto confession too. Here cross and swift questions have their use, but besides them, for my part, I should not be unwilling that an experiment be made whether accused parties can repeat the Lord's Prayer, or those other systems of Christianity which, it seems, the devils often make the witches unable to repeat without ridiculous depravations or amputations. The danger of this experiment will be taken away if you make no evidence of it, but only put it to the use I mention, which is that of confounding the lisping witches to give a reason why they cannot, even with prompting, repeat those heavenly composures. The like I would say of some other experiments, only we may venture too far before we are aware.

VI. But what if no confession can be obtained; I say yet the case is far from desperate. For if there have been those words uttered by the witches, either by way of threatening, or of asking, or of bragging, which rationally demonstrate such a knowledge of the woeful circumstances attending the afflicted people, as could not be had without some diabolical communion, the proof of such words is enough to fix the guilt. Moreover, I look upon wounds that have been given unto specters, and received by witches, as intimations broad enough, in concurrence with other things, to bring out the guilty. Tho' I am not fond of assaying to give such wounds, yet the proof such when given carries with it what is very palpable.

Once more, can there be no puppets found out? and here I would say thus much, I am thinking that some witches make their own bodies to be their puppets. If therefore you can find that when the witches do anything easy, that is not needful (and it is needful that I put in that clause "not needful" because it is possible that a prestigious demon may imitate what we do, tho' we are none of his) I say if you find the same thing, presently, and hurtfully, and more violently done by any unseen hand unto the bodies of the sufferers, hold them, for you have catched a witch. I add, why should not witch-marks be searched for? The properties, the qualities of those marks are described by diverse weighty writers. I never saw any of those marks, but it is doubtless not impossible for a chirurgeon, when he sees them, to say what are magical, and if these become once apparent, it is apparent that these witches have gone so far in their wickedness as to admit most cursed succages, whereby the devils have not only fetched out of them, it may be the spirits of which they make vehicles, wherein they visit the afflicted, but also they have infused a venom into them which exalts the malignity of their spirits as well as of their bodies; and it is likely that by means of this ferment they would be found buoyant (if the water-ordeal were made upon them).

VII. I begin to fear that the devils do more easily proselyte poor mortals into witchcraft than is commonly conceived. When a sinful child of man distempers himself with some exorbitant motions in his mind (and it is to be feared the murmuring phrensies of late prevailing in the country have this way exposed many to sore temptations) a devil then soon presents himself unto him, and he demands, Are you willing that I should go do this or that for you? If the man once comply, the devil hath him now in a most horrid snare, and by a permission from the just vengeance of God he visits the man with buffetings as well as allurements, till the forlorn man at first only for the sake of quietness, but at length out of improved wickedness, will commission the devil to do mischief as often as he requires it. And for this cause 'tis worth considering, whether there be a necessity always by extirpations by halter or fagot every wretched creature that shall be hooked into some degrees of witchcraft. What if some of the lesser criminals be only scourged with lesser punishments, and also put upon some solemn, open, public, and explicit renunciation of the devil? I am apt to think that the devils would then cease afflicting the neighborhood whom these wretches have stood them upon, and perhaps they themselves would now suffer some impressions from the devils, which if they do, they must be willing to bear till the God that hears prayer deliver them. Or what if the death of some of the offenders were either diverted or inflicted, according to the success of such their renunciation.

But I find my free thoughts thus freely laid before Your Honor, begin to have too much freedom in them. I shall now therefore add no more but my humble and most fervent prayers to the God who gives wisdom liberally, that you and your honorable brethren may be furnished from on high, with all that wisdom, as well as justice, which is requisite in the thorny affair before you. God will be with you. I am persuaded He will; and with that persuasion I subscribe myself, 　　　　　　　　　　　　　Sir, Your very devoted servant,

To John Cotton

DI/AAS 　　　　　　　　　　　　　　　　　　　August 5, 1692

Reverend Sir,

Our good God is working of miracles. Five witches were lately executed, impudently demanding of God a miraculous vindication of their innocency. Immediately upon this, our God miraculously sent in five Andover witches, who made a most ample, surprising, amazing confession of all their villainies, and declared the five newly executed to have been of their company, discovering many more, but all agreeing in Burroughs being their ringleader, who, I suppose, this day receives his trial at Salem, whither a vast concourse of people is gone, my father this morning among the rest. Since those, there have come in other confessors; yea, they come in daily. About this prodigious matter my soul has been refreshed with some little short of miraculous answers of prayer, which are not to be written; but they comfort me with a prospect of a hopeful issue.

The whole town yesterday turned the lecture into a fast, kept in our meeting-house; God give a good return. But in the morning we were entertained with the horrible tidings of the late earthquake at

Jamaica, on the 7th of June last. When, on a fair day, the sea suddenly swelled, and the earth shook and broke in many places; and in a minute's time, the rich town of Port-Royal, the Tyrus of the whole English America, but a very Sodom for wickedness, was immediately swallowed up, and the sea came rolling over the town. No less than seventeen-hundred souls of that one town are missing, besides other incredible devastations all over the island, where houses are demolished, mountains overturned, rocks rent, and all manner of destruction inflicted. The Non-conformist minister there escaped wonderfully with his life. Some of our poor New England people are lost in the ruins, and others have their bones broke. Forty vessels were sunk—namely all whose cables did not break; but no New England ones. Behold, an accident speaking to all our English America. I live in pains, and want your prayers. Bestow them, dear Sir, on Your,

To John Foster

TLHSQ;HM/*   August 17, 1692

Sir,

You would know whether I still retain my opinion about the horrible witchcrafts among us, and I acknowledge that I do.

I do still think that when there is no further evidence against a person but only this, that a specter in their shape does afflict a neighbor, that evidence is not enough to convict the [word missing] of witchcraft.

That the devils have a natural power which makes them capable of exhibiting what shape they please I suppose nobody doubts, and I have no absolute promise of God that they shall not exhibit mine.

It is the opinion generally of all Protestant writers that the devil may thus abuse the innocent; yea, 'tis the confession of some popish ones. And our honorable judges are so eminent for their justice, wisdom, and goodness, that whatever their own particular sense may be, yet they will not proceed capitally against any, upon a principle contested with great odds on the other side in the learned and godly world.

Nevertheless, a very great use is to be made of the spectral impressions upon the sufferers. They justly introduce, and determine, an inquiry into the circumstances of the person accused, and they strengthen other presumptions.

When so much use is made of those things, I believe the use for

41

which the great God intends them is made. And accordingly you see that the excellent judges have had such an encouraging presence of God with them, as that scarce any, if at all any, have been tried before them, against whom God has not strangely sent in other, and more human and most convincing, testimonies.

If any persons have been condemned, about whom any of the judges are not easy in their minds that the evidence against them has been satisfactory, it would certainly be for the glory of the whole transaction to give that person a reprieve.

It would make all matters easier if at least bail were taken for people accused only by the invisible tormentors of the poor sufferers and not blemished by any further grounds of suspicion against them.

The odd effects produced upon the sufferers by the look or touch of the accused are things wherein the devils may as much impose upon some harmless people as by the representation of their shapes.

My notion of these matters is this. A suspected and unlawful communion with a familiar spirit is the thing inquired after. The communion on the devil's part may be proved, while, for ought I can say, the man may be innocent; the devil may impudently impose his communion upon some that care not for his company. But if the communion on the man's part be proved, then the business is done.

I am suspicious lest the devil may at some time or other serve us a trick by his constancy for a long while in one way of dealing. We may find the devil using one constant course in nineteen several actions, and yet he be too hard for us at last if we thence make a rule to form an infallible judgment of a twentieth. It is our singular happiness that we are blessed with judges who are aware of this danger.

For my own part, if the Holy God should permit such a terrible calamity to befall myself as that a specter in my shape should so molest my neighborhood as that they can have no quiet, although there should be no other evidence against me, I should very patiently submit unto a judgment of *transportation*, and all reasonable men would count our judges to act, as they are like the fathers of the public, in such a judgment. What if such a thing should be ordered for those whose guilt is more dubious and uncertain, whose presence [thus?] perpetuates the miseries of our sufferers? They would cleanse the land of witchcrafts, and yet also prevent the shedding of innocent blood, whereof some are so apprehensive of hazard. If our judges want any good bottom to act thus upon, you know that besides the usual power of governors to relax many judgments of death, our General Court can soon provide a law.

Sir, you see the incoherency of my thoughts, but I hope you will also some reasonableness in those thoughts.

[Cites a witchcraft case in 1645.]

Our case is extraordinary. And so, you and others will pardon the extraordinary liberty I take to address you on this occasion. But after all, I entreat you that whatever you do, you strengthen the hands of our honorable judges in the great work before them. They are persons for whom no man living has a greater veneration than, Sir,

Your servant,

To William Stoughton

U/* September 2, 1692
(typed transcript at AAS)

Honorable Sir,

I have made the world sensible of my zeal to assist, according unto my poor capacity, the weighty and worthy undertakings wherein almighty God has employed Your Honor as His instrument for the extinguishing of as wonderful a piece of devilism as has been seen in the world; and yet I hope I may say that the one half of my endeavors to serve you have not been told or seen. But one of my feeble essays that way, I would not use till I have in the first place asked your direction, with your countenance.

I have been extremely sensible of the duty lying upon the ministers of the country to do some singular thing in a way of testimony against those evils which lay people most open to the present annoyances of the devil, and unto those duties whereto we are now extraordinarily obliged. Because others have not hitherto done anything considerable that way, I have myself, not without the advice of others, drawn up an address unto my neighbor, on the prodigious occasion that is now before us. Throughout the whole of that attempt I would both propound your service, and enjoy your conduct. Wherefore,

I. I have labored to divert the thoughts of my readers, even with something of designed contrivance, unto those points which help very much to flatten that fury which we now so much turn upon one another.

II. I would ask Your Honor's leave that I might give a distinct account of the trials which have passed upon some of our malefactors, which being inserted in this treatise will much vindicate the country, as well as the judges and juries.

III. I have not only set our calamity in as true a light as I can, but also, where I have let fall, as once or twice, the jealousies among us, of innocent people being accused, I would humbly submit all those expressions unto Your Honor's correction, that so there may not be one word out of point. In short, I have all along aimed at expressing such a temper as, I believe, Your Honor wishes the whole people at this time to be filled withal.

IV. To rectify further the opinions of men, as well about the nature of our distress as about the justice of your proceedings, I would publish a short narrative of the Swedish story, especially those articles of it which most agree with ours.

V. For me to beg that either Your Honor singly, or the judges jointly, would in a line or two signify unto the world that my labors have your approbation, or being not only an agreeable account of the calamity now upon us, but also a profitable representation of the duties whereto we should apply ourselves on this occasion.

This were an arrogance whereupon I dare not presume. Although a favor of that kind bestowed upon me would somewhat lay before the world an intimation of that holy, pious, fatherly frame of spirit, with which you are herein concerned for us, yet, I say, I dare not aspire so far as to ask it. I shall think myself highly favored if you do but let me see that you approve my cares to sanctify the terrible hand of God, which is now upon us. [Sends along part of *The Wonders of the Invisible World*.]   Your sincere and most humble servant,

To Stephen Sewall

NEHGR; Upham/NEHGS   September 20, 1692

My dear and very obliging Stephen,

[He is beset by "objectors" to the Salem trials.] . . . that I may be the more capable to assist in lifting up a standard against the infernal enemy, I must renew my most *importunate request*, that you would please quickly to perform what you kindly promised, of giving me a narrative of the evidences given in at the trials of half a dozen or, if you please, a dozen, of the principal witches that have been condemned. I know, 'twill cost you some time; but when you are sensible of the benefit that will follow, I know you will not think much of that cost. And my own willingness to expose myself unto the utmost, for the defense of my friends with you, makes me presume to plead something of merit to be considered.

I shall be content if you draw up the desired narrative by way of letter to me; or at least, let it not come without a letter, wherein you shall, if you can, intimate over again, what you have sometimes told me, of the awe which is upon the hearts of your juries, with [respect?] unto the validity of the spectral evidences. Please also [torn] some of your observations about the confessors and [torn] the credibility of what they assert; or about things evidently preternatural in the witch-crafts, and whatever else you may account an entertainment, for an inquisitive person, that entirely loves you and Salem. Nay, tho' I will never lay aside the character which I mentioned in my last words, yet I am willing that when you write, you should imagine me as obstinate a Sadducee and witch-advocate as any among us; address me as one that believed nothing reasonable; and when you have so knocked me down, in a specter so unlike me, you will enable me to box it about among my neighbors, till it come, I know not where, at last. . . . Sir, Your grateful friend,

[Mentions in a postscript that Governor Phips himself prompted his request to Sewall.]

To John Cotton

Holmes/BPL   October 20, 1692

My kindest and my dearest Uncle,

[Mentions sending along a book and invites Cotton's comments.]

There are fourteen worthy ministers that have newly set their hands unto a book now in the press, containing *Cases of Conscience* about witchcrafts. I did, in *my* conscience, think that as the humors of this people now run, such a discourse going alone would not only enable our witch-advocates very learnedly to cavil and nibble at the late proceedings against the witches, considered in parcels, while things as they lay in bulk, with their whole dependences, were not exposed; but also everlastingly stifle any further proceedings of justice, and more than so, produce a public and open contest with the judges, who would (tho' beyond the intention of the worthy author and sub-scribers) find themselves brought unto the bar before the rashest *Mobile*.

For such causes, and for one more, I did with all the modesty I could use, decline setting my hand unto the book, assigning this reason: that I had already a book in the press which would sufficiently declare my opinion; and such a book, too, as had already passed the censure of the hand which wrote what was then before us.

With what sinful and raging asperity I have been since treated, I had rather forget than relate. Although I challenged the fiercest of my accusers to find the thousandth part of one wrong step taken by me in all these matters, except it were my use of all humble and sober endeavors to prevent such a bloody quarrel between Moses and Aaron as would be *Bitterness in the latter end;* no other fault has yet been laid before me. At last I have been driven to say, *I will yet be more vile!* and quoting Math V 9 I have concluded, *So, I shall not want a father!*

Since the trial of these unworthy treats, the persons that have used them have endeavored such expressions of sweetness toward me as may make me satisfaction. But for the great slander with which they have now filled the country against me, *That I run against my own father and all the ministers in the country,* merely because I run between them when they are like mad men running against one another, they can make me no reparation; however my God will!

[Expresses confidence that God will bless the purpose of his book.]

My friends have now happily gained a point which has been long wished for; even for *me* to become unconsidered. I confess, things become every day more and more so circumstanced, as if my opportunities of serving my neighbors were after a sort expiring; alas, that I have made no better a use of them, while I had them! I seem now to have little to do, but to die; and oh blessed be the free-grace of God, by whose help, I hope, I can do that! [Asks him to write.] God preserve you, and all yours, from a crafty, busy, prevailing devil. Farewell. And think on,

Your honest cousin,

To John Richards

IV Coll 8/MHS   December 14, 1692

Honorable Sir,

Many months are now past, since I laid before Your Honor my judgment, my desire, and with God's leave, my purpose, to administer the baptism of our Lord unto such as were instructed and orthodox in the Christian religion, and should bring testimony signed by more than one among the people of God that they are of a virtuous conversation, and should after their names have been publicly propounded (and objection cannot be made against them) openly and seriously give themselves up to God in Christ, according to the terms of the covenant of grace, with a declaration of their study to prepare themselves further for the table of the Lord.

I have intimated unto you that I look upon such persons as visible subjects in the Kingdom of our Lord Jesus Christ, although they have not proceeded so far in Christianity as to be constituent members of the corporations, the particular churches in that Kingdom; and I have intimated that baptism is an ordinance that belongs to visible Christians, or those that are visibly of the catholic church, before and in order to their joining to a particular.

In this thing, the Scripture-pattern seems plain; and among the people of God, I have the concurrence of the most able, the most learned, and the generality, an army to a man.

Now that I might after many a prayer and fast, and after a thousand most solicitous thoughts, know the way that God would have me to take, I was willing to try the mind of the dear people to whom I am related; and this with as little clamor or dispute as may be. Accordingly, the instrument which I once put into your worthy hands, I gave to two or three discreet men, who carried it unto almost every one of the brethren belonging to our church that were not then abroad at sea. I directed not their coming to you, because, I told them, I would myself do that part. But they almost every man of them, did sign with their hands their desire that I would immediately put in execution the persuasions and proposals wherewith I had entertained them. Indeed, there were three or four that forebore signing the address which the church thus made unto me; but even of these, one told me he agreed unto my persuasions, and another told me he thought I sinned by delaying to proceed unto the practise of my proposals. Briefly, I have seventy-five hands (whereof three are of their Majesties' Council) and I suppose I could for asking have when I will, ten more, soliciting me to go on.

'Tis a good part of a year ago, that this thing was done; and I have ever since let it rest. But when I have seen that the devils have been baptizing so many of our miserable neighbors in that horrible witchcraft, for the extinguishing whereof God has made a more than ordinary use of your honorable hand, I must confess it has increased my uneasiness under that sin of omission wherein I reckon myself to live.

I cannot be well at ease until the nursery of initiated believers, out of which this garden of God is from time to time to be supplied with the trees of righteousness, be duly watered with the baptism, as well as with the teaching of the Lord. I would mark as many as I should, that the destroying angels may have less claim unto them.

I do most fully agree with you that no unregenerate person is to be baptized. But then, I also think that a person so qualified as has been described, and one so sensibly submitting to the laws of our Lord, should not be pronounced unregenerate. Except I own that such persons may be baptized, I declare that they are visibly the subjects of the devil; but I think that is to do them a very visible injury.

If it be said, Why then don't they come to the table of the Lord: I answer, first, because they are themselves under doubts and fears which discourage them; and for us to punish those doubts and fears in them, with declaring of them to be infidels, or to have no other consideration in the Kingdom of God than the infidels have, is, in my poor opinion, very unreasonable. Secondly, because the supper of the Lord, requiring not only grace but some growth in grace, and being a sacrament of confirmation for those who have heretofore in baptism had their initiation, we may justly expect more positive attainments for the one, than for the other; and so the primitive churches practised.

But where shall we stop? I answer, the instrument which our brethren have signed sets a sacred and a glorious bound; if we go hitherto and no further, we shall be safe, and none can fairly demand us to go any further. It was in part for this cause that I was willing to have this instrument so circumstanced; namely, because if hereafter you should have a pastor who may not be so concerned for purity or administrations as I hope you have always found, and may yet find, me to be, you may have an everlasting clog upon all endeavors of any man to prostitute an ordinance.

In short, this dispensation of baptism, to such as have received the messages of the Gospel, which I bring unto them unto whom I am to seal the truth of the covenant so received by them, in the baptism of that covenant, it is properly *my* work. And I have therefore so cautiously stated the whole matter that I avoid entangling any of our brethren who may be scrupulous, in any act which they may not see light for. And yet I resolve also, in all my admissions, to have the particular assistances of two or three or more of our understanding brethren; and particularly of some that have been most scrupulous of enlargements, until we have a consistory of elders more fully settled.

I am ever now and then visited by well-disposed people who, I believe, have the fear of God in them; and these tell me, *Sir, Your ministry has broke our hearts for us; we would willingly become the professed servants of Jesus Christ; it is a trouble to us that we, or ours, are not by baptism dedicated unto Him: will you baptize us? Sir, if you can't, we must be forced to seek that blessing elsewhere, and so leave your ministry, which we would not leave upon any other terms whatsoever. It is true, we should come to the Lord's table; but such is our weakness, we dare not; pray don't punish us for that weakness; and when we are a little better confirmed in Christianity, we shall come.* These persons I do in my conscience judge that I ought to baptize; and yet, scores of such have I banished from my ministry merely because I have been loath to go against the sense of *but two* very good men, whom I value at so high a rate; and of these, dearest sir, you are the chief. *Quere,* whether my dear Major himself would not advise me to do otherwise? Say, my excellent friend, say, whether this be not *hard!*

God forbid that ever I should pollute the sanctuary! But I think the way of the Lord which I have offered is the most ready way to prevent feared pollutions. For my part, I shall not be able to hold up my head before the whole Christian world, until I do more than I have done in this regard; no, nor can I answer it unto the Lord Jesus Christ Himself, before whose judgment-seat I set myself, when I am going to take any steps in this affair.

All that I now ask of my ever-honored Richards, to whom I have signalized my perpetual respects before the whole world, and whom I can't endure to dissent from, is but thus much. Tell me that if I proceed in what I propound, it will be (tho' perhaps not easy, yet) not grievous to you. Tell me that if I go on, you will still hold a joyful communion with me in the points wherein we are agreed, and not be roiled in your heart about those wherein we are not. For my part, I observe it that the more men grow in grace, the more they abate of rigidness in many matters where extension of charity is to determine. And you being now grown to a high degree in grace, and apace ripening for Heaven, it gives me no little encouragement with reference to this very matter. Say then, ought I not to do what the church has in the most explicit manner called me to? And this, when 'tis my burden that I have so long deferred the doing of it? I am confident that almost all men living would say, I ought! Let my Major then say it. And so let me not want that countenance in the work of God which upon all other accounts you have always comforted me withal. God has made you a singular blessing and honor to me; and I am very confident of my having Heaven itself, a little while hence, the sweeter for your being there. Pray, let what is now before us cause no diminution of that satisfaction. Upon some temporal accounts, I suppose, few ministers of our Lord in this poor land have been more incommoded than I have been; and yet, as I never did complain, so let me not be inconvenienced upon spiritual accounts, and I never shall. But let what will happen, I will be of Your Honor, and of Madam your virtuous consort, Sir, a very sincere servant,

To Robert Calef

Calef/*   January 15, 1694

Mr. R. C.,

Whereas you intimate your desires that what's not fairly (I take it for granted you mean truly also) represented in a paper you lately sent me, containing a pretended narrative of a visit by my father and self to an afflicted young woman, whom we apprehended to be under a diabolical possession, might be rectified, I have this to say, as I have often already said: that I do scarcely find any one thing in the whole paper, whether respecting my father or self, either fairly or truly represented. Nor can I think that any that know my parent's circumstances but must think him deserving a better character by far than this narrative can be thought to give him. When the main design we managed in visiting the poor afflicted creature was to prevent the accusations of the neighborhood, can it be fairly represented that our design was to draw out such accusations, which is the representation of the paper? We have testimonies of the best witnesses, and in number not a few, that when we asked Rule whether she thought she knew who tormented her, the question was but an introduction to the solemn charges which we then largely gave, that she should rather die than tell the names of any whom she might imagine that she knew. Your informers have reported the question, and report nothing of what follows as essential to the giving of that question. [Says that Calef misrepresented him.]

[Charges that Calef's narrative also contains some outright lies.] 'Tis no less untrue that either my father or self put the question, how many witches sit upon you? We always cautiously avoided that expression, it being contrary to our inward belief. All the standers-by will

(I believe) swear they did not hear us use it (your witnesses excepted) and I tremble to think how hardy those woeful creatures must be to call the Almighty by an oath to so false a thing. As false a representation 'tis that I rubbed Rule's stomach, her breast not being covered. The oath of the nearest spectators, giving a true account of that matter, will prove this to be little less than a gross (if not a doubled) lie; and to be somewhat plainer, it carries the face of a lie contrived on purpose (by them, at least, to whom you are beholden for the narrative) wickedly and basely to expose me. For you cannot but know how much this representation hath contributed to make people believe a smutty thing of me. I am far from thinking but that in your own conscience you believe that no indecent action of that nature could then be done by me before such observers, had I been so wicked as to have been inclined to what is base. It looks next to impossible that a reparation should be made me for the wrong done to, I hope, as to any scandal, an unblemished tho' weak and small servant of the Church of God. Nor is what follows a less untruth, that 'twas an attendant and not myself who said, if Rule knows who afflicts her yet she won't tell. I therefore spoke it that I might encourage her to continue in that concealment of all names whatsoever; to this I am able to furnish myself with the attestation of sufficient oaths. 'Tis as far from true that my apprehension of the imp about Rule was on her belly, for the oaths of the spectators, and even of those that thought they felt it, can testify that 'twas upon the pillow, at a distance from her body. As untrue a representation is that which follows, *viz.* that it was said unto her that her not apprehending of that odd palpable, tho' not visible, mover was from her fancy; for I endeavored to persuade her that it might be but fancy in others that there was any such thing at all. Witnesses every way sufficient can be produced for this also. 'Tis falsely represented that my father felt on the young woman after the appearance mentioned, for his hand was never near her; oath can sufficiently vindicate him. 'Tis very untrue that my father prayed for perhaps half an hour against the power of the devil and witchcraft, and that God would bring out the afflictors. Witnesses of the best credit can depose that his prayer was not a quarter of an hour, and that there was no more than about one clause towards the close of the prayer which was of this import. [Says there are many other mistakes in Calef's account, arising from his reliance on hearsay.] Whereas you would give me to believe the bottom of these your methods to be some dissatisfaction about the commonly received power of devils and witches, I do not only with all freedom offer you the use of any part of my library which you may see cause to peruse on that subject, but also, if you and any else whom you please will visit me at my study, yea, or meet me at any other place less inconvenient than those by you proposed, I will with all the fairness and calmness in the world dispute the point. [Promises to send a full narrative of his visit, if Calef wants it.]   Your sincere (tho' injured) friend and servant,

V

ALMOST no letters written by Cotton Mather between 1694 and 1699 have survived. His diary indicates that his correspondence in those years was extensive and his creative energy, as always, torrential. Thanking God for his many publications, he was particularly gratified by the reception of his life of Phips in England. The Bishop of London sent to Boston to learn how to charge him with treason and sedition, a sign, he noted, of his growing fame. He learned Spanish, glowed over the consistently large audiences that turned out to hear him preach, yet still prickled under Calef's needling and still suffered recurring pains in his jaw and head. He witnessed the death of one daughter and the birth of another. Born to him on July 9, 1699, was the son who would become a source of infinite concern and grief later on—Increase Mather, Jr., called "Cressy." Secretly and rapturously he pondered the "advice from Heaven" he often received. Angels assured him again that his father would be taken to England; French Catholicism would be vanquished; the "Half-Reformation" marked by the publication of Luther's Theses would give way, around 1697, to the New or Full Reformation.

Cotton Mather's entry into prominence and maturity coincided with the death of one of his dearest relations, his uncle John Cotton. In 1695 John Cotton began a heated, three-year controversy with a member of his Plymouth congregation. Some members of his church withdrew from communion. In October, 1697, he was forced to resign his pulpit for breaking the Seventh Commandment and for "undue carriage in choosing elders." Mather thought that his uncle had been justly reprimanded but prayed that he would not be dismissed. Cotton reconciled himself to his flock by making a public acknowledgment of the charges against him.

But before that, he had been invited to preach in Charleston, South Carolina. Leaving his wife in Plymouth, he accepted the new post. Before departing south he visited his nephew Cotton in Boston and prayed with him.

Less than a year later, in September, 1699, a ship from Barbados introduced yellow fever into Charleston. The disease carried off nearly two hundred people, John Cotton among them. Mather thanked Heaven that his uncle had died in the service of the church, and he wrote again to his "Plymouth mother," JOANNA COTTON (1642–1702). One of her eleven children, her son Josiah, described her as a "comely, fat woman" who had some knowledge of Latin, poetry, and medicine. Of her dead husband, Mather wrote: "I had not many friends on earth like him." In Cotton Mather's new prominence, that banality would become a plain statement of grim fact.

To Mrs. Joanna Cotton

IV Coll 8/MHS   October 23, 1699

My dear Aunt,

[Letters from New York tell us that] by an infected vessel arriving at Charleston the horrible plague of Barbados was brought into the town. About the latter end of September it had been there little above a fortnight. In this little time it had made an incredible desolation. I think many above a hundred were dead, and so many more lying at the point of death that the dead were carried unto their graves in carts.

Mr. Fenwick, and others, write that all the ministers in Charleston were dead; but they mention the death of their precious pastor, my uncle, as the most killing disaster they had yet met withal. In their confusion, they tell us not the precise time of his death, nor do they relate any circumstances of it, only that he lay sick two days and he died the third, which is the period whereat the sick of that pestilential distemper use to die. That circumstance will make you think of Lazarus, and you'll join with me in hopes that my uncle was one whom the Lord loved.

I need not say unto you, how near the death of so beloved a friend goes to the heart of his relations in this town, and in a special manner to mine. I had not many friends on earth like him.

[Consoles her for her loss.]   Your kinsman and servant,

CHAPTER TWO

1701–1714

The Brattle Street Church; publication of the *Magnalia*; the Dudley government; Queen Anne's War; death of Abigail Philips, courtship of Elizabeth Maccarty, and marriage to Elizabeth Hubbard; earliest correspondence with John Winthrop and Samuel Penhallow; beginning of the "Goods Devised"; earliest correspondence with Scotland and Malabar; the New England Company; the Royal Society and *Curiosa Americana*; early financial problems and difficulties with Increase Mather, Jr.; attempts to publish *Biblia Americana*; the public bank scheme; end of the Dudley government.

I

By 1700 Cotton Mather had established what political and religious power he would be able to wield in New England. A measure of his prominence is his struggle with the most prominent political figure in the province, JOSEPH DUDLEY (1647–1720), who became governor of New England in 1702. Nothing explains Mather's relationship with Dudley but the whole history of Massachusetts in the early eighteenth century.

Born in Roxbury, Massachusetts, and trained for the ministry, Dudley switched to civil affairs as an Indian fighter and a commissioner of the United Colonies. In 1682 he was appointed to accompany John Richards to England in the hope of saving the charter. His moderate position made him unpopular at home but popular at court, and in September, 1685, James II appointed him to be president of New England until the installation of Andros. During his brief presidency he reorganized the courts and sat his close friend William Stoughton at their head. Andros later placed Dudley on important committees and made him censor of the press and chief justice of the Superior Court. With the overthrow of Andros, Dudley was imprisoned for ten months, ostensibly for his own safety. He asked Cotton Mather to help him; he was released but confined to his own house and in January, 1690, allowed to return to England.

Dudley had a gift for staging political comebacks. In London he was soon appointed deputy governor of the province of New Jersey. Later he became chief justice of New York and presided over the court which tried and executed Jacob Leisler. In 1693 he was made lieutenant governor of the Isle of Wight for eight years. Despite these successes he strove to return to the administration of Massachusetts—his wife still resided in the province and his father, Thomas Dudley, had been the second governor. He was nearly appointed to succeed Sir William Phips, but most of Massachusetts hated Dudley as a royal puppet: the instrument for destroying the charter, the willing recipient of an illegal commission, the president of the council not by popular choice but by royal favor. Dudley was also opposed in London by the influential SIR HENRY ASHURST (1645–1711), a London merchant, alderman, and agent for Massachusetts. Ashurst had helped Increase Mather win compromises in the new charter and had attempted to justify the overthrow of Andros to the king. While Ashurst tried to check Dudley's ambition to return, Dudley improved his time in England by acquiring polish in court circles, befriending Sir Richard Steele, and writing papers on scientific matters.

Dudley's chance came when Richard Coote, Earl of Bellomont, died in New York on March 5, 1701, after reigning only fourteen months as governor of New England. His regime had been lively, if brief, and revealing. Personally benign and moderate, Bellomont was a nobleman, and the first governor of Massachusetts who was not an immigrant or a native. The appreciation and respect that Bostonians showed to his high tone suggest the increasing worldliness and new social pretensions of the city. William Stoughton, the lieutenant governor, also died in 1701, and in July of that year the administration temporarily passed to the Council. As soon as news of Bellomont's death reached London, Dudley again began to press for the governorship. But the king proved unwilling at first to appoint a governor he believed the people disliked, as they did. A petition urging Dudley's appointment was sent from New England to sway the king. In his own behalf Dudley produced a flattering letter—probably the one included here—from Cotton Mather.

Why did Mather support Dudley, a man whom all the earlier

historians, and most later ones, damn? Bancroft took him for "as good a governor as one could be who loved neither friends nor his native land"; Palfrey depicted him as a self-seeking snob. Indeed, throughout his regime Dudley was threatened with violence. Some historians have viewed Mather's support for Dudley as a shrewd strategy for placing in power someone he felt able to manipulate. But of the human qualities Mather lacked, the first was shrewdness. Rather, he seems at the beginning to have been fond of Dudley. He looked out for Dudley's safety during the Revolution and tried to have him released from jail. He was also indirectly related to Dudley: the "Col. Page" Mather refers to in his letter was his own niece's husband, who had posted a thousand-pound bond for Dudley's release from prison. Given his temperament, Mather must also have respected Dudley's literary and scientific accomplishments. Besides, he saw many advantages in having a New England man head up the government. His first letter to Dudley shows him apprehensive again that the charter might be dissolved, and hopeful that Dudley desires to preserve it. (Actually, it seems that the Pennsylvania, not the Massachusetts, charter was under consideration; the bill, anyway, was dropped in the House of Lords.) Finally, Dudley and Mather had enemies in common. Increase Mather wanted to return to England as agent for Massachusetts, but he was opposed by Elisha Cooke, against whom Dudley pledged himself.

If any one thing explains Cotton Mather's support of Dudley, it is his feeble political judgment and his lack of foresight. Whatever he imagined Dudley able to do or to be, the governor was not. From the moment Dudley arrived in Boston, on June 11, 1702, Mather's friendship with him curdled. At once Dudley became his archenemy, until in 1708 Mather turned against him a righteous contempt he never had shown to any man before.

The extremity of Mather's loathing of Dudley was no doubt propelled by disenchantment, an outraged sense of favors betrayed. Yet it was occasioned by the whole life of New England at the time —the new Brattle Street Church, the fate of Harvard, the publication of the *Magnalia*, the revived Indian wars. From the beginning, Dudley antagonized the old-line clergy. Five days after coming to Boston he visited his sponsor Cotton Mather. By some accounts, Mather warned him against coming under the influence of Nathaniel Byfield and John Leverett; then Dudley went to them and told them what Mather had said. By his own account in the diary, Mather merely urged Dudley to remain neutral and to favor neither the Mathers nor Byfield-Leverett; then, Mather said, Dudley went to them saying that Mather had urged him not to take their advice. In either case, the man whose governorship Mather called in August, 1701, "a blessing almost too great for to be expected" became in his diary by June, 1702, a simple "wretch."

Bad enough to Mather that he no longer had the governor's ear, and galling that other ministers had. That among these were the newly organized Brattle Street Church group and Solomon Stoddard was insufferable. The Brattle Street Church had been erected in 1699 as a rival to Mather's. It offered a free baptism and the election of ministers by the baptized congregation. Mather disliked its very open use of the Lord's Supper, found its ministers "ignorant, arrogant, obstinate, and full of malice and slander," and believed its very existence subverted the hard-won and precious design of the New England churches. Like others, he accused the Brattle group of imitating Episcopalian gentility (Benjamin Colman was criticized for powdering his hair). When supporting Dudley in England in 1701, Mather had not known that aside from acquiring polish during his long stay in England, Dudley had also converted to Episcopalianism. His resentment over Dudley's attachment to the Brattle Street group was compounded by the appearance of Robert Calef's *More Wonders* late in 1700, renewing the sore memory of his supposed leadership of the witchcraft proceedings. At the same time *The Gospel Order Revived,* an anti-Mather tract probably by Benjamin Colman, appeared in New York. By his alliance with the Brattle Street Church, Dudley merged in Mather's mind with Colman and Calef as fomenting scandal against him and strangling his authority in Boston. (The anti-Mather mating of the Brattle group and Dudley continued to the end of Dudley's reign. When the Mathers attacked Dudley in a pamphlet in 1707, some ministers counterattacked with a petition in Dudley's favor, the list headed by Solomon Stoddard.)

Mather's hatred of Dudley, spurred by Dudley's involvement with the Brattle Street Church (although Mather learned to superficially accommodate himself to it, especially to Benjamin Colman), was further complicated and infuriated by the intertwining of Dudley, the Brattle group, and Harvard College. Mather had been proposed as president of Harvard to succeed Samuel Willard, Dudley's brother-in-law. But the Harvard Corporation elected John Leverett instead, to Mather's disgust and Dudley's delight. Leverett, a religious liberal sympathetic to the Brattle Street group, had been appointed a judge of the probate court by Dudley. During Leverett's administration of the college, Mather attended the Board of Overseers' meetings only once (although he later made a quasi-peace with Leverett also). Leverett introduced some liberal measures into the college, offering French and the reading of Anglican theologians. Mather dismissed him as an "infamous drone" and thought the college might as well be given to the Bishop of London.

A more personal indignation fed Mather's rage at Dudley. In June, 1700, Mather sent his completed *Magnalia* to London for publication. His diary notes with distress the many "clogs" that hindered its publication, Dudley among them. In London before sailing for Boston to assume the governorship, Dudley read proofs of the book and changed some words in Mather's life of his father, Thomas Dudley. Mather felt, justly, that Dudley took it upon himself to edit and censor his work. On the other hand, Mather had not memorialized Thomas Dudley with a perfect respect for the facts. In the deceased Dudley's pocket was found an epitaph he had written on himself. The verse ended: "Mine epitaph's—I did no hurt to thine." Mather changed this in the *Magnalia* to: "My epitaph's, I died no libertine." Whether he intended to flatter Dudley's piety or to question his good works is debatable. It is likely that he intended to hint at Thomas Dudley's lower-class origins when he called him a "servant" to the Earl of Lincoln. Joseph Dudley changed this, in the manuscript of the *Magnalia*, to "guardian."

In his diary, Mather packed this assortment of grudges, envies, and resentments into epithets describing Dudley as "our wicked

Governor" or, simply, "Ahab." At once he set to work to have Dudley replaced. His leading candidate was SIR CHARLES HOBBY (d. 1715), whose appointment he would urge unsuccessfully for years. Hobby had been knighted for bravery during the great Jamaica earthquake of 1692, although he never overcame the suspicion that he paid for his title not in derring-do but in hard cash. While his physical bravery seems real enough—he later acted as senior officer at the capture of Port Royal in 1710—Hobby has been seen by the historians of Massachusetts as having been vain, licentious, and the owner of half of New Hampshire. And, surprisingly in the light of Mather's choice of him, he was an Anglican. The fragmentary evidence suggests that it was the worldly Hobby who tried to ingratiate himself with Mather, whom wealth and titles seduced with pathetic ease. The diary affords glimpses of Hobby accompanying Mather on several trips outside of Boston, "for no reason," Mather innocently surmises on one such trip, "but that he might keep me company." But Hobby probably desired the governorship as much as Mather desired it for him. Mather's official justification for choosing Hobby, as he gave it to the queen's Principal Secretary of State, the EARL OF NOTTINGHAM (1647–1730), was that Hobby would not set himself against the council. Throughout his administration Dudley treated the council with a notoriously high hand. (The "trampling" Mather mentions in his letter to Nottingham probably refers to Dudley's negating the choice of councillors and trying to negate the choice of a Speaker.)

Mather's chance to even scores with Dudley arose through the revived Indian wars. Dudley's handling of the war turned much of Massachusetts angrily against him and gave Mather wide popular support. Although the Treaty of Ryswick in September, 1697, had formally ended King William's War, the hope for peace was short-lived. The Indian fighting, which had never really stopped, erupted again in the War of the Spanish Succession (also called Queen Anne's War), which coincided with the beginning of Dudley's reign. In 1707 Dudley asked the Massachusetts General Court to underwrite an expedition against Port Royal, partly because Boston fishermen there were being driven away by privateers. The expedition, consisting of about a thousand soldiers and five hundred sailors, sailed on May 13; it disintegrated into a wrangling mob. In August, Dudley called for a second try. Again the New England forces withdrew ignominiously, despite their numerical superiority and their capture of the French commander. An aroused Boston greeted the returning army with cries for court-martial; boys flourished wooden swords; housewives emptied chamber pots on the troops and called out, according to Wait-Still Winthrop, "Is your piss-pot charged, neighbor? So-ho, souse the cowards." Mather followed the events closely in his diary and wrote about them to JOHN BARNARD (1681–1770), a minister at Marblehead who had defended the Mathers against Calef and was looked upon as their tool. Barnard accompanied the Port Royal expedition as a chaplain and was publicly disgraced in Boston for playing cards during it.

Mather, and many others, blamed the failure of the expedition on Dudley. Dudley had instructed the army not to attack the fort at Port Royal, but only the surrounding countryside. He gave as his reason the queen's supposed intention of sending ships against the fort. But his enemies charged that he wanted to preserve the fort only to share in the unlawful trade with its inhabitants. The evidence against him was an invoice for a hundred thousand nails which he allowed to be shipped at the request of the governor of Port Royal. Without these supplies, many charged, the French could not have moved against Newfoundland, damaging New England's commerce. The invoice only seemed to bear out earlier suspicions that Dudley's agents had been trading with the enemy in 1706, a charge which some extended at the time to Dudley himself. Among those accused of carrying on the trade was Cotton Mather's brother-in-law John Philips. This did not prevent Mather from preaching a sermon in June, 1706, clearly directed at Dudley, on the love of money as the root of all evil. Because of the failure at Port Royal, a petition to the queen was drawn up condemning Dudley and accusing him of treason with the French. Mather inflamed the petitioners further by telling them that Dudley's son Paul had remarked, "This country will never be worth living in for lawyers and gentlemen till the charter is taken away." Heading the list of signatories to the petition was Nathaniel Higginson.

Dudley gave a copy of the petition to the council and demanded that they vindicate him. Thereupon the council and the House of Representatives voted their opposition to it, although as Mather mentions in his letter to Stephen Sewall, Samuel Sewall refused to join the vote of censure. Anticipating this vindication of Dudley, Mather had prepared a mighty counterblast, a forty-page pamphlet entitled *A Memorial of the Present Deplorable State of New-England . . . by the Male-Administration of their Present Governor, Joseph Dudley, Esq. and his Son Paul*. It denounced Dudley for the losses at Port Royal and accused him of arranging pardons for men who traded traitorously with the French. The bitter tone and content of the work reappear in Mather's letter to Dudley in January, 1708, where his stored-up grievances against the governor, finding a well-substantiated cause for expression, finally explode in cold, furious exultation. Despite the climactic tone of the letter, Dudley succeeded in remaining in office for another eight years. And in October, 1710, an expedition under General Francis Nicholson captured Port Royal.

Mather's struggle with Dudley did not absorb all of his energy. The angels who assured him of the overthrow of the Brattle Street Church also gave him a "particular faith" of the recovery of his wife Abigail, who in June, 1702, miscarried and became desperately ill. Her illness, complicated by the return of smallpox to Boston that July, lasted until December. Mather spent many nights lying on the floor half-clothed and "crying to God," his anguish relieved only by "particular faiths" that foretold her restoration. In October, in the midst of a deathwatch for Abigail, and on the same day that his daughter Nibby was stricken with smallpox, he joylessly received the long-awaited *Magnalia* from London. After languishing for seven months, Abigail died. Mather had been married to her for sixteen years. Her death moved him to prolonged fits of weeping and depression. It also unsettled his belief in "particular faiths." In the future he would treat them, he wrote, with "a more exquisite caution than ever I had in my life. . . ." Abigail's death turned him away from the supernatural side of Puritanism and toward a religion of benevolence and good works.

It also led to one of the oddest escapades in Mather's life. In February, 1703, he began to be pursued by a "young gentlewoman of incomparable accomplishments." His diary for the next six months is taken up with his bumbling, halfhearted efforts to end the affair. The gentlewoman visited him repeatedly and confessed to being charmed by him. He received her, but feared a scandal in Boston. People began to talk. Abigail, he well knew, was only two months dead, and the gentlewoman had a bad reputation because of the people, undesirable for some reason or other, who visited her father. He found even his own relatives turning against him. (The Dudley faction may also have used the affair to discredit him. Mather's anti-Dudley pamphlet of 1707 was countered by a pro-Dudley tract entitled *A Modest Enquiry into the Grounds and Occasions of a Late Pamphlet* which charged Mather, among other things, with having consorted with "a gentlewoman of gaiety, near Boston." Perhaps the affair of 1703 was scandalous enough to still serve as a smear four years later.) What few details can be added to Mather's very general account in his diary come from his un-addressed letter of June 16, 1703. The gentlewoman who alternately pleased and pestered him was Kate Maccarty (d. 1723). Her mother, who clearly pushed her to the match and kept pushing, was Elizabeth Maccarty (c. 1641–1723), the wife of Thaddeus Maccarty of Roxbury. Mother and daughter both apparently died during the later smallpox epidemic. "Mrs. S——n" in Mather's letter may be the wife of John Saffin. "Mrs. Bant" was one of Mather's neighbors, for whom he wrote a no longer extant funeral sermon. He frequently mentions her husband John Bant, a ship captain.

Mather's feelings about Kate Maccarty conflicted. He desired to marry. He confessed in his diary that since Abigail's death he had often been tempted to "impurities." He was also drawn to Kate's accomplishments, as he was invariably drawn to people of learning and imagination, however heretical or bothersome. Despite his obvious liking for her he repeatedly tried to turn her conversation from amorous to religious matters. To dissuade her he described his life unpalatably as one devoted to "continual prayers, tears, fasts, and macerating devotions." What clearly decided him against the match was that Kate's doubtful reputation among so many people would cost him many opportunities to be useful. To renounce marriage with a woman he liked and respected, but whose name was questionable, became an example of the self-sacrifices he would feel increasingly compelled to make in the interest of his flock, of Boston, and of worldwide reformation.

But Mather underestimated Kate Maccarty's determination. She and her mother went in person to Increase Mather in May, 1703, to enlist his influence on his son. Mather meanwhile shifted his amorous attention to his neighbor Mrs. Elizabeth Hubbard, a widow nearing thirty, and wrote that he believed the storm was passing. Actually, his visits to Elizabeth enraged the Maccartys and Kate threatened to remain "a thorn in my sides" if he married. Somehow she had a change of heart. Elizabeth Maccarty wrote to Mather to assure him that she and her daughter would respect his wishes and not continue the suit. Freed of this seriocomic entanglement, Mather married Elizabeth Hubbard on August 18, 1703, and found her "a most amiable consort."

To this same period belong Mather's earliest extant letters to perhaps his two dearest friends, JOHN WINTHROP (1681–1747) and SAMUEL PENHALLOW (1665–1726). Winthrop was the great grandson of the governor of Massachusetts, the grandson of the governor of Connecticut who served from 1657 to 1676, and the son of Wait-Still Winthrop, who served as chief justice of Massachusetts. Mather's respectful awareness of this distinguished lineage pervades all of his letters to John Winthrop. In the first of these he pays Winthrop's ancestry subtle homage by denigrating Peregrine White, the "blockhead" born on board the *Mayflower* in Cape Cod harbor, who died in 1704. Mather's respect for Winthrop was largely ancestor worship, and out of proportion to his accomplishments. Winthrop dressed extravagantly, dabbled in verse, and like his forebears pursued science and alchemy, even signing his name with an hermetic emblem. Otherwise he seemed content to play the part of a young man of wealth and to coast on his name. At the time of Mather's first letter to him he had married Ann Dudley, the daughter of Mather's archfoe, even though Dudley and Winthrop's father had been political enemies. Whatever political advantage the match promised, Winthrop gave up by moving to New London, Connecticut, the site of the family estate, where he lived as a gentleman, preserved his grandfather's noted science library, and dabbled with experiments. Mather periodically tried to get him to return to Boston, his birthplace, for he thought of Winthrop as a kindred spirit. He well understood Winthrop's feeling of being put upon by his neighbors and of having his talents choked off by what Winthrop called "rude and unfurnished America." In Mather's eyes Winthrop was, like himself, something of a pearl among swine.

The merchant Samuel Penhallow, originally from Boston, lived in Portsmouth, New Hampshire. After marrying the daughter of the president of the province he became its treasurer, speaker of the general assembly, and in 1717 chief justice of the Superior Court. He kept a careful record of the Indian wars and in 1726 published *The History of the Wars of New England with the Eastern Indians*. Part of the value of Mather's correspondence with Penhallow is its occasional discussion of slavery. Late in 1706 Mather applied to officials in England for aid in financing his scheme to Christianize Negroes in America and the West Indies. A month before writing his note to Penhallow dated February 6, 1707, Mather had himself been given by his congregation a slave named Onesimus. Onesimus, one of several slaves Mather owned, had been purchased for forty or fifty pounds and was "a mighty smile of Heaven upon my family."

Special notice should be taken of Mather's single surviving letter to MICHAEL WIGGLESWORTH, poet and fellow clergyman, whose funeral sermon he preached at Malden in June, 1705, not long after writing to him.

To Joseph Dudley

U/Hunt   August 25, 1701
(BL 259; not in Mather's hand)

Honorable Sir,

For the silence which hath brought me under your censure, I must (having some instance in antiquity to countenance that method of proceeding) appear before you with your son in my arms. Besides the apology with which the miscarriage of letters, I suppose, may furnish me, I have this to plead, that my frequent letters to your excellent son I hoped would speak for me to his honorable father, and be seen by him as written to him.

However, I have obtained for myself a most agreeable pleasure in the rebuke which I have incurred from you. For what can be more pleasant than to be rebuked, when the rebuke itself is the greatest expression of kindness and service, only to chastise me and reduce me into the ways of having the rays of your kindness fall the more sensibly upon me.

I fall to writing then, but not without hopes that what I write will come too late, by reason of your being actually upon the seas in a commission for the government of your country.

The Earl of Bellomont had not long been dead before the symptoms of death grew very fast upon our Lieutenant Governor, who hath now also left our helm. And I think I may assure you, the tribes of New England are now generally conspiring in their wishes to see Your Honor brought back in the highest capacity of usefulness unto them.

'Tis a wonderful thing to see, nor can I see the providence of God in it without wonderment and reverence, that the most considerate people of New England concur (so far as I see) in their opinion that your succession in the government would be a blessing almost too great for to be expected.

See our good God humbles us, and pardons us, and doth us good in the latter end!

Indeed, those rash men who have abused this country with their false representations, that we might have had our old charter if their counsels had been followed, and who used to say that if the King sent us a governor, the worse man he sent it would be the better (for a reason too vile to be mentioned) these are very angry at my father, and at myself, on your account. You know (or if you don't, our friend Col. Page does) who makes this broth.

But their anger has not hindered us two from letting the country hear us on all fit occasions, declaring that we are confident, if you return in our government you will serve the King so faithfully, and yet at the same time so study to oblige people, as would be for the interest of both, beyond what could be expected from any other person.

Indeed, if so unacceptable a thing befall us as the loss of our charter by act of Parliament, tho' it would be an uneasy circumstance of your coming to arrive with the first effect of that change upon us, yet it would certainly be a prudence (as well as a favor) in the Court of England for us to begin our new condition with the government in the hands of a gentleman that is our own countryman, and perfectly understands how to serve the King, as well as how to ease the people.

We ought perfectly to continue our kind respects unto our honorable friend Sir Henry Ashurst. And if in this one point we should happen to dissent from him, such is his goodness that it will not impair the friendship that is between us. But if we may help to bring you into it (and, *utinam Tertius esses!*) and if, all things in the former age being forgotten, you may enter this new century (which you will neither of you live to the end of! and should that consideration be of no force for it?) in a state of reconciliation to each other, it would certainly be to the advantage of us all. [Florid close]

Your obedient servant,

Unaddressed

U/UVL   June 16, [1703]

Very dear Sir,

The obligations which your letter yesterday laid upon me, are so great as to swallow up all my expressions, and for that only reason I now say no more of them.

You will find the defensive armor of righteousness wherewith you have supplied me, so silently lying by me, that I do suppose you will never hear mention of it (tho' you so generously offer it); if it be exposed, it will be on some very unforeseen and most allowed occasion.

I perfectly conformed (and shall do so) to your directions about the appendiced informations. I may take a convenient season to correct the Colonel's mistakes. For I still aver to you that I never showed the letter talked of to any woman under Heaven in all my life.

My faithfulness and innocence in my conduct towards the gentlewoman so inexorably displeased at me is my minutely [sic] consolation.

I wrote yesterday to Mrs. M——y my desire that not "only she, but her child, would forbear making Mrs. S——n any more of the theme of her invective discourses where she comes. And, that I would myself take my opportunities to say that it was not so criminal and unfaithful a thing in Mrs S——n to say to me what she did, as it might at first seem to be."

She wrote me an excellent answer (as she is indeed a gentlewoman of an excellent spirit). And among other things she tells me that her child will never any more mention the matter which I have thus forbidden to her.

I went yesterday to Mrs. Bant's (as you directed me) and there used these words (several gentlewomen being present): "It would be a great satisfaction to me that there might be no clamor against Madam S——n on the score of her fidelity to me, in the late instance that has been discoursed on. Her action, which has been censured by some, has appeared unto me not so criminal and unfriendly, as some have thought it. And much wiser persons than I do think she did as became a good woman to do."

They all (especially Mrs. Lilly) promised me to endeavor the allaying all the storms on this occasion as they had opportunity.

The affair hinted to you by my father last Friday, will not be proceeded in.

Continue an interest in your loves and prayers for, Sir,

Your sincere brother and servant,

To Lord Nottingham

U/Brit Mus   November 26, 1703

May it please Your Lordship,

[Florid salutation]

. . . the generous temper of Your Lordship towards the people of those dispositions in religion at home in England, which are professed by a small nation in these parts of America, and the service you did unto England, yea, the justice you did unto mankind in the influence you had upon that act of Parliament upon which they enjoy so much of liberty as they do, invites all persons of my character to speak of Your Lordship with a profound veneration. And Your Lordship will not wonder at it, if they who are not writing of other business, yet count it business enough to burden you with letters of thanks, and even stifle you with the number of roses which they cast upon you.

But it is another matter that procures unto Your Lordship the trouble of these letters.

The gentleman who bears them is Colonel Charles Hobby, a gentleman whose capacity and affection for Her Majesty's service are not of the smallest elevation. [Mentions Hobby's services to the crown in Jamaica and his loss of ten thousand pounds.]

But the best friends of New England . . . applied themselves unto him with their earnest solicitations, that he would wait upon Your Lordship to see whether the government of this province might not be obtained for him, inasmuch as 'tis understood that the gentleman who is our present governor has rendered himself so universally unacceptable that there is a likelihood of his removal.

My Lord,

It is by persons of the most consummate prudence among us believed, that Colonel Hobby will not by an imprudent and improper management cause a fatal prejudice to Her Majesty's affairs in the province.

Colonel Hobby is one who worships God in the way of the Church of England; and tho' they who do so in this country are one very little congregation, yet he is of that congregation.

But he has propounded unto himself Your Lordship's excellent example for his imitation; and he is for treating the Non-conformists with the respects which are due to conscientious Christians. [Hobby has served the queen well, particularly in his command of the militia.]

He will not irritate either the councilors or the representatives of our General Assemblies by so disobliging a way of trampling on them, as to render them intractable. And yet he will, with an inviolate integrity, pursue Her Majesty's gracious intentions. [Elaborate close]

Your Lordship's most humble and obedient servant,

To Michael Wigglesworth

U/Hunt (HM 22326)   April 17, 1704

Reverend Sir,

My father's tutor must not wonder at it, if I gladly put myself under his tuition. And one of the interests for which his grandson (for I must pretend unto the honor to be so) must petition his counsel and succour, is that great one of his health.

Spring advancing, Sir, I find my health must be looked after. Cathartics I have a mean opinion of. Your good *Elixir proprietatis* is, in my opinion, the best remedy for all that threatens me. The bottle which your bounty once filled, now therefore again waits upon you. You see how I presume upon your paternal affection to the unworthiest of them who (as all do) rejoice in the wondrous prolongation of your life and strength, to serve your generation.

And who can tell what the servant of the Lord, who was as a dead man almost forty years ago, may yet live to see!

The whole world is [in?] such a combustion as never was known. [Detailed news of the warfare and turmoil in Europe.] You have heard of the horrible tempest which made havoc on a great part of Europe, November 27. In France, many places were as if bombarded by an enemy. A fourth part of Friezeland was laid under water. England suffered extraordinarily. Many towns were woefully battered, many people destroyed, many vessels ruined. Thousands of poor sailors lost their lives. The Queen, in a proclamation of a fast on that occasion, admires the infinite mercy of God that she and her people were not utterly slain by so prodigious a judgment of Heaven. But behold, the impenitency of the nation! On the very day of the storm, as soon as it was over, it, and the thunder and lightning and falling of houses that accompanied it, was acted on the public stages and made a ridicule. A conformist (and one that was none of the best men) writes, that the fate of Sodom was like to be the fate of England! After the storm, the House of Commons passed a bill against *occasional conformity*, which made it a more unqualifying thing once to worship God according to the word of Christ than to be guilty of atheism and ten thousand debaucheries and immoralities. But the House of Lords threw out the bill.

Another storm is begun; God knows how it will terminate. The Prince of Wales has a strong party in Scotland; the Highlands and the High Church are for him. He has dispatched his commissions to his friends in both nations. In the Highlands, upon the government's beginning to seize the heads of the clans, the rest are upon their own defense, and mischief is hatching there; there is breeding a whirlwind out of the north. In Ireland, the papists have actually begun to form themselves into bodies and declare for King James III and commit several depradations.

—But who can reckon up the astonishing disturbances of the world! I will only add: Monsieur Du Cosse is coming to America with a squadron of eight men-of-war. God grant he may not visit New England!

I have now left room only to subscribe myself,

Your son and servant,

To Samuel Penhallow

DI/MHS   December 4, 1704

Sir,

[Thanks him for the gift of some "papers"; mentions that his children are ill with scarlet fever.]

About our friend Colonel Hobby, all that is proper to be spoken at present, is that the principal ministers of state offered him to introduce him into the government of New England, if either he, or the gentlemen of the country, would prefer any complaints against the present Governor. He generously answered, that if the gentlemen of the country had no complaints to make, for his part he should make none; whereupon there was at present no further proceeding. I confess, herein he did but follow my poor advice, for I had said unto him that I would by no means have him do anything to unhinge the present gentleman. [The next lines crossed out but clearly legible and meant to be read:] But things were operating, and Colonel Hobby chose to delay what services he had to do for the country till our ships were gone, for there were some to come over in them who were very much in the interests of him that is now at our helm; you know them, etc. etc. . . . [Close]   Sir, Ever yours,

[Possibly to Stephen Sewall]

U/AAS   January 30, 1706

Sir,

[Wishes to be serviceable to his correspondent.]

I am sensible that you take the *Boston News-Letter* for a thin sort of diet, and that you are more solicitous to know what the Duke of Marlborough does at Vienna, or the Earl of Peterborough does in Catalonia (both of whom are mightily decried and maligned by the *High-flyers* of this day), than what a *fop in boots* does at Piscataqua. [Supposes that Oliver Noyes has communicated Mather's feelings about current affairs to the correspondent.]

At this time I will only entertain the leisure of a winter evening or two with the Life of a Merry Bishop. Let it be returned in a fortnight or three weeks by some safe hand.

[Promises to send other entertaining reading.] I constitute you a sort of a feoffee in trust, that what I send may be applied unto the use of our excellent friend Mr. Noyes, but limited still with your inspection; for else, his employments are so very many, he will forget that he has what I send and it will be a long, long while before it find the way back again. [Sends something for Noyes.]

Sir, Your obliged friend and servant,

I suppose we shall have Sir Charles Hobby here by May. He comes in purely on the Whiggish interest. . . .

To Stephen Sewall

NEHGR/*

May 2, 1706

My Friend,

Because I suppose your patience will hold out until our *Boston News-Letter* has given you the detail of the public occurrences, I shall confine my short letter at this time to such as perhaps that paper may take little notice of.

I know your first and great inquiry will be, what of Sir Ch. H.! Answ: I cannot learn that about the beginning of February he had yet received the commission commonly talked of. I learn that people there, at that time, had their various discourses and conjectures about it, some very confident it was as good as done, others very suspicious it would never be done. I learn that at the time when it was just upon the point of won, the game again went on our side, and Col. D——y had his interest wondrously revived by the arrival of the £5000 of Portuguese gold, with advantageous representations. I learn that for all this, the establishment of our side is yet very uncertain and contingent, and that we have no advice at our Court that has much comfortable assurance in it. Finally, I learn that for certain Sir C. H. is coming home, and in a month or two to be expected. And so, let this content you for the present. Horrid! In England, they know nothing, they think nothing, of the descent upon the Islands in the West Indies!

[Affairs in Poland.]

There is a mighty calm all of the sudden on the minds of the people in England. It is admirable to see it. And to see how the moderate Church-men grow amicable to the Dissenters. I have lately read a letter of a late Lord Mayor of the city of London, written about the

Church-History of New England, full of such high compliments to it
as truly I little expected from a Church of England man.

I can add no more because dear Sammy sends for my letter. God gives
you comfort in this dear child. He is newly joined unto one of the
religious societies in our neighborhood. [Close]   I am, always yours,

To Stephen Sewall

NEHGR/*   October 11, 1706

Child,

[Has sent a transcript of the Connecticut appeal.]

I had made my applications to England before the last intimations
to me about Nova Scotia and Canada, and as expressively as I could,
particularly to my Lord High Treasurer.

But because your representations of the matter had a certain peculiar
emphasis or two in it, I took the pains to write another letter to
Sir Ch. H. wherein I transcribed that paragraph of yours, and let him
know whose it was, and whom you meant by an *American Marlborough.*

I can't but suggest that it was weakly done of your gentlemen to
sign a petition against Sir Ch. H. (for it was nothing else) when our
Nathaniel Higginson & Company were petitioning for him. It may
happen only to give an honest and sincere servant of the country an
opportunity to know who are (under their hands) his declared enemies. There is very great probability of its coming too late; or if not,
yet what will it signify? Everyone knows that the officers of the militia
are the enemies of the captain-general.

If things continue in the hands where they now are, there will not
be one man in all the country easier than I am. Yet I will not sign a
petition for it. I will much sooner sign that I am,

                                          Your very hearty friend,

P.S. The learned have sometimes given us a rule to put the principal
business of the letter into the postscript of the letter. Let it meet with
such an interpretation, that I take this place to render you may hearty
thanks for the great civility and long entertainment wherewith you
obliged my daughter. Your kindness to her father brings you under
a necessity of being also kind to his offspring, but you are never weary
of laying us under obligations. I thought this letter would have come
to you on Saturday.

To Samuel Penhallow

DI/MHS   February 6, 1707

Sir,

Many months ago I sent you by a captive-woman (who went by water from hence; I think her name was Jurdain) a number of little books entitled *The Negro Christianized*, with my desire to know from you, what number of Christian families in your province you could learn to have Negroes in them. Inasmuch as I have never since heard from you, it makes me suspect whether my packet ever came to your hands. [No news to report.]   Sir, Your sincere servant,

To John Barnard

U/MHS   July 1, 1707

My dear Friend,

You will easily believe that the retreat which our army has made from Port-Royal produced great uneasiness among us. As our mob expressed themselves intemperately on that occasion, so our more serious and pious people were greatly uneasy because there seemed a defeat therein given to as great an army of prayers to Heaven as we had employed on any occasion.

When your return to Port-Royal was resolved on, it was admirable to see how all the storm fell at once. No more intemperate speeches were heard, and those that had been used seemed universally repented of. If you'll go on, everything that has looked like a mistake is forever forgotten! And that you may be the better strengthened in going on, we have sent you (à la mode of Holland) our field-deputies, whose orders from time to time you must comply withal.

What remains is that we cry mightily to our glorious Lord for you, which you may be sure we shall do, and keep our hands lifted up with agony. The most of the good and great things that have been done for the people of God, have been done with *second essays*. Yea, we shall never see good times until a *Resurrection!* Who can tell what may be the effect of your new attempt? Especially if the French store-ship arrive not at Port-Royal in your absence.

I conclude, that you and the rest of the worthy chaplains in the army, keep watching all opportunities to do all the good that ever you can. [Close]   Your hearty friend and servant,

To Wait-Still Winthrop
IV Coll 8/MHS   November 21, [1707]

Honorable Sir,

[Congratulates him on his marriage to Catherine, the daughter of Thomas Brattle.] Otto de Guerick says, that fifty ciphers headed with one figure will contain the number of poppy-seeds that would fill the vast space between us and the stars.

I may declare to you that I wish you, and the Lady that makes you happy, more blessings than could be numbered in the septendecillions aforesaid. My letter all filled with figures could not number them.

Tho' earth has not, yet Heaven has so many for you! Heaven, from which you cannot be far.

I will confess one thing more, tho' you will smile at me. You will excuse me, if you don't see me presently. I durst hardly be seen walking to your end of the town until a certain indignation be overpast. A just punishment upon me, for the fault of a letter I wrote six or seven years ago. I wish I knew the best ways of approving myself,

Sir, your most hearty servant,

To Stephen Sewall
NEHGR/NEHGS   December 13, 1707

Sir,

Supposing the late public ferments to be so far allayed (tho' far from over) that you may be at leisure calmly a little to look back on something of them, I have here sent you an account of one small article that occured in them.

I pray you, that you expose it unto nobody, nor let it be a moment out of your hands; but return it [at?] the first safe opportunity. You may, if you please, give the sight of it unto our worthy friend Mr. Noyes. (Tho', by the way, a couple of malignant fellows, a while since, railing at me in the bookseller's shop, among other things, they said— And his great friend Mr. Noyes *has cast him off!*—at which they set up a mighty laughter; 'twas a matter beyond a mere *ovation* with them. 'Tis possible I may know the meaning and the reason of what they said, tho' I know not all the occasions which *he* may have given them to say so. All this is only a parenthesis which you may employ as you think fit. Only I beg your pardon for my mention of a matter which I should hardly think worth mentioning.)

There are too many things to be written about.

No doubt, you understand how ridiculously things have been managed in our late General Assembly: voting, and unvoting, in the same day, and at last the squirrels perpetually running into the mouth open for them, tho' they had cried against it wonderfully. And your neighbor Sowgelder, after his indefatigable pains at the castration of all common honesty, rewarded before the court broke up, with being made one of your brother-justices, which the whole House, as well as the apostate himself, had in view, all along, as the expected wages of his iniquity.

Not only ridiculous, but very barbarous, was the proceeding of the Council (and afterwards the other House) on their contriving their vote so as to stigmatize by name such an excellent person as Nathaniel Higginson. It had been easier to have said, they were sorry such worthy persons as the subscribers of the petition had been imposed upon by false informations. Even this had been too much. For this infamous Nathaniel Higginson, etc., whom we have in print vilified as an author of *scandalous and wicked accusations,* had the oaths of credible witnesses before his eyes to assure him that his petition was true. And he with his honorable companions will doubtless pursue a public vindication, for which they will not want materials. They will particularly prove, that a hundred thousand nails are iron, and that furnishing an enemy to shingle a thatched fort is high treason. The attempts of our councilors to blanch Ethiopians and blacken honest men, will expose them to ridicule. The history of the late proceedings in the General Assembly will, by a number of themselves, be sent over; yea, 'tis already done; and there will be other gentlemen, with their characters and their oracles in print, as well as Nathaniel Higginson.

And, the ingratitude!—But, *Brutus* among them too! *John Higginson* one of the stigmatizers of *Nathaniel Higginson!*—Tell him, (not from me, 'tho; 'tis none of my business!) how grievously the gentlemen in Boston generally resent the inhumanity!

Your excellent brother will be the darling of the oppressed people for what he has done. He has done bravely! 'Tis incomprehensible, what a contempt the rest of our Council have brought upon themselves. They wonder, that in a Council chosen by the people, they do not find half the fidelity and integrity which is exemplified by the councils in the other plantations, where none of them are chosen so!

If things continue in the present administration, there will shortly be not so much as a shadow of justice left in the country. Bribery, a crime capital among the pagans, is already a peccadillo among us. All officers are learning it. And, if I should say, judges will find the way to it; some will say, there needs not the future tense in the case; but it may qualify them for our clergy to recommend them to be, not examples, but—Everything is betrayed; and that he on the top of our House may complete all, our very religion, with all the churches, is at last betrayed—the treachery carried on with lies and fallacious representations, and finished by the rash hands of our clergy.

Tho' there are few men to be trusted, and you see your best neighbors *will lee a little*, yet you see how much I can trust *you*, in the freedom I use with you (Mal III 16).

I am surprised to think what work Mr. Benjamin Brown's brother-in-law will make with our Piscataqua-men, who have lately so scorched him; and with the rest of our New England men. There are those going over in the fleet who will certainly furnish him with matter enough to fill many *Observators*.

If the letters of our best intelligence have any truth in them, our filthy and foolish *News-Letter* here will within this half-year be served *à la mode* of *Piscataqua*!

I long to see you, tho' I take it for granted I shall not do it again at Salem. [Close]   Sir, Your sincere servant,

To John Winthrop

IV Coll 8/MHS   December 16, 1707

Sir,

If there be a family in the world which I have endeavored always to treat with all possible service and honor, 'tis the *Winthropian*.

If there be a person in that family for whose welfare I have even travailed with agony, 'tis *you*; whereof the walls of a certain *bibliothecula* in the world are but some of the many witnesses.

[Congratulates him on his marriage to Ann Dudley, daughter of the governor. Desires the publication of his sermon at the funeral of John Winthrop, governor of Connecticut, who died in November, 1707.]

I do it for a hundred reasons, needless to be mentioned. I will only mention one that comes after the ninety-ninth. Our paltry *News-Letter*, when it reports the death of that meritorious gentleman, takes care that not so much as one honorable word shall be spoken of him —an omission like to which it was never guilty of, no, not when such a blockhead as old White of Marshfield was to be spoken of.

[Urges that the sermon be published soon.]

The famine of paper creates a difficulty. But one ream will print more than two hundred copies, which may doubtless be found in some store-house or other. And so many copies may present every magistrate and minister and deputy in Connecticut colony with one, and reserve some number for other particular friends, both here and in England.

. . . I heartily desire, (what I do indeed with pleasure see daily accomplishing) that you may be turned into your *uncle*, be a lover of your country and inherit the true spirit of a gentleman.

The dreadful elegies, or epitaphs (or What-shall's-call-em!) whereof you gave me the sight this day, moved my indignation so far that tho' I am an old man, I could hardly forbear a verse of my own.

I have some thoughts of adding such a thing at the end of your sermon, when I shall understand that it is in the printer's hands.

[Close]   Your true friend and servant,

To Governor Joseph Dudley

I Coll 3/*   January 20, 1708
(inaccurate copy, not in Mather's hand, at LC)

Sir,

There have appeared such things in your conduct that a just concern for the welfare of Your Excellency seems to render it necessary that you should be faithfully advised of them. It was not without a design to introduce and exercise this faithfulness that I have in diverse letters to Your Excellency sought out acceptable words, and acknowledged everything in the world that might at all dispose you to give me the hearing. In some of those letters, I have indeed, with the language of the tribe of Naphthali, insinuated unto you what those points were, wherein I earnestly desired that we might observe and confess you laudable. And I still imagined that you would at the same time understand my apprehension of there being points wherein you were too defective. But Your Excellency compels me to see that the schemes of speaking and modes of addressing used among persons of the most polite education will not answer the expectation I have had of them. You will give me leave to write nothing but in a style whereof an ignorant mob, to whom (as well as the General Assembly) you think fit to communicate what fragments you please of my letters, must be competent judges. I must proceed accordingly. And tho' I may complain of it, that the letters which I have written formerly to Your Excellency have been improved unto my damage, yet I will now venture another, which if it may be for your service, I care not tho' it be as much for my detriment as any of the rest, and exposed as an appendix unto them. A letter of mine, the reading whereof to King William was (as I have heard) of some small service to you in obtaining his royal determination that you should have his commission for the government, brought upon me an extreme displeasure in the country. I proposed therein to return good for evil, to conquer evil with good, and retaliate (in my own way) the venoms which you poured upon me in your last conference with my father, at your leaving New England. And if I never saw after this an expression of your gratitude, yet I saw all that I proposed. However, to hand such a gross untruth about the country, as a report (which I hear some of your counselors do as from you) that at the time of my writing that letter I wrote another quite the contrary, to do you a disservice, is but a very mean requital.

When that letter was written, I weakly believed that the wicked and horrid things done before the righteous Revolution, had been heartily repented of, and that the rueful business at New York, which many illustrious persons of both Houses of Parliament, often called a barbarous murder, and which the King, Lords, and Commons, by an act of Parliament invited all persons to think so, had been considered with such a repentance as might save you and your family from any further storms of Heaven for the revenging of it. I flattered myself with a belief that you would know no interests but those of a glorious Christ, and of His people and kingdom, and study what you should render to Him for His wonderful dispensations towards you in restoring you to your family, with the government of a people with whom you had been in such evil circumstances. [Stresses that he always presented Dudley to the people as "a good man."]

Sir, your snare has been that thing, the hatred whereof is most expressly required of the ruler, namely *covetousness*. When a governor shall make his government more an engine to enrich himself than to befriend his country, and shall by the unhallowed hunger of riches be prevailed withal to do many wrong, base, dishonorable things; it is a covetousness which will shut out from the Kingdom of Heaven; and sometimes the loss of a government on earth also is the punishment of it. Now, Sir, much of this has appeared in your administration; and the disposition to make haste to be rich, has betrayed you unto things from which many have wondered that the natural goodness which they thought was in your temper has not restrained you. [Others have censured Dudley even more harshly.] The main channel of that *covetousness* has been the reign of bribery which you, Sir, have set up in the land, where it was hardly known till you brought it in fashion. When you were going over to exhibit articles against Sir William Phips, as others have done and will do (I hear) against you, you said *you could put him in a way to make the perquisites of his government worth twelve hundred a year.* He did not understand the way, and said *he was sure he must not be an honest man if he did so.* But, Sir, you have made the way now to be understood. It was unaccountable which you let fall at the Council Board, *that a governor could not be guilty of bribery.* Yes, Sir, in Paul's time one could; and there lie affidavits before the Queen and Council which affirm that you have been guilty of it in very many instances. I do also know that you have. You may expect that many more such instances will in time be declared. In the meantime the most infamous things done by your son this way (to whom I design more particularly to apply myself) do many of them reflect upon you, because the marks of a most intimate communication between you on this head are on the view and talk of all the world. [Bribery was abhorrent even to pagan governments.] This iniquity, and that one branch of it, a demand of cruel pensions for places, does fearfully betray and deprave the country. It brings in a flood of confusion, and it is now come to pass that lesser officers begin to do villainous things in that way of iniquity, to which bribends and robberies they embolden themselves because they think they have a great example. The dishonor done to the Queen's government by this iniquity is irreparable; it begets a low and vile idea in the minds of the people. But the worst wounds of all are given to the guilty person himself, because there is an essential ingredient of a sincere and saving repentance in the case which the person will usually run any hazard rather than comply withal; and that is restitution, I say, restitution. And this it is that many do firmly believe has drawn you in to countenance that unlawful trade with the enemies which has been carried on by some grateful merchants, and the bitterness whereof, I am afraid, is not yet over. The House of Representatives did by their vote several times over, generally declare that they could not clear you from that unlawful trade, and tho' they were drawn at last into a vote of a more particular aspect about it, everybody sees through the fallacy. Nor will such men of honor as diverse of the pensioners at home (I believe) be so negligent of their own vindication from the impolitic essays to stigmatize them in the votes which you have (and this untruly) procured to be published in your *News-Letter* as unanimous, but they will pursue the inquiry, who shingled and boarded the barracks of the soldiers at the forts in Port-Royal.

The whole affair of the trial of those grateful merchants will by degrees be brought to light; yea, is already so, and the communications between Roxbury and the prison are discovered, and will be published on the house top; and some fear will be found, *minor fuit ipsa infamia vero.*

A trial of that nature by the General Assembly is a thing which you always decried with the greatest abhorrence; yet you permitted it; yet you promoted it; yet you managed it, when a personal advantage might come out of it. The people were ensnared by what you drew, Sir, them unto, the country endangered. And I must now tell you, Sir, that a certain letter to Sir Charles Hobby had never been written if there had not come to the writer some gentlemen of your Church of England (among some of whom your conversation on the Lord's-day, after the public service is over, has been by many serious Chrisians a little wondered at!) pressing for such a letter to be written, because they protested with indignation that they perceived by some of your own private discourses among them that you intended to improve that illegal trial unto the disadvantage of the charter.

[Charges that Dudley has impaired Mather's own effectiveness, and hurt the general welfare of both Massachusetts and Connecticut.]

Connecticut, I say, because the late Governor whereof has sent over large packets to England, and among the rest a letter or two from Northampton, demonstrating a wonderful falsehood in the charges which you have loaded this poor people withal.

We have long since had sent over to us your son's letter to a kinsman, which declares your good will to the charter, expressed more ways than one. And, Sir, why should any more charters be envied, maligned, unhinged? The destruction of them would open the floodgates for a world of inconveniences, tho' particular men might be gainers thereby.

Shall I go on with my expostulations in behalf of my poor people? Before the Port-Royalers knew (tho' we did) that the war was broke forth, you were earnestly solicited (as Haraden tells) by some who would have put the country to no charge about it, that you would but give them leave to go, and at once put an end unto all possibility of any future trouble from that quarter, that [word missing] unto us. I beseech you, Sir, why did you reject that proposal, and send them away with grief, and make them fear and say, *that a seat of trade was to be reserved there?* This one thing has undone us.

When Church afterwards went with his forces thither, he could as easily have taken the fort at Port-Royal as have done anything in the world; but the reason which he has often given of his not doing it, is because you absolutely *forbad* him; you peremptorily *forbad* him. The cause you assigned was because the matter had been laid before the Queen, and the Queen had *sent over no orders* for it. Anon the fort will not be taken, and tho' the Queen has sent no orders, we send a pretense to take it. But this story grows now too black a story for me to meddle with. The expedition baffled. The fort never so much as demanded. The forces retreating from the place as if they were afraid of its being surrendered. An eternal gravestone laid out on the buried captives. A nest of hornets provoked to fly out upon us. The back of the country broken with insupportable expenses. A shame cast upon us that will never be forgotten. And all possible care taken that after all, *nobody shall be to blame!* I dare not, I cannot meddle with these mysteries. There are abler and better pens will do it. All I say is, the country is ruined, and the premises declare whose conduct very much of the ruin is owing to.

[Charges that Dudley does not allow the council to deliberate, and blames everything on them; that he often grossly contradicts himself, takes no notice of grievances submitted by the assemblies, and finally that he is on "ill terms with Heaven." Urges Dudley to repent "in the methods of piety."]

No usage that I can meet withal shall cause me to lay aside the temper towards you which multitudes of witnesses can say I have expressed on all occasions. I have been desirous that you should not hurt my poor country, for it is dearer to me than Your Excellency. It would make me cry out that I was the dumb son of Croesus. When things have looked incurable, I have declared my sorrows to a private friend, and there at the instigation of those whom I thought were friends to the public. It was never intended, but the contrary with all importunity demanded, that any of my simple conversation with a private correspondent should be made public, and that when I have spoken what the best men in your Council will speak upon occasions, it should reach any further than the private conversation. At the same time I can, with all the sincerity imaginable, acknowledge your abilities and accomplishments, talents whereof a great account must be given to the Lord of all. And I have always done so. I can heartily mourn for all the calamity wherein you make yourself obnoxious; and I have done so. I can heartily set myself about to seek the prosperity of your family; and I have done so. I can heartily pray that you may enjoy an old age full of good fruits, and be blessed in both worlds; and I do so. Secret places can testify it. Every service that can be done for you consistent with what I apprehend fidelity to the public interest, even so far as these altars, where all personal respects must be sacrificed, you may with assurance command me to do.

Scores of times have my most intimate friends heard me formerly say, that although in the time of your government you have treated me with much aversion (and would affront a gentleman for nothing but the crime of giving me a visit, and would throw affronts upon gentlemen, merely for being inhabitants in that part of the town where I have my habitation) yet if the troubles you brought on yourself should procure your abdication and recess unto a more private condition, and your present parasites forsake you, as you may be sure they will, I should think it my duty to do you all the good offices imaginable.

Finally, I can forgive and forget injuries, and I hope I am somewhat ready for sunset, the more for having discharged the duty of this letter.

It is now so near it that I take leave to subscribe, Sir,

Your humble and faithful servant,

To George Vaughan

NEHGR XVI (1862)/*   March 3, 1708

Sir,

You demand my thoughts upon the date of the instrument in which the Indian sachems of Piscataqua convey to Mr. Wheelright and his friends the country whereof your people are the present possessors: How a date in the year 1629 could consist with the true time of Mr. Wheelright's coming into the country?

I cannot but admire at the providence of Heaven, which has all along strangely interposed with most admirable dispensations, and particularly with strange mortalities, to stop the proceeding of the controversy about Mason's claim upon you, still as it has been just upon a crisis, just in the most critical moment of it. There seems to have been a remarkable display and instance of that providence in the finding of this instrument just before the sitting of your last court about this affair, and after it had been for very many years discoursed of among the good men who knew of such an instrument, but with regret concluded it lost and gone beyond all recovery.

I suppose you are making your application to those who will be far from the opinion *that dominion is founded in grace.* Titles to lands are not more or less valid according to the profession of Christianity in the owners. There is no Protestant but what will acknowledge that pagans have titles that are incontestable, and that they have not by their paganism forfeited their titles to the first Christians that shall therefore pretend unto them.

Let the date of Wheelright's instrument be what it will, there seems an instrument of some such importance on Mason's party necessary to render Mason's claim effectual. When the kings of England have given patents for American lands unto their subjects, their virtue and justice has been such that they have not therein designed ever to give away the properties of the natives here, but always intended that their subjects here should honestly agree with the natives for what lands they should get under the protection of these patents, before they should call them their own.

Briefly, you expect a decision of your case, where Indian titles will have a due consideration. And I suppose your antagonists can hardly show such a one as yours.

[Argues on several grounds that the document is authentic: the testimony of Wheelright's aged daughters that he came over in 1636, is unreliable; the document shows "indisputable and irrefragable marks of antiquity"; it is unthinkable that Wheelright himself would have been involved in a forgery.]

There was a time in the year 1637 when he was persecuted, with too much violence, in the Massachusetts colony; but it was only from a disturbance made about certain speculations which were thought to be of an Antinomian tendency. His worst enemies never looked on him as chargeable with the least ill practises.

The blinding heat of those troubles procured an order for his remove out of the colony. 'Tis remarked in the books then published, that he did not go to Rhode Island, the most inviting part of the country, whither all they went that were censured at the same time with him. No; he removed then into Hampshire, and unto Hampton, which would invite one to think that he had a peculiar interest in that province.

I have heard that when he was a young spark at the University, he was noted for a more than ordinary stroke at wrestling, and that afterwards waiting on Cromwell, with whom he had been contemporary at the University, Cromwell declared unto the gentlemen then about him, *that he could remember the time he had been more afraid of meeting this gentleman at football than of meeting any army since in the field, for he was infalliably sure of being tripped up by him!*

I know not whether the instrument of his now in your hands will have as good an efficacy as its owner had; you will doubtless think it has, if in wrestling with your adversaries it trip up their cause, and give them a fall.

I should abhor that the cause of my best friends, and a very good cause, ever should be served by any indirect means. Yet I verily think this instrument ought very much to be considered, and to have a very great weight allowed unto it.

Sir, I wish you a good voyage and a good issue, and subscribe,

Your sincere servant,

P.S. I forgot to tell you that when my parent lay at Plymouth bound for New England on March 24, 1692, Mr. Sherwit, a minister then living near, told him that his grandfather, and our Mr. Colman and another, had a patent for that which Mr. Mason pretended unto at Piscataqua. You may do well to inquire further concerning it.

Unaddressed

DI/AAS   September 21, 1708

Sir,

Your case is, whether a baptism received from a deacon employed to baptize by a society of Anabaptists and rigid Separatists, who also hold several other errors, be a valid baptism!

Doubtless 'tis not an orderly and regular baptism. Nevertheless the answer which is generally given by Protestants to that problem, whether the baptism received from laymen or women in the communion of the Church of Rome be so disallowable as to make a new baptism necessary, may serve on this occasion.

You know, they generally make use of this old rule: *Multa fieri non debent, quae tamen facta valent.* The army of them who have written on this point and against the repetition of a baptism, tho' attended with such very defective circumstances, is very numerous; and the reasons they bring are as powerful as the writers are numerous. They are so well-known, there is no use of repeating them neither [*sic*]. Here was a society of Christians, and a church, tho' laboring under very great corruptions. Here was an administrator, authorized, according unto their opinion, to the work of baptizing. The popish baptism, which compels not Protestants to repeat their baptism, has rather more exceptions against it than this, in the case now before us.

There is a distinction to be made between a *Vitium in actu baptismatis* and a *Vitium in persona baptismatis.* Here was a baptism, a sacred washing, in the name of the glorious and eternal Trinity, tho' he that performed this washing had not all the qualifications that he should have had. They also distinguish between one that has no manner of call at all to baptize, and another that has a call, tho' not a lawful one. In many churches of the Reformation, those persons have no manner of call at all, who are allowed in the church of Rome to baptize in a (pretended) necessity. If a baptism have been received from one of those persons, then such Reformers as Beza and Cartwright will afirm, *Ejusmodi ablutionem, nihil magis ad baptisuum fac[ent?], quam ordinariam aliam aliquam et quotidianam lavationem.* Certainly, in our days, and among us, a baptism of the *Boyes of Alexandria* would not be judged sufficient. It was not so, in the baptism we now have to consider. There was a profession of a call and power to baptize in the administrator. Yea, you know who, besides Anabaptists, do ordain deacons to baptize. But after all, while the baptized person has not a plerophory, which puts him out of all doubt that his baptism is a mere nullity, the judgment and custom of the Reformed Churches has been to commend the modesty of those who do not make haste unto a new baptism. For, *Non privatio sacramenti, sed contemptus damnat.* And, as Voetius observes, the repetition of baptism is usually founded in the same error that produced the disorders of the first baptism, that give the occasion of desiring to have it repeated. Namely, *Imaginare necessitas baptismi tanquam medii.* [Close]

Your faithful brother and servant,

To Samuel Penhallow

DII/MHS   May 22, 1710

My honored Friend,

After a thousand obligations which you have heretofore laid upon me, you have by your late kind presents entered pretty far into another chiliad. Should I write you as many letters of thanks as I have obligations, I should make you but an ill requital and but oppress and injure you with a load of acknowledgments. In one word, I thank you, I love you, I wish I could serve you.

I proceed unto the next part of my duty, which is to inform you that the arrival of our ingenious, generous, and prosperous friend, Capt. Wentworth, surprises us with a large cargo of intelligence. I will offer you nothing that you may expect from our public *News-Letter*. But—we may every day expect the Dragon as a forerunner of six men-of-war, with a thousand marines, of whom Col. Nicolson is General, to pursue an expedition, first against Port-Royal. The arrival of our mast-fleet, and the Maquas, may perhaps a little retard and alter some of the motions and measures—but the thing will go on; and you will foresee that it is like to be a summer of extreme distress unto us.

The Parliament were willing to exert a trial of skill on the High-flyers in the nation, and impeached one Sacheverel before the House of Lords for some fiery sermons which he published. He had a long trial of ten days; and the friends of his cause in the House of Lords were so many, that a very easy sentence was passed upon him, of three years suspension from the preaching part of his priestly function. Immediately a High-Church mob was raised by some incendiaries, who did horrid things and pulled down Six Presbyterian meeting-houses (Burgess's, Bradbury's, etc.) and were proceeding to pull down the Bishop of Salisbury's house, and endless outrages. But the city trained bands suppressed the formidable tumult. Almost all men of thought expect a civil war; at least, as soon as opportunity shall be given for it, by a peace with France, which now is diverted until some further decisive action.

[Return of Rev. John Emerson from England.]

Your very obliged servant,

II

IN 1711 Mather began to enter in his diary each day a "G. D." or "Good Devised." He would continue the practise for the rest of his life, proposing, often quite imaginatively and wittily, and then enacting some good work for a friend, neighbor, relative, or for the cause of reformed religion. After 1711 his diary is largely a record of the good he sought to do, and did. To Do Good had long been a driving force of his life. It made him give up a valuable love-match, plan to Christianize the Negroes, establish a Society for the Suppression of Disorders; it got his work done. But now Doing Good grew from a motive into a motto. By it he could explain everything that happened to him and to New England. Consciously he began to equate his own reputation with the Errand in the Wilderness, until Getting Ahead and Reformation became, in his mind, one.

Mather would henceforth try to Do Good to every man and to become like Christ. To his enemies, as he explained in March, 1711, he would return only good: "I can't recall to mind any person in the world who has injured me and abused me, but I have requited them with good." Although the possibility of such a self-view lay within the Puritan injunction to lead a Christlike life, any delusionary identification of self with Christ was always aborted by a humbling sense of man's dependence and inherent evil. For this reason Mather's near-identification of himself with Jesus cannot wholly or singly be attributed to his Puritan upbringing. Into the metaphor there also entered features of his own complex personality. Lacking any adequate vocabulary for describing those features, it is enough to say that his pleas of Christlike humility often seem nothing more than guilty checks on a resistless pride and ambition. His master plan for Doing Good seems at times nothing more than a transparent version of Getting Ahead, put in a form acceptable to his conscience. At the beginning of his diary for the year 1712 he quoted Proverbs: "He who diligently seeketh good, procureth favor." Mather's imitation of Christ sometimes seems the self-deluding effort of an extraordinarily ambitious man to demonstrate his superiority and to explain why others dislike him, while disowning any wish to prove himself their superior.

This does not mean that Mather's efforts to Do Good were illusory. They were tangible and without end. After the great Boston fire of 1711, which destroyed whole streets, he collected almost two hundred pounds from his congregation for the relief of victims. Despite gout, despite constant toothaches and pains in his jaw, he increased the number of his pastoral visits and convinced his wife to also make such visits with families in the immediate neighborhood. His letter to JOHN SAFFIN (1626–1710) typifies many such letters, largely omitted here, which he wrote to compose quarrels within families. (It is an ironic sidelight, too, on the domestic tribulations in old age of New England's leading male love poet.) He hoped to Do Good especially by circulating his many writings around the country. His letter requesting patronage for his works from the Boston merchant JOHN MICO (d. 1718) will also stand for many such letters (similarly omitted because of their sameness). These illustrate the circuitous, subtly flattering manner that Mather came to adopt whenever he wanted someone's help in Doing Good. In all of the letters, his hunger for recognition and fame is tantalizingly indistinguishable from his devotion to spreading the Truth. This ambiguity is what makes him at once splendid and contemptible.

The same ambiguity expresses itself in Mather's letters through a tone of awkward and designing stooping. For example, he softsells the merchant Mico by punning on the word "account," both heavenly and bank. A further example is the uneasily jocose letter on January 11, 1712, to Samuel Penhallow, his friend. The circumstances of this letter are revealing, and not very flattering to Mather's character. He invited Penhallow to prompt a "Mr. Archer" to contribute three or four pounds toward publishing one of his discourses. An unstated element of extortion here perhaps prevented Mather from approaching Archer directly since the gentleman had recently joined his flock. Penhallow did write to Archer and asked for fifty shillings. Mather's follow-up letter to Penhallow on January 28 thanks him for doing the part of a "cunning Archer." The pun and the good-humored tone draw attention away from the fact that it was he, Mather himself, who asked Penhallow to approach Archer; he even wrote out a letter for Penhallow to use. By making it seem that the idea originated with Penhallow, he obscures his own wish to have the work published. One can only guess whether he wanted to deceive Penhallow or himself—more likely the latter. The deception seems a consequence of Mather's effort to disburden himself of the feeling of his overweening ambition and to make himself not seem pushy. The result was the same Doing Good, but the mask of Christ often hid the face of Horatio Alger.

Mather hoped to Do Good—thus to spread his fame—not only in Massachusetts, but around the world. By writing to correspondents living abroad he also tried to keep himself up on the latest currents of European thought, and to show Europe in turn what a cultivated American could produce. His letter to ANTHONY WILLIAM BOEHM (1673–1722), a German chaplain at the English court and a voluminous writer and translator, marks the beginning of Mather's correspondence with Bartholomew Ziegenbalgh and August Hermann Francke. Ziegenbalgh was a Danish missionary who converted Hindus at Malabar; Francke was an apostle of Pietism who ran a university and an orphan home in Halle, Germany, where Boehm had studied. Through Boehm, Mather transmitted to these men his disturbed thoughts on the spreading revival of Arianism, and sent letters, packets, and money to forward their work. Despite some reservations about the Pietists, he looked upon Ziegenbalgh in southern India, Francke in Germany, and himself in Boston as working for the same end, and wrote to them hoping to bridge the divisions within Protestantism. Little of this correspondence has survived except Mather's twelve-page Latin letter to Ziegenbalgh in December, 1717, which he later expanded and published in 1721 as India Christiana. In that work he applauds Francke's distrust of "extraordinary gifts," and, indeed, the importance of Ziegenbalgh and Francke to Mather was that they stressed benevolence over mysticism, the orphan home over the retreat, Doing Good over Particular Faiths.

Mather also began corresponding abroad with notable ministers in Scotland, where his works were highly regarded during the eighteenth century, as Increase Mather's had been earlier. In 1710 the University of Glasgow awarded him an honorary Doctor of Divinity degree. With the degree came a signet ring depicting a tree with a verse from Psalms I:3 under it, the image encircled by *Glascua Rigavit*. Mather wore the ring, and justified its display by interpreting the Fifth Commandment to mean that one should assert any honor which providence has given. He was immensely proud of the degree as a symbol of his transatlantic fame and was deeply honored by this correspondence with men of venerable age, learning, and reputation in Protestant circles. He also felt a special kinship with Scotland as, like Boston, another provincial outpost of the English empire and as, again like Boston, a choice target for the encroachments of the "high-flying party," that is, the Church of England. He despaired when in 1712 an act of Parliament tolerated episcopacy in Scotland. But more than anything else he admired the orthodoxy and, as his father had, the Presbyterian organization of the Church of Scotland. His admiration grew the more he felt isolated and put-upon in liberal Boston, and by the end of his life he clearly preferred a Presbyterian to a Congregational form of church organization.

Mather's Scottish correspondents in the following group of letters are SIR JOHN MAXWELL OF POLLOCK (1648–1732) and JOHN STIRLING (1654–1727). Sir John was an ultra-orthodox Presbyterian and long-term rector of the University of Glasgow (1691–1717), which together with Stirling he virtually ruled. The minister John Stirling, a controversial figure, was accused during his tenure as principal (1701–1727) of having spent too much money on a house for himself and even of embezzlement. Much of the faculty disliked him, although later historians of the University of Glasgow depict him as an effective administrator who added professors of humanities, built up the divinity faculty, and generally improved the school. The sympathy for Stirling's position that underlies Mather's remarks to him on the American colleges must have sprung from Mather's own difficulties with Harvard.

Mather found another important instrument for Doing Good in SIR WILLIAM ASHURST (1647–1720). Ashurst was a staunch Dissenter with many important political and business ties in London.

He served as Lord Mayor of London from 1693 to 1694, later as a member of Parliament for the city, as a director of the Bank of England and, following the death of his brother Sir Henry Ashurst in 1710, as the Massachusetts agent in London. Most important to Mather, from 1696 to 1720 Ashurst was governor of the oldest Protestant missionary organization, the New England Company. Founded in 1649, the New England Company was the chief rival to what Mather calls the "new Society," the Society for the Propagation of the Gospel in Foreign Parts (SPGFP), an Anglican missionary group chartered in 1701. (In New England, the New England Company was called the Society for the Propagation of the Gospel in New England. The representative body on the American side was known as the Commissioners of the United Colonies.) Most members of the company were rich Puritan merchants in London, along with a few Presbyterians. Ashurst himself was highly regarded in New England—Mather dedicated *Bonifacius* to him—although toward the end of his life Ashurst's interest in the company waned and he rather neglected it.

The New England Company was founded to convert the Indians in New England. It invested funds and, on the interest, sent money to the commissioners in New England, who then paid the missionaries' salaries. Cotton Mather had been named a commissioner in 1698 (Increase was also a commissioner), and although the commissioners performed gratis, the company awarded him twenty-five pounds for his work. New England was not an altogether fertile territory for the company's designs, for with such notable exceptions as John Eliot, the New England Way was unevangelical. The minister's role was to care for the elect. The extraordinary intellectualism of Puritan theology and the heavy dependence of Puritan society on middle-class family life would not very well appeal to the Indians anyway. Mather, like most of the commissioners, felt just the same that the Indians could not be converted in their own language and social groupings, but would have to be Anglicized and civilized first.

All of these many efforts to Do Good, Mather feared, might be aborted by a Catholic victory in Queen Anne's War and a French invasion of New England, or through a Catholic victory in negotiations after the war. In December, 1711, the English opened negotiations for the peace with France in Utrecht, Holland. Although Queen Anne's War was essentially a continuation of King William's War with a brief interruption, it had lasted for eleven years. News of the queen's proclamation of an end to the hostilities reached Boston on October 24, 1712, shortly after Mather's letter to Wait-Still Winthrop. The death of Queen Anne doubled Mather's fears. He foresaw a Catholic king proclaimed in England, further encroachments by the Anglican Church in Scotland, and an increasing clamor for episcopacy and Anglican ordination.

Mather's domestic life at this time was itself becoming ominous. His need to ask John Mico and Samuel Penhallow for patronage indicates that he was beginning to be devilled by the financial problems that would later plague him. In 1709 he wrote in his diary that because of the size of his family and the negligence of "those that should have been concerned for me," he found that "I had not clothes fit to be worn; I was clothed with rags." Despite this pinch he soon began to care for his orphaned nephew Mather Byles, the son of his sister Elizabeth (Elizabeth was still living, but Byles's father had died). While he struggled to buy clothing for his nephew, he was forced to accept hand-me-downs from others for his own son Increase. Increase, too, disturbed Mather by episodes of wildness, keeping to bad company, and signs of lack of piety. In July, 1712, "Cressy" was proposed for admission to Harvard. For reasons not clear he never went there, a disappointment Mather faced with as good-humored a resignation as he could.

To Anthony William Boehm

U/AAS   July 8, 1710

My most honored Brother,
    [Regrets not having heard from Boehm in a long time.]
    I remember the thoughts of Mr. Teelman, a Dutch divine, on Matth XXIV—But if the Church in the condition of a carcass may be a sign of the times, alas, we have enough and enough of it. If our glorious Lord will make His descent unto us, when the condition of a carcass

invites Him unto it—*Lord, what an invitation have we given to Thee!*
It is prodigious to see what a withdraw of real and vital piety is everywhere to be complained of. The very few in whom it yet lives do in
every country pour out their sad complaints upon it. My country as
well as the rest that profess Reformed Christianity is languishing under
the common apostasy. My dear friend, what shall we do? [But he will
not despair.] Yea, but will you allow a professor of chiliasm to say,
can any [thing?] be done to purpose until our Lord Himself, attended
with the Eagles of Heaven, make His descent unto Us? *Come, Lord
Jesus, come quickly!*

[Sends along a dozen copies of his *Coheleth* and asks Boehm to
distribute a few at the Frederician University.]

I am, for certain unmentionable reasons, very desirous to get into
some correspondence with Geneva, and particularly with Mr. Pictet
there. But how can a poor pilgrim in America accomplish it! None
but my dear Boehm can accomplish it.

No [news?] yet from our lovely brethren at Malabar!

Because piety is gone, behold Arianism and Gentilism coming in. My
friends complain of me, that in all my projections for the union of
good men in a syncretism of piety, I insert clauses that exclude the
Arians. Dear Sir, permit me to exclude them. They set up another
Christ. Their Christ is an idol. They destroy piety and the life of God
in the soul. I perceive some of my brethren publish and scatter thro'
the nation my poor letters, written on this deplorable occasion. I am
content. Let them go on to do so. I cannot lay aside my sentiments.
We must keep to this, that our blessed Jesus is over all, God blessed
forever, or we are undone. [Close]

To John Saffin

Hutchinson/Mass Arch   July 19, 1710

You will give me leave to proceed in offering my poor advice upon
your distressing affairs.

I am informed that M. Saffin is inviting you to take your quarters
where she has hers, and enjoy the best assistances her person and estate
can give to render your old age honorable and comfortable.

My humble opinion is that you will do well to accept this offer, and
spend the rest of your very little time in as easy and as pious a manner
as 'tis possible.

'Tis my opinion that your acceptance of this offer should be attended with two agreeable circumstances.

The one is (as I have heretofore taken the leave to tell you), that all *former and crooked things must be buried.* There must be no repeating of matters which never can be exactly rectified. This would be an endless and useless embroilment. It can have no tendency to any good in the world. There is a Scotch proverb that you must keep to: *Bygones be Bygones, and fair play for the time to come.* That must be an ample satisfaction for all that is past. [Stresses that this is the best attitude for Saffin to take.] As to your controversies with Mr. George, let there be no disputation between you and Madam about them. Say to the gentleman himself what you have to say. If Madam study to make your condition easy, certainly you will make your conversation with her forever so. It is, you know, Sir, better than I, the true spirit of a Gentleman to make his conversation easy to every one, especially to such a companion as Madam will be to you.

The second is, that you do the part of a GENTLEMAN in securing Madam's interest from any future destruction or detriment, while she is devoting it, as far as may be, unto your present service. You have known what it is to treat a wife as becomes a Gentleman. And you have told me that in your former conduct towards this gentlewoman you have not forgotten the laws of complaisance and of tenderness. Good Sir, hold to them. And take it not amiss, if others should be made to you, such overtures as judicious and indifferent friends may approve on this occasion.

My opinion for your coming into such a cohabitation has a thousand reasons.

If you decline it, it will be improved vastly to your disreputation. It will cause them to forsake you, that are now desirous to assist you. If you were furnished with stores enough to carry on the wars, yet your age forbids it. You must cheerfully entertain the reputable character of a *Miles Emeritus.* There is nothing more decent than for old men to be aforehand in such a sense of themselves. You have the honor of an age wherein the men who have done worthily in their day must have done with the world; and especially with the wars of it. I have a hundred times assumed the liberty to tell you, Repose is the milk of old age. I hope your piety will render it no ungrateful message to you, that you are just arrived unto the period of your days. Doubtless you are so wise, as to live in a daily expectation of your dissolution. It will be the worst thing imaginable for you now, Sir, to be vexing yourself with business of a wrangling importance. No, dear Sir, you must now be wholly swallowed up in praying, in reading, in assiduous meditation on the heavenly world. The affairs of your husbandry at Bristol, methinks, you should rejoice in an opportunity to cast them off. *No more EARTH now, Sir, but all for HEAVEN!* [Urges him to lay aside all bitterness.]

You will ask, what assurances you shall have that Madam will do you good and not evil all the rest of the days of your life. My answer is, we must all be guarantees. That is to say, if there be any point in which you think yourself unkindly dealt withal, we must any of us, on the least intimation, readily offer to Madam our sentiments. And we persuade ourselves, that she will readily hearken to us. [Close]

Pardon this freedom of, Sir, Your faithful friend and servant,

To Sir William Ashurst

Ford/Guildhall   November 9, 1710

Honorable Sir,

[Greeting]

I humbly tender unto your acceptance a book newly published under the title of *Bonifacius*, the intention of which book, I am well assured, will be very agreeable unto you. But for the freedom I have used in the preface, I do need, and must beg, your pardon.

Therein, if I am guilty of a trespass on the modesty which might have disposed you to forbid what I have done, mankind will make my apology; and we always look to come off easily, when—*crimen amoris erat.*

The appendix, which relates the present state of religion among our Indians, is inserted not only for Your Honor's more particular satisfaction, but also as our vindication from an envious passage in a sermon of the Bishop of Chichester's, which allows it as a true matter of reproach, that our colonies have made no application to the conversion of the natives. It seems, no good must ever be owned to be done, but what is done under the influence of the mitre. Let the gentlemen of the new Society then be prevailed withal, to send a missionary or two, for the Christianizing of the Iroquois Indians, whose princes (as they were fabulously called) appearing among you, made so much noise the other day on your side the water. This would free your faithful and thoughtful commissioners here from one of our most uneasy

solicitudes, and the objects are without the bounds of New England.
[Close]   Your Honor's most obliged servant,

To John Mico

U/HCL   February 17, 1711

Sir,

Few men in the world have more labored under the misunderstandings and misrepresentations of other men, than he that now addresses
you. Yea, and I have never been worse misconstrued than when I
have most of all endeavored to do my duty and set before me (according to my best apprehension of it) the pattern of my admirable Saviour.

My conduct under such things has been with patience and silence
to bear them, and be at little pains for their confutation.

One reason for that conduct has been a deep sense, not only of the
wisdom and mercy of Heaven in multiplying for me such thorns in
the flesh, but also of the Divine Justice in chastising me for the secret
errors which the eye of the Holy One hath seen in me, tho' no man
on earth could ever tax me for them.

Another has been the sweet satisfaction I have had in that conformity to a Lord who was despised and rejected of men, which by
contempt and reproach and multiplied exinanitions is carried on; and
in that precious opportunity which I have had to love, and wish well,
and do well, to those who have been pleased to declare themselves my
adversaries. I know not one of them all on whom I have pursued any
personal and unchristian revenges; yea, I know not so much as one of
them on whom I am not continually seeking to revenge myself with
kindness, with services, with good offices.

But a third has been my exceeding aversion to that loss of time
from employments of a much better importance, which I must have been
betrayed into if I had sacrificed so much of a short life as must have
gone to fending and proving and vindications. And this has been accompanied with a persuasion that wise and good men would in time, and
upon after consideration and experience, find that they have been
imposed upon. An innocent and a virtuous, or a justifiable behavior,
will at last clear itself; and when ferments are over, wise and good
men will of their own accord come in a true sight of men and things.
Judgment shall return unto righteousness, and all the upright in heart
shall follow it.

I have had it more than once hinted unto me, that you, Sir, in particular, have entertained such moderated and favorable sentiments of me, that I may without indecency, venture upon the action which I am now a-doing.

'Tis not to ask any regards unto myself, but it is to pray your acceptance and perusal of a book, whereof a good part was written for such as you.

I cannot be without regards for a son of such an excellent father as yours. May you be the true son and heir of his excellencies. What augments my regards for you, that I have known the instances wherein you have Done Good. But that which carries the regards on to the action wherein they now express themselves, is your capacity to Do Good; not only on the score of your temporal interest, but also in your temper, and genius, and good thought, which being directed by Heaven (and may you always enjoy the happy direction!) is capable of accomplishing very many good purposes in the world.

I propose nothing, I desire nothing, in this address, but that I may be a small instrument of promoting your Good Account in the Day when we shall both of us give an Account of ourselves and of our conduct unto the glorious Lord. [Close]

Your sincere friend and servant,

To John Stirling

U/UVL   March 25, 1711

Honorable and most reverend Sir,

The honor which your University has lately done to the most undeserving of men, lays him under uncommon obligations to make some returns. He is inexcusable if he don't study all possible demonstrations of an agreeable gratitude.

And, Sir, I know none that you will so well approve and accept as endeavors to do that service to the cause of Christianity, unto which it was your purpose to encourage me.

The token of your unmerited respect found me in the midst of such endeavors; and from all quarters in these colonies, I have received the congratulations of good men for the new strength which our glorious Lord has by your hands given to my capacity of doing such things as those wherein they see me laboring.

There has no part of the Church of God in the world, for many years appeared so valuable to me as that in Scotland. Thousands of times I have wished myself in its arms; times without number I have projected whether I might find within my reach any opportunities to be at all useful unto it. When you surprised me with your commands, *To look on myself as one of you*, you could not have done it unto any person on earth more disposed that way, more satisfied in such a relation.

You will then easily believe, sir, and you may justly expect it, that as I shall not now abate of my poor essays to do good (wherein Heaven by the way of Glasgow sends me such an excitation), so, Scotland will employ more than ever of my thoughts on what may be done, for the cause of Christ, and of His Holy Religion.

[Sends along a few of his "two hundred several treatises, on various arguments, in various languages," including *Bonifacius*.]

Your sincere and grateful servant,

My aged parent commands me in his name to salute you with his most affectionate remembrances.

To Samuel Penhallow

DII/MHS   January 11, 1712

My honored Friend,

[Thanks him for his many services.]

My book of *Pastoral Desires*—which is to set before my neighbors the *Excellent Things* we desire for them—now waits for some help to be given unto it. I was thinking about a line or two of yours unto Mr. Archer, to this effect: 'That C.M. having delivered in the public, as he knows, a discourse of *Excellent Things*, and having signified, as he also knows, his intention to publish the discourse and lodge it in all the families of the neighborhood for the assistance of their piety, it would be a noble thing in him, and a demonstration of his own piety, to enable the said C.M. to prosecute his good intention, by a generous tender of three or four pounds unto him, to help him in the charge of the impression. And it would be an excellent offering, both unto Heaven and unto the church whereto he has the happiness to be now related.'

But I know not whether I am not guilty of a great impertinency in this proposal. I pray you consider it with the candor that always accompanies you, and by no means do anything but what you shall upon

deliberation judge will best square with the nicest rules of discretion.
[Close]   Your very obliged friend and servant,

To John Winthrop

IV Coll 8/MHS   January 23, 1712

My dear Friend,

Neither your distance, nor your silence, nor the congelation which an unusual winter has brought upon us, has caused me to forget you. . . .

Among the old Virginians, one that had been well *huskanaw'd* [Indian puberty rites] forgot everything that was before it, and began the world anew, and was thought fit for public services. We have in the severity of our winter undergone a sort of *huskanawing*. Yet I hope we have not quite lost the memory of one another.

[Sends along some essays.]

At the same time, I enclose in the packet my *Fisherman*. But I had not appeared unto you like Peter with my fisher's coat about me (a new form of appearance for me) if it had not been to ask you, that you would please to bestow the book upon some fishing vessel (if you have any such, as I suppose you have) belonging to New London.

Of public affairs, you will expect nothing from me. . . . Only, *a peace, a peace*, is now all the cry.

I ought to add that we have a very deep sense of the calamity you suffer from a more than ordinary mortality in your colony. We mourn for you, we pray for you, we are studying how you and we may be the better for such grievous and speaking dispensations.

And we rejoice in the particular preservation of you and your family.
[Close]   Your hearty friend and servant,

To Samuel Penhallow

DII/MHS   January 28, 1712

Honored Sir,

'Tis a very cold time, 'tis true; but you take a course to make me even sweat under the heap of obligations that you lay upon me.

[Thanks him once more for his many services.]

I have not yet had opportunity to see our friend Master Archer, on whom you have done the part of such a *cunning Archer*. But I make no doubt, I shall suddenly feel the operation of your letter to him. [Close]   Your obliged servant,

To George Corwyn

U/BPL   March 11, 1712

Sir,

[Asks him to forward a letter.]

When my calash comes from Salem I should be glad if the servant were directed to call upon me, for your Dr. Friar to be lodged in the box, for a safe and clean conveyance. Having wintered with me 'tis time he should, with the other geese, fly back to the northward. In the mean time, and at all times, I must employ the quits of one, to return my thanks to you for the loan of him.

[Asks what will be the results of the peace.]

Your brother and servant,

To Samuel Penhallow

DII/MHS   April 17, 1712

The negotiation of peace is going on, and all things conspire to give us a strong expectation that it will speedily be accomplished. [Names the terms of the peace.] On the whole, the public writers are pleased to express themselves in these terms, That here is much more promised unto the English than was even demanded in those famous and numerous articles, fallaciously termed *preliminaries*, which were signed by the Duke of Marlborough and the Lord Townshend, at this place in the year 1709. And, indeed, as we have nothing left now to fight *for*, so we have as little to fight *with*. The difficulty which the Exchequer finds, to pay what it owes, causes a general discontent. Our debts amount unto more than fifty millions. A great part of the revenues of the Crown are mortgaged. We have brought upon our grandchildren such encumbrances as their posterity will hardly see themselves discharged of. We may add, the Queen and the present ministry seem resolved upon a peace, if it can be in any tolerable manner accomplished.

[Describes the fate of the Duke of Marlborough, "thrown down with all the indignity imaginable."]

The Act against Occasional Conformity runs to such a height that if a man be present at any one meeting of the Dissenters for the exercise of religion, he is *ipso facto* deprived of all places and offices of any trust or profit whatsoever. Not only the Dissenters, but all that part of the nation who have been distinguished by the title of the Moderate Party are treated on all occasions as an Undone Faction (the term expressly given to them) and insulted with all manner of provocations. The conduct of the Whiggish Lords (in whose House the bill was passed first, and went, *Nemine Contradicente*) in this matter was very wonderful. The Earl of Nottingham hired their concurrence to the bill by a bargain to bring over unto them so many Lords of the High Church as would break all the measures now taking, and save the nation. So they sacrificed the best friends they had; and, if my Lord fail in his part of the bargain, let them get their Act repealed again how they can.

The ferments in the nation are boiled up to such an astonishing and prodigious height as fills all people with consternation. [The king of Prussia is trying to promote union among the Protestant nations. Describes affairs in Turkey and Sweden.]

The Canadian fleet upon their arrival filled the court and nation with clamors against New England. The country was charged with treachery and stubbornness, and accused as having designedly ruined the expedition. Mr. Dummer did the country the justice and honor of publishing an elegant and sufficient vindication, even before the arrival of Col. Nicolson, who carried with him a great addition of materials. Whereupon the clamor was very much abated, and Col. Nicolson thanked for his activity and fidelity. My Lord Privy-seal, our plenipotentiary at Utrecht, gave particular thanks to Mr. Dummer for that vindication, and assured him he would at the congress prosecute the claim which he had therein so well made out unto Canada. [Quotes a report from Glasgow of a likely alliance between Scotland and France.]

To John Stirling

U/AAS   June 3, 1712

Most honored Sir,

[Sends along his *Concio ad Populum, Psalterium Americanum,* and some other recent treatises.]

But so 'tis ordered by the sovereign and infinite wisdom of our most glorious Lord, that while the things which have had most of my design and study and elaboration employed upon them lie buried in obscurity, the things which I have bestowed least thought upon have been, some hundreds of them, drawn forth into the service of His Kingdom.

[Wishes well to the Church of Scotland and its ministers.]

Doubtless we are entering into those dispensations whereby the second of Daniel and the thirty-fourth is to have a tremendous accomplishment. But it is a consolation unto me to think how little there may be found in the dear Church of Scotland for the all-consuming stone to strike upon. May our God prepare us for those awful works of His providence, wherein His voice will shake not only the earth, but the heavens also. [Close]   Your most affectionate servant,

To John Maxwell of Pollock

U/NLS   August 12, 1712

Honored Sir,

[Thanks him for his letters.] Tho' my correspondences are very many, and it engrosses more than a little time and care to answer the expectations which a great many correspondents, in many parts of Europe as well as of America, are pleased to honor me withal, yet I know none I shall be more fond of cherishing than yours. I wish I may not carry it on to the degree of troublesome [*sic*].

One of my first essays to give a public testimony of my esteem for you is to be seen in a little book of pastoral offices which I now humbly tender to your acceptance, and to your university. There is a famous book in the English nation entitled *The Whole Duty of Man,* which I take to be but a corrupt and a very defective one. I shall be sorry if our brief plain American *Whole Duty of Man* do not handle the matter . . . with more regard unto those points of duty which are of all the most considerable, and I shall be glad if it find a favorable reception with you that are among the best judges. Our presses in this town are continually bringing forth new productions for the service of our holy religion; thereof more than two hundred, such as they are, have passed from the mean hand that is now writing to you. [Says he desires to be useful to the Church of Scotland.] And the necessary labor of all the pastoral offices to the greatest congregation in America, and one of the greatest in the [world?], and the continual resort which all the churches in all these northern colonies have to the meanest of men on their frequent occasions, and many more employments both at home and abroad, needless to be mentioned, require a greater strength than mine to do the things that are to be done in any measure as they ought to be done. Having thus intimated the reasons you have to expect the marks of much feebleness on all my poor essays to serve you or any good interest, I will go on to give you some account of our American circumstances.

The churches in the New English colonies are multiplying; every year brings forth new ones in our swarming plantations. The City of God is building among us in these troublesome times. The difference between Presbyterian and Congregational is hardly known in our churches, few being rigid in either way, and both freely agreeing in a temper which makes all run upon substantial piety. In this large town of Boston, which contains near 10,000 souls, there are as I suppose not near half of 1000 who profess themselves of the Church of England, tho' that church has all the encouragements imaginable from our Governors given to it; yet it increases not, except from strangers coming in amongst us. We live in a very quiet and easy neighborhood with them in this town. But . . . in two or three country-towns, a small number of people, scarce the proportion of seven families to a thousand, and many of these having a vicious character as well as a factious intention, have grown vexatious, as your episcopal Jacobites are at you. They declare for the Church of England, tho' they know no more of it than the religion of Confucius. [And they ask for special privileges.]

The supply of churches has been from our College. But how long that may continue after High-Church Governors come to manage us, God only knows. An act of the Assembly did once incorporate the College, and in that year (before or after which the College has never had power to do such a thing) they presented my father with his doctorate. The King repealed that act with a direction [to?] it, with more power left for the Royal visitation. One retardation fell out after another, so that it was never done; but the College has a subsistence altogether precarious, with about fifty students in it; and tho' it holds commencements wherein the degrees of Bachelor and Master are dispensed, yet it has been rather by a connivance of the Governor affording his presence with them, than with any legitimate proceeding.

Many of our candidates for the ministry prove serious and hopeful young men. But I could wish more of them were more qualified and inclined for evangelical undertakings at places which are at some distance from us, where there is a want of such desirable instruments. In this, your students begin to set an excellent example.

I have been in extreme distresses for the colonies of North America which are to the southward of ours: New York, Jersey, Pennsylvania, Maryland, and Virginia. Our glorious Lord has a precious harvest there, but the laborers are too few, and the enemies pretty powerful. The ministers who are laboring there are very valuable men, and the late accession of Mr. George Gillespy to them, doubtless gives them no small consolation. I have writ to him and to the people there as much as I can for his encouragement. But if a fund could be settled for the support of suppose two missionaries, for a year or two, and then for a succession, it being supposed that the predecessors will in time have gathered a church and become settled in the charge of it, it would unquestionably be attended with excellent consequences. In the meantime we are alarmed with an advice that the French of Canada (who by the base treachery and cowardice of the expedition which miscarried a year ago are left in a condition which threatens the extirpation of the whole British interest in America [a few words illegible]) have poisoned all the Indians at our backs from Canada down even to Carolina, so that they begin everywhere to make hostile appearances. If such a calamity goes on, all the British colonies, especially in the more upland parts of them, will have an uneasy time of it; and yet who can tell how far calamity may prepare them to receive a Glorious Gospel. . . . [Close]

Your Honor's most sincere and humble servant,

To John Stirling

U/NLS   August 16, 1712

Most reverend Sir,

The letters which I have done myself the honor to write you by this opportunity have not fully answered the expectations which a fresh review of yours to me makes me sensible I ought to satisfy. I owe you some account of our College; and I wish I were able on all accounts to give a better.

While the Massachusetts colony flourished under its ancient charter, the College passed thro' its vicissitudes with a charter on which our government had founded it. On the dissolution of the charter of the colony, about the year 1686, the charter of the College was also supposed to be dissolved. The subsistence of the society has ever since been very precarious, and upon little better foundation than the connivance of our Governors. Once, indeed, an act of the Assembly did incorporate it with full power to give all the degrees of a university. And while that act was in force, they presented my parent, who had long been the president, with a Doctorate. But the King soon repealed that act, with his Royal permission and direction to renew it, with more of room left for His visitation. Thro' a variety of supervening accidents this was never carried thro'; but unto this day the society jogs on, lying entirely at the mercy of our Governors. It annually dispenses degrees, but pretends to none other than those two of Bachelor and Master of Arts; and these also having little else but the presence and countenance of our Governors to legitimate them. There are about fifty students at this time in the College, with a president and three tutors. And many hopeful and worthy candidates of the ministry are continually proceeding from this nursery.

Besides this Harvard College, from which the most of our churches have been happily supplied, the colony of Connecticut, adjoining to ours, hath of late years formed another college, which annually also gives degrees like ours. But that seminary is yet in its infancy, and the number of students there is not so great as ours, tho' several valuable young men have had their education there. [Close]

Your obliged and most affectionate servant,

To Wait-Still Winthrop

IV Coll 8/MHS October 6, 1712

Sir,

[Congratulates him on his recovery from illness.] The truth is, the times now in our next view seem to be as good times to die in as any that we have seen in the whole period of our pilgrimage.

The wrath of God against a sinful and woeful world! *Peace,* it was always reckoned a good thing. The word *peace* implies all good. But there is now a *peace* accomplished at which the reluctant nations make a roar that reaches up to Heaven; they toss their waves unto the very welkin. The war produced a distress of nations and greater perplexity. The peace distresses them with a ten times greater perplexity. They apprehend that the world is delivered up for the united power of France and wealth of Spain to impose what chains they please upon it. They expect an irresistible torrent of slavery, popery, and confusion!

Dr. Lloyd, the aged Bishop of Worcester, eighty-eight years old, got himself carried up in a horse-litter, and waiting on the Queen warned her against a peace with France, and told her that France was devoted of God unto destruction in four years, and expounded certain prophetical scriptures unto her, and would by no means have her involve herself and kingdoms in the fate of such an enemy of God. But Her Majesty had not studied the Revelation so much as my old Doctor! In the House of Lords there were forty-two who made a protest, that for certain reasons they feared the Duke of Ormond had some orders that restrained him from giving battle; if so, there had been very ill advice given to Her Majesty, and such as betrayed the common cause and had a tendency to a separate peace, which had been in Parliament declared, *foolish, knavish, and villainous.*

The states of Holland presented a memorial to the Queen on their having found it actually so. And they declare that this being done without the knowledge of the allies, and at a time when they had the bravest army which had been seen since the war began, and in force much superior to the enemy, and with the ordinary blessing of God they might have expected a very decisive action, the force of all humane ties is hereby brought to an end, and no treaties, alliances, or obligations will after this be of any significancy.

[Mentions the fall of Dunkirk and the defeat of the Dutch by the French.]

Dr. Fleetwood, the Bishop of St. Asaph, printed some old sermons, with a preface in which he paid some honor to the memory of King William and Queen Mary, and justified the Revolution. The House of Commons voted this preface to be malicious and factious, and ordered it to be burnt by the common hangman, and the sheriffs of the city to attend with the Sergeant of their House at the execution. This was done on June 10, the Pretender's birthday. In Scotland a violent party kept that birthday in very riotous excesses, and at Edinburgh and Leith set up his arms, with flags, and J.R.8. upon them.

This is the sum of our story, besides what our weekly piece of blockheadism will please to favor you withal.

I leave you, Sir, to your own remarks upon these things.

I was going to urge your speedy return; but I know not whether I should not rather solicit you to find out some retreat in some village of the colony where you are now sojourning, in which I may lie sheltered with you until the *Nubecula citò transitura* shall be blown over, and until the old Bishop of Worcester's period.

For we must expect here all the efforts of an arbitrary government in the hands of infuriated Flanderkins, except—the Watchers and the Holy Ones obtain what they are asking for. [Close]

Your Honor's most affectionate friend and servant,

III

MATHER was determined to turn all of his abilities, religious or secular, to Doing Good. He wrote in his diary on November 26, 1712, that he had been "entrusted with some small talents wherewith I had not yet glorified my Lord. In my acquaintance with natural curiosities I was made capable of communicating something that might give an agreeable entertainment unto the ingenious and inquisitive students of nature. Accordingly I made a collection of such things, and with some artifice digested them into thirteen letters. . . ." In this characteristic state of mingled self-sacrifice and self-aggrandizement Mather began his extensive and fascinating correspondence with the Royal Society of London.

It was not an abrupt beginning. Increase Mather, while still a young man, had formed a philosophical society in Boston whose members discussed natural history and submitted communications to the Royal Society. Cotton had been reading the society's *Transactions* by at least his early twenties, as well as its German counterpart, the *Ephemerides*. By the time of his death he had sent to the society fifty-nine very lengthy letters comprising his *Curiosa Americana* and several dozen related letters and summaries. The *Curiosa* have never been published as a whole, although Mather grafted scraps of them onto some other works, particularly *The Christian Philosopher*. Although he intended the *Curiosa* as a book, they belong with his correspondence for they are genuine letters, containing some of his most polished and shapely epistolary prose. The believe-it-or-not aspect of these stories of monstrous births and mermen drew from him some of his most high-spirited writing, and some of his worst puns. On one letter he sketched diagrams of the planetary motions and amusingly doodled into the sun a smiling face and halfmoon eyes. In his genial effort to keep in touch with the other learned men of his time, he appears as very much the model of the Enlightenment virtuoso. The simplicity and concreteness of the letters express both his essential seriousness as a scientist and the nationalistic impulse behind the *Curiosa*. He hoped to describe as accurately as he could the remarkables of the New World and to demonstrate what America uniquely was and what an American could do. He often reminds his readers that his subjects are American curiosities, reported by an American. Perhaps no other pre-Revolutionary writer except Crèvecoeur was as aware of living in the New World and as preoccupied with seeing how it differed from the Old World. As a result, the *Curiosa* provide some of the freshest descriptions of nature in colonial American literature.

In Mather's time the Royal Society was less a scientific organization than a fashionable men's club. Mather's temperament befitted the society's blend of real curiosity and real snobbery. As were the English members, those in the colonies were primarily professional men who dabbled in science. For example, Mather's correspondent RICHARD WALLER (d. 1714), secretary of the society from 1687 to 1709 and again from 1710 until his death, was a businessman who wrote on physiology, zoology and linguistics. The lack of full-time, professional scientists among the members on both sides of the Atlantic diminished the importance and quality of the society's work despite the fact of Sir Isaac Newton's presidency. Still, the society kept a close eye on American science throughout the colonial period. Mather himself was the first Fellow to have been born in the colonies; other colonial Fellows were William Byrd, William Penn, Governor William Burnet, Francis Nicolson, John Leverett, Elihu Yale, Paul Dudley, the Harvard tutor Thomas Robie, Dr. Zabdiel Boylston, John Winthrop, Robert Morris of New York, and Benjamin Franklin—a list which includes many of Mather's friends and acquaintances.

The most important of Mather's correspondents at the society in this earliest group of letters was his close contemporary DR. JOHN

WOODWARD (1665–1728), a geologist and physician who acted as the society's Provincial Secretary. In 1693 Woodward became interested in fossils, collected them all over England, and in his still-celebrated *An Essay Toward a Natural History of the Earth* (1695) called attention to the existence of strata in the earth's crust. An accomplished botanist and a founder of experimental plant physiology as well, Woodward served on the council of the Royal Society until he was expelled in 1710 for insulting the wealthy Sir Hans Sloane, who shared the secretaryship with Waller. Mather found Woodward—who sent the society a paper on small-pox inoculation—particularly congenial and useful. He took the occasion of his first letter to Woodward to ask his help in publishing the *Biblia Americana*. Mather's outline of the work closely follows his *New Offer to the Lovers of Religion and Learning* (1714), a pamphlet describing the *Biblia* for prospective patrons, first appended to *Bonifacius* in 1710.

Mather emphasized in his diary that he had digested his scientific findings "with some artifice." Originally he gave the *Curiosa* a deliberate structure. He planned to ascend from subterranean to terrestrial to celestial phenomena. But he soon abandoned the plan. The earlier *Curiosa* are shapely, polished, calligraphically neat; the later are often uninspired, chaotic, and scrawled. It was probably because the society failed to publish his letters that Mather relaxed his efforts. He acquired his material from personal observation, from his reading, and from his friends. He personally visited the twin daughters described in his letter of October 15, 1713, and took John Winthrop and Samuel Sewall with him. A remarkable instance of his use of first-hand observation is his letter to Woodward on November 22, 1712, describing a cure appearing in a dream. An ill woman "whom I may do very well to keep alive in my memory" was instructed in her sleep to apply warm wool from a living sheep to her breast. Mather has here described a dream of his wife Abigail as she languished in the last days of her life. At other times he based his reports on material donated by Winthrop, Penhallow, Samuel Mather of Connecticut, and others. These borrowings, it will also appear, sometimes bordered on plagiarism, and perhaps crossed the border.

Mather's exuberant hopes that the *Curiosa* would extend his reputation and benefit mankind begot equally powerful worries that they would become lost in transit to the society, as some did. He spent much time anxiously anticipating the reception of his letters in London. At first his hopes were rewarded. After withstanding nearly a year's wait, he rejoiced in his diary on October 12, 1713, over a "marvellous favor of Heaven to me": by a ship just come from London he learned that his letters had been read before the membership and that at the next meeting for elections he would be made a Fellow. (The society's records show that after the reading of Mather's letters, the Fellows judged him "a very inquisitive and proper person," inquisitiveness and propriety being, apparently, equal recommendations for membership.)

To Dr. John Woodward

U/RS   November 17, 1712

Sir,

Your excellent *Essay towards the Natural History of the Earth* has obliged and even commanded the true friends of religion and philosophy to serve you with as many communications as they can that may be subservient unto your noble intention.

[Discusses the recent unearthing of a giant's bones.]

It seems not improper for me to give you first of all some account, how and where I met with the discourse which I am now to lay before you. And herein also I shall do that which perhaps may gratify the inquisitive genius of a person who wishes very well unto the commonwealth of learning. It is fetched from an amassment of treasures which I could wish did not lie too like the subterraneous ones; and that the library in which they lodge may not be so like the horrid cellars of Indoustan, where your silver and gold, after they have been brought out of their subterraneous condition, and circulated thro' the business of the world, again return into it, and are again buried by the covetous Mogols, and have no more to do on the face of the earth. My meaning is, tho' I need not explain what I mean, I wish they had the publication which they are waiting for, and that your presses would return to print something else besides your politics, and serve to better purposes than to vent the ill humors of your nation. I wish it may come into the minds of ingenious and opulent men to do mankind the good office of bringing forth what has been prepared for common benefit.

There is an American friend of yours who, tho' he never travelled out of America, has had the honor to be related unto one of your European universities, and has been desirous to oblige a number of the best people in Europe with a composure which now arises to two considerable volumes in folio, wearing the title of *Biblia Americana*. He had long since been of your excellent Boyle's opinion, that *you should no more measure the wisdom of God couched in the Bible by the glosses and systems of common expositors, than estimate the wisdom He has expressed in the contrivance of the world by Magnus's or Eustuchius's Physics*; and agreed with him in hopes that learned men would go on to make more admirable explications and discoveries in that wonderful Book than what usually occurred in the vulgar (tho' very useful) *Annotations*. Having the honor of a correspondence with the incomparable Witsius, one of the greatest men that the last age produced, he laid before him the plan of his undertaking, and received the encouragement of that great man to go on with what he had in hand. And the truth is, that hero (for I know not why learning also should not have its heroes) was himself not the least in furnishing this author with rich materials for him to work upon, and in verifying his own report. [Says that while compiling the work "your author" continued his many other writings and pastoral employments.]

He [Mather] has given us the Sacred Scriptures in the order of time wherein the several and successive occurrences may direct the [making?] and reading of them. This alone were itself a valuable commentary. But then, the common translation is here also amended and refined, with a due modesty, 'tis true, and only where the most judicious philology has offered much reason for it. You have here also a rich collection of antiquities which the laborious researches of learned men in our days have recovered, for a sweet reflection of light on the heavenly oracles; the agriculture, the architecture, the tactics, but above all, the idolatry of the former ages, you will find explained in this collection. The types in the Bible are here accommodated with their antitypes, and those paragraphs of it that appeared the least fruitful with instructions, are now to be perused with vast mixture of holy profit and pleasure. The laws of the Israelitish nation in these pandects of Heaven are here interpreted, and the original and intention thereof rescued from the misinterpretations of some famous writers. Gold is here fetched out from the dunghill of the Talmuds, and other Jewish writers, not only to illustrate the oracles once committed unto the distinguished nation, but also to demonstrate the truth of Christianity. Natural philosophy is here called in. The fairest hypotheses (and yours, my most honored Doctor!) of those grand revolutions, the making, and the drowning, and the burning of the world, are offered. The meteors, the minerals, the plants, the animals, the diseases, the astronomical affairs, and the powers of the invisible world, mentioned in the Book of God, are here considered, with the best thoughts of our times upon them. The chronology of this Book, and of the world, is here cleared from all its difficulties, and the clock of time set and kept right in its whole motion from the beginning of it. The sacred geography is here surveyed, Paradise and Palestine are particularly laid out. And many notable and enlightening things are contributed unto this work, from the modern travellers. Here is a particular history of the city Jerusalem, in its marvellous vicissitudes, from the days of Melchizedek down to ours, with an account of its present condition. But this is not all; for you have here what the author calls a sort of twenty-ninth chapter of the Acts, or an elaborate and entertaining history of what has befallen the Israelitish nation in every place from the birth of the glorious Redeemer to this very day; and the present condition of that nation, the relics of the ten as well as of the two tribes, and of their ancient sects, yet (several of them) existing also in the several parts of the world, where they are now dispersed at this time, when their speedy recovery from their sad and long dispersion is hoped for. More than so: you have here the histories of all ages, brought in to show how the prophecies of this invaluable Book have had their most punctual accomplishment, and strongly established conjectures on such as yet remain to be accomplished. With the true doctrine of the chiliad brought in as a key to very much of the wealth which the church of God enjoys in this Book of the Kingdom. Sir, all these things are but a part of your entertainment in the work, which I may presume to call, as they did the *Octapla* of Origen long ago, *Opus Ecclesiae*, and which yet lies like the impotent man at the pool of Bethesda, waiting till Heaven stir up the inclinations of some generous minds to appear as benefactors in the publishing of it. [Ends with an eleven-page extract from the *Biblia*, on giants.]

Your sincere friend and humble servant,

To Dr. John Woodward

U/RS   November 19, 1712

Sir,

You expected from me a communication of my subterraneous curiosities; and I have in one remarkable instance endeavored it. I will go on to endeavor your satisfaction, but in things that are so far from subterraneous that they shall be rather of a celestial character and residence. In this, you will not charge my friendship with the solecism of that actor, who when he cried O *Terra!* pointed up unto the heavens. But you will accept from your American friend everything that may entertain and gratify a mind that would know what is observed in our hemisphere.

I shall not attempt an addition to the treasures of your ornithology. As we have most of your birds (indeed our being without rooks and buzzards and magpies and woodcocks and cuckoos has been improved by some aiery gentlemen as a piece of banter on our behalf), so you have, I suppose, the most of ours. 'Tis true, some that we have in common with you, yet here make almost a different species from yours, particularly our wild turkies, which are bigger and blacker, and their flesh tougher, than your tame ones, and whereof some weigh forty, yea, some sixty pounds. We will not boast of our pilhannaw, a mighty kind of eagle, four times as big as a goshawk, with a head as big as a child's of [a] year old, who when he soars aloft makes the feathered tribe in his view to hide themselves. We behold as much beauty and glory in our humming-bird, the least of all the things that are cloathed with feathers. Their feathers glitter with variable colors. Their bills are long, and like a needle. With these they suck the honey which they find on the blossoms and flowers in our gardens. They build little nests in the spring, made up like a bottom of soft matter, like silk. Here they lay their eggs, no bigger than small peas, whereof they hatch three or four at a time. We can rarely catch them unless by shooting them with pistols charged with sand; when weighing of them we find them with feathers and entrails and all, to make but eight or ten grains. [Discusses the abundance of pigeons in America.]

It was my learned friend, Mr. Charles Morton (whose nephew and namesake is at this time a worthy physician in your city), who first led me into the conjecture (I had almost said, hypothesis) which I am now laying before you, for your judgment upon it, how far it may pass the ordeal of reason and experiment.

The little birds, which we may call season-birds, do seem to have their annual recesses in some remote and upper quarters of the Heaven, within our atmosphere. They are not only *Birds (of) Heaven* but also *Birds (IN) Heaven* (Jer VIII 7), from whence at their appointed times they take their journey hither. It seems as if they found something either in the temper of their own bodies, or in the alterations of their lodgings above, or in the effluvia of the earth upon the new reflections of the sun thereupon, which invites them to change their quarters, and so they know their seasons. If these birds during their absence from us, did reside in any part of this earth, methinks we should after so many ages at last have heard where it is. But no man hath yet seen any numbers of them out of their seasons, nor have we any but old wives' fables concerning the finding of any except a bird or so, that by some lameness has been left behind his fellows. [Notes that the birds come by "dropping down from above upon us."] Moreover, at the first coming of these birds, they are generally of a texture very different from what they have after they have been here a while. Their taste is finer, they eat short, their flesh is tender, they have little or no blood in them. Which argues that they have had another nourishment than what this earth affords. Once more the flight of these birds, while they abide among us, for the most part is only short; and, I am told, those which on your island of Great Britain are found near the seashore, being disturbed, never will offer toward the sea; wherefore, 'tis probable they never came thither from beyond the sea. Finally, there are very odd phenomena among these birds at or near the time of their departure. They don't grow duller, their flights are higher, their notes are brisker, they gather together as having a noble design for another world. [Notes that this has also been observed of the storks in the low countries.] Everything looks as if they sought a comfortable repose by flying directly upward, which is not the way to any other land on our earth.

[Discounts the possibility that the birds fly to the moon.] But then, it seems no unreasonable presumption to imagine, that there are nigh unto our terraqueous globe, sundry minute planetary bodies, which partly from the smallness of their bulk, and perhaps also from some other causes, may not be visible unto us without the help of instruments. Until we were assisted with telescopes, who ever dreamt of the satellites which move about the superior planets; or who ever thought of catching Saturn by his ears? If glasses were a little more improved, and men's attention to the discovery of their glasses a little further awakened, it is possible we might soon discern some very significant globules in our supreme regions, without coming under the scoffs employed upon those who build castles in the air. Yea, the greatest [a few words faded] of them who died in the former century, did affirm in private conversation that some crystalline or semi-pellucid bodies between the earth and the moon have already been discovered. Certainly the Negroes on the coast of Barbary, that know not of such a rock as the Isle of Ascension, which tho' it be thirty miles in compass has no fresh water on it, will ignorantly think the prodigious multitude of sea-fowl which visit them from the rock, to be bred on their own shore, because they know not of such a retirement for them. And why may not this illustrate the case before us?

[He must close.] My presumption that my season-birds might happen to prove not unacceptable unto so great a philosopher, and unto one who makes the *Natural History of the Earth* a favorite article of his philosophy, but one who at the same time loves to see the oracles of the Sacred Scripture illustrated, this is my apology for the freedom I have used in the exhibition of them. With a quill taken from one of them, I will now presume on subscribing myself, Sir,

Yours in the bonds of the most inviolable friendship,

To Dr. John Woodward

U/RS   November 22, 1712

Sir,

It has doubtless been somewhat of a surprise unto you to find what operations of the invisible world there have been in communicating the knowledge of medicine unto us. You remember how a dream taught (the gentleman whom the Persians call Irsenius) Galen himself which way to cure a malady upon himself. You are well acquainted with what antiquity has related concerning the usual method of dreaming for a cure, after the observation of certain ceremonies and superstitions in the temple of Aesculapius. You have particularly considered the Greek inscriptions on the marble table found in the isle of Tyber, where the temple of Aesculapius formerly stood, and now to be seen in the palace of Mapheo. Among the modern examples, that of Wallace cured of a consumption by a few leaves of red sage and bloodwort steeped in small beer, from the instruction of a genius, has not escaped you. And you have no doubt employed a particular thought on old Napier's way of practise, and the *responsa raphaelis* which he entered in his manuscripts, to be seen in the *Museum Ash-moleanum*, where I understand they are now reposited.

[Claims that in his own neighborhood he has met with several cures appearing in dreams.] A gentlewoman whom I may do very well to keep alive in my memory, fell into grievous languishments wherein a pain of her breast and an excessive salivation were two circumstances that were become as insupportable unto her as they were incurable. She apprehended (in her sleep, no doubt) that a grave person appearing to her directed her, for the former symptom, to cut the warm wool from a living sheep and apply it warm unto the grieved part; for the latter symptom, to take a tankard of spring water, and therein over the fire dissolve an agreeable quantity of mastick and of gum-icinglass and now and then drink a little of this liquor to strengthen the glands. The experiment was made, and she found much advantage in it. However, other distempers growing upon her did a few months after put an end unto her days.

My third instance will be so remarkable that I believe you will not repent the pains you bestow on the reading of it. A young woman of Boston, called Lydia Ingram, after other languishing illnesses, fell ill of a fever. Her fever was at length attended with a very great swelling of her stomach and sides, and a total suppression of urine for ten days together. Several of our most able physicians did what they could for her, but at length desisted from doing any more, because they saw her case was altogether hopeless. While she lay in this condition, she dreamt that there came into the room a gentleman with the circumstances of a venerable old age upon his head and face, but of a very comely countenance; of a middle stature, and having a light-colored chainlet-coat for his habit. This gentleman said, that overhearing the groans of one in distress as he passed by the house, he could not but come in; and now, having the distressed case of the young woman more particularly related unto him, he gave her this advice: *Take a glass of white wine, and put into it a little alum; and add the powder of a burnt beef marrow-bone, as much as may lie upon the lid of the civet box now in your hand* (which happened now to be there, and was about as broad as a sixpence). *Drink this off; do it twice in three hours; by the fourth you shall have relief.* So he went away. She awoke, and informed her physicians of what passed, only had forgot the third ingredient. They allowed her to take the white wine and alum, if she pleased, for they were able to do no more. She took it, but without any effect. Hereupon she fell asleep again, and the same venerable person come again unto her. He asked whether she had followed his advice. She said she had, but found no good of it. He asked, *What have you done?* She told him. He replied, *Don't you remember the powder I told you of, to take as much of it as might lie on the lid of your civet box? Alas, you have almost fooled your life away. But however—go take what I bade you. I believe it may do you good yet. There is nothing too hard for God, and so you'll find it!* Which last words he also repeated at his then going out of the door. She then awaking told her physicians of the remedy, whereof she now gave them a more perfect account. The remedy was immediately allowed and prepared, tho' the physicians derided it at the same time as a mere notion, and an improper one too. She took it, and by the fourth time she had the relief that was promised her, and voided five pints of urine at one time; and from Wednesday at one o'clock to Friday at one o'clock, there came from her by measure six gallons. The suppression returned and continued three days. The same venerable person then a third time returned unto her in her dream. He said, *How dost do now, child?* She said, *I grow weaker.* He said, *Did you do as I advised you?* She said, *Yes.* He said, *Did you repeat it?* She said, *No.* He said, *Why not?* She said, *I could get no white wine.* He looked very much displeased, and said, *No white wine! There's enough in the town; but people that want a will seldom want an excuse!* She said, *I am almost gone!* He replied, *you are almost gone indeed. However, take it again; all things are possible with God!* He then went unto the door, and there turning about again, he said with a more cheerful and pleased countenance, *Take it, and give God all the glory; give God all the glory. Farewell!* And so he went out. She accordingly followed his advice, and found present relief. She went on taking the remedy twice or thrice a day; and God blessed it so that she recovered, and quickly came abroad, and has been since married successively to two husbands, and been a mother of children, and is to this day alive, which is fourteen years after the occurrences that have been related.

[Cites Boyle and some classical writers.]

I am not so forgetful as to offer any of my remarks on these things to a person of your sagacity. I leave them with you, for *yours*; but among them, I hope, you will not fail to make one on the forward zeal which you find in me to make you a tender of everything in our American world which may give you any sort of entertainment, and to approve myself, Sir,　　　　One who always loves and honors you,

To Dr. John Woodward

U/RS　　　　　　　　　　　　　　　　November 24, 1712

Sir,

You will allow me to think that in your noble profession, chirurgery was the elder sister to pharmacy; and your father, shall I say, or idol, whom you call Aesculapius (or Asclepius) does in his name, *Ish Calaphet*, that is to say, *a man of the knife*, carry the remembrance of his principal profession; or, take Bochar's etymology for it, *Ish Calabi* or, *a man of the dog*; you know that he carried a dog with him, to lick the sores of his ulcerous wounded patients.

I am writing to an accomplished and experienced physician who has at some time or other had his thoughts employed upon that problem of chirurgery, what wounds are to be esteemed mortal. [Cites stories of minor wounds that have resulted in death, and of grievous wounds that have not.]

The Indians making an assault upon Deerfield struck a hatchet some inches into the skull of a boy, and even so deep that the boy felt a sensible wrench used by them to get it out. There he lay a long while weltering in his blood. At length we found him; we dressed him; considerable quantities of his brain came out from time to time when we opened the wound. And yet the lad recovered. I know not whether the story told by Plato be true, that one Herus Armenius (whom Clement will have to be Zoroaster) being slain in war, lay ten days among the dead, and then being brought away, and on the twelfth day laid on the funeral pile, came to life again. But it is true that one Simon Stone being here wounded with shot, in *nine* several places, lay for dead (as it was time!) among the dead. The Indians coming to strip him, attempted with two several blows of a hatchet at his neck, to cut off his head, which blows, you may be sure, added more enormous wounds unto those port-holes of death, at which the life of the poor man was already running out as fast as it could. Being charged hard by our forces, they left the man, without scalping him, which else they would have also done. And ours now coming to bury the dead, one of the soldiers perceived this poor man to fetch a gasp, whereupon an Irish fellow then present, advised them to give him another dab with a hatchet, and so bury him with the rest. Our English, detesting this barbarous advice, lifted up the wounded man, and poured a little fair water into his mouth, at which he coughed; then they poured a little strong water after it, at which he opened his eyes. The Irish fellow was ordered now to haul a canoe ashore, to carry the wounded men up the river unto a chirurgeon; and as Teague was foolishly pulling the canoe ashore, with the cock of his gun, while he held the muzzle in his hand, his gun went off and broke his arm, whereof he remains a cripple to this day. But Simon Stone was thoroughly cured, and as he was born with two thumbs on one hand, his neighbors have thought him to have at least as many hearts as thumbs.

[Six more pages of such cases, several in Latin.]

Wishing you a perpetual freedom from all that may wound or hurt you, I now take leave, but remain, Sir,   Always at your service,

To Richard Waller

U/RS   November 24, 1712

Sir,

[Sets forth a table for computing the Julian period; states his intention of writing a letter a day to the Royal Society for the next five days.]

Only I must aforehand pray you to pardon an infirmity that I find that I do [word illegible] easily fall into; which is, that while I am writing to a learned friend (tho' it be in the most autoschediastic manner that can be) I find a difficulty to forbear my little excursions into more of reference and quotation than may be decent in so free a conversation. Indeed, I should be more ashamed of this infirmity if I were conscious (which I find I shall be, ere I aware [sic], of committing it, even in the very moment when I am asking pardon for it!) of its proceeding from the humor which Austin reproached in Julian, who was ever citing of authors to make a vain ostentation of his erudition. But tho' I may plead the great examples which I find of reading being made and thought much more pleasant for being so *dulcified,* and the real advantage (especially when the subject is none of the greatest) of having what is written somewhat justified at least, if not also embellished, by a style with some spirit this way put into it, I rather choose to say that you shall, if you please, in your friend who now writes, let it pass for one of those natural weaknesses which all men of breeding indulge in one another. However, I will so far keep a restraint upon it, that it shall be within the bounds of mediocrity, and be confined unto my first thoughts, with facility flowing through my pen at the moment of their occurring, into these mean and coarse originals whereof I have had no time to take and keep a copy. They are but a few of your and my subcessive hours, which these letters are like to call for; and you will permit me a little of the air of a Camerarius in writing of them. [Close]

Your friend and servant,

To Richard Waller

U/RS   November 26, 1712

Sir,

Having been informed that you were desirous to be confirmed in the truth of a relation which had reached you, concerning an apparition to one Mr. Joseph Beacon, a gentleman in my neighborhood, I address myself to discharge that part of my duty.

The relation is this.

On the second of May in the year 1687, a most ingenious and religious young gentleman, Mr. Joseph Beacon by name, about five o'clock in the morning as he lay, whether sleeping or waking he could not say (but judged the latter of them) had a view of his brother then at London, although he was himself now at our Boston, distanced from him the whole breadth of the great and wide Atlantic Ocean. This his brother appeared now unto him, having on him a Bengal gown, which he usually wore, with a napkin tied about his head. His countenance was very pale, ghastly, deadly, and he had a bloody wound on one side of his forehead. *Brother!* says the affrighted Joseph. *Brother!* answered the apparition. Said Joseph, *what is the matter, brother! How came you here!* The apparition replied, *Brother, I have been most barbarously and inhumanly murdered by a debauched fellow, to whom I never did any wrong in my life.* Whereupon he gave a particular description of the murderer, adding, *Brother, this fellow, changing his name, is attempting to come over unto New England, in Foy or Wild. I would pray you, on the arrival of either of these to get an order from your Governor to seize the person whom*

I have now described, and then do you prosecute him for the murder of me your brother. I will stand by you in the prosecution. And so he vanished. Mr. Beacon was extremely astonished at what he had seen and heard; and the people of the family where he sojourned, observed an extraordinary alteration, which continued many days upon him, in which time he also gave them an account of this apparition.

All this while, Mr. Beacon had no other advice of anything amiss attending his brother at such a distance from him. But about the latter end of June following, he understood by the common ways of communication that some time in the preceding April, his brother going in some haste by night, that he might call a coach for a gentlewoman then with child whom he was attending upon, met a fellow who had his doxy in his hand and too much drink in his head. Some way or other the fellow thought himself affronted in the hasty passage of this Beacon, and immediately, with a transporting fury, ran in to the fire-side of a neighboring tavern, from whence he fetched out a fire-fork, wherewith he grievously wounded Beacon on the skull, even in that very part where the apparition showed his wound. Of this wound he languished until he died, on the second of May, about five of the clock in the morning at London, so that the specter, it seems, took the same time that the sun takes to pass over the degrees of longitude into America. The murderer, as we are told, was endeavoring the escape which the apparition affirmed; but the friends of the deceased Beacon in London seized him, and pursued the law upon him; but he found the help of such friends as brought him off without the loss of his life.

[Quotes some affidavits in support of the account.]

I know not whether for a story of this nature, a fuller evidence can be with any reason asked for. But the matter of fact being thus incontestable, we are still in the dark about the manner wherein spirits do make these apparitions. There is that which we may call an internal apparition of spirits. The ancients called such things *phantasmata* and *idola* (not because, as a foolish philosopher of Malmsbury will tell you, the things are nothing more than a mere fancy, but) because they thought spirits did appear nextly to the fancy. They operate immediately upon that internal faculty, and exhibit themselves merely by smiting on that, and moving of it, and so are as well to be seen when the eyes are shut as when they are open, as well sleeping as waking. But then, there is that which we may call an external apparition of spirits, wherein the spirits do really present themselves unto the ocular view of those to whom they make their visits. Dr. Burthogge thinks the spirits make the bodies, wherein they thus appear, by the plastic power of imagination (whereof the signatures made by the imagination of the mother on a fetus, are a pregnant instance!) and that what gravity is in respect of elementary bodies, that a strong inclination, disposition, passion, or will is unto spirits. We seem to be left at a loss, which of these was Beacon's apparition! Yea, you are well aware, Sir, that it is not easy always to determine whether the spirits appearing in the shapes of deceased persons are truly the spirits of those persons, or may not be other demons. You may remember, perhaps, how Chrysostom in one of his sermons about Lazarus, affirms that oftentimes demons would appear, pretending to be the souls of the dead. And what shall we make of this, that the shapes of persons have been seen in distant apparitions, while the persons themselves have been yet alive? Of this, Mr. Baxter gives you a famous and a modern history. I am not yet apprised of any infallible rules to distinguish the real apparitions of the dead from diabolical personations. [Cites other cases in classical writers, and another, similar case from America.]

. . . if there appear anything defective in the evidence of these relations, I will do my best that there shall want no evidence of my desire to approve myself, Sir,   Yours most heartily,

IV

WHILE pursuing his scientific interests Mather also busied himself with the work of converting the Indians. His many letters in this period to Sir William Ashurst show him specially involved with the Indians at Martha's Vineyard and at Natick, and with the reprinting of John Eliot's Indian Bible. In 1641 Thomas Mayhew purchased proprietary rights to Martha's Vineyard and fourteen smaller islands. His son tried to convert the Indians there and opened a school for Indian children. Mather's uncle John Cotton succeeded him, but quarreled with his father and moved to Plymouth. In 1670 a church was gathered in Edgartown with an Indian pastor and teacher who administered communion to the whole population. By any Puritan standards, however, the worship was corrupt, nominally Presbyterian but mixed with Quaker practises. Urged on by Samuel Sewall, Sir William Ashurst purchased these lands for the New England Company in May, 1711, the negotiations being handled by Jeremiah Dummer. Mather felt that the company had made a splendid bargain. Since Gayhead Neck was used for grazing sheep, the land would yield revenues, and these could be turned back into the missionary venture. Meanwhile, the Indian communities would be protected from Anglican encroachments. (So Mather hoped and supposed; later this ambitious missionary attempt fell apart in squabbles over the ambiguous land titles.)

Natick, some eighteen miles from Boston, had been the site of a large community of Puritanized Indians. In 1650 John Eliot settled the Dorchester Indians there on two thousand acres granted by the Massachusetts General Court. In 1660, after much opposition from conservative Puritans, the Indians in Natick formed their own church, which became a model for later Indian churches. But by 1700 the church membership had dwindled to seven men and three women. Mather visited the expiring community in July, 1712, accompanied by other Indian commissioners—Sewall, Sir Charles Hobby, and John Leverett—to preach to and discourse with the Indians. Afterward he wrote to Sir William Ashurst in the hope of revitalizing it. He also appealed to Ashurst for particular exertions to Christianize the Mohegan Indians of Connecticut who lived, Mather thought, in a uniquely scandalous, pagan condition. Since he opposed as futile any plan to convert the Indians through their own language and within the framework of their own cultures, he tried to dissuade Ashurst and the company from reprinting John Eliot's Indian Bible, a project the company began considering in 1708. Its futility, he pointed out, was compounded by having to choose for the translation one out of many Indian dialects in use, and by the inevitable distortion of Scripture which would result no matter which dialect was chosen. His arguments against the translation seem sound enough, and familiar, yet one may reasonably feel that he was motivated as much by petty envy as by logic. He never objected to the company reprinting some of his own works in Indian translations made by Roland Cotton.

Although Mather felt grateful to the New England Company

for enlarging his opportunities to Do Good, his role as an Indian commissioner proved uncomfortable. In his diary in December, 1712, he complained that the commissioners' activities were disrupted by "the boisterous, clamorous and impertinent loquacity of one man," namely Governor Dudley. Dudley's manner grated Mather enough to make him want to resign his commission and write to England to have himself replaced. He also felt discouraged by the often successful competition of the Anglican SPGFP. This society threatened to investigate the New England Company's affairs in New England and one night sent the Anglican Sir Charles Hobby to Samuel Sewall's house demanding to see the company's commission. The episode surely contributed to Mather's eventual estrangement from Hobby. Mather's letter to the English Calvinist divine DR. JOHN EDWARDS (1637–1716), the author of *Theologia Reformata* (1713), explains his deeper distrust of the Anglican group. Under cover of converting the Indians to Christianity, he believed, the SPGFP was really trying to turn Congregationalists into Anglicans.

Mather's letters on these larger public affairs avoid any reference to his personal trials. His worsening money problems made it difficult for him to pay the higher postal rates levied by the House of Commons in 1710, fixing the rate for a letter from New York to London or Boston at a shilling, and between Boston and sixty miles distant at four pence. Worse, the adolescence of his son Increase was troubled and disappointing. Deciding in 1713 that Increase had best be applied to a secular career, he helped Cressy to perfect his reading and ciphering, and looked for a merchant to whom Cressy could apprentice himself. All we know of the outcome are the many cryptic laments in his diary at the time: "My poor son Increase!" As Mather's fame grew, his detractors multiplied. In June, 1713, "knots of riotous young men" gathered under his window in the middle of the night and sang "profane and filthy songs." The demand in Boston for new meeting houses hinted to him that his own flock might scatter, as it eventually did. This rash of building, he felt, reflected a craving for lax religion, fashion, and special privilege among a growing Boston nouveau riche class, a "proud crew that must have pews for their despicable families."

More poignantly, during the measles epidemic of 1713, which swept through New England and Europe, Mather suffered a ghastly succession of deaths in his family. On October 30, twins were born to him, his last children, who both died in November. On November 8 his wife Elizabeth was taken ill with sudden violence; she died the next afternoon. On November 18 his son Eleazer died. Two days later his daughter Martha died. The day after that his daughter Jerusha died. No trace of these six deaths in two weeks appeared in the letters he wrote, on virtually the same days, to Sir William Ashurst and to the Royal Society.

Perhaps the most numbing sentence Mather ever wrote is the entry in his diary for December 13, 1713, scarcely a month after these castastrophes. With stupefying callousness, he confesses to finding a sort of relief in the new tranquility in his family, owing to "a release from the hurries which the number of infants in it formerly always gave unto it." Certainly the New England insistence on authentic private experience—"grace" to Mather, the "transparent eyeball" to Emerson—invited egoism and self-cultivation at the expense of social and family ties. For the earlier Puritans such an attitude must have provided a defensive armor against the omnipresence of death in wilderness New England. But in Mather's case it seems not a self-defensive hardening of soul but a desire to have his own way—the fewer encumbrances the better. Presumably his "release from the hurries" of his children freed him to Do More Good.

To his list of correspondents in Scotland Mather now added the important Scottish minister and ecclesiastical historian ROBERT WODROW (1679–1734), a distant relative of Sir John Maxwell of Pollock. Wodrow was a sort of Scottish Cotton Mather, engrossed in all of the religious and political events of his time. He wrote a *History of the Sufferings of the Church of Scotland* (1721–1722) in two volumes, of which Mather published an extract in his *Palm-Bearers* (1725). Wodrow also dabbled in natural history, and Mather often told him of his doings with the Royal Society. A prodigious correspondent himself, Wodrow wrote also to Increase Mather and, frequently, to Benjamin Colman, to whom Cotton Mather introduced him. Intensely interested in the fate of the Reformation in America, Wodrow prized Mather's friendship and newsy letters.

PROBABLY TO SIR WILLIAM ASHURST

U/Hunt (HM 22318)   December 10, 1712

Honorable Sir,

The American colonies, whereto belongs the hand that now addresses you, can afford nothing that is great, and little that is new, to entertain you. The only subject that I can propose at this time for the conversation whereto you admit me, is an affair whereto you have a near relation; and that is enough to render it proper to be somewhat insisted on.

You are doubtless desirous to know how your commissioners proceed in their care about our Christianized Indians. And, I hope, the account of our proceedings will be something for your satisfaction.

We have employed visitors to go unto all the villages of our Indians and bring us an exact information of their condition: their numbers, their desires, their wants, and how things are carried on among them. And this information lying before us, we consider from time to time what may be done to preserve and promote all good interests among them, according to their various occasions. That we may the more effectually pursue these ends, we hold our meetings with a much greater frequency than formerly; and since the loss of our state-house (which is now almost rebuilt) we have the pleasure of being in our turns at each other's houses.

Your purchase of Martha's Vineyard was a very seasonable action; and it being worth, at a moderate computation, six thousand pounds, the bargain made for it was a pretty good one, for which, I hope, our industrious and ingenious agent, Mr. Dummer, has had some grateful acknowledgment. The intention of putting it into a condition of yielding some agreeable revenues, to help the support of our main interest, will be a business of some time; and it is what we are in convenient methods prosecuting.

One of our most languishing and withered Indian villages is that of Natick (with some not far distant from it), which our famous Eliot made the more distinguished and peculiar object of his travels. That which has reduced them to scarce thirty families at Natick, and scarce half so many at either of the next villages, has been chiefly their exposed situation in this grievous time of war, and perhaps a little hard usage from some superiors, who know how to make their penn'orths out of them. But we are employing our most exquisite studies to form a more considerable town in that place, by bringing their neighbors to a cohabitation with them, and having them under a good government and protection.

The grand concern of reprinting the Indian Bible often comes under our consideration. The most of your commissioners are averse to doing it at all, and rather hope to bring the rising generation by schools and other ways, to a full acquaintance with the English tongue, in which they will have a key to all the treasures of knowledge which we ourselves are owners of. My own poor opinion is that the projection of anglicising our Indians is much more easy to be talked of than to be accomplished. It will take more time than the commissioners who talk of it can imagine. 'Tis more than you have done to this day for your Welsh neighbors and captives. However, I will humbly show you my further opinion: that the reprinting of the Bible will be much sooner and cheaper done at London, than at Boston. The experiment we made in printing the Psalter not long ago, convinced us what a tedious and expensive undertaking that of the Bible must be, if in this place it be gone upon. Seven years would not be enough to finish the work at our presses, whereas little more than a seventh part of the time would perhaps dispatch it with you, if such a person as Mr. Grindal Rawson or Mr. Experience Mayhew (both of whom are most expert masters of the Indian language, and preachers to the Indians in it) might pass over the Atlantic and keep close to the supervisal of the press-work. And the cost there would be surprisingly short of what it must be with us. (Except you should rather choose to send over a couple of operators hither, who might follow no other work but that, while that is a-doing.) And how far the capacity of your stock must be considered in such a matter as this, you are very able to form a judgment. I am sure that small stagnation upon the remissions hither, which the Martha's Vineyard purchase has occasioned, compels us unto the borrowing of several hundreds of pounds to answer our obligations for necessary salaries and services. In this, there are of your commissioners, who generously offer to tax themselves for disbursements on emergencies. [Thanks the company's treasurer for his help.]

[Recommends that Adam Winthrop be appointed a commissioner, and asks to be dismissed himself from the commission because of his many other obligations.] I do not remember, that ever I have taken more than one journey, and that was lately and no very long one, personally to visit and inspect and instruct the Indian villages. And the truth is, considering the pastoral care of the largest flock in the English America lying on me, and the expectations which all the churches in these colonies have to be served by one in my circumstances, and the many correspondencies which I am to cultivate, and the many societies I belong to, and the publication of treatises on many arguments demanded of me faster than I can well dispatch them (whereof I now take leave to tender one or two of the latest small ones to your honorable Lady), I am rendered less capable of doing what I could wish to do in this particular affair. However, I hope that whether my relation to your commission be superseded or no, I shall, as long as I live, continue to do everything that I find myself capable of doing, for the cause of Christianity among the Indians. What I am now pressing is the introduction of Christianity among the Monhegin Indians of Connecticut, who, alas, remain obstinate pagans to this day. And I am not without hopes that the excellent Governor of that colony, whose heart is in the cause, will one way or other help us to accomplish it. [Close]

Sir, Your most obliged servant,

To Dr. John Edwards

U/Brit Mus   December 10, 1712

Reverend Sir,

[Thanks him for a recent letter.]

Your works (I must continue to inform you) are of great esteem in this country, and besides the many that have been sold, those which I have been the owner of I have caused by way of loan to visit many parts of these colonies, especially our two colleges. Your *Theologia Reformata* is longed for, and you have many friends here who pray for your life. . . .

Our High Church here, in imitation of their brethren in Scotland, seek all advantages to disturb us, and if in a town of two or three hundred well-instructed families, they can find half a score of an abject and vicious character to declare for the Church of England, tho' they understand nothing of the matter, they promise them a release from their parish duties to the established ministry, and send over to your Society for missionaries, whose business here cannot be for the propagation of religion, but the molestation of it. The Society is in this matter extremely imposed on, and the reputation of it in these parts of the world suffers to the uttermost.

[Sends along some "American composures."]

Sir, Your most sincere servant,

TO JOHN WINTHROP

IV Coll 8/MHS   January, 10, 1713

My dear, and never forgotten (but I had almost said, forgetful!) Friend,

Si terrena spernas et superna quaeras, benè est—ego quoque conatus sum.

Do tell me how I shall entertain and gratify you. Our domestic intelligence has nothing but folly and baseness in it. And here, *he that increaseth knowledge, increaseth sorrow.* So I'll offer you nothing of that. The foreign is bad enough; but a formidable and comfortable passage in the second of Daniel, which has the word *consume* in it, is now upon a speedy accomplishment. [Sends one of his works.]

Our friends of the Royal Society do strangely neglect us (or packets miscarry). I hear of many things of mine published; but I never saw them.

We must no longer let our letters go into the post-office; they render it so very chargeable! [Close]   Yours as ever,

Did I ever send you a little dissertation of mine upon a *Seventh Son?* A passage in one of your letters looks as if I did, tho' I don't remember that ever I did it.

TO WAIT-STILL WINTHROP

IV Coll 8/MHS   January 19, 1713

Honorable Sir,

[Relates an anecdote about the French king.]

. . . by our last advice from Europe, it looks as if a blind and mad nation were beginning a little to open their eyes and come to themselves.

I am in continual expectation to hear of Dan IV 13, 14—which will bring on a mighty revolution.

The Church of England by their late act of Parliament have cut themselves off from the communion of the Catholic Church, and cease to be a part of it. This looks but ominously upon that unreformable society! A coalition with the Gallican Church must now be the game. And yet, I have more than once heard of a vessel bound for Rome suffer shipwreck, and so we shall again.

Our reprinting of the *Letter of the Aged Non-Conformist Ministers* put our High-flyers into a strange ferment. You know what followed —namely, Dr. Williams's virulent vindication of the Common Prayer worship, and Dr. King's heap of sophistries and calumnies. My aged parent's *Remarks* hereupon did not produce a hundredth part of the clamor he expected. Our people are generally gratified, edified, established. The Church of England party resolve to publish no more. Harris is under some attrition for his *unhappiness* (that's the word) in writing his preface, which was indeed almost universally decried. Our Newbury faction are coming off and putting themselves under the conduct of one of our ministers. For the rest, I know nothing, but all peace and quietness. [Close]   Sir, Your sincere servant,

To John Stirling

U/NLS   April 24, 1713

Most honored Sir,

[Asks that a recent work of his be distributed among the students at the university.]

This country has afforded little that is remarkable since I had the honor of my last writing to you. Only it will be some satisfaction unto one who loves our country, as you do, to be informed that we are in a fair way to a peace with our Indian savages, and that the waste-places which the late fire had made in this capital town of the province are already rebuilt, to a degree and in a beauty that is to everyone's admiration. In the meantime, we are trembling for the Ark on your side the water, and fear such things coming upon you as will require the pen of another Gildas to relate the story of them; and are afraid of our own sorrows, from the share which our poor lean-to must have in the fall of a house which the XII chapter of Matthew has but a sad prediction for. We particularly have at heart the plots of your neighbors, the Church of England, against your tranquillity, whereof we are the more heartily sensible because a little party under that name are playing just the same game among us, that they are with you. [To demonstrate the validity of Presbyterian ordination, Mather now quotes a number of authorities: Gothofred Voigtius, Lewis Seckendorf, Dr. Osiande of Tübingen, Dr. Bebelius of Strasburg, and Joachim Hildebrand.]

I am unawares gone too far. I call to mind an old rule about our epistles: *Animi candor, epistolis exprimendus, non eruditio ostentanda.* The whole purpose of this is obtained if you may perceive in it the dispositions of my soul towards you, which are none but those of love, honor, esteem, and the most profound respect. You expect not Asiatic epistles from America, and it would be a wrong to take up your better spent hours in reading such. If long ones have gone under such a denomination, I ask that *American Epistles* may become the technic term for such as are no other than brief, honest, sincere declarations of love and value in the writer. [Close]

Sir, Your most obliged and most obedient servant,

To Robert Wodrow

U/NLS   August 21, 1713

Reverend Sir,

[Repeats his complaints against the Church of England missionaries, as in the preceding letter to Stirling.]

You did the *Eleutheria* and the *Letter of Advice to the Dissenters* too much honor, when you imagined my venerable parent the author of them. He smiled when he read it, and complimented me with, *Hos ego versiculos.* The marvellous old man, at seventy-four, continues to do notable things, and preaches to the greatest auditory in America, where I have had the honor to be for three and thirty years his assistant. I suppose he takes this opportunity of letting you hear from him.

[Peace with the Indians, as in the letter to Stirling.]

Sir, Your most affectionate brother and servant,

[To the Royal Society]

U/MHS

October 15, 1713

(A Monster)

The conversation which you allow me the honor of maintaining with you, you may depend upon my entertaining you with nothing but what upon the strictest inquisition will be found so true, that I shall even challenge the name of the late Inquisitor-General in Portugal, whose name I find was *Dom Verissimo*. What I now relate I beheld October 15, 1713.

A woman in my next neighborhood was delivered of two daughters, which were so united as to afford us a shocking spectacle, whereof I was myself one of the spectators. They were in all points entirely two lusty children, only from near the top of their breasts to near the bottom of their bellies, they grew together in such a manner that without a destruction to both, it would have been impossible to have parted them. The union was for the whole breadth of the chest; and their four paps were on their sides, below the arm-pits. Their heads lay on the cheeks of each other; their arms in a mutual embrace of their bodies; their legs all stowed close, that the whole might lie in as little room as could be. It was a little surprising that the mother had no harder a travail in bringing such a burthen into the world. Had these united miserables lived, our first thoughts cannot but in a minute or two suggest a variety of cases which might have occurred in their circumstances, not easy to have been encountered or answered. What must the one have done, if this or that which were easy have been supposed, had befallen the other? But the cases were all superseded at once by their dying as soon as they were born.

[Cites another case of monstrous birth.] And it is not amiss that the displays of the divine providence in such things be observed, if it be done with a due regard unto the rules of modesty, and of charity, and with the reservation which our Saviour made upon the case of the man blind from his nativity.

[Cites another case, in Latin, and mentions a cow that gave birth to three differently colored calves.]

But that my epistle may not grow to a monstrous bigness, and into the dimensions and arguments of two, I shall here conclude it, and subscribe,   Sir, your most hearty friend and servant,

To Samuel Penhallow

DII/MHS   October 21, 1713

Sir,

. . . I wish my pen were able to entertain you with anything like what the poet says dropped from the lip of Nestor, whose Greek verse I have turned into this English hexameter:

His lip dropped language, than sweet honey, sweeter abundance. But such as it is, I pray your acceptance of my last publication.

Our friend, for whose arrival we made so many smokes above a week ago, has now exhibited his commissions and instructions—in which, *Nihil invenio bonis moribus contrarium*, or that has any hurtful aspect on these colonies or churches.

The next day after his arrival, he (with an army of the same religion) was present at an ordination in Charlestown—where, among other things, a speech was made that asserted the validity of our ordination, and the legitimate vocation and investiture of our ministry, with great freedom and assurance; and affirmed that all the churches of God on the continent of Europe do subsist on an ordination received from an order not superior to that of our pastors. Nevertheless he declared afterwards, not without appearance of some impression, that he *had never seen such a spectacle before, and it was a solemn, serious, affecting transaction.*

His commission relating to these provinces is, I suppose, only to examine accounts; which, I hope, you gentlemen-treasurers, etc., are not afraid of.

I was going on with my intelligence, but at this moment your lovely children stop at my gate, calling for my letter. . . .

Yours always,

The measles is got into my family and is like to prove an heavy calamity to all the town.

To Richard Waller

U/MHS draft   December 1, 1713

(A Woollen Snow)

Sir,

You cannot but form some very strange conjectures concerning the matter which upon the first opening of this letter you find enclosed in it, if you allow any time for conjecturing before you have read all the letter over.

If I make so much haste as to tell you that you have here enclosed a *snowball*, you will wonder what the American snow should be made of; and you will affirm this is the first time that ever a gentleman sent his friend a parcel of snow wrapped in a letter to him, at least at such a distance as the breadth of the wide Atlantic.

When you have read of Heaven *giving snow like wool*, I know you have taken it as it is, for a poetical expression, and very much approved and admired the sacred poetry.

But a *snow of wool* without a metaphor is a thing so unusual as to be almost incredible; and yet I must ask that such a thing may find some credit with you.

For, Sir, I do assure you that this wool did fall from Heaven, and a considerable quantity of it, at a time when more common snow was falling.

I have unhappily mislaid the large, and full, and well-asserted account of it with which I furnished myself at the time of it, which was a few years ago; so that I cannot be so particular in my relation as I shall be if I happen to recover it.

But however, my memory sufficiently serves me to assert so much as may afford you a tolerable satisfaction, which is that at a town in one of our colonies, called Fairfield, in the depth of winter, there fell a snow, as at other times; but there was a large frozen spot, of I know not how many acres, which instead of the snow that lay in other places, was covered with a very considerable quantity of this wool whereof I now tender a specimen to your acceptance.

The stories that you have read about a rain of blood, I can guess what you think of. And what a Roman historian relates about a rain of gold, I can guess what some others would be glad of. Thuanus will tell you of corn rained for the space of two hours, and of two miles together. You are so well acquainted with such relations that it would be a perfect rudeness in me to mind you of them. A snow of wool, and of what would be proper to make us a double cloathing, that we may not be afraid of the snow, I do not remember that I have anywhere met withal.

[Gives a few stories about snow from classical literature.]

My letter, Sir, affirms itself to be a faithful messenger; it uses always all possible fidelity in its relations. It brings indeed another sort of snow; I shall rejoice if it at all *refresh the souls of my masters.* . . .

A most humble and obedient servant,

[To Dr. John Woodward]

U/MHS draft   [written late 1713, but apparently sent later]

My most honored Doctor,

For the most acceptable present, which I received, when you honored me with your defence of your *Natural History of the Earth*, I return you all the thanks of a mind filled with gratitude.

Your triumphs over the doctor of Tübingen do but whet our appetites for that most valuable work, whereof I find my excellent friend Dr. Edwards, in a learned essay with which he favored me, raising also our expectations.

I am overwhelmed with some confusion that I have not all this while yielded a due obedience to the commands you laid upon me, to make a collection of our fossils. I can plead nothing for my delay of my duty in this matter but my being overwhelmed with employment. For truly, Sir, I am far from what some have put into their litany *Homo unius negotii*. But I am forming the best projection I can, in an infant country entirely destitute of philosophers, to have this and other intentions answered.

In the meantime I pursue my design as well as I can to make my annual presents of American curiosities.

I am very much afraid whether one of my collections did not miscarry, in which I also enclosed a couple of guineas or Louis d'ors (I forget which) to be spent by you and our dear Mr. Waller when you should (with your treasurer) undergo the trouble of reading over my tedious letters. I therefore looked out some imperfect copies which I kept of those letters, and have thr[ust?] them into the packet now before you. If you have had 'em, 'tis well. There is no hurt in the repetition.

[Mentions sending his packets with Samuel Woodward.]

If Dr. Halley would please to enrich his *Transactions* more plentifully with communications of what we call natural philosophy, and also of medical curiosities, as well as of mathematical rarities, whereof he is so great a master, but how few able to be so much as learners from him!—it would much help to recommend the treasures wherewith mankind is obliged from him. [Close]

Your most affectionate friend and servant,

[To the Royal Society]

U/MHS draft   [late 1713, sent 1716]

(Surprising Influences of the Moon)

Sir,

Tho' our incomparable President, Sir Isaac Newton, than whom philosophy has never had a dictator more justly submitted to, has at length obliged us with a theory of the moon which has performed that which all former astronomers have thought almost impossible, yet the history of the influences which the moon has upon sublunar bodies is among the *desiderata* of our philosophy. With my consent, he shall merit more than the title of a Solomon Iarchi who gives it unto us. [Mentions various observations on the moon's influence by Dr. Grew, Borellus and others.]

. . . If our chestnut wood, whereof we sometimes make our fuel, be felled while the moon is waxing, it will so sparkle in the fire that there shall be no sitting by it in safety. If it be cut while the moon is waning, there will be no such inconvenience.

The other [observation] is this. Whatever timber we cut in two wanes of the moon in a year, the wane in August and the wane in February, it will be forever free from worms. No worms will ever breed in it. Unto these I will add a third, which relates unto the weather. We very much observe it in our country, and govern our affairs by the observation that *as the winds are in the last quarter of the moon, so they generally govern in the next three quarters.*

[To the Royal Society]

U/MHS draft   [late 1713, sent 1716]

(The Pigeons)

Sir,

[Gives various classical and biblical accounts of pigeons.]

A better dish than that [locusts] you would have in our pigeons, a bird which in almost everything resembles your turtle-doves, only that it is a little bigger. The numbers of these that visit us in their seasons are such that I am almost afraid of giving you a true report of them, lest you should imagine a Palephatus were imposing his incredibles upon you. Yet it will a little answer the intention of the correspondence wherewith you favor me, if I do report something of them.

I affirm to you, then, that sometimes we have mighty flocks of these pigeons flying over us, thousands in a flock, the best part of a mile square occupied by a flock, these passing along, the welkin in a manner obscured and covered with them; and several hours have run out before the appearance of these birds thus making the best of their way have been over. They have been frequently sold for two pence or three pence a dozen, tho' two or three of them, roast or boiled or broiled, may make a meal for a temperate man; yea, they are sometimes killed in such plenty that the country-people feed their hogs with them. [In the margin: one of my neighbors has killed no fewer than two and thirty dozen at one shot.]

Gentlemen have complained unto me that they have lit in such numbers on their trees as to break down the limbs thereof, and spoil their orchards.

They will sometimes roost at night in such numbers among our thickets, that our people, with no other weapons than sticks and poles, kill thousands of them.

One worthy person of my acquaintance had a descent of them in his neighborhood, in the month of December, a very unusual time of the year, while there was yet no snow, but many acorns, on the ground, which, 'tis thought, might then draw them thither. At their lighting on a place of thick woods, the *front* wheeled about, the *flanks* wheeled inward, and *rear* came up (Sir, he was a Captain who gave me the written relation!) and pitched as near to the center as they could find any limb, or twig, or bush to seize upon. Yea, they sat upon one another like bees, till a limb of a tree would seem near as big as a horse. 'Tis incredible to tell how large and strong and many limbs were broken down by this new burden upon them. The breaking of them was heard at a mighty distance. The birds filled more than half a mile about from the center; and the noise they made was like the roaring of the sea. The night was dark; but this gentleman and his sons, with guns, and some other less noxious tools, laid in among them, and some they took alive with their hands, and in the morning found the number of their slain to be one hundred and three dozen, besides what some other people had carried away. A few days ago, I was at a table of a superior gentleman, relating some of these things. And one, whose veracity was not to be disputed, said he had a story that would cap all of mine; for (said he) *I have catched no less than two hundred dozen of pigeons, in less than two minutes of time, and all in one trap!* The pleasant mention of this whetstone on the occasion, obliged the gentleman immediately to explain himself, and add: *Such a number broke into my barn, and but by shutting the doors I had them all at my mercy.* [Other stories about pigeons.]

Heartily and forever at your service,

[To the Royal Society]

U/MHS draft   [late 1713, sent 1716]

(Uncommon Idiots)

You find India to have been among the ancients a term for ignorance; and where they knew no further they still termed India. If you European gentlemen still count India a seat of ignorance, we poor inhabitants of the Western India must humbly acknowledge we give you too much occasion. If you look upon us as generally *idiots,* or but a little superior to such, we ought not to complain of you as having wronged us. And therefore you will not wonder at it that you are entertained from hence with a story of some *idiots,* but rather, that we have anybody in any tolerable manner to relate the story. I remember Strabo says, that all the geographers who had written of India had given the world nothing but lies. But you shall have none such from the pen which is now writing from thence unto you.

I have been told that the famous Dr. Sydenham, having that question put unto him, *What he took to be the greatest cure that ever he wrought?* replied, *The restoring of reason to an idiot!* How much mankind in general may want such doctors is not the present subject of remark. But I know not what our Sydenham could have done upon two deplorable objects in our town of Dunstable.

A gentleman there, whose name is Mr. S——, under paralytic affects, is yet the father of two daughters, whereof the one is now nine, the other three, years of age. They continued for several months after their nativity in the same circumstances of sensibility that other infants of their age use [*sic*] to have. But anon they were taken with odd convulsive motions, which carried a little of an epileptical aspect upon them. The fits would be short, and many of them in an hour; but after some while the fits grew seldomer, and lasted longer, and the screeches of the little wretches in them would be very doleful. These fits anon left them wholly deprived of almost everything in the world, but only a little sight, and scent, and hunger. Nothing in the whole brutal world so insensible! They move not their limbs: you may twist them, and bend them to a degree that none else could bear, and they feel it not. They take notice of nothing in the world, only they seem to see and smell victuals, at the approach of which they will gape, and be very restless, and make something of a bray. They are in good health, and eat rather more than other children of their age. But they let their excrements pass from them without the least regard. The elder is ever drivelling, the younger never has any salival discharge. They shed no tears. They never sneeze. They have no speech. They have no way to discover any sentiments of their minds. They never use their hands to take hold of anything. Was *idiocy* ever seen so miserable!

I have sometimes beheld and admired the display of the divine providence in this thing, that a total deafness and a total blindness has hardly ever been known to concur in one subject. The concurrence of two such incapacities in one subject must have made the miserable so uncapable of being subsisted, that it seems the compassion of Heaven forbears the infliction of it. This example is the nearest unto it of any I have met withal.

But so much for my Dunstable idiots. I shall but bring myself into the number if I once imagine that I can impose long letters upon a person of your superior circumstances, without hazard of making you weary with them. I will break off seasonably, with some evidence of my being so far from idiocy, that (besides my wishes that I were no worse a one than honest Raymund the Abbot, who under the name of

Idiota wrote the famous *Contemplationes de Amore Divino*) I understand my duty, which is to subscribe, Sir, for many reasons, and with no less respects, Your most obedient servant,

[To the Royal Society]

U/MHS draft [late 1713, sent 1716]

(An Unusual Discharge)

[Relates various classical stories about "attempts to discharge such things as may be noxious to our bodies."]

At a town called Concord, about eighteen miles distant from me, a young woman was taken with a grievous fit of coughing, which held her for an hour or two, and [until?] she was near strangling. At last the cough grew more moderate; but still it was troublesome, and she became very much indisposed. One of her indispositions was a tumor, which in a little while began to appear about her left shoulder-blade. The chirurgeon applied his plaster to it; one morning, about a fortnight after the first inconvenience, her father, taking off the plaster, saw a speck in the skin, of such maturity towards a suppuration, a little below the shoulder-blade, that he resolved upon opening it. He did so, and unto his astonishment pulled out a large ear of rye, after which the place healed fast enough, and she returned unto her former health and ease. It seems that the young woman going in too much ha[ste?] with an ear of rye in her mouth, upon the action of driving some hogs out of the field, received a fall, the violence whereof drove the ear of rye down the *aspera*. But then, for the safe passage of the ear of rye out a little below the shoulder-blade, I leave this to your investigation, who have gone beyond *Mundimus* in your study of anatomy. . . . [Close]

V

In his diary for 1714 Cotton Mather announced his intention of publishing *Biblia Americana* and spreading it across America and Europe. Eight years earlier he had announced that the gigantic book was finished. Both announcements proved premature and heartbreaking. He would revise the *Biblia* on and off for the rest of his life but would never see it published. In 1714, just the same, he wrote off to THOMAS REINOLDS (or REYNOLDS, 1687?–1727), an English Presbyterian minister associated with the bookseller Thomas Bradbury. What perhaps recommended Reinolds to Mather was his biography of Mrs. Clissold (reprinted in Boston with a preface by Increase Mather), which Mather regarded highly enough to give to his children as pious reading, and the fact that Reinolds had studied in Utrecht under Herman Witsius, a Dutch theologian whom Mather greatly admired. Mather's May, 1714, letter to Reinolds is an enclosure; in the covering letter he asked Reinolds to address this enclosure to three London ministers of his choice. Simultaneously Mather applied to John Stirling in Scotland, asking him to write a few lines in favor of the *Biblia* and send them to Reinolds and others in England. These efforts to find a publisher failed because, as Mather complained to Sir William Ashurst, the English Dissenters betrayed him and because Englishmen looked down on Americans, especially Nonconformists, as cultural inferiors.

Although pained by this setback, Mather continued his efforts for Ashurst and for the New England Company. He renewed to Sir William his special pleading for the Connecticut Indians, who so far had been preached to without success. The company promised greater financial support, but the missionaries in Connecticut found the Mohegans hostile and cynical. Still hoping to derive revenue from their land on Martha's Vineyard, the company ordered six hundred acres of it leased in June, 1714, to Ebenezer Allen for ten years. Ashurst still believed that if the Indians there could be brought into "fixed settlements," and made to employ themselves on husbandry, they could be civilized and after that Christianized or, more accurately, Puritanized.

Another problem that hindered the missionary work was the difficulty of transferring funds from England to the colonies. The New England Company at last decided to use bills of exchange. What brought the problem into being was a larger fiscal difficulty that had begun making itself felt throughout the province. As a result of the decision to issue bills of credit in Massachusetts (a decision Mather had supported), more and more paper accumulated, worth less and less, while gold and silver were drained off to Europe. By 1714 silver had nearly disappeared from Massachusetts, and the cost of living had doubled. A group of Bostonians associated with the councillor Elisha Cooke, issued a pamphlet titled *A Projection for Erecting a Bank of Credit Founded on Land Security*. They proposed using land as security for incorporating an independent, public bank. The bank scheme, pushed through the General Court in November, 1715, begot a pamphlet controversy into which Mather entered. When Governor Dudley learned that the bank group intended to secure a charter for itself in London, he tried to prevent them and sent instructions to the Massachusetts agent in London, Jeremiah Dummer. But without Dudley's intervention the bank scheme was defeated by the London Board of Trade. Its supporters in Boston, however, blamed Dudley for the defeat and exerted their influence to oust him.

Mather's stand on the bank reveals the way Mather operated in secular affairs. As he freely confessed, and without any smugness, he never had a head for business. Indeed, his letters on the bank to Ashurst and to Sir Peter King are essentially requests for counsel. As far as he could see, Mather considered Dudley's arguments against the bank wrongheaded, and he certainly opposed merely issuing more paper money. Yet there were also, he clearly felt, arguments to be made against the bank. To the extent that he favored the bank, he did so without conviction and with a sense that he was not qualified to judge. Typically, despite his confessed ignorance of such a worldly matter, he decided to take a hand in it. First he wrote to SIR PETER KING (1669–1734), chief justice of the Court of Common Pleas, Fellow of the Royal Society, friend of Newton, uncle of John Locke—the sort of man Mather always felt close to. He must have known, however, that King was also a member of the Anglican SPGFP and a defender of the Arian William Whiston. Mather's cordial letter to King suggests that he could be both ecumenical enough and practical enough to distinguish religious from worldly affairs and that he could put aside his ministerial role entirely, with shyly innocent and often fumbling results. At the same time, one suspects that his interest in the bank and in a sound currency grew from the fact that, as a salaried minister, his income was coming to be worth less and less under the inflation.

It might be expected that as a matter of course Mather would support anything which Dudley opposed, such as the bank. But, in fact, by 1714 the intricate relationships between Mather, Hobby, and Dudley were recombining in unforeseen patterns. For one thing, by 1708 Hobby—Mather's chief candidate to replace Dudley—had himself been won over to Dudley's party. He infuriated Mather by showing Dudley some of the letters which Mather had written urging Hobby's governorship. Also, Sir William Ashurst turned out to be against the bank and now strenuously supported Dudley in the fear that someone worse might succeed him. Mather respected Ashurst's reputation and influence and was anxious to stay in his favor. And, as previously noted, Hobby had acted for the SPGFP, the Anglican rival of the New England Company. The result was that Mather began turning towards Dudley and away from Hobby. As the bank party tried to get rid of Dudley, Mather found himself interceding for him. His mediation, he remarked in his diary, was "unexpected," but he told Ashurst that he had "of late months lived in good correspondence" with the governor, and that he now looked on Sir Charles Hobby as "our former friend." Some other unforeseen events helped to swerve Mather's allegiances. He always sympathized with the aged and infirm, and Dudley, growing old, was in poor health. Besides, Mather found irresistible any opportunity to forgive his enemies in a Christlike way.

Dudley's reputation in Boston had also changed. A new generation, less fiercely protective of its independence, began to see Dudley as some recent historians do—as a devoted servant of the crown carrying out the policies of Queen Anne. Those who see Dudley in this way see Mather's new friendship for him as a Machiavellian gambit—Mather calculating that the death of the queen spelled the end of Dudley's power. Upon the queen's death Dudley did lose his influence in England, and a new governor— Elizeus Burgess—was appointed on April 21, 1715. After leaving the governorship Dudley continued to regain some of his popularity, and at his death in 1720 he received a lavish funeral.

To Sir William Ashurst

U/Hunt   December 7, 1713

Sir,

[No considerable news to report since his last letter.]

The most considerable [news] has been an essay to send the gospel of God our Saviour unto some forlorn and wretched companies of Indians in the colony of Connecticut, who formerly have rejected the tenders that have been made them of the great salvation, and continue to this hour in horrid paganism, tho' they have been for seventy years together in the bowels of a Christian colony. I formerly wrote as pressing a letter as I could unto the General Assembly of Connecticut, that the government there might be prevailed withal to exert their care, with the advice of their ministers, to revive the work of Christianizing the Indians that are under their influences. They began to do something, which yet came to nothing. But, I hope, this new essay of ours, under the countenance of their excellent Governor, will have a harvest anon to be rejoiced in. I suppose our secretary, Judge Sewall, will send Your Honor the journal of our missionary.

I made so bold with the honorable Governor of New York as to address him lately with another letter, soliciting for something to be done, that a body of Indians yet in the darkest and vilest heathenism upon Long Island may be Christianized. That most valuable gentleman will do what he can; but I wish he may not find his generous intentions clogged, by some English people of a very bad character, with insuperable difficulties.

A peace now being after some sort restored with our Frenchified Indians at the eastward, we shall soon be upon projections, what may be done that they also may be Christianized. You must give me leave, Sir, and excuse me from the guilt of a solecism, that I oppose *Frenchified* and *Christianized*.

I am very particularly making certain motions for the instruction of one among them, concerning whom I have a pretty odd story to tell you. An English woman, whose name is Cloyse (now a widow), at a town called Wells, had a little infant son taken from her about four or five and twenty years ago, by some skulking Indians who were then in their hostilities; and by all her inquiries of captives or others, she could never hear what was become of him. T'other day, since the peace, an Indian of a complexion that had hardly quite so much copper in it as the rest of his company, came into a house where Mrs. Cloyse was present. She began to entertain some suspicions that this blade might be her son, tho' he were now so Indianized. Upon examination it was then found that he was never known to have any kindred among the Indians, never any one person in the least related unto him. And upon further examination, there were found several very notable marks upon his body, which his mother successively declared, before they were searched for, that if he were her son they must be there. The issue was that upon entire satisfaction, with floods of tears on both sides, they acknowledged one another, and she admits him as her son, to inherit some of his father's estate; and he blesses himself that he had not killed his father, as diverse times in the progress of two long wars he had been upon the point of doing of it. This man, I hope, will anon have the acclamations of the prodigal in the parable made upon him.

[Promises to send an account of how the Indian lands are being made to yield revenues.] . . . you see, Sir, how I am unawares led into it, to take upon me the quality of your intelligencer for the state of affairs among the Christianized Indians. [Close]

Your Honor's most sincere servant,

To George Corwyn

U/HSP   December 22, 1713

Sir,

[Regrets not having seen Corwyn during his recent visit to Salem.]

You are sensible that it has been a time of much calamity in this town, and that I, whom am far from being the least sinner in the place, have not been the least sufferer in the calamity.

In the three sad weeks that passed over my family, my cross (tho' the cross be but a dry sort of a tree) produced six or seven publications, whereof I now tender some to your acceptance. You will divide the fruits with your valuable neighbor.

The fury of the measles is a little abated in the town, especially in the north part of it, where the trouble began. I pray God, the succeeding fever, which kills many young men, may have no further commission.

The inhabitants of this town did in four several congregations the last Thursday, endeavor to present their supplications before the glorious Lord our Healer. And their alms with their prayers went up as a memorial. Tho' it were a very bitter season for the cold, and many hundreds of our people did not plough by reason of the cold, yet near four hundred pounds were gathered for the relief of our poor, whereof we have many that conflict with grievous difficulties.

I am in distress for the sorrows that poor Salem will see, if the distemper should become so epidemical with you as it has been with us. It will require a very nice management, else it will be attended with many pernicious consequences. For which cause, there is in the press a sheet of plain directions, to be dispersed where they may want skilful physicians. [Sends along a book by his father.]

Sir, Your brother and servant,

To Sir William Ashurst

U/Hunt (HM 22323)   December 31, 1713

Sir,

[Has no news to report.]

Only there is one thing in which your willing and faithful servants, the commissioners for the evangelical affairs among the Indians here, do need and ask your favor.

Expenses that have appeared necessary for the support of those affairs, have insensibly grown upon them, until at last they find that the remittances from London do not fully answer them. Several generous gentlemen of their number have with ready disbursements advanced for the payment of the annual salaries for the ministers and school masters among the Indians, as the time of the year has recurred for them, when the treasury here has been empty. But their just hopes of being reimbursed must have long stops upon them if the expenses here exceed the capacities of the spring with you that must supply them. There can be therefore nothing more seasonable than a direction from your honorable Board unto this, to set some limits unto them, and regulate their expenses with limiting them to a sum within what you know you can afford them. They will then walk in a better light than they find by a sensible recollection they have done of some later years, and they will also act the more advisedly and regularly in applying that pinching-stroke here, to which they begin to find themselves necessitated, and make suitable retrenchments. It is true, the gentlemen are pursuing it with all the projection they can, to render the land interest of the Indians here serviceable to the great interest of all, in yielding revenues to it. But this will be a work of some time, and all the effects of what is projected will not be presently accomplished. In the meantime, a virtuous gentleman, Major Thomas Fitch, who has the honor to be in your commission, and who has already done his part more than once in lending us what money we have wanted, has offered unto us to serve all present necessities for payments, as far as five hundred pounds or more, when your treasurer here happens to be out of money, if his action therein might be so acceptable to you, that you would answer his bills in London, at an exchange that shall be stated and settled by the most indifferent judges. But your treasurer here hath such a remembrance of the aversion you once expressed for any bills drawn from hence, that this matter is proposed but with all the deference imaginable.

[Encloses a printed letter.]

Your Honor's most obliged and obedient servant,

To Governor Robert Hunter

U/AAS draft [early 1714?]

Sir,

[Sends along a printed letter.]

Your Excellency gave life and form to my first written copy, and I had no reason for dropping the distinction that I had used in it, but only my complaisance to Your Excellency's repose, inasmuch as your *Cornburian* crew might improve it unto your disadvantage for Your Excellency to have been known corresponding with a person of my well-known circumstances. And indeed, besides Your Excellency I am not aware of any one person in your city whom I can suppose to have any other sentiments of me but such as are full of contempt, and the greatest aversion. [Close] Y.E.ˢ most humble,

To Thomas Reinolds

DII/AAS draft [c. May, 1714]

My most honored Brethren,

It is a consolation of God, which cannot be small with you, that you have American colonies, who have an ambition to be acknowledged as your United Brethren, are ambitious to be bound up with you in one bundle of life and of love. We believe we enjoy the benefit of your prayers for us, and are sure our prayers for you, our solicitous concern for your prosperity, and our sympathizing distress in all your adversity, are such as will become our declared brotherhood. And if any service for the church of God, worthy of any notice, be performed by His Grace granted unto any person here, it recommends itself unto you under that consideration: 'tis done by *one of you;* 'tis one of *your own* performances.

Behold, now laid before you, A *New Offer to the Lovers of Religion and Learning,* made by one of yours, at a thousand leagues distance from you, which will, no doubt, sufficiently explain itself in the perusal.

That the things promised in this offer are indeed prepared, I suppose, will be unquestionable unto such as may think the author could not otherwise be so senseless as to make a tender of them; for I can assure you, there will be found rather more than what the bill of fare has mentioned.

It has not been any disadvantage unto your particular profession of dissent from the irregularities in the worship imposed on the nation, or unto the cause of pure and undefiled religion in general, which is your cause more than any people's, that so many of your way have had their pens used by the glorious Head of the church, to do things that have proved advantageous and acceptable to the reasonable part of the world. [Mentions, as examples, Poole, Williams, Calamy, Henry, and others.]

That your American servant may obtain some share in the candid sentiments of the churches pursuing the Reformation in London, and wherever you may see cause to command the essay which he now tenders you, he might plead that as far as the publishing a variety of [crossed out: of many more than two hundred] some lesser, some larger treatises and composures, on various arguments and in various languages, may secure him the reputation (if not of having talents rendering him in some degree capable of his undertaking, yet) of his pure, innocent, confessed orthodoxy, you may depend upon it that no disservice will be done to the Kingdom of God by your encouraging of what you find thus undertaken.

Some eminent persons in the church to the rites whereof we are Non-conformists, have given me such a prospect of encouragement from them for our *Biblia Americana,* that if you should wholly cast it off, it may happen by their means to make its way into the world. But, I think my duty to you obliges me to choose that it should rather be by yours.

If you, my dear Brethren, (and those who meet you on the common affair, to whom you may if you please communicate these my letters) do judge it worth your while to concern yourselves for the forwarding of this work, I shall request that you three accept the t[rou]ble of advising, directing, ordering [what] shall be done about it.

That you single out the booksellers whom you would have to go through with it.

That you give effectual injunctions for the press-work to be well done: fairly, neatly, correctly, and according to the directions I may in time give concerning it.

That you exert as full power in agreeing upon terms for everything about the work, as if it were your own.

Only, I would entreat that my dear and only brother, Mr. Samuel Mather of Witney, may interpose his sentiments with yours, if there may be occasion.

I delay sending over the copy till I have some return from you, to make my way more plain before me. When you say *let it come*, we will do our best that it may be no longer detained here.

In this country, my friends begin to send me in such *indefinite subscriptions* for the work, as the proposals have spoken of, supposing that the two volumes will not cost much more than five pounds of our money to the subscribers. And your booksellers may have a rational expectation of having subscriptions for many more than one hundred sets of the work, to be paid in upon their arrival here, if they will run the risk thereof. [Close]

Your sincere brother and most humble servant,

To John Stirling

U/NLS   May 17, 1714

Very reverend and most honored Sir,

[Has not heard from Stirling for a long time.]

These parts have afforded little that is remarkable since my last. We have our share in the general peace, and we share with you also in the apprehensions of what is to arise, *when they shall say peace and safety!* In the mean time, our churches are considerably multiplying; and within a little while, above twenty new congregations have been formed in this country, generally with the countenance, concurrence, and satisfaction of those from whom they swarm into distinct societies.

Attempts to propagate the Church of England among us, by a most conspicuous and marvelous blast of Heaven upon them, do very much come to nothing. Even the organs introduced into the chapel in this metropolis of the English America, signify very little to draw over our people unto them. The only hope of that interest prevailing here, is in a prospect of that church's arising into a capacity to persecute, which 'tis hoped by some that the third and fourth verses of Obadiah's prophecy will put a bar unto.

[Mentions his attempts to publish *Biblia Americana* in London and asks Stirling to "write a line in favor of the work."]

Considering that the American churches owed a testimony unto the truth, against which a modern giant has appeared with some open defiances, the meanest servant thereof, (and yours), devoted a little more than a week's time, in the midst of many returning and unceasing labors, unto the service. I sent it the last fall to London, and the famous Dr. Edwards writes to me from Cambridge that he had written a preface unto it. But I cannot yet hear whether it be published or no. For which cause I [tender?] a manuscript copy of it unto your kind acceptance. If it should by your advice be honored with a publication at Glasgow, I would pray that you would allow the title to be changed into *Testimonium Glascuense*. For, I assure you, it had been first of all so entitled, and sent unto you, that it might have come forth as from a poor member of your famous university, had I known of any way for its conveyance unto you. But the merits of the performance are so very mean, that I cannot flatter myself with a promise of its finding so favorable a reception. [Asks him to show the work, and the letter, to Jameson and Brown.]

Sir, under many and lasting obligations, your most affectionate friend and servant,

To Sir William Ashurst

U/Hunt (HM 22316)   June 1, 1714

Sir,

As I would miss no fair opportunity of giving Your Honor, and the Company, an account of what your commissioners are doing in pursuance of the trust with which you have honored them, so I would impose it as a law on myself, which for some while I have observed, that every letter shall be accompanied with some Indian entertainment that may afford you a little refreshment and satisfaction.

We meet this day to agree upon an address unto our General Assembly for certain guardians of the Christian Indians to be furnished with legal powers, whereby their unoccupied lands may not only be rescued from English encroachments but also be applied to such uses, and be disposed with such leases, as to bring in a considerable revenue, which may be united with yours, for the support of the main interest.

I must ask pardon of some in the world, if I presume to say that I know of a mighty Society for the Propagation of Religion in Foreign Parts, whose revenues are much more ample than yours, and who for number and figure are such as to raise the greatest expectations concerning their performances; and yet they are not able to show such considerable effects of their great pretensions and advantages, and such valuable services to the Kingdom of God, as you, Sir, and the Society at the head whereof you are placed, can show of your lesser ones.

What I now entertain you with is a poem in the three learned languages, all formed and written by an Indian youth whom we are educating at our college for your service, not yet got beyond the standing of a Junior Sophister. Considering the person from whom it comes, it may hope for some acceptance with you, as one or two little treatises now also do, with your excellent Lady, from another hand, who takes leave again to subscribe, Sir,

Your most obliged and obedient servant,

[To Daniel Parker and Zacheus Mayhew,
agents for the Indian commissioners]
U/AAS draft   [c. August, 1714]

Gentlemen,

The commissioners for the evangelical affairs among the Indians have in pursuance of the care committed unto them found it necessary that the portion of land allowed for the Indians to occupy at Gay-head on Martha's Vineyard should be more equally divided and improved among them than heretofore. We therefore entreat of you, with all convenient speed, to visit the land aforesaid, and exert the powers which we now put into your hands, by assigning to each Indian family there, together with such as we now direct to be removed from the land we have leased unto Mr. Ebenezer Allen (whom we have desired to assist you with his best advice on this occasion) such proportions of the land as you may judge proper for their cultivation; and appoint and adjust the payments of suitable quitrents for the same, as an acknowledgment of those on whom they have their dependence. In the managing of this affair, 'tis our desire that all due and discreet provision be made, that such as have no cattle may not unreasonably suffer in their tillage and herbage, especially from those who have so great stocks that they must be obliged to hire pasturage from those that have none. We would also desire you to put these Indians into the best way of improving their lands, and that they may not be left unto a liberty of perverting their allowances unto purposes that will not well agree with our grand intention. [Close]

[To the Indians on Gay-head]

U/AAS draft   [c. August, 1714]

Our good Friends and Brethren,

The commissioners love you, and seek your good in everything.

We direct the sixteen families of you which are now on the land that we have leased unto Mr. Ebenezer Allen, to remove unto that land which we think most suitable to be inhabited by the Indians.

And unto you and all the Indians upon the Gay-head, we say that we have given power to Mr. Daniel Parker and Captain Zacheus Mayhew to visit you and settle your bounds and assign to every one of you a suitable portion, that you may all live comfortably and that the rich may not oppress the poor among you.

We expect that you comply with the orders of those gentlemen. And tho' we would have you own your dependence on the good and great protectors you have in London, who have bought this land for your benefit, yet we shall use all the care of kind fathers to make your condition comfortable. Every penny of the money received of Mr. Ebenezer Allen, or of any other, is all laid out only to make you a happy people. And we hope you will be glad that you have those to look after you, who love you like their children and are desirous that you may know and serve the Lord Jesus Christ, your only Saviour, and in all things fare as well as we do ourselves.

We are, Your loving friends,

To Sir William Ashurst
U/Hunt (HM 22309; AAS draft in DII)   October 12, 1714

Sir,

Your grand Revolution on the first of August has affected these plantations in a very uncommon manner; and we comfort ourselves with hopes that our King will extend his benign rays to his American colonies, where he has diverse hundreds of thousands of subjects, but none more loyal and faithful to him and his house than those of New England.

Our Governor, with whom I have of late months lived in good correspondence, commands me to give you his service.

Many (whereof your servant who now writes was one) were of the opinion in the reign of the late ministry that we should be much easier and happier in him, notwithstanding some dissatisfactions, than in any such disbanded, boisterous, terrible *Flanderkin*, as it was feared might come in the succession; and therefore heartily desired his continuance in the government, and so much the rather because all agree him to be a gentleman of fine accomplishments.

I perceive that some are even still of the opinion that we had better still have him for our Governor than some that may be *strangers to us,* or *not of our nation.*

And I myself cannot well shake off a certain principle which obliges me to wish him all the good that may be obtained for him, and particularly as much quiet as may be when his *Quietus est* shall be granted him.

Nor have I forgotten what Chrysostom did for Eutropius.

While I was in the midst of these contemplations, I was entertained with the comfortable advice of the safe arrival of our former friend, Sir Charles Hobby; yea, and a fresh prospect which he might now have of a succession to our government.

As my whole conduct in relation to that friend of ours has for many years been a perpetual series of civilities to him, and wishes and essays for his prosperity—nor can any one living tax me with one act or word inconsistent with the friendship I have ever treated him withal, tho' some things have happened that looked a little discouraging, especially when the unaccountable publication of my letters to him did so extremely expose me to the revenges of our Governor and his partisans— so I am still full of all due regards unto him.

[Mentions that Hobby has always spoken well of Ashurst.]

If the divine providence bring into the hands of that gentleman the royal commission for our government, I hope the many and severe afflictions with which the Holy God has exercised him will have a tendency only to render him the more serviceable to the world, and the more capable and the more disposed for to be a generous benefactor unto the people that shall be committed unto him.

I hope likewise that all old personal animosities between him and our present Governor will be so laid aside, that nothing shall be done in any point but what the public welfare shall call for. Behold, the most unlikely and improper person in the world interposing in a most unexpected mediation. [Close]

Your Honor's most sincere and humble servant,

To Sir Charles Hobby

DII/AAS draft   October 15, 1714

Sir,

[Has just heard of Hobby's arrival in London.]

I may truly say, you never had a friend upon earth more sincerely and assiduously concerned for your prosperity, and more heartily sympathizing with you in every article of adversity; or that preserved a more inviolable friendship under circumstances that perhaps might have shocked it in some other person. When I have been diverse times told that you have spoken to my disadvantage, my constant answer has been, That gentleman knows me so well, I am sure he never spoke an ill word of me! You might therefore justly wonder at it if I should let slip an opportunity of expressing to you my satisfaction in the good providence which has thus far watched over you.

Our Governor desires me to do him all the good offices which my poor pen may serve him in. And you may be sure that the fifth chapter of Matthew will compel one of my principles to do all good offices for one to whom I am so obliged.

I know nothing that I am capable of doing, but only to entreat of you that when a certain point, about the revival whereof you have been long since apprised of my apprehensions and expectations, is accomplished, you do him what good may lie in your way.

154

He has powerful enemies, (as well as friends,) and some that are gone from hence, no doubt, carry terrible representations of him; and I wish that he had given them less occasions.

But tho' Governor Eutropius had very much maligned Chrysostom, and loaded him with indignities, yet when Eutropius, likely to be overwhelmed with his enemies, fled unto Chrysostom to defend him, the honest old man spoke, as far as his conscience would let him, if no farther, on his behalf. [Close]

    Your Honor's most sincere friend and humble servant,

To Sir William Ashurst

U/Hunt (HM 22307)   November 17, 1714

Honorable Sir,

[Is sending along his *Duodecennium Luctuosum* and "one or two more little things."]

I should not have put into this packet my *New Offer* of our *Biblia Americana* but that you may be sensible that one of your servants, who always counts that you put an undeserved respect upon him when you lay upon him any of your commands, has also found the time to do some other things, unto which your commands have not extended.

Tho' I may without vanity pretend that this work is grown a wealthy preparation, and tho' among the many others who in these plantations have subscribed unto it, it has had the countenance of three Governors who are all of them uncommon literators, yet I have no expectation of its ever getting without the walls of a private library while the character of a New Englander and a Non-conformist must run so low as it does on your side the water. From the Dissenters I must expect nothing, for such reasons as I am not fond of mentioning, especially since the death of Mr. Matthew Henry, who diverse times offered me his best assistances for the publication of the work. Except some gentlemen of a moderate and catholic (and your) spirit in the Established Church, favor the work, it will remain where it is; but why should I expect any such thing as that? I have been taught such submission to the will of the glorious God that I am satisfied in my having endeavored what I have done, tho' my poor endeavors be not accepted. [Close]

    Your Honor's most obedient servant,

To Sir Peter King

DII/AAS   December 22, 1714
(not in Mather's hand, but with his corrections)

Honorable Sir,

[Recommends the people of New England as pious and honest.]

New-England is now grown a populous country, and by consequence the business therein carried on must be considerable. But for some well known causes 'tis come to pass that it may say, *Silver and gold have I none.* The main subsistence for our business these many years has been upon bills of credit, issued out from the public treasury of the province, the fund whereof has been in our immense debts contracted by our grievous wars; for the payment of which the faith of our General Assembly has been engaged, that certain heavy taxes should be annually levied on the people, until the whole sum in the bills of credit thus emitted, should return into the treasury. The debts of the province have thus been the riches of it, and in the circulation of these bills, a medium of trade and a method for our conveyance of credit unto one another has been kept in motion.

But our extraordinary debts are hastening, we hope, to a period. Our bills of credit are apace going into the treasury, where having done what they have to do, they expire, as the theater on which they have done their part, at length is to do, in flames. What number and value of them we have now circulating is, as our gentlemen of business express it, no more than *a sprat in a whale's belly,* and bear so little proportion to the business of the country, that our people are plunged into inexpressible difficulties. The most uneasy of the four grand Jewish pains, *Vacuitas marsupis,* is come upon us. The blood in our veins is much of it exhausted, and what little is left is by some wealthy and hoarding people stagnated. We find the name of Truck-land (which your honor knows is that name of Germany) will scarce do for New England, but throws us into inextricable difficulties. For the relief of these difficulties, not a few of our more ingenious gentlemen formed a projection of a bank in partnership among themselves, the bills whereof might somewhat answer the necessities of the country. The persons concerned in it are many of them such as in all accounts are in superior circumstances. From all parts of the land they pray

156

to come into the partnership. Their interest is very potent, and very much carries the new elections for our General Assembly.

I forbear to give Your Honor the several articles of the projection, because it will be laid before you by certain gentlemen who will wait upon you with it. What I have to relate is that some gentlemen (for some reasons which in the *Monarchia Solipsorum* are very passing ones) have appeared violently against this projection, and partly by their share in the government, and partly their way of gaining their points upon it, they have drawn upon it a discountenance from the government. At the same time the government has been drawn into an action which many think to be not advisable, and hardly justifiable; even to order the making more bills of credit like our former, and letting fifty thousand pounds of them out upon interest unto such as will borrow them, the principal with the interest to be paid in five years, or the mortgaged lands are seized by the government. However, many who dash hard and with much noise against the projected bank, do it really from a public spirit, and from a real persuasion that the public will be best served in the way whereof the government is now making an experiment. In this exigence the gentlemen [about eight words torn] prostrate themselves before the Throne for the Royal favor; and what I have to request of Your Honor is that, if in your deep penetration you see their proposals to be wise, and just, and allowable, you will please to cast a benign aspect upon them. Your Excellency's character assures us, that if you see what is proposed will be for the service of the Crown, and for the encouragement and consolation of a well-disposed people, willing in all things to live honestly, it will be made partaker of your favorable influences. [Close]

Your Honor's most sincere and humble servant,

TO SIR WILLIAM ASHURST

U/Hunt (HM 22314)   December 24, 1714

Honorable Sir,

[Encloses a circular letter from the Indian commissioners.]

Our country grows full of people and full of business. But a medium of trade almost wholly failing among us, we find ourselves plunged into inexpressible difficulties. For the relief of these difficulties, a great number of our best gentlemen began to form a projection of a bank, which Your Honor finds in the packet that now waits upon you. The projection meeting with opposition from some who can do what they will in our government, the gentlemen prostrate themselves before the King for His Royal favor to it. And it is humbly desired by the gentlemen concerned in this affair, that our honorable and most valuable friend Sir William Ashurst will please to bestow a few thoughts on their projection; and that, if a person of his deep and clear discernment, judge it a wise, and a just, and a good thing, he would, as he has opportunity, express his good will unto it. [Close]

Your Honor's most sincere servant,

CHAPTER THREE

1715–1719

Courtship of Lydia Lee George; attempts to establish
Increase, Jr., in business; renewed efforts to publish *Biblia
Americana*; correspondence with Jeremiah Dummer; the
memorial to the new king, George I; membership in the
Royal Society; controversy with visitors from Scotland;
worsening financial difficulties; *Lapis è Monte Excisus*; relations with Governor Shute; slavery; founding of Yale
College and relations with Harvard; successful conversion of
the Indians in Connecticut; the plight of John Winthrop;
further efforts to publish *Biblia Americana*; prophecy.

I

LATE in 1714 or early in 1715 Cotton Mather began courting the
woman who became his third wife and worst tormentor. She was
LYDIA LEE GEORGE (d. 1734), a daughter of the Reverend Samuel
Lee. Her husband had died in November, 1714, only a month or
two before Mather began seeing her. What remains of this courtship are the following letters and drafts. Mostly undated, they leave
the chronology of the affair, and to that extent its atmosphere, a
bit uncertain. This group also includes the first extant letter from
Mather to BENJAMIN COLMAN (1673–1747), minister of the Brattle
Street Church, to which Lydia belonged. Mather's earlier dealings
with Colman had been unfriendly because of the liberal religion
Colman introduced into his church, because his church drew
members away from Mather's church, and because he wrote an
anonymous pamphlet attacking Mather. While they never became
friends, by 1710 they at least stopped being enemies. Indeed, the
differences between the two men seem generational rather than
temperamental, and they had much in common. Had Mather been
born a decade later he might have been very much like Colman.
Even so, like Mather, Colman was a literary man with an extensive
correspondence; like Mather, he had an honorary doctorate of
divinity from the University of Glasgow and a fondness for the

Church of Scotland. Mather sought Colman's advice on his courtship because Lydia Lee belonged to Colman's church, but perhaps also because Colman was known as something of a poet and ladies' man, who while in England had befriended the poetess Elizabeth Rowe.

Mather's courtship of Lydia reversed the roles of the Kate Maccarty affair. He was now the pursuer; he now went in and out of favor. Yet in both affairs he saw the same pattern. With Lydia as with Kate, he felt, he would have to renounce an enviable love match as one more of the infinite sacrifices demanded by Doing Good. At first he complained to Colman ("Mr. C.") that he had no desire to remarry, and was too old and impoverished besides. He changed his mind, however, and then had to break down Lydia's reluctance to entertain any of his correspondence or visits. To help him he recruited Lydia's relative THOMAS CRAIGHEAD (d. 1739), a minister and physician who had only recently arrived in New England from Ireland, apparently to escape persecution. Craighead preached at Freetown, forty miles from Boston; later he moved to the middle colonies, where the records lose sight of him (Mather mentions him in A Sorrowful Spectacle, 1715). As Craighead tried to bring Lydia over, the Boston "mob," as Mather called them, again began gossiping, this time about his "unseasonable overture" to a two-months widow. Lydia herself continued to repulse his advances. After visiting her on March 21, 1715, Mather wrote up a memo, apparently for no other reason than to relive the event. The meeting, lasting several hours, was "as pertinent and as obliging as my dull wits could render it." But Lydia told him to desist, assured him that another woman would be "more agreeable," and forbade him to write her any more letters. Vacillating between his usual willingness to sacrifice himself and a keen desire to have a wife, he wrote to MRS. GURDON SALTONSTALL (c. 1665–1730), the third wife of the governor of Connecticut, asking her to promote him to Lydia. Mather had a long, and to him useful, friendship with Mrs. Saltonstall and her husband. She apparently paid for the publication of his important Ratio Disciplinae (1726) and bequeathed a substantial scholarship to Harvard and other money to Yale.

Mather married Lydia George on July 5, 1715. The unusually good cheer of his early letters to and about Lydia suggest that the marriage was initially happy, more exuberantly happy indeed than his first two marriages. Mather told Mrs. Saltonstall that Lydia was a "very valuable fish." When Lydia had to be away for a few weeks, it seemed "ten years at least" and he did penance by not cutting his beard until she returned. Fondly and admiringly he addressed her as "Mathmadgnenai"—a portmanteau word combining a pun on "Mather" with "well-born" and "well-informed." Aside from revealing his delight in Lydia's accomplishments and breeding, "Mathmadgnenai" ironically anticipates the outcome of this tragic and dreadful marriage, when Mather would write his diary in Greek and Latin to conceal his thoughts from Lydia's prying eyes and unbalanced mind.

Mather's courtship of Lydia was part of his larger effort to order his household affairs after Elizabeth's death. While seeing Lydia he worked to set up his son Increase in business. He arranged for Cressy to be taken abroad, primarily to learn something about the shipping business, but also to remove him from bad company at home, to improve him by stays with several pious relatives and friends in England, and perhaps to make certain that Cressy's unpredictable behavior did nothing to antagonize Lydia. Circumstances would increasingly force Mather to such subterfuges as the extraordinary letter which he forged in Cressy's name to JOHN FRIZZEL (d. 1723), a bolder version of the letter he half-wrote for Samuel Penhallow to send to "Mr. Archer." John Frizzel (or Frizzell) was a very prosperous Boston merchant and later burgess and guild brother of Glasgow, whose name occasionally appears in the *Boston News-Letter* advertising slaves for sale. He frequently paid for the printing of Mather's works, which Mather repaid by writing a funeral sermon on him (*Euthanasia*, 1723) and on his wife (*The Widow of Naim*, 1728). When Cressy departed for London, Mather gave him a letter of introduction to Sir William Ashurst. Its subtly flattering manner implies a hope that Ashurst will do something for Mather's "tame Indian" son.

Cressy stayed for a long while in Witney, England, with his father's brother SAMUEL MATHER (1674–1733). As a child Samuel had studied under Cotton and had accompanied Increase on his charter agency. He apparently did not share the family's reverence for itself since he declined to take over the pulpit of the Second Church and, having inherited a fortune from his aunt in London, married a wealthy widow and settled as the first Congregationalist minister in Witney, near Oxford. He undertook to produce an abridged edition of his brother's *Magnalia*, but never finished it. The surviving, somewhat curt letters from Samuel to Cotton intimate that Samuel envied his brother's prestige and found his consciousness of it annoying. Rather than abridge the *Magnalia* he preferred and felt competent to write a history of his own, as he did in his *Compendious History of the Rise and Progress of the Reformation* (1715), pointedly subtitled "of the Church here in England."

Samuel found Cressy no less difficult than Cotton found him, and Cressy proved as capable of getting into trouble in Witney as in Boston. Samuel wrote to his brother in July, 1715, that he had to keep a "pretty thick eye" on Cressy to help him "escape ruin in a place of temptation." Cressy arrived in Witney with only ten shillings in his pocket and tainted with the Mather weakness, which Samuel accurately summed up: "to spend inconsiderately and take no thought about providing against future unavoidable occasions." Thus Samuel directed Cotton to send a "genteel remittance" so that Cressy could pay his bills, but urged him to deposit the money with a "Mr. Soden" who would manage it for Cressy.

Mather also wished to resolve the fate of his massive, unpublished *Biblia Americana.* As his frustration over it continued, his bitterness toward the English Dissenters who, he felt, rejected and betrayed it grew; and he began seeing the *Biblia* as another sacrifice appointed for him. But he was, finally, unwilling to give the book up, and he began gathering forces. He bombarded a host of correspondents with agitated requests, just short of demands, that they use their influence to have it published. His disgust at Thomas Reinolds' failure to publish the book he made clear to DR. DANIEL WILLIAMS (1643?–1716), the English divine who founded the famous Dr. Williams' Library in London, and who wrote a preface for Mather's *Family Religion Urged* (1713). He also appealed to

Sir William Ashurst, who had been involved in writing and printing an Indian library for the New England Company. To the campaign he impressed his lifelong, sometime friend JEREMIAH DUMMER (c. 1679–1739), whose learning, polish, and influence made him valuable to the cause. Dummer, a fluent Latinist whom Increase Mather considered the best scholar of his time at Harvard, studied philosophy and theology at Leyden under Herman Witsius and afterward took a Ph.D. at Utrecht. Trained for the ministry, he opted for business and went to London where he acted as the agent for Massachusetts, to which he never returned. Some recent historians have justly begun to view Dummer as the most skilled colonial diplomat and negotiator before Benjamin Franklin. While in London, Dummer shed his native Puritanism: he played cards, flirted with fashionable ladies at court, got to know Steele and Newton, wrote verse for the *Gentleman's Magazine,* and had his portrait painted by Godfrey Kneller. As a result, Samuel Sewall and others in Boston never fully trusted him. (The complex relationship between Mather and Dummer will be explored in the later correspondence, where Dummer appears prominently.)

Mather protested to Dummer bitterly about the fate of his work among the English Dissenters. He interpreted their neglect as a sign not only of how deeply the English were prejudiced against colonial culture, but more worrisomely, of how far English Puritanism had drifted from the sincerity, orthodoxy, and reforming zeal of Puritanism in New England. Mather was not only worried and bitter, but also crushingly offended: on his side he had worked long and hard to form the English Dissenters, the Brethren in Scotland, and the American Puritans into a single phalanx of the Reformation. In failing to have the *Biblia* published, the English Dissenters were breaking ranks in Christ's army. Mather repeated this tale to ISAAC WATTS (1674–1748), pastor of the distinguished congregation of Mark Lane and one of the most popular writers of the day, author of educational manuals, a catechism, a Scripture history, philosophical works, popular divinity, poetry, and of course the famous hymns with their endless editions. In complaining to Watts that he had not heard from Reinolds in a year and a half, Mather was either lying, or else Reinolds' letter of June 9, 1715, had not yet reached him when he wrote to Watts. Far from displaying any unwillingness to publish the book, Reinolds said that the *Biblia* was "great and worthy of yourself," but that the bookseller chosen to publish it had recently died. Since then, he said, he had been unable to raise subscriptions because of the public turmoil and other disheartening circumstances. In fact, there is no evidence that any heterodoxy, snobbery, or ingratitude among the English Dissenters prevented the publication of the work, which remains unpublished today largely due to the cost of printing it. Mather could not see the issue in practical terms. It meant to him what almost everything had come to mean to him: The man who Does Good is betrayed.

As Reinolds explained, England was in turmoil. A new king, George I, had acceded to the throne. Mather, like the rest of Massachusetts, was relieved that Anne's Romanist brother had been turned aside and that the new king was a religious liberal and a Francophobe. As he told TIMOTHY WOODBRIDGE (1656–1732), minister at Hartford, Connecticut, he counted the first of August, when the queen died, a greater revolution than that twenty-six years ago when the Prince of Orange landed at Torbay. He felt it important for the New England churches to at once address the new king and ingratiate themselves by expressing pleasure in his accession. He declared the importance of a speedy address to his Scottish correspondent WILLIAM JAMESON (fl. 1689–1720), a blind lecturer on history at the University of Glasgow, whose knowledge of antiquity he flattered and respected. Mather desired to present the memorial himself, but his flock disapproved. Anxious to give the king a favorable first impression of Massachusetts, he wrote the circular letter of February or March, 1715, asking the ministers in Connecticut and Massachusetts to help choose a different representative. But his letter to Dr. Williams in May, 1715, reveals that they again chose him. When a group of New England ministers was agreed upon, he noted, they met with "unexpected encumbrances," and at last the delayed memorial was presented by several English divines—Dr. Williams, Edmund Calamy, Reinolds and, very grudgingly, Samuel Mather of Witney.

The importance of the memorial went beyond New England.

Besides desiring to have the country accurately and flatteringly represented, Mather hoped to portray New England, Scotland, and the London Dissenters to the king as a united front. Becoming ever more moderate and international in his religious views, he hoped for a Protestant union having Scotch Presbyterianism, New England Congregationalism and English Dissent for its base, broad enough to include Baptists and the Brattle Street group but sharply enough defined in its polity to exclude Arians and Anglicans. What probably drove Mather to this ecumenical hope were signs of Protestant disunity and of growing Anglican strength in America. His letters to Scotland at this time laugh off as insignificant the incursions of Anglican missionaries in America, and such signs of religious breakdown as the writings of John Wise, that "hot-headed, crack-brained Furioso." Mather similarly writes off the Church of England missionaries as ignorant and few and those persons who convert to Anglicanism as the tax-evading nouveau riches who want to be rid of paying salaries to the regular ministry. Gloatingly and repeatedly he insists that the Anglican efforts defeat themselves because the missionaries sent to America are uniformly "ignorant, vicious, debauched wretches."

But for all his derision of the Anglican program Mather feared what it could do, and his fear took shape in his vision of a defensive Boston-Glasgow-London Protestant league. In fact, as is well known, Anglicanism failed to take hold in New England, despite its help from the mother country, until around the time of Mather's death. Andros' attempts to establish Anglican worship in Boston were broken off by the Revolution. And although the SPGFP sent many missionaries to America, invested vast sums, and enrolled such colonial officials as Governor Robert Hunter of New York, they were hampered by the absence of American bishops to supervise discipline and by the second-rate abilities, which Mather only exaggerated, of the missionaries themselves.

Mather's letters of this period mention two further, unrelated events. He wished to have Adam Winthrop, a member of his church, appointed to the commission for Indian affairs, for which Winthrop had been acting unofficially earlier. Made a commissioner in March, 1714, Winthrop did much toward recovering money owed to the commissioners and later became treasurer of the company—unfortunately for them: in 1741 he found himself six thousand pounds in debt, sold his estate, and began using the company's money to extricate himself; he died before paying off the debt.

Written in his most elegant hand, Mather's letter thanking Richard Waller, secretary of the Royal Society, for being admitted to membership, again expresses the snobbery and curiosity that equally inspired his scientific investigations, and the pleasure and pride he took in the honor.

To Benjamin Colman

U/Maine   January 3, 1715

My dear and honored Friend,

Misunderstanding! [The word crossed out, but perfectly legible and intended to be read.] Away with it, I beseech you, term and thing. There is none at all. As I have dealt with the term, so let the thing be dealt withal.

Adoni Avi, with his usual prudence and all possible tenderness, let fall a hint, as having learned from you that some thought our children's visit, as well as mine, where it was then talked of, had some inconvenient constructions made of it. The hint was friendly and prudent. But it was not improper for me to mention it unto the children, that there might be nothing said or done incautelously. This is all I know. Of any misunderstanding or disaffection or disesteem raised on the occasion—I entreat you to be very easy. Everybody is so, for ought I know. 'Tis all well, just as it was; and as it should be.

As to my own visit (which I endeavored altogether to avoid, by a letter which I hoped would answer all the intentions of it), I could give you a pretty satisfactory account of it. But it is needless. I knew, at the very time of it, I did imprudently. I was aware of what has happened. I said so. But my best account will be that even before the prudent hint you gave (even on the Friday before, from something I then met withal) I had fully made and spoke the resolution you would most advise unto. And the neighbors will no more have the least occasion given them to suspect me of any designs not proper for me.

To be free with you: I have too high an opinion of the discretion,

166

as well as other good qualities in your excellent friend, to entertain any imagination that (suppose we should live a year more, which for myself I do not suppose; but—Psal LXXXVIII 3) one of my many unrecommendable circumstances could find any acceptance there.

My friend, I have no manner of prospect of returning into a state wherein I have sometimes lived in a somewhat agreeable and gentlemanly manner. Tho' I have not hitherto taken anywhere one step that way, yet I have by the edges had hints enough to satisfy me, that my grandfather's will has forbid all such prospect unto me.

It is, I confess, too natural for us foolish old men, when we have a whimsy from every quarter buzzed into our ears, to think a little, *what there may be in it.* I have, no doubt, foolishly enough been ready to fall into this weakness. But as yet my old age has not got so far but that I presently recollect, I presently am sensible of the *delusion,* presently bring all to rights, as a dying man ought to do.

My life is full of sacrifices. And, if I had not a very deceitful heart, I would have said I know nothing in this world that I have not in some degree (or desire) sacrificed. I have also got into the delight of sacrificing what I *have not,* as well as what I have.

A late King of Argier, called *Medio-morto,* that is, Half-dead, had a name which it seems more proper for me to challenge than any other. I am sorry it so much suits me in regard of the *mortification* wherein one so nigh *death* ought to be exemplary. I ask your prayers that I may *go through* with that work, not leave it done *by halves.*

Old Jerome (I confess, a very sour sort of a man) has given me good advice. *Cogita te quotidie moriturum, et de secundis nuptiis numquam cogitabis.* My heart would reproach me if I had not more than one hundred thoughts of my death to one of the fancy my neighbors talk of. Your advice, which I must always value and request, leaning and leading that way * would sensibly strengthen my dispositions.

I hope you will out-live me; and I shall endeavor to deserve it that at my death you may remember me as one studious many ways to approve himself,

Sir, Your true brother and hearty and constant friend,

Having both with tongue and pen told my opinion to your invaluable friend, That your conversation would be so profitable and so comfortable there would never be the least need of any other, I hope I need not ask you to continue in affording as much of it as is possible

* Jerome

to one so very worthy of it. When you have perused the cruel pamphlet I now send you, you will permit as quick a return of it as may be.

To Timothy Woodbridge

PCSM V/MHS   January 20, 1715

Reverend Sir,

[Has no news from England.]

'Tis a great thing that we have so great a King, so little in the French interests.

It appears evidently [*sic*] that he is looking about for a stick to beat the dog. And so probable is his finding it, that your politicians expect the breaking out of a new war in a little while.

One of the most expressive things which discover the temper and freedom of a great many people, is a book entitled *The Conventicle*. Because I cannot send you the book itself I will transcribe and enclose a few select passages, which doubtless you will count bold enough and coarse enough; but they are some of the roars of the waves of the betrayed and enraged nations.

The memorable first of August makes a revolution rather greater than that of November twenty-six years ago. And it is made hitherto so peaceably, and in so strange a manner, that your common newswriters, who do not use to burden their papers with too much piety, can't forbear frequent confessions, *That it is the work of almighty GOD*.

What our share is like to be in the consolations and advantages of it, is as yet unknown unto us. I wish none of our people have written letters home unto the late ministry, which were so far from dictated by a prophetic spirit that when they come to be exposed, the writers will find very inconvenient consequences. [Close]

Sir, Your brother and servant,

To John Frizzel

DII/AAS draft   January 25, 1715

Honored Sir,

The constant kindness you express to my father's family makes me fly to you with some hopes that you will also be my father.

'Tis too well known that my inclination is more for business than for learning. And being inclined unto the business of the sea, my friends have a prospect of my arriving sooner to some figure on that element than on the long wharf or the dock.

I have pretty well perfected myself in the theory of navigation. And it is now necessary that I take a few voyages for the practick part. I must go aboard some ship as a school for my education; and some very good commanders who have been advised withal, think it is not absolutely necessary, nor perhaps convenient, that I should enter at the cook-room-door.

I confess my desire that the ship whereof your son is the commander may be my school.

Here I would most heartily submit unto my father's expectation that I apply my hand unto every action aboard, whereof the master and mate shall judge me capable, and yield an exact obedience to all their orders.

And that when I come to London, I should stay aboard, stick to the ship, and attend both the unlading and loading of it, and only ask one fortnight's leave to visit my uncle. I hope I am every way so disposed, that there will be no difficulty in my obedience to the commands of those aboard whom I shall acknowledge as my superiors.

My father is willing to have me under all the government of a sailor, and to do all possible duty and service aboard, and yet to pay for me as a passenger.

Sir, I cast myself upon you in this matter, and pray to be considered as your younger son, who, by consequence, must pay obedience to the elder.

But I do it with submission, that if you think any better advice can be given to prepare me to do some good in the world, I shall be sensible that it ought to be complied withal.

So I take leave, Sir, Your most obedient servant,

To Thomas Reinolds

U/AAS draft   [c. February, 1715]

Reverend Sir,

My disappointments are very great, but will be submitted to, if you have not received my many packets, whereof I have yet no advice that they have reached you. And if I be disappointed of what you will find

I have proposed when you have received them, that also will be submitted to.

Our *Biblia Americana* will have a time to be acceptable and serviceable, when the Lord in whose Hand are all our times will please to order it.

Tho' our correspondents on your island seem very much to cast us off, and count us what we really are, of too little use or worth for them to converse withal, yet we cannot but continue our strong affection to them. . . .

I am—

[To Ministers in Massachusetts
and Connecticut]
DII/AAS draft   [February or March, 1715]

Honored Sirs,

The happy accession of a King so much wished and prayed for, as him whom we now with unspeakable satisfaction see sitting on the throne of the British empire, opens to us a fair prospect of considerable services to be done for the churches in these American colonies.

Our brethren in the Kirk of Scotland have sent five of their most eminent ministers to wait upon His Majesty, with proper congratulations. And the Dissenting ministers about London have also personally addressed the Throne on this great occasion. And it is thought by men of sense among ourselves, that we shall be exceedingly and scarce excusably wanting to ourselves and unto the best interests, if we do nothing after their example.

'Tis to be feared, there will be those who will take all opportunities to misrepresent us; and as we have already felt some ill effects of the misrepresentations which have heretofore been made of us unto our superiors, thus we cannot but rationally look for more, if we do nothing to rectify them.

If His Majesty might have in his royal view the true state of our country in regard of the religion and the disposition which prevails among his loyal subjects here, and his great ministers of state be duly apprised of our condition, and at the same time such a good correspondence established between us and our United Brethren in the Church of Scotland and the Dissenters in England, that they may look on what is done unto us as done unto themselves, it would no doubt be followed with a long train of desirable consequences, too many to be at once enumerated.

For this cause, the ministers of this town have had serious thoughts of desiring that an address may be presented unto the King, on the behalf of the ministry and of the churches in the country, to congratulate his accession to the throne, and the succession of the crown in the illustrious House of Hanover; and humbly to pray his royal protection in our peaceable and undisturbed possession of our sacred liberties, and in prosecution of the main end of these plantations; to have churches established on those terms of communion which our great Lord-Redeemer has instituted, and wherein all good men ought to be united. We have made the proposal unto the honorable Council, at a very full board, and the return we have had from thence is, that it is very acceptable to them, and that they desire it may be proceeded in.

But we cannot proceed in this matter till we have obtained the judgment of our brethren throughout the country upon it, and their consent unto it.

We do therefore humbly entreat that the brethren in your association or vicinity would as soon as 'tis possible, procure an interview, and communicate from thence unto us (either by letters or messengers) your apprehensions about the important matter that is now proposed, in the several points of the design and the best method of prosecuting it, particularly whether by any hands that may be sent from hence of our own order, which is by some thought worthy of consideration. We say, *as soon as 'tis possible,* because 'tis an affair which requires expedition, and there should be no time lost about it. It is more particularly desired, that on the second Wednesday in April next, we may enjoy an interview with such delegates from you as may think fit to afford their presence at the house of Dr. Mather the elder on this occasion.
[Close]   Your affectionate brethren and servants,

[TO LYDIA GEORGE]
DII/AAS draft   [c. March, 1715]

Madam,

A person of your good skill at making inferences, having a little considered what you know of him who now addresses you, will easily infer some things that will be very much to his advantage.

If he be one who looks upon love to his neighbor as a very essential article of his religion, and who so loves every man that the offer of an opportunity for the doing of good unto any one, is the sweetest pleasure that can be given him; and his life is entirely spent in the doing of good unto all sorts of people, in all the ways imaginable—yea, if upon any people's abusing and injuring of [him], he presently prays for them and sets himself to do good offices for them—it will be very reasonably inferred from hence, that the gentlewoman who comes one day into the nearest relation unto him will be loved by him as much as can be wished by her.

Especially if he be one of a singular fondness in his temper; fond to a fault, and never more obliged than when the objects will give him leave to let them know how fond he is of them. Were the gentlewoman one of no more than common circumstances, yet might she expect here to be honorably and comfortably treated. But how much more, when he shall have the sense of all the world concurring with his own, that she is a gentlewoman of endowments and endearments exceeding what can anywhere else be met withal!

Madam,

The person to whom you have done the honor of admitting him sometimes to your tea-table, has that high opinion of your wisdom, that he hopes never to be guilty of taking a step which may not have your approbation.

He will entirely wait the allowances of your wisdom for the more finishing strokes of the conversation which has been begun, and will press for no public appearance, or procedure, that you shall judge unseasonable.

Nevertheless, he begs your leave that it may not be thought too soon for him to tell you, that your bright accomplishments, your shining piety, your polite education, your superior capacity, and the most refined sense, and incomparable sweetness of temper, together with a constellation of all the perfections that he can desire see related unto him, have made a vast impression upon him. If ever he should be so inexpressibly happy as to enjoy you, he could not but receive you as a wondrous gift of God unto him; a token that the unworthiest of men had yet obtained favor of the Lord. Such an idea he has conceived of you, that everything you shall be or say or do, will forever please him; and the pleasing of you will be his continual study and rapture.

His tenderness for you will be the effect not only of the natural sense he must have of your merits, or of a disposition in him always to oblige; but also of a strong apprehension he will be ever under the power of, that the more of love and of goodness he shall express in his carriage to you, the more his conformity to his great Saviour will be exhibited.

It will be yet augmented by the strange and kind providence of God, which has been at work to bring about what is proposed. Especially the answers of prayers, which always bring blessings with them.

Truly, Madam, as it happens that the gentleman is one whom the eyes of all the country, and many more, are much upon, so the general vote and voice of the country has been that way, which he is now agoing. His purposes (which [word illegible] have eagerly waited for) are already a common subject of discourse, but with universal satisfaction. Especially among the more praying people, whereof there have been many concerned for him, and these now begin their praises for the prospect which they have of a precious harvest.

I know not what is in the enclosed letter; but I believe it may be something of such a tendency. 'Tis from a mother and sister of yours, and one of the best of women.

What remains is to entreat that it may be no offence unto you, Madam, if hereafter I may take the liberty to speak unto you such things as I have now written, and that such talk in our interviews may not be grievous to you, as will be an unspeakable satisfaction to, Madam,   Your most affectionate servant,

To Mrs. Gurdon Saltonstall

U/AAS draft   [c. March, 1715]

Madam,

[Rejoices in the Governor's recovery from illness.]

Our interregnum for about seven weeks has been attended with some difficulties and altercations, whereof you will hear from other hands. A proclamation from the King dated November 22, for the continuance of all officers, arriving on Saturday night from New York, our Governor does this day resume his authority, with no little celebrations.

And since we are upon the [ceasing?] of Interregnums—It is time for me to confess (inasmuch as you are pleased to tell me, 'tis so), that I have struck for a very valuable fish, one so agreeable on all accounts that everybody tells me, if Heaven had given me leave to kill [sic] and make and do as I pleased, I could not have done so well for myself, as the divine providence gives me hope of its doing for me. But the manner of the whale-catchers is then to let the fish run for a considerable and convenient while; which, I suppose, I am to do for a number of months yet unknown to me.

I know not whether your acquaintance with the gentlewoman may be such, that [you] may judge it proper for me to request from you, at your leisure, a letter unto her to add unto her sense that in treating me honorably, she does nothing but what the best of people throughout the country give their approbation to. [Close]

Your most obliged servant,

[TO LYDIA GEORGE?]

DII/AAS draft   [March, 1715?]

My—(Inexpressible!)

I am afraid you been't well, because my head has ached pretty much this afternoon.

The pain of my heart will be much greater than that of my head if it be really so.

But I imagine you are growing well, because my headache is going off. Your little daughter waits upon you, to bring me the agreeable satisfaction.

May you tomorrow (and preparatory to it) have sweet interviews with Him whom your soul loveth!—what is He, more than any other beloved! And infinitely more. All others, pretenders to your esteem, and I among the rest, are black and base and vile things. Yea! and the brightest angels in Heaven are mean things in comparison to Him.—O sun in the firmament, thou too art all blackness before that Sun of Righteousness.

Think so, my dear, grow in such thoughts; and lose the sight of all things but Him.

I mightily wish that you may love nothing that is mine. My wishes are, that I may be so happy as to exhibit unto you some reflection of His Image. If you can discover any thing of [illegible] in the meanest of men, 'tis well. Everything else, dislike it. And the more will you be liked and loved by one who loves you inexpressibly (and [a word or two illegible] most affectionately and compassionately).

To Richard Waller

U/HCL (another, in Mather's   March 10, 1715
hand, at RS; MHS draft
published in PCSM XIV)

Sir,

Among the valuable circumstances which have brought you into knowledge and esteem with men of letters, as far off as the regions beyond Thyle [sic], and even on the western shore of the wide Atlantic, one is the relation you sustain unto a SOCIETY which is one of the most illustrious in the world.

It was very much by your favorable recommendation that an admission into that SOCIETY has been granted unto an American, of so obscure a character that a place in the Academy of the *Nascopi* at Milan, or the *Innominati* at Parma, or the *Incogniti* at Venice, would by their titles doubtless have been more suitable for him, than a room among your honorable virtuosi.

And for *these*, as well as other causes, an inscription to you belongs unto a performance which was hereby awakened and animated, and which now prays for a favorable reception with you.

No man of any reasonable thought can consider your noble undertaking: how worthy it is to be pursued by gentlemen who would *show themselves men*; how useful it has already been to mankind, and capable of being yet more applied unto the *best of purposes*; a tendency it has to refine and sweeten the minds of men, and reconcile them unto *just regards* for *true merits* in one another; with an extirpation of that noxious clamor-wort, the *party-spirit*; and, finally, how generously the more polite literators of the world go on in it, with a decent contempt on the banters of the *brutish among the people*; but the result of his consideration will be, that it will be a greater honor to be taken into the list of your servants, than to be *mixed with the great men of Achaia*.

[In thanks to the Society he sends along his *Philosophical Religion*.]

He is aware of what has been said about *the religion of learned men*. But as the religion here exhibited, under the advantage and incentive of the most improved philosophy, will be what men of learning and of breeding will have a relish for, so, if they will unite in *this*, the consequences will be glorious.

If the author had been a *man of but one business,* or if many scores of observations proper for this collection had not been lodged in several apartments of the *Biblia Americana* (yet unpublished) from whence he did not think it proper to transfer them hither, or if he had not been afraid that a *great volume* would have been reckoned a *great evil,* and that more than a *sufficiency* would have been reckoned a *superfluity,* the treatise had been much bigger than it is.

But of the two poets, he who *knew what to say* wears not so many laurels as he who *knew what not to say.* Perhaps 'twill be not much otherwise among philosophers.

However, the *Libri Elephantini,* or a book that should require *twelve hundred and sixty oxhides for a covering,* would not be of a bulk proportionable either unto the dignity of the copious and excellent subject, or indeed unto the respects I owe unto the person to whom I now make the dedication.

Of the many things *left unsaid,* this must not be one: That I am, Sir,
Your most affectionate friend and obedient servant,

To Thomas Craighead

DII/AAS draft   March 23, [1715]

Sir,

'Tis with a grateful surprise that I reflect upon it, that one so much a stranger and so lately arrived as he to whom I am now applying myself, should be admitted into such an intimate acquaintance with us, and with our most important and reserved affairs. But since the divine providence has brought you into circumstances of so much friendship and freedom with us, I take the liberty of entreating you do the good office wherein this letter terminates.

The best of women, having in express and severe terms repeated her prohibitions that the hand which now writes (and which has written some few things in its time that have been of a little use to others) should at all write unto her, I am under a necessity of writing to you what I desire she may be acquainted withal.

A worthy relative of hers just now gives me to understand that nothing will satisfy her but such a conduct in me as will put a total stop unto the discourse of the people, about my intentions to pursue a reception with her. And he seems to be of the opinion that the method I am now taking is the most proper that can be taken.

For my past conduct, I thought, I followed such advice as would prescribe no wrong measures to me; but I perceive I have hitherto done just nothing that is right. And it is a killing thing to me to think that I have been led into steps that have been so very offensive, and have occasioned so much trouble, to a person for whom I must always have so great a veneration.

Some of my last words to her were, *That I would sacrifice all my satisfactions unto hers.* And I know not how 'tis possible for me to give a fuller demonstration of my vast value for her, than by saying it over again, and keeping her charge unto me upon it, *Say and hold!*

Wherefore, tho' the earth could not afford me a greater pleasure than her most agreeable conversation, and I envy you the felicity that you enjoy in it, yet I will totally deny myself of it for as many months as her wisdom, to which I pay all the deference imaginable, shall order me.

You were proposing to me one interview more with our incomparable friend. But this will prove, perhaps, to both of us a disadvantage.

First to her, because it will be impossible for me to come there unobserved; and the least observation of my being there will keep alive the talk which gives her so much uneasiness. And I cannot be guilty of anything that shall have any tendency to make her uneasy, tho' I never so much cross my own inclinations in forbearing it.

Secondly to me, because, as I gather from what I just now meet withal, I cannot but expect from her over again such afflicting passages as I received when I last waited on her. And I must from experience confess unto you my weakness to be such, that they will make too deep an impression upon me. My tender spirit and health will suffer so much, and I shall be so unhinged for my employments, which are what they are, by wounds from a hand I so much admire, that I am loathe to have them renewed upon me.

If the people [crossed out: *mob*] that are to govern us knew how cold a reception I have hitherto had, and what a perpetual care Madam has used in all her expressions to discountenance anything that I might hereafter propose relating to her, and how she did at last, when I came to speak more plainly, as plainly signify her wish that I would come no more, there would be no room left for the censures whereof she is afraid. It would indeed be sufficiently for my dishonor, if this ever come into their knowledge (whereof, I hope, I shall be very patient). But it is enough that I omit the visits which are thought so obnoxious to misconstruction. And that I say no more than this to my friends:

That gentlewoman is too discreet to allow of any unseasonable over-tures. What I have to request of you, is to assure that excellent person that my resolutions to keep out of sight (even until those two very precious friends to both of us, Mr. C. and Mr. B., whose good will to me I very much value myself, and unto whose prudence I can entirely refer myself, shall direct me to do otherwise) oppress my own mind with violence, which could be well borne, by none but one of my age and one so much used unto sacrifices. But they are formed merely to gratify her, whom I can undergo anything to oblige, even while I have never yet received one favorable word or look from her; and it may be naturally inferred, how much more I should do so if ever anything reciprocal should invite unto it.

And then, give her assurance of this also, That my vast regards for her will continue inviolable. She may depend upon it (tho' I know not whether a total deliverance from me would not make her yet more easy) that I can by no means lay aside those vast respects, but must renew my endeavors one day to make her yet more sensible of them.

However, to be free with you, I have strong apprehensions that my dying hour will intervene (which, oh! join with me in my praises to our dear Saviour for it, I often even long for, and hope it will be the best hour that ever I saw). I leave all with Him, I am, Sir,

Your affectionate brother and servant,

To Sir William Ashurst
U/Hunt (HM 22305; AAS draft in DII)   March 29, 1715

Sir,

[Congratulates him on the new king.]

In my letters I have still taken care to treat you with some Indian curiosity. But all that I have at this instant for you is the hand which brings you a paper of our squash seed, from our worthy friend Mr. Sewall.

It comes by a *tame Indian,* for so the Europeans are pleased some-times to denominate the children that are born in these regions.

More plainly, 'tis my own son, a youth not sixteen years of age, but one who having passed thro' the learned and polite education of our schools, has chosen a life of action rather than of study, and having been so long with an acute merchant as to acquaint himself with the methods of business, the death of his master opened a new scene and hope to him of arriving more speedily to significant business by the sea than in any other way. Accordingly, he is aboard in the quality of a passenger, but with a design to accomplish himself in the practick part of shortly commanding a good ship, whereof he has already got much of the theory.

I have been perhaps too willing to indulge and follow the genius of a child in the choice of a business for him, as knowing that if that be not very much consulted, a child will never prove considerable.

'Tis an alleviation to my dissatisfaction in this choice that it may give the lad an opportunity of waiting on Your Honor, and bringing to your Lady the enclosed little treatises. [Close]

Your most affectionate and humble servant,

To Dr. William Jameson

U/AAS draft   [c. March or April, 1715]

Sir,

Could the people among whom I am stationed have been made willing to live a while without me, I might have been sent over by the churches of this country with their Address and Memorial unto the King, which they have now transmitted unto Dr. Williams, and one or two more, to be presented.

If I had embarked on such an agency, I might have attempted a journey from London to Glasgow and have sought the satisfaction of seeing a delectable garden of God. And of more particularly seeing a person, the sight of whom would be more grateful to me than any man upon earth. . . . I am now denied all of this, but have an abundant compensation in our hopes of meeting in a better world. [Close]   Your most affectionate brother and servant,

To Jeremiah Dummer

DII/AAS draft   May 4, 1715

My dear and most valued Friend,

As you are sure when you are opening any letter which by the hand in the superscription you know to be mine, that you shall find nothing to render you uneasy in it, so I perceive my task sometimes must be to find you uneasy, and cure it.

First and foremost, it will be in vain for any evil instruments, or any trivial occasions, to break that generous friendship which has hitherto been cultivated between us. Nobody shall persuade me that my Pamphilus is not a person of bright accomplishments, and one of a singular goodness in his temper, and ready forever to do good offices, and a lover of his country, and an honor to it. Nobody can persuade him, that his Eusebius has not a high esteem for him, and is not of those principles which will cause him to do him good and not hurt all the days of his life.

Whoever tells you that I have ever spoken anything to do you the least mischief in the world, is a talebearer, and wrongs me unaccountably.

If Adoni Avi [Increase Mather] should happen to express any dissatisfaction at anything, it is an injustice to make me responsible for it.

The only thing that I have ever spoken that can have the least aspect of what you may dislike is, that I have expressed (and this but very privately) a concern lest the open appearance of *Irenaeus Americus* to blanch the late ministry might prove some disadvantage to him with the present. But I know not that ever I have heard that matter spoken of without my adding, *I am sure that his country ought to love him for it; for it was nothing but a noble zeal to secure his capacity of serving them, that caused him to appear so far on that side. But I am not much afraid; he will have sense enough to make a good retreat.* And how often have I added, *We are too much at a distance from Europe to be competent judges of our friend's conduct there.*

And suppose I should once take the liberty to express myself not mighty well satisfied in one book of yours; does not my dear Pamphilus, without the least offence to me, let me know, concerning some hundreds of mine, *He likes not my writing of them!*

[Asserts his continued good will toward Dummer.]

My simple essay on *The Balances of Equity* was designed by me for the public with the more of alacrity because I proposed in it a very public, solid, lasting testimony of my value for you. I cannot be of the opinion that the raising of envy was any objection at all against my doing the part of a Justin Martyr for my country, who have deserved it, indeed, as little of me, as of any that serve it. I am very willing to encounter that envy and shall count it my glory. But I entirely resign my own opinion to yours. Do as you please about it. Only don't think to proselyte me unto that persuasion, that my writing so many books procures me any damage, which is to be esteemed so much as the light dust of the balance, when weighed against the service done by them to the Kingdom of God.

Nor is it easy to beat me out of that persuasion that our *Biblia Americana* must be an amassment of most valuable treasures, and that it has not been amiss to make an offer of it unto the lovers of religion and learning. [Charges that the English Dissenters neglect the work.] An eminent Non-conformist minister in the country wrote me only that silly condemnation upon the work: If it were for Mr. Baxter, a great part of the Non-conformists would set them against it. If it were against him, a greater part would do so. As if the *Biblia Americana* had anything to do with Mr. B. But, my friend, I am very easy if the rest of the world be as indisposed unto a work of this nature as my brethren the Dissenters. I can easily resign the disposal of it unto the Glorious Head of the church, who knows how and when His interests are to be served; and I would have none of my own. I only add, you will not in the least measure disoblige me if you never take one thought more about this work, while you have such a ponderous load of other cares upon you. [Close]

To Sir William Ashurst

U/Hunt (HM 22304; draft at AAS)   May 10, 1715

Honorable Sir,

[Notes having written to Ashurst recently.]

It is not very long ago that an unknown author published an instrument of this title, *Ter Mille querelae de corrupto christianismo.* And I find my excellent and illustrious friend Dr. Franckius, in the Lower Saxony, making on that instrument this reflection, *At verò myriadem earum facilè aliquis dederit.* But I hope I may without any trespass upon modesty observe, that for ought I can see we have in our New England near two hundred churches, wherein Christianity is maintained with as little a taint of the epidemical corruptions as any part of the Christian world can pretend unto. And some of those churches are of the Indians under your influences.

[Hopes that on this account Ashurst will continue to favor the colonies.]

. . . I will take the leave to mention a small proposal in relation to our valuable friend, Col. Adam Winthrop, whose accession to the number of your commissioners is a very sensible advantage to our affairs; and indeed a gentleman of more capacity and integrity is not ordinarily to be met withal. He was lately saying to me (but with the modesty which perpetually accompanies him in all his motions) that if in your annual remittances hither, you thought fit that they should be constantly made by bills, which Mr. John Loyd, an eminent merchant in the city probably known to you, may draw upon him, you would be perpetually sure of all honor most punctually paid unto them. And perhaps this constant and steady and certain way of re-mitting may be some ease to you, as well as afford a little convenience unto him, whose merits among us do indeed something distinguish him. However, this is proposed with all the submission that ought forever to be paid unto your management. [Close]

Your Honor's most affectionate servant,

[PROBABLY TO THOMAS CRAIGHEAD]
DII/AAS draft   [c. late July, 1715]

Sir,

I am now *there*—
But remembering my vast obligations to you for the many good services you did me with so much sincerity and alacrity in my grand affair, and believing the share of satisfaction which your hearty friendship will dispose you to take in my felicity, I thought it my duty to inform you, That the fifth of July is the brightest day in my calendar.

Then it was that one whom you love, saw himself invested with a constellation of blessings which you do not imagine me capable of language enough to set off in their proper luster.

Instead of making a vain essay to declare my just sentiments of gratitude unto Heaven upon so illustrious an occasion, I shall only ask that you would go on to oblige me with your supplications to the Glorious One, whom I have in this most joyful experience found a prayer-hearing Father, that I may by a vast improvement in sanctity and industry and usefulness, walk in some degree worthy of the great things which have been done for me, when I have so obtained favor of the Lord.

I long to take a walk with you in an upper-room of a house, which I hope to see illuminated the next week with the presence of one that shines forever with a thousand lovelinesses.

In the meantime I am preparing to entertain, on the Lord's-day approaching, a church which I am robbing of an invaluable treasure and beauty, with a discourse on I Sam I 27. And I am, at all times, my dear friend, Yours in bonds never to be forgotten,

[TO INCREASE MATHER, JR.]

DII/AAS draft   [c. August, 1715]

Child,

Solicitous I am that you may return unto me as fast as you can, and come into new methods as soon as may, to qualify you for usefulness in the world.

But much more solicitous that you may return unto God and be withheld from sinning against Him.

A thing, for which it is impossible for me to express the pain of mind wherein you have long held me distressed.

You know not the child upon earth which has been more prayed for, and more talked to, that he might be converted unto God. And unto all the former means for your good there have now been added the admonitions of a pious uncle.

God forbid that you should be so infinitely unhappy as you must be if all these be lost upon you.

I hope you let not a day pass you without prayers to the glorious God. And that all the vices of dishonesty, debauchery, and false-speaking are abominable to you.

[TO LYDIA GEORGE]

"Thursday morn. 10 d."

U/AAS draft   [Probably 1715]

Dear Mathmadgnenai,

It being ten years at least since I parted with you, I could not for my life any longer forbear to acquaint you how I, and the rest of yours, have done this long while.

Not that we can expect any return in writing to inform us whether you live, or how you live; because there are no pens where you have your present habitation.

Our daily informations about you, we expect by your faithful

Mercury, John Cominy; when we hope to hear, you are *much as you were.*

But so are not we. For ever since you left us, a palpable darkness is come upon our whole family. Nothing was heard but lamentations, and those very sincere and hearty ones, among all your children, when that word, *Mother not come home,* was heard among us. We enjoy nothing as we use to do. We are not sensible that the sun shines into any room in the house, nor that our chocolate has any sugar in it.

As a token of my own disconsolate condition, while the best creature I ever saw is out of my sight, I scarce allow Cutbert once with his razor to render my face visible, till you return.

[TO SAMUEL MATHER]

DII/AAS draft   [c. September, 1715]

My dear Brother,

The first advice that I had of the circumstances wherein my son has been detained with you, was the last week, and a few minutes before the departure of a ship just ready to sail.

I had then an opportunity only to render you my thanks for your paternal civilities to the child, which I now repeat, and assure you of my speedy care to make the remittances you direct me to.

I am since advised that it is much easier to obtain bills of exchange from England hither, than from hence to England. If with nobody else, yet among the masters of ships coming over hither, it may be easy to find those who will disburse what shall be necessary on this occasion, and accept your bill drawn upon me for it. I am also at a loss what sum will be necessary on this occasion, and my condition won't invite me to superfluous expenses.

What I therefore choose to do is by a vessel which is to touch at Plymouth to hasten my direction to you, that whatsoever sum you order me to advance for my son Increase, that so his return to me [crossed out: which I desire may be with all possible exhibition] may be hastened, you would please to draw your bill upon me for it, and it shall be punctually answered.

I confess, I flatter myself, that you will use all prudent frugality in assigning what shall be judged necessary on this occasion, and that it will not much exceed twenty pounds.

I again and again renew my thanks to you and my sister for your civilities to the child, especially for the admonitions of piety which you have been continually distilling upon him, and which, oh! that they make a due impression!

I hope I have put you out of pain as to the library about which you seem to have such an uncommon tenderness. [Asks him to give his *Christian Virtuoso* to the Royal Society.]

To John Stirling

U/NLS   September 16, 1715

Sir,

'Tis a sensible infelicity that opportunities for communication between Glasgow and Boston occur so very rarely. But that which now offers, I do with much satisfaction embrace, that I may treat you with a few more of our American entertainments.

Indeed we cannot entertain you with anything that shall be very considerable, any further than your brotherly affection for us may dispose you to esteem it so. But small things coming from a far country, and especially from those whom we love as brethren there, will always hope for a kind acceptance.

Our churches are multiplied and edified, continually but very peaceably swarming into new societies.

There has been a late essay to disturb their tranquillity by a certain hot-headed, crack-brained Furioso who has published a libel against some of us, as being in a plot to betray our churches because we have Presbyterianized with a little more study to have our churches well-consociated among themselves, and recommended unto those whom we honor as our United Brethren, than the little, stingy, narrow souls of some, who affect the most unsociable and arbitrary Independency, give their approbation to. But by using the *Magnum contumeliae remedium*, and by observing the twenty-sixth of the Proverbs and the fourth, or by giving little other answer than what an archangel has furnished us withal, such furies and follies will die away, and come to nothing.

We are somewhat, tho' not unto your degree, your fellow-sufferers in regard of emissaries from the Church of England imposing themselves now and then upon us.

We live in all amicable correspondence with the congregation of that way in this populous town, whose chapel is chiefly filled from strangers coming in among us. But we have had some instances in the country, that in a town of near two hundred Christian families, a little crew of litigious people have had some factious intentions to be gratified. And this crew, which perhaps know the Church of England as little as they do the religion of Confucius, yet will declare for the Church of England that so they may have our Governor's appearing on their side. These, tho' they are for number, and on all other considerations, the most contemptible and scarce regardable part of the town, apply themselves to the Society for Propagation. But they expect therewithal to be released from all obligations to pay their parochial dues, assigned by the law of the province to the established ministry. And that Society, very little for their honor, send forth and support their missionaries on these occasions, to maintain confusion in towns of well-instructed Christians; while at the same time, whose [sic] plantations in the southern colonies that are perfectly paganizing, are left wholly uncared for. And what is much less for their honor, but yet proves for the service of our tempted churches, is that the missionaries have been so many of them such ignorant, vicious, debauched wretches, and such finished rakes, that their hearers have in a little while with shame deserted them, and the Church of England has been laid under the greatest contempt imaginable among the well-disposed people of the country. Whereon we can't forbear saying to them *ouk athee tauth' hemin epiginetae*. To enable themselves the better for the molestation of our churches, the Society have sent their briefs unto the churches of the Dissenters in England, to raise money for them. While it is at the same time also observable, that in the more southern colonies, their missionaries (blades for their morals, too often, like those which we have been blessed withal!) unaccountably neglect the paganizing plantations, but choose to screw themselves in where a Presbyterian church is gathered; and if a Presbyterian make a sally to do good in any of the aforesaid plantations, they will presently follow him, to persuade the people that all his administrations are but nullities. No remonstrances will put a stop to these unaccountable proceedings; nor perhaps anything but the eighteenth chapter of the Revelation.

The miserable colony of Carolina, as I am informed by three worthy Scottish ministers, refugees from thence now sojourning in my next neighborhood, was in a hopeful way to be a religious country, under the influence of Presbyterian ministers, which began to be sprinkled as a salt from Heaven upon it. But the missionaries of the

Church of England no sooner arrived there, than a torrent of wickedness broke in with them, and carried all before it. The people grew so wicked that the patience of Heaven would bear no longer, but the savages, who had been greatly injured and provoked and scandalized by them, are broke in upon them and have destroyed multitudes of people, with such barbarities as no Myrmidons before them have ever perpetrated. They have laid the country, in a manner, all waste, but the capital town by the sea-side, which, 'tis thought, can hold out but a little while. And thus a flourishing colony is come under a fearful desolation! But it is feared lest the savages have entered into a very extensive combination which may be animated by the French Canadians, whereof some other colonies, which are on the most unhappy accounts too obnoxious thereunto, may soon feel the tremendous consequences.

[Repeats the tale of his failure to have the *Biblia Americana* published in England.]

. . . what fitter conclusion can I make, than with most hearty supplications that the Great Shepherd would graciously preserve the dear flock of His heritage in Scotland from the designs of our common enemies, and give them to feed as in the days of old. And yet more particularly, that He would prolong and prosper your precious opportunities to serve His Kingdom in the world, and remarkably bless the famous university which flourishes under your auspicious influences, and cause the streams of the Clyde to make glad the City of our God. [Close]   Sir, Your most sincere and humble servant,

To Robert Wodrow

WII/NLS (AAS draft in DII)   September 17, 1715

Sir,

When the distance of the huge Atlantic separates brethren from one another, one method unto which we must resort for maintaining the communion of saints, is the epistolary.

[Repeats at length his attack on John Wise, his account of the SPG, and of the Indian attacks in South Carolina, as in the preceding letter to Stirling.] In the prosecution of this descent upon the miserable Carolinians, the barbarities perpetrated by the Indians are too hideous to be related; there were a sort of inhumanity in the very relation of such things. But yet I will venture to mention one instance that—*crimine ab uno*—you may apprehend the rest. One Major Cockrain, a very honest man, had been a trader with these Indians; yea, their leader in expeditions and their feeder very often at his hospitable habitation, and they had a reciprocal esteem for one another. Nevertheless, he was one of the first seized by the Indians, who bound him—and then stripped his lady—and abused her with all possible and infamous prostitutions—before his eyes. Then they stuck her flesh with splinters of that only wood which they burn for candles —and set them on fire. In this condition, and [in the?] lingering torments—but how horrid!—she was two or three days broiling and roasting to death—which time they roasted her sucking infant—and compelled her to eat of it. And when these diabolical operations were gone thro'—they finished all by barbecuing of the gentleman!—*Quis talia fando!*

[Declares his expectation of a union among all Christians on basic points of doctrine, and sends along his *Nuncia Bona*.]

Sir, Your brother and servant,

To Isaac Watts

U/AAS draft September 27, 1715

Sir,

[Congratulates him on his recovery from illness.]

Your excellent composures have been much dispersed and valued, and some of them reprinted, in this country, by means of the friend who now tells you so.

And I have a commission from the principal ministers in the country to solicit you that you would expedite the version of the Psalms whereof you have given us an expectation.

A year and half, I think, has rolled away, since I addressed my valuable friend Mr. T. Reinolds with repeated importunities that I might know whether my brethren, the Dissenters in your city, would cast any favorable aspect on our *Biblia Americana*; but I have not unto this hour one word from him nor any of the rest in the city, since the death of Mr. Henry, who diverse times wrote unto me to forward that work. At the same time, from Scotland and from Ireland, and from other parts of England, and from eminent persons in the Church of England, the procedure of the work is urged with kind assurances of large subscriptions.

But I would with all possible resignation leave unto the glorious Head of the church the disposal of my poor essays to serve His Kingdom, and have done expecting any countenance to my offers.

Tho' I am a little prone to flatter myself—[The sentence breaks off here. Close follows.]

To Dr. Daniel Williams

DII/AAS draft [fall, 1715]

Reverend Sir,

[Hopes the memorial to the king has reached Williams.]

You will pardon me if I repeat my humble wishes, that my brethren, the Dissenters, would please to take it into their consideration, whether it may conduce unto the best interest, and their own, for our *Biblia Americana* to meet with some countenance among them. I have diverse times addressed my excellent friend Mr. Reinolds for his advice on that head; and I have waited a year and half, without the least word of return; which has held me in a little suspense as to some other applications.

[Introduces the bearer, "Mr. P.," and encloses some publications.]

To Sir William Ashurst

U/Hunt (HM 22308; AAS draft in DII) October 18, 1715

Sir,

[Encloses his *New Offer*, and assures Ashurst that "there is more performed in the *Biblia Americana*, more than all that is promised in the advertisement."]

I have sometimes flattered myself with an imagination, that if the treasures with which this work is enriched were so acceptable in their separate state as to render many copious and costly volumes vendible, certainly there would be at some time or other so much common sense operating in the world as to believe that a close and thick amassment of these treasures, refined from the superfluities among which they have lain diffused, with an addition of many never before exposed, would be not altogether unworthy of some acceptance. I did not know but that a composure which may pretend without vanity to be the richest collection of the most valuable treasures in so little a room, that ever the church of God was entertained withal, might hope for a favorable reception with people of religion and ingenuity.

But I find, and I do not wonder at it that I do so, the work laboring under discouragements.

The booksellers are generally such that a celebrated author thinks the most opprobrious term he can put upon them is to say, *In one word, they are booksellers.*

It is complained unto me, how truly I know not, that the Dissenters do not seem to overvalue literature, and that a public spirit is much lost among them, drowned in their mutual emulations. Nor do they seem to think that it is much for their interest or honor to have any of their number do things of much consideration in the commonwealth of learning. It has truly been surprising unto me to read the little, absurd, ridiculous exceptions which have been made against this work among some of my brethren.

Indeed, the good-spirited Mr. Henry several times in his letters to me expressed his good will to this undertaking. But Mr. Henry is dead. I am sensible, he is dead.

The surviving seem to be of the opinion that a poor American must never be allowed capable of doing anything worth anyone's regarding, or to have ever looked in a book. And the truth is, we are under such disadvantages that if we do anything to purpose, it must carry in it a tacit rebuke to the sloth of people more advantageously circumstanced.

[The London ministers have failed to answer his pleas for help in publishing the work; if "persons of quality" aided him, "vast subscriptions would soon be sent in."]

Had not the work been in the English tongue, my correspondents in the most illustrious Frederician University, who have put singular marks of their favor upon me, would soon bring it into the light.

One considerable article in the work, namely *The Christian Virtuoso,* one would think might procure some favorers to it among the members of the Royal Society, which have allowed my relation to them.

It may be, God our Saviour will in His time dispose the minds of some eminent and opulent persons to cast a benign aspect upon a work which may hand down their honorable names, with lasting acknowledgments, unto late posterity. [Close]

Your Honor's most affectionate servant,

II

MATHER'S transatlantic admiration and fondness for the Church of Scotland throve on the distance separating him from it. The Atlantic removed, he had difficulty getting along, and two affairs with actual Scotsmen in America especially disillusioned him. The first involved JOHN SQUIRE (c. 1685–1758), a minister from Forres, Scotland. Mather's letters say almost everything about Squire that needs to be said. Squire had arrived in America at least by 1715, when Samuel Sewall mentions going with him and Mather to Rumney Marsh. Mather became affronted when Squire refused to take communion with the Boston churches. Squire's criticism of the ways of New England rattled Mather not only by its rudeness, but also because at the time Mather looked to Scottish orthodoxy for a united front against the Church of England and for some appreciation of his reforming labors. But Squire had gotten a taste from Mather of the obsequiousness that often went with Doing Good. Replying to Mather's two letters of January, 1716, Squire told him that his "civilities savor the worse to me that they are cast so frequently in my teeth" and that "I'm not the only person that thinks you need much more wisdom than you have . . . that you may know better how to meddle with things that concern yourself." He snubbed Mather's peacemaking offer to stay with him and enjoy his library, and boarded instead with the Frizzels. The second affair involved another young man, named [Patrick?] Erskine, who probably came to New England with Squire. This man, the son of Colonel Erskine of Carnock (a close friend of Robert Wodrow), insulted Mather by not responding to his invitations, then by marrying without his consultation, finally by having the marriage performed by Mather's sometime friend Benjamin Colman. The upshot of the first affair is Mather's stinging letter to John Stirling on June 26, 1716, the only angry letter he ever wrote to the Church of Scotland, which he otherwise loved and served faithfully throughout his life.

Mather's chronic disappointment with Cressy gave way to sudden concern when in April, 1716, he learned from his brother in

Witney that Cressy had become seriously ill with rheumatism and had lost the use of his limbs. For all Cressy's failings in the methods of piety, Mather always thought him uniquely good-natured and amiable. Much disturbed by the news, he was relieved when on May 22, 1716, Cressy returned hale from his stay abroad, and, surprisingly, "much polished, much improved," he declared in his diary, "better than ever disposed." In a hopeful mood he wrote to his brother's wife in Witney, thanking the couple for their pious influence on Cressy. In April, 1717, Cressy prepared to marry (Mather himself seemingly arranged the match) and to go into partnership with his intended brother-in-law. Mather began to see a useful future for him.

Mather's pleasure in Cressy's improvement was dampened, however, by the death of his daughter Kate. Kate was exemplary in every way that Cressy was not. Mather saw in her and in his son Samuel the real continuators of the family tradition of piety. In 1716 he tried to find a suitable match for Kate, as for Cressy. But late in the year Katie became ill. Mather wrote off to John Winthrop hoping to obtain a medicinal root cultivated by one of Winthrop's Connecticut neighbors. But after a long and terrible illness, Katie died on December 16, 1716. Mather memorialized her in *Victorina* (1717), but his family, he observed on the day of her death, was coming to "a mighty diminution."

A few months later Mather's vision of Cressy's useful future also began to dissipate. By May, 1717, as before Cressy went to England, he was left questioning, "Oh! when! when shall I see my son Increase converted unto serious piety!" He called Cressy into his library to importune and pray with him, and set aside three days of supplication to the Lord. His prayers brought him a new "particular faith" that God had heard his prayers for his son.

And again his particular faith collapsed. On November 5, 1717, he learned with astonishment that "a harlot big with a bastard accuses my poor son Cressy and lays her belly to him. Oh! Dreadful case!" It comforted him that "the most sensible judges" thought Cressy innocent, yet he set aside further days of fasting and secret prayer, by himself and with Lydia and Cressy. But nothing worked: on November 19 the rebellious Cressy made "a worse exhibition of himself unto me than I have ever yet met withal." The threefold result in Mather was anguish over Cressy, fear for his own reputation, and a further "heartbreaking intimation" that his "particular faiths" were nothing but delusions.

On top of his domestic griefs, and continuing aguish pains in his jaw and head, Mather had to bear his chronic financial worries, made weightier now by the shortage of money in New England and the debts Cressy had accumulated abroad. To help clear his debts, he sent off on February 21, 1716, an angry dunning letter to his cousin ATHERTON MATHER (1663–1734), of Suffield, Connecticut. Two years before, he had received from Atherton what his diary calls "a considerable accession to the temporal interest of my family." Atherton apparently repaid his debt to his cousin by April 30, 1717, when Cotton records caring for the "temporal interest" of his family by securing a farm in Connecticut "which is made over to me." His financial straits drove him not only to angry notes but also to subterfuges that must have been painful and embarrassing, as for example the unaddressed letter of late 1715 or early 1716, included here, intended to recover money spent during Increase Mather's charter agency. The agency, after all, was twenty years past. In the perspective of Mather's life at the time, this letter must seem a dodge, a way of getting money for himself to pay off his debts, disguised as a plea for his father. (His sermons following, as always, the course of his life, Mather published in 1716 *Fair Dealing between Debtor and Creditor. A very brief Essay upon the Caution to be used about coming into Debt, and getting out of it*, which he sent along to John Stirling.) Another such unseemly maneuver is the letter on November 11, 1717, to Wait Winthrop, who was the chief justice of Massachusetts and one of Mather's patrons, asking for a promised forty or fifty shillings toward publishing one of his works. Unknown to Mather, Winthrop had died four days earlier. After learning the news, Mather immediately wrote to Winthrop's son John, asking him for funds to publish something on the chief justice (later printed as *Hades Look'd Into*).

This untimely wheeling-dealing resulted not from Mather's financial straits alone, of course, but from his added, unquench-

able mania for publication. The *Biblia Americana,* still in manuscript, tormented him so that hardly a letter in these years fails to
rehash broodingly his disgruntlement with the English Dissenters.
Still, his publishing activities were prodigious. To the recipients of
his *Curiosa Americana* at the Royal Society he added DR. JAMES
PETIVER (1663–1718), an English apothecary, botanist, entomologist, and Fellow of the society. Petiver published many botanical
studies in the *Transactions,* one concerning plants from Maryland
sent to him by the Reverend Hugh Jones. Mather also began
writing to DR. EDMUND HALLEY (1656–1742), the noted astronomer
and assistant secretary of the society, after whom the comet is
named. Second only to Newton among English scientists of his
time, Halley accurately predicted a solar eclipse in May, 1715,
and observed it from the roof of the society building. Of special
interest is Mather's letter on July 12, 1716, to John Woodward,
describing the circumstances that led him to the method of inoculating against smallpox.

Among the large number of Mather's works published during
this period appeared a brief and very little known pamphlet which
he considered one of his most important writings: *Lapis e Monte
Excisus. The Stone Cut out of the Mountain. And the Kingdom of
God in those Maxims of it that cannot be Shaken* (1716). It is a
brief work, containing only twenty-six pages, thirteen of Latin and
thirteen of facing English translation. The spirit of the work de-
rives from the growing ecumenicalism in Mather and his growing
fear of Anglicanism. In the *Lapis* he attempted to reduce Reformed Christianity to fourteen maxims on which all Reformed
Christians could agree. These gems refined from the mountain of
doctrine, he wrote in the book, would "smite all the kingdoms of
the papacy and break them to pieces, and consume them. . . ."
Like the rest of Mather's theology, there is nothing doctrinal in the
fourteen maxims that would offend a John Cotton. But to a
fundamentally conservative view of doctrine Mather has added
large-scale social benevolence, great leeway for dissent on inessential
matters, and approval for the pleasures and activities of at least
the pious business class. While insisting on three persons in one
God and on hard grace—a religion for John Stirling or John Cotton

—Mather also offers religion to a John Frizzel or to any man who would "not frowardly refuse the blessings of God in the comforts of this life."

Mather doted on this brief work as a special favorite. It was, he wrote to the English minister Henry Walrond, "of greater expectation with me than anything that I have ever yet been concerned in." He sent copies of it along to all of his correspondents (even to Geneva), proposed that it be translated into Dutch, had the maxims recited in some Massachusetts schools, and suggested prize money for schoolboys who could memorize all of the maxims. To Mather, the fourteen maxims of the *Lapis* formed a rock on which the floundering Reformation could reunite and preserve itself. At the end of the work he warned that the year 1716 would date the collapse of the Roman Church. The warning marks an interest in prophecy that more and more infiltrates his diary as he feels more and more set upon. The prophetic undercurrent of the *Lapis* expresses the evolution of Mather's personal myth onto a cosmic scale: his good works would be rebuked, the Reformation would perhaps fail, but everything would be redeemed in the not very distant Judgment Day. In this sense the *Lapis e Monte Excisus* is both an epitome of Mather's whole religion and a personal testament.

Of course Mather was not content to further the Reformation merely through his writing. In the case of JOSEPH PARSONS (1671–1740), as in many others, he took a direct hand in ecclesiastical affairs. Parsons had studied under Increase Mather and married the daughter of the poet Benjamin Tompson. Parson's gossiping and his reputation as a talebearer lost him two ministries in Connecticut and, in 1708, the ministry of the New North Church in Boston. In 1716 he was rejected for posts successively at Haverhill and at Boston's New South. By the latter he was rejected for having charged a man named Whiting with sitting up all night drinking and playing cards. As Mather's letters indicate, Parsons collided with his old teacher Increase Mather when Increase emphatically discouraged him from pressing for a ministry at the New South. Increase decided to respect the will of the congregation, which did finally reject Parsons (and had no pastor until September, 1718).

Partly as a gesture of Christlike mercy, but also to get Parsons off his hands, Cotton Mather wrote to recommend him for a post at Tiverton, adding that if Parsons has begotten any "misunderstandings which have sometimes been a disadvantage to his improvement, I hope those will be no prejudice to his future usefulness." In the end Parsons settled at the newly formed Second Church in Salisbury, Massachusetts.

As always, Mather worked to further the Reformation by taking ing a direct hand in politics as well. To ingratiate New England to the crown, he wrote to EDMUND CALAMY (1671–1732), the English historian of Nonconformity and editor of Richard Baxter's works, asking him and JONATHAN BELCHER (1682–1757) to present to the new king a second memorial. Belcher was an urbane and rather hot-tempered Boston merchant who later became governor of Massachusetts. Together with Jeremiah Dummer he bribed the newly appointed governor, Elizeus Burgess, to vacate his office for two thousand pounds in favor of SAMUEL SHUTE (1662–1742). Burgess had been partial to the private bank scheme, and his appointment was largely unwelcome in the province. Shute arrived in Massachusetts on October 5, 1716; Jeremiah's brother William Dummer, a son-in-law of Joseph Dudley, was made lieutenant governor under Shute. Mather preached a eulogistic sermon upon Shute's arrival and immediately wrote him a long, flattering letter. His delight in Shute's appointment was unbounded, mostly because Shute was a Dissenter. He consistently valued Shute above any other governor who ruled Massachusetts. In Shute he saw his greatest chance to be influential, to extend his powers of Doing Good, to continue the work of Calvin and Luther, and at the same time, to advance himself.

But from the beginning, Shute's administration was stormy and Mather had to weather the governor's trials with him. An early wrangle involved Jeremiah Dummer, who had warned Shute against the bank party. In return, the bank party tried to oust Dummer from his agency in London, although he had been enormously useful to Massachusetts. The case against Dummer was bolstered by a letter that had been shown to Samuel Sewall in April, 1716, claiming that Dummer had gotten Sir Alexander

Brand drunk, picked his pocket, and brought two prostitutes into a tavern. Sewall dismissed the charges, although considering Dummer's reputation as a London rake, they are not inconceivable. In May, 1716, the council ordered Sewall to reprimand Dummer, who was his cousin; he was forced to do so. At the front of the opposition to Dummer was OLIVER NOYES (1675-1721), a politician, real estate speculator, founder of the Brattle Street Church, physician to the Sewalls and Dudleys, and from 1714 until his death, a member of the General Court. As an important land speculator Noyes favored the bank and belonged to the "popular party," headed by Elisha Cooke, that formed Shute's opposition throughout his reign. Noyes and some Representatives from Boston met at Mather's house to discuss Dummer's fate. Despite the conciliatory tone of his letter to Noyes, Mather detested him as a radical, a "misleader and enchanter of the people," and exulted in his death.

Mather's feelings about Dummer, on the other hand, were politically influenced and ambivalent. On the one hand he tried to defend Dummer before his opponents in the House, and he had some personal affection for him. He also recognized that any move against Dummer at home would jeopardize the favor toward Massachusetts that Dummer had built up in London, and would alienate Dummer's influential London friends. On the other hand, Mather had reasons for being dissatisfied with Dummer and was not above using him as a political football. He suspected Dummer's religious leanings and privately said harsh things about him, apparently when he felt his listener wanted to hear them. Even when writing to Dummer his tone is often peevish. His double-dealing letter to Noyes is significant of how far Mather would go to retain favor in London. He discredits Dummer, whom he liked, to Noyes, whom he hated, and tries to win Noyes over by suggesting that it is merely good politics to keep the otherwise uncommendable Dummer in office. In *realpolitik* Mather was not above betraying his friends and pretending friendship for his enemies if it ultimately meant keeping Massachusetts under Congregational rule.

This is not to say that Mather was by nature crafty or wily. He was merely overreaching himself, playing Napoleon as well as Christ. He chose to make use of the squabbling political powers of Massachusetts at a time when, because of his own domestic and financial tribulations, he could least afford involvements. Moreover, to make use of them he was forced to adopt the tone of, and to become the dupe of, the sort of worldly and powerful men like Oliver Noyes who were beginning to flourish in the political life of Massachusetts, where bribes and betrayals of confidence were becoming everyday occurrences. A pitifully unworldly man without the smallest gift for political intrigue, Mather was drawn by his prominence and his desire to Do Good into matters he did not understand and could not handle except by the most devious, unethical, and unbecoming stratagems, which he brought off with a bludgeoning lack of finesse.

Mather wrote several essays and letters at this time on the treatment of slaves. He was a slaveholder himself, and many merchants in his congregation were engaged in the slave trade. He did grant freedom to his slave Onesimus, but only because Onesimus proved recalcitrant and difficult to govern. He replaced him with a new slave, a boy named Obadiah.

The slave remained invisible to Mather as a man. Otherwise he looked upon the slaves with compassion for their plight, curiosity about their nature, missionary zeal, and later on, with fear. As he wrote to Anthony Boehm, he grieved over "the sweat and blood of slaves treated with infinite barbarities." But ultimately he was less concerned with the slaves' emancipation than with their conversion. He had tried to promote with Sir William Ashurst a scheme to Christianize the slaves in New England and the West Indies. Different difficulties, he felt, presented themselves in converting red Indians and black slaves. He was consistent in believing that the fact of color had nothing to do with the chances of salvation, but inconsistent on the question of whether the widely alleged stupidity of the slaves would stand in the way. In *The Negro Christianized* he wrote that the slaves were stupid, but that their stupidity made their conversion the more imperative. Yet, in his *Small Offers towards the Tabernacle in the Wilderness* (1689), he implied that the supposed stupidity of the slaves was only the invention of their masters, used as a justification for keeping them "as horses or oxen to do our drudgeries"; in fact, black souls "are as white and good as those of other nations."

For himself, Mather was not above learning from his slaves. He told John Woodward that it was his slave Onesimus who first showed him the method of inoculating against smallpox. Mather's reliance on the word of a slave was even used against him by his antagonists during the inoculation controversy (see the letters at the end of chapter four). His chief opponent, Dr. William Douglass, derided his "negroish" evidence and, to defile him, some people in Boston renamed their slaves "Cotton Mather." Despite this slightly greater respect for the slaves' intelligence and reliability, Mather's feelings about slavery did not differ from those of most Puritans, as Winthrop Jordan has characterized them in *White over Black*. Puritan theology required that Negroes be seen as possessing the same nature as whites; but Puritan tribalism and its sense of the messianic group insured the exclusion of blacks from Puritan society.

Unaddressed

DII/AAS draft   [late 1715 or early 1716]

Sir,

It will doubtless be an honor unto our country that it has been equal to the best in the world for the justice exercised in paying the debts of the public. And a sensible addition is made unto its honorable character when there are done such things as are done in the present session, and unto justice there is added gratitude.

Good men are pleased when they see the country grateful unto those worthy gentlemen who ventured over the Atlantic ocean in a dangerous time, and underwent the inconveniences of an absence from their families and businesses in an agency for us.

But, I perceive, many good men do express their wishes with some concern, that there may not be at the same time a total neglect of a person who bore a part in that agency with some distinguishing circumstances of service, when all the gentlemen concerned for us found the prosecution of the former charter become hopeless, and united in a petition for another, which produced what we now enjoy. Many are concerned lest such a total neglect of that person may carry an aspect with it, which, I make no doubt, would be far from the intentions of gentlemen of such consideration, as we have the happiness to see both Houses filled withal.

To confess the truth, some very considerable persons in both Houses have given me to understand that if the motion be brought forward on his behalf, they believe the Assembly will readily give to that person also, some testimony that they accept with thankfulness, the pains which he also took to obtain for us the things by which we have enjoyed great quietness. And I am very sure that if any objections happen to be offered, a very little discourse with him will presently set things in so true and clear a light as to remove them all and render his merits incontestible.

'Tis true, when the first great and general Assembly of this province offered him a recompense at his arrival, he, considering the grievous debts then lying on a distressed people, answered, He would have his recompense adjourned unto the Resurrection of the Just. But, certainly, the sentiments of the province at this day, and under the influence of the generous dispositions which are now operating, will not be the less favorable to him for so noble and Christian an answer.

'Tis also true that he now declines to take any step himself in this affair. But you will be so far from censuring, that you will rather commend a son, for thus doing the part of a remembrancer, and stepping in with a memorial for his aged parent.

Briefly, it will not seem strange if the Assembly hear a proposal of this importance. 'Tis their own goodness towards two worthy persons that has introduced the thoughts of not leaving a third forgotten. But it might very well seem strange if a son, so advised and so directed as I have been on this occasion, should not have addressed you as I now do, with an action the like to which I never did in my life before. For I never in my life asked any beneficence unto myself from any society in the world. And verily, if I had now been on my own account, you should not have [torn].

Sir, your most hearty servant,

To John Squire
DII (there assigned the date January, 1717 *)/AAS draft

[January, 1716]

Sir,

When you (and the brethren with you) arrived here, we did with unspeakable pleasure lay hold on the opportunity to express our communion with the dear Church of Scotland, and the precious sons of Zion therein, whom we valued as our most United Brethren.

Accordingly we have all along treated you with all the civilities imaginable, as we have always done other ministers of your nation upon their arrival among us.

You are the first that ever we have known to decline and renounce communion with the churches of God in this country, albeit I am very certain that for you to have held an occasional communion with them would have been very grateful to your excellent mother, the Church of Scotland. The Elect Lady, I am very certain, would have been pleased with it, and your treating of it in such a manner as you have done has much reproached her.

You must not wonder if declarations that it would be a wrong unto conscience to hold communion with our churches, and insinuations thrown among the people, that our ministers can admit you no otherwise than as laymen, and that our baptism is little better than none at all, should be things at which we are dissatisfied. Nor can it, without a folly equal unto the rest, be called a *persecution for righteousness' sake* if in our discourse with you we'll tell you so.

This does not hinder me from telling you that I am afraid your hasty leaving of the hospitable and religious family where you have always been honorably treated, may expose you to some inconveniencies.

* The two following draft letters to Squire are undated. That the affair Mather mentions took place in 1716, not in 1717, is established by Mather's dated letter of June 26, 1716, to John Stirling, included in this section. Mather discusses the affair with Stirling, in language that echoes his letters to Squire. Perhaps what misled the editors of Mather's *Diary* is a letter from Squire to Mather (AAS) dated January 10, 1716, in reply to the first of Mather's letters to him. Squire was almost certainly dating his letter in the New Style and not, as the editors may have thought, in the Old. In the case of January the difference is a full year, since in the New Style January is the first month, while in the Old Style it is the eleventh month.

Wherefore I do in the most brotherly manner invite you to my own habitation, where your diet and lodging shall cost you nothing while you stay in the country, if you see cause to accept thereof, or are not provided more to your satisfaction. Your accommodations here will be inferior to few in the town, and in respect of the library, superior to any. To which this easy circumstance will be added, that all the while you stay you shall not hear those things which we take to be your weaknesses uneasily insisted on. Do what you please—I shall always endeavor to approve myself, Your friend and servant,

To John Squire
DII (there assigned the date January, 1717)/AAS draft
[January, 1716]

Sir,

In answer to what I this moment received from you, I have at present nothing to say, but only desire you to forbear filling the town with a false story, that I have said the government of the Church of Scotland is a *Tory-government*.

All that ever I said (as the gentlemen in the company can witness) was, that I doubted a great part of the church-government in the world had a little touch of (what I called, in a way of perfect pleasancy, and all the company took me so) *ecclesiastical* Torism [sic].

I said nothing of the Church of Scotland. It was you ran upon *that*. And I explained myself that my meaning was, the people in some things seemed to want the due exercise of their liberties.

If you go on to traduce me on this occasion, you will persist in a violation of the Ninth Commandment. No man in America has a juster veneration for the Church of Scotland than I must always maintain, and shall do so.

And I am sorry for the wrongs that you have done to that venerable body.

I pray God forgive you all the sins of your abusive and virulent letter, as well as your endeavors to sow discord in a town that ought to be more gratefully treated.

I have something else to do with my time than to spend it in altercations with a person of your disposition.

More humility, meekness, and wisdom would render you more amiable and more serviceable.

You will expect nothing further from your abused friend,

To Atherton Mather

DII/AAS draft   February 21, 1716

Dear Cousin,

To all the other inconveniences which I have of late suffered in my temporal interest, there is this added, that my brother having detained my son in England, I have been thereby put upon such difficulties as are not yet known unto me; but this I know, that I have already a demand of [crossed out: thirty pounds] more money made upon to defray my son's charges there, than all that you have borrowed of me.

And now, after all the wrong things that you have imposed upon me, what is it that you design to do!

I have many months ago freely told you my thoughts about your conduct, and the rules of charity and of discretion violated in it. But I now again desire you to pay your debt unto me, without which I must be put unto extreme trouble to discharge mine unto other men.

If you refuse to do this, I have then another proposal to make.

Never till the last night had I any discourse with Mr. Oliver Noyes concerning you and your affairs. And now I perceive that he has had the same account of you that I have had from every quarter.

However, for your debt of a hundred pounds unto him, you have invested him in two thousand acres of the land in your new plantation. If you deal no worse with me than with him, you can do no less than invest me in six hundred acres of as good land in your plantation, if it be not all disposed of. I desire you to let me know by the first opportunity what you will do, and what you would have me to do, and no more deal with me as you have done hitherto.

The Eighth Commandment will oblige me to do some justice unto my family, as well as the Fifth, to approve myself,

Your kinsman and servant,

If you don't give me quickly to hear from you, I must put over my business into the hands of an attorney in your parts of the country.

To Sir William Ashurst

U/Hunt   March 5, 1716
(HM 22306; AAS draft in DII, dated 1717)

Sir,

[Repeats the story of *Biblia Americana*.]

. . . will Your Honor forgive my rudeness if I presume to say that should a person of your great esteem and figure prevail with two or three more persons of quality, to appear as patrons and favorers of a work so evidently calculated for the service of the interests which the best of men have thought it their honor to serve, and thereby obtain the lasting monuments and memorials of their generous goodness to be erected for them, which would become their due, the thing desired would be soon accomplished.

[Repeats his story of the failure of the Dissenters to value the work.] Those distresses upon the nations, which may perhaps for a while retard the publication of our *Biblia Americana*, will doubtless be so hot as ere long to melt all good men down into a compliance with the sentiments in an instrument which I now humbly offer to Your Honor, and which is getting into the heart of revolving France, as well as other parts of reforming Europe—the *Lapis è* [*sic*, although no accent appears on the published title] *Monte Excisus*.

Behold, Sir, a *system of religion* consisting of and confined to such articles as all good men (for the most part at least) are united in! Articles which afford a sufficient basis for a union among all the good men in the world: the articles of their goodness, the choice grain of the purged floor, an essay never yet so explicitly made in the church of God! Behold, the religion of living unto God! A most rational and substantial religion, and what the most critical *wise men of inquiry* will never find cause to be ashamed of. The religion which with all them who die not without wisdom, is justified in the approaches of death, and will be so by all the sons of wisdom while they live. All the controversies agitated upon any point of religion, by all them who handle the pen of the polemical writer in the world, pretend forever to serve one or other of these maxims. And therefore, if the contending managers will but agree to the maxims, their controversies are now either ended, or must come under a management full of moderation. The treatise ostentates very little erudition, but is the effect and result of more than a little contemplation. St. Barnaby's Day would not be long enough to recite all the views which the author had in the composing of it. The millions of people in the world who are pressing and heaving after a *real and vital religion* are here accommodated, and with a brevity, I suppose, not ill-contrived. God will go on distressing the sinful nations till there be produced a people that will unite upon these maxims; and this people will grow into a mighty mountain. 'Tis not amiss for an obscure American, as well as others, to make offers unto the grand service that is *now* to be prosecuted; yea, and to do it in the language which will speak unto every nation.

I may not break off without a word upon the evangelical affairs among our Indians. After I had solicited the Governor of New York with addresses for the Christianizing of the pagan Indians on Long-Island, but found him so encumbered with his enemies, who were all the High Church party, that *the good he would have done, he did not*, I obtained a promise that our ministers on that island would set themselves to do what they could for that intention, and especially for catechising the children of the Indians, which are now generally in English families. And for their assistance in that work, a servant of yours has prepared for them an essay, which you will find here enclosed. But the same essay is like to have a much more extensive usefulness not only for the Indians in the eastern, as well as the southern parts of the Massachusetts province, but also in many of our families where we have Negroes as well as Indians, and perhaps in some other countries. In the packet you will find it accompanied with some other small things which are humbly tendered unto your excellent Lady. My wife (in whom a good God has made me one of the happiest of men) has the honor to be known to her, and the book entitled *Utilia*, consisting of sermons on subjects which were at her desire preached upon, she 'tis, that with her most humble service, presents that book to your Lady's acceptance. [Close]

Your Honor's most sincere servant,

To Mrs. Samuel Mather

DII (as August, 1715)/AAS draft   [c. May, 1716]

My dear Sister,

My value for you has been very great, ever since I understood that you made my only brother one of the happiest men in the world.

I have thought that Mademoiselle de Gournay, the lady who a while since wrote an essay to demonstrate the *equality of women to men,* might victoriously enough defend her problem (tho' that learned and famous and wondrous lady, A. Maria Schurrman, had the modesty to disallow it) while she had such as you as friend, who help so notably to render your husbands useful and considerable.

It was the acclamation made by spectators in the primitive times of Christianity, *what rare women are to be found among the Christians!* By such as you the occasions for it [are?] continued in our days.

Go on to love him and serve him, and felicitate him, and become accessory to all the good which he may do in the world; and consider him as a valuable minister of God, and one of whom our Lord will say, of what you have done for him, you have done it unto me.

As you have obliged me in all you have done for him, so you have these obligations in what you have done for my son in the many months of his residing with you. Your maternal tenderness for him, in the time of his long illness, and the many civilities he at all times received from you, as well as the excellent accomplishments wherewith he saw you adorned, he never mentions without a sensible passion of gratitude and admiration.

I return you my most hearty thanks for all your kindness to the lad; and, if God bless him, he will one day be able to return you his own thanks in a manner more significant than mere verbal acknowledgments. [May God take delight in her.]

The best of women in the American world accompanies me in the most affectionate remembrances, which you have in the heart of,

Your obliged brother,

Unaddressed

U/AAS draft   [c. late May, 1716]

Sir,

Your civilities to my son Increase Mather will be acknowledged by me with a perpetual gratitude.

But the first of my acknowledgments must be the discharge of a debt of fifteen pounds sterling unto you, to which my brother directs me, which I now do immediately upon his arrival.

I could by no means procure a bill of exchange for the sum. Wherefore I ship silver to that value upon the ship Hanover commanded by

Captain William Chadder, the very ship which brought my son home, and which with an uncommon dispatch is upon the return.

The child comes home to me so very much improved that I think this money well-bestowed; and at his first arrival he steps into so lucriferous, agreeable, and honorable a business, that I cannot but be surprised at the gracious providence of a God and Saviour in what He pleases to do on this occasion.

May the glorious Lord multiply His blessings on you and yours,

To Dr. Edmund Calamy

U/AAS draft   [c. June, 1716]

Sir,

A year ago we presumed so far upon your good affection unto your United Brethren on the American strand, that we prayed your appearance for us, to present our address unto His Majesty.

Except in one letter from our excellent friend Dr. Williams unto me, none of our brethren have by their letters given us to understand the more particular circumstances of our obligations to you. We only know that we are very much obliged and that you have been the happy instruments of bringing us to *stand right in the King's esteem.* And we render our utmost thanks accordingly.

[Notes the death of Dr. Williams.]

We have directed a gentleman of ours, Mr. Jonathan Belcher, who is now in London, to wait upon you and three or four other ministers (and such others as you please) with our humble request that you would repeat the favor you showed us the last year, and join with him in presenting another address unto His Majesty, wherein you will pardon us that our design to serve you as well as ourselves is rendered so very legible. Yea, this emboldens us further to add, that if Mr. Belcher [a word or two blotted] be absent we must prevail with our Dr. Calamy to take upon him the whole administration. [Close]

Your hearty brother and servant,

To John Stirling

U/NLS (draft at AAS)   June 26, 1716

Sir,

[Must write hurriedly, as a ship bound for Scotland awaits.]

You have brought me so much into your debt by your favors, that I know no other method of solvency than by sitting down on the *Lapis Opprobrii.*

[Sends along *An Honest Debtor* and other publications; notes that the New England churches are flourishing.]

And the true character which, especially by the means of my dear Dr. Williams (whose death, as well as that of our excellent Carstairs, is greatly regretted among us) our King has received of us, has been extremely much to our advantage.

Very particularly, in the change of our Governor. It is impossible to express the love, the honor and esteem, and brotherly affection with which the North-British Christians, and especially ministers, are embraced in our churches, and the rapture with which we lay hold on all opportunities to testify our delight in them as our United Brethren.

We know not any of your ministers, formerly arriving among us, but what have treated us with reciprocal regards; and there are more than two or three of them that are at this very time the pastors of our churches; and our churches do rejoice in their gracious influences.

I am sorry we have lately had some occasion to wish that when Scotch ministers come among us, and we invite them into our pulpits, and privately as well as publicly load them with ponderous and all possible civilities, and are even proud of asserting our brotherhood unto you in them, all the return may not be a disdainful and ungrateful carriage towards them that have deserved infinitely otherwise from them:

A behavior, in which a loathsome display of united ignorance and arrogance;

A provoking declaration that they cannot with a good conscience hold communion with our churches;

A setting up of private conventicles, and baptizing in a private house—with foolish insinuations that they know not what covenant we baptize into;

Scurvy reflections on the College of Glasgow, asserting it to be no university;

A vast indiscretion in their whole conduct, with attempts to sow discord among our people;

—among whom some of the more loose and profane sort (and scarce any but such) siding with them;

And while the churches here not holy enough for their communion, at the same time their own conversation full of a levity not usual among our ministers, beheld with wonder and scandal by our more pious people;

—Drinking of healths, and pleading in defense of the games of lottery—

All having an unhappy tendency to make our people take up a mean idea of the most venerable church in the world, as if it were a stingy, narrow, froward, and very uncatholic sort of a body, and as if some of us had represented her in more beautiful colors than we had reason for.

All the strangers that shall come into this country these twenty years will be treated with the more of jealousy and reservation for the sake of some that have lately been among us.

I do not aim at the hurting of any man by what I have intimated; I had not given so much as the least of these intimations if it had not been to make a just provision that if any returning to you go to do any ill offices, with invectives and calumnies against a country, or any particular gentlemen in it, from whom they (as well as other strangers) have received such kindnesses as no other part of the world would have shown unto them, you may be fortified against ill impressions by this *true account* of the persons who may seek to make them.

Every word of my account is known by this whole city to be *matter of fact*. [Close]   Sir, yours under many obligations,

[To the Royal Society]

U/MHS draft   [July 3, 1716]
(A Monstrous Calf)

Sir,

Among the stores of a more than royal treasury which are amassed in the stock of the Royal Society, from the communications of inquisitive and ingenious men, you have allowed a particular class to the monsters, whereof a relation communicated now and then has found a good reception. [Notes that accounts of monsters are worth collecting.]

The reasonable philosopher will not be too ready to imagine that monsters carry omens in them, and that the name of monsters does for that cause belong unto them. Even Fortunius Licetus himself will furnish two small reasons to confute the superstition, the one because monsters are nowhere more frequent than in the solitudes of Africa, where there are few people capable of receiving admonition from them. The other because they often are of too criminal an original to have it supposed that the Holy God would employ them to be our monitors. And yet, monsters may no doubt be sometimes attended with such circumstances that they who are more nearly concerned may do well to be sensible of a voice from Heaven therein unto them.

[Cites various monsters compounded of human and bestial features, drawn from Arrianus, Vincentius, Volaterran, Petrus Damianus, and others.]

. . . passing by the cow that brought forth *vitulum semi-hominem* in the days of Albertus Magnus, who delivered the cow-keeper from the suspicion of his neighbors by persuading them, from his wonderful skill in philosophy, that the stars were concerned in the business, that whereof I am now to give you a short narrative is that this year a cow in our vicinity brought forth a calf, which had so much of a human visage as to make the attentive spectators apprehensive that the poor animal had been impregnated by a beastly Negro. My shortest and [plainest?] account of the monster will be in a lively icon of it, which you have here annexed.

That my letter may not for its bigness grow into that which has been the subject of it, I here finish it, and subscribe, Sir, Your,

[To the Royal Society]

U/MHS draft [July 5, 1716]

(A Triton)

Sir,

Long was I no other than Pyrrhonian upon the common tradition of tritons, or fishes in a shape near human, sometimes coming from the watery world unto us. [There follow five pages of examples of tritons drawn from various authors: Demostratus, Theodore Gaza, Scaliger, Gillius, Albertus, and many others.]

But now at last my credulity is entirely conquered, and I am compelled now to believe the existence of a triton; for such a one has just now been exhibited in my own country, and the attestations to it are such that it would be a fault in me at all to question it.

On February 22, 1716, three honest and credible men, coming in a boat from Milford to Brainford (which towns lie near one another on the south-shore in our colony of Connecticut) when it was young flood, about the hour of two in the afternoon, as they drew near the shore of Brainford-harbor, they were surprised with the view of a creature that seemed a man, lying on the top of a rock, about a dozen foot from the water. When they were about three or four rods from the rock, the animal seemed affrighted, lifted up his head, looked forwards and backwards, then clapped his head close to the rock, as willing to hide himself, and after this, lifting up his head again to discover what was approaching. The three men rowed unto the leeward of the rock, and two of the three went out of the boat, with a design to take him, the one in the front, the other in the rear. He that went behind the rock had a purpose to strike him with a pole, and was come within a rod of him; the other was two rods off, and the third, in the boat, might be three. The person who approached, purposing to strike him, trod on the ice, the breaking whereof made a noise which frighted the animal, so that he jumped off the rock, and with all possible expedition flounced into the water. They had a full view of him, and saw his head, and face, and neck, and shoulders, and arms, and elbows, and breast, and back all of a human shape. Only his arms were little more than half the length of a man's. He wanted not for hair, which was a grayish color. However—*desiuit in piscem.* [The] lower parts were those of a fish, and colored like a mackerel. His tail was forked, and he had two fins about half a foot above the tail. The whole animal was about five or six foot in length. He scrabbled with his arms, and wrought with his tail, to reach the water; and being safely lodged there, and having dived out of the sight of his persecutors, until he was near twenty rods from them, he there lift up his head again to look at them, as high as his arms, reaching down to the water, would allow; and having thus taken a view of them, he took his leave.

[Compares this account with a recent one from England.] If the story in your accounts be Grubstreet, mine is not so. All that I have to regret is that my honest friends missed of taking my triton. For tho' I should not have thought fit then to have trusted him with the conveyance of my letter to you, yet I should have been able to have given you a more punctual and entertaining account of him. [Close]

Sir, Your,

[To the Royal Society]

U/MHS   [July 9, 1716]

(Strength of Imagination)

Sir,

The surprising force of imagination has doubtless appeared unto you in so many instances as to set your philosophy to work upon some solution of its very strange appearances. And I make no doubt that the insipid philosophy of a [Fierius?] writing on that subject, which seems to lie very much in a few school-terms, which are a mere jargon invented for an ostentatious cover of ignorance, give to your sagacious inquiries very little of satisfaction.

[Notes examples of "*potentia imaginativa*," drawn from Avicenna, Agrippa, Pomponatius, Medina and others: mental telepathy, miraculous cures by laying on of hands, hypnotism, power of suggestion; mentions in passing the strange death of Moliere.]

My story now is this, and I have it well attested unto me. A gentleman of Carolina, whose name is [Mr.?] Edwards, in his repentance of the errors which the too free use of wine had once led him to, came to entertain an aversion for that liquor, equal to what Lancelot's instance in the German *Ephemerides* has told us of. The least approach of it distressed him. The minister of the place (who is my author for my story) persuaded him to present himself unto the communion, for which he thought so good a penitent was well prepared. He objected his incapacity to partake of the cup, which he had so much of a Calixtine and a Protestant in him as to think essential unto the eucharist. The minister exhorted him and overcame him to make the experiment; which he did, and found not the least inconvenience in the world. The wine sat well upon him, and he continued a religious communicant. And yet, after this, the minister seeing the wife of this gentleman making of a famous dish which they call a pudden, prevailed with her, utterly unknown unto her husband, for to put a few drops of wine into it. When it came to the table, tho' no mortal else would have been apprehensive of any wine in it, the quantity being so very small, yet he was extremely sensible of it, extremely disturbed

212

with it; it made him very sick, and produced very ill effects upon him. How a gentleman of such an antipathy for wine should so inoffensively drink it at the table of the Lord! Whether something superior to mere imagination may not operate in so rare a case?

Could I by the force of imagination transport myself, I would immediately try to converse with you on this and some other subjects. In the meantime, I must be content with subscribing, Sir,

[To Dr. John Woodward]
U; (extracts in Proceedings XLV)/MHS draft

July 12, 1716

(Curiosities of the smallpox)

The history of that grievous and wondrous disease, the smallpox, would no doubt be as grateful as the distemper itself is loathsome.

I shall presume at this time to entertain you with no more than two or three American curiosities upon it.

The famous Fernelius in his treatise *De abditis rerum causis* makes the smallpox to proceed *Ab occuleo quodam coelesti influxu*. We have been almost ready to think this, and even suspect a peculiar agency of the invisible world in the infliction of the smallpox upon our city of Boston, when we saw that from the first foundations of it, in the year 1630, down to the year 1702, it observed the precise period of twelve years in its mortal visits unto us. Now and then a vessel would in the intervening space bring in the distemper among us. However, it would not spread. But on the twelfth year, still no precaution would keep it off. In the twelfth year it must be epidemical. So raging, so reaching, that it may come at unborn children; they have been born full of it upon them. But at last, when a seventh period for a variolated twelfth year was arrived, our observation has met with an interruption. We had not the usual return of that contagion. The compassion of Heaven would not add that calamity unto what we suffered the year before (1713) in the measles, which at once arrested almost the whole city, and proved so strangely mortal to a multitude of people that we buried above a hundred in a month. Of this disease, at this time, there were no less than five of my own family. . . . [Relates several curiosities about the measles.]

[The smallpox] has usually proven a great plague to us poor Americans, and getting among our Indians hath swept away whole nations of them, and left not living enough to bury their dead.

When our last visitation was beginning, and I was full of distress about the misery I saw coming on my neighborhood, I accidentally lit on a hint in the *Philosophical Transactions*, that the famous Dr. Sydenham had saved more lives than the wars of Ireland had destroyed, by teaching the true method of managing the smallpox. I presently consulted h[is] method, and pressed our physicians to come into [it?], and the success was answerable. Few died in comparison of the numbers we formerly destroyed, when by our unseasonable alexiphamacks, we killed one another with kindness, and put nature out of the course, which ought not to be disturbed.

[Mentions various other methods of treating smallpox.]

. . . many months before I met with any intimations of treating the smallpox with the method of inoculation anywhere in Europe, I had from a servant of my own, an account of its being practised in Africa. Inquiring of my Negro-man Onesimus, who is a pretty intelligent fellow, whether he ever had the smallpox, he answered, both *yes* and *no*; and then told me that he had undergone an operation which had given him something of the smallpox, and would forever preserve him from it, adding that it was often used among the Garamantese, and whoever had the courage to use it was forever free from the fear of the contagion. He described the operation to me, and showed me in his arm the scar which it had left upon him; and his description of it made it the same that afterwards I found related unto you by your Timonius.

This cannot but expire in a wonder, and in a request, unto my Dr. Woodward. How does it come to pass that no more is done to bring this operation into experiment and into fashion in England, when there are so many thousands of people that would give many thousands of pounds to have the danger and horror of this frightful disease well over with them? I beseech you, Sir, to move it, and save more lives than Dr. Sydenham. For my own part, if I should live to see the smallpox again enter into our city, I would immediately procure a consult of our physicians, to introduce a practise which may be of so very happy a tendency. But could we hear that you have done it before us, how much would that embolden us! [Close]

Sir, Your most sincere servant,

To Anthony William Boehm
DII/AAS draft   August 6, 1716

Reverend Sir,

[Has received his letter, and the accompanying one from Ziegen-balgh.]

. . . It is among the singular felicities with which the good hand of Heaven has favored me, that I enjoy a correspondence with my invaluable Boehm (which alone is to me an inestimable treasure); yea, and that by his mediation I am let into a correspondence which carries my precious opportunities to serve the Kingdom of God into a vast extensiveness.

I rejoice to find the *Magnalia Christi Americana* fallen into your hands. And I verily believe the American Puritanism to be so much of a piece with the Frederician Pietism, that if it were possible for the book to be transferred unto our friends in the Lower Saxony, it would find some acceptance, and be a little serviceable to their glorious intentions.

Your inquiries after the history of the introduction of Christianity into the other English plantations of America must meet with a short and melancholy answer. For one must make very free with that worthy name, if it be said that Christianity is yet well introduced into them. Our islands are indeed inhabited by such as are called Christians; but, alas, how dissolute are their manners! And how inhumane the way of their subsistence, on the sweat and blood of slaves treated with infinite barbarities! What little worship of God they have: as it is confined unto the English liturgy, so it is too commonly performed by parsons, of a very scandalous character.

[Tells how the Society for the Propagation of Religion has ruined the piety of Carolina.] The other colonies have such a religion as your Church of England maintains in many parts of the realm at home; and are, as your neighbors usually are, afraid lest the Dissenters break in to show men the true methods of living to God, and instruct them in a religion that shall not wholly consist in lifeless forms and ceremonies expiating for a vicious life. In Pennsylvania and the Jerseys, and some adjacent places, a congregation of more serious Christians is now and then formed, under the conduct of a godly minister. But then presently some of those missionaries, whose bigotry for their High Church follies is usually more conspicuous than their piety, presently pursue them with all possible disturbances. New England is the only country in America which has much of real and vital religion flourishing in it; and here also your missionaries, who are of little use but to propagate impiety, come to disturb well-ordered churches of God. In many of the other colonies, there are numbers of ungospellized plantations, which have no public worship of God among them. Your society sends not its missionaries unto these. But a country filled with holy churches and pastors cannot have a dozen litigious families in a village where the name of the Church of England pretended by odd people, who know nothing of the matter, may be of use to serve their political and vexatious purposes, but presently the Society dispatch their missionaries hither. [But the Society ruins its own cause by the dissolute character of its missionaries; repeats the story of his difficulties with the *Biblia*.]

Sir, Your most affectionate brother and servant,

To Dr. James Petiver

U/MHS draft   September 24, 1716

(Curiosa Botanica)

Sir,

'Tis high time for me to make you some return that may express my sense of the obligations which your letters with what accompanied them have laid upon me.

[Mentions enclosing six or seven plants thought peculiar to America.]

. . . I hope annually to treat the Royal Society also with such a number of communications that if every member of that illustrious body whose name stands in the catalogue (an honor not yet granted unto mine) will do but half as much, the stores in your collection will soon grow considerable. [Close]

Your most affectionate friend and servant,

The virtues of the
Caltha Sylvatica.

It is the greatest vulnerary in the world. Make a balsam of the green leaves with oil-olive, it cures the most grievous punctures of the nerves, and cuts of all sorts, with an admirable efficacy and celerity. Ordinary wounds are cured with it in four or five hours unto the astonishment of the patient, and extraordinary ones in a few days at farthest. The Indians are extremely venturesome in their fighting, if this traumatic be near them.

Consolida Lappata

For internal wounds, it will do wonders. It relieves oppressions from clotted blood in the stomach. For the spitting of blood it affords a relief hardly to be paralleled.

Ophiophuga

Bruise it, and lay the cataplasm to the part bitten by the rattlesnake; it infallibly and immediately fetches out the horrible poison, which else would in a few hours bring a miserable death upon the patient. It is a marvellous gift of Heaven to the countries which have these venomous vipers in them. 'Tis remarkable that if a man put it in his shoes, no serpent will dare to come near him. The decoction of it is also a good opthalmic.

Fagiana

It grows nowhere but under beech-trees, in shady places. It appears in the summer, and expires in the autumn. An infusion taken inwardly, and a cataplasm used outwardly in cancerous and scrophulous maladies, does things to be wondered at. A tea of it will strangely refresh under and against weariness. And is [word illegible] grand use in malignant fevers.

Formosa

It grows near six foot high. Red flowers on the top give it a lovely aspect. The water in which it is boiled cures inflammations of the eyes that are washed with it. T[wo?] spoonfuls of the said water [will?] cure the malady we call the stomach-ache.

Geranium Americanum

[In the margin: Called by our Indians, Taututtipoag] Inwardly the infusion, and outwardly the cataplasm. [Margin tightly bound, concealing the ending of several words.] 'Tis gr[and?] medicine for [?] foul disease. The whole pl[ant] with the root, boiled [and] applied unto the face, it cures w[hat] we call the ague there, as [well as?] any tumor. A tea of the root is good in fevers, and the palpitation of the heart.

To Dr. James Petiver

U/Brit Mus   September 24, 1716

Sir,

[Thanks Petiver for his letters.]

I perceive that botanic studies are those to which you have more singularly applied your inquisitive and ingenious mind. And now that I may find something which may be a little relishable for you, after that I have mentioned one or two curious observations upon some occurrences in the vegetable kingdom, I will fulfill a promise which I made unto my most valuable Dr. Woodward a few weeks ago, concerning certain American plants which I was collecting for you.

In a field not far from the city of Boston, there were lately made these two experiments.

First, my friend planted a row of Indian corn that was colored red and blue, the rest of the field being planted with corn of the yellow, which is the most usual, color. To the windward side, this red and blue row so infected three or four whole rows, as to communicate the same color unto them, and part of the fifth, and some of the sixth. But to the leeward side, no less than seven or eight rows had the same color communicated unto them, and some small impressions were made on those that were yet further off.

Secondly, the same friend had his garden ever now and then robbed of the squashes which were growing there. To inflict a pretty little punishment on the thieves, he planted some gourds among the squashes (which are in aspect very like 'em) at certain places which he distinguished with a private mark, that he might not be himself imposed upon. By this method, the thieves were deceived, and discovered, and ridiculed. But yet the honest man saved himself no squashes by the trick, for they were so infected and embittered by the gourds, that there was no eating of them.

Several useful hints relating to vegetation and agriculture may be taken from these experiments, which I wholly leave to your sagacity and that of the philosophers to whom you may see cause to mention them.

What remains is to make you a tender of six or seven plants which are here esteemed peculiar to America. I have not yet found them in any European herbals, and if you find that I have been mistaken, you will pardon my ignorance, and still accept my intention.

I have preserved the plants, as well as I can, in a book of brown paper, and have presumed so far as to impose names upon them, and have added schedules declaring the virtues and uses for which our Indians have employed them, and in which our English have been also confirmed by their experience. [Hopes to send other plants.]

. . . I hope annually to treat the Royal Society also with such a number of communications, that if every member of that illustrious body whose name stands in the catalogue (an honor not yet obtained for mine) will do but half as much, the stores in your collection will soon become considerable. [Close]

Sir, Your most affectionate friend and servant,

To John Winthrop

IV Coll 8/MHS   October 15, 1716

My dear Friend,

Si philosopharis, benè est; Ego quoque philosophor—tho' very indifferently, and not likely to do so much more without your friendly assistances. [Regrets not having written in a while, and sends along a book by John Woodward.]

But how obliged would both he [Woodward] and I be, if your inquisitive ingenuity employing the leisure of a gentleman of erudition (which you are) for that purpose, would make as full a collection as may be of the fossils (the names written on each little bundle) to be in *your name* transmitted unto him!

Favor us also with as many communications as you can, and let not the various treasures of natural knowledge wherewith you are enriched, and are daily growing richer and richer, lie by you uncommunicated. A true Winthrop cannot but be generous!

Give me the true story of your Pelton's feeling what was done to his arm at a distance.

But such is the calamity of our time, that philosophy as well as theology is all swallowed up in politics. Yea, I am afraid my poor letter too will hardly be welcome, even to such a friend as you are, without something political in it.

I will not insert anything that you may expect to find among the antiquities of our *Boston News-Letter*. But I will mention to you a curiosity, an occurrence, which is in a letter I received from a famous German divine two days ago. There has been of late a strange and miraculous motion from God upon the minds of the Jewish children in the city of Berlin. The little Jews from eight to twelve years of age, fly to the Protestant ministers, that they may be initiated in Christianity. They embrace it with such rapture that when they see the name of Jesus in a book, they kiss it a hundred times, and shed floods of tears upon it. No methods used by their parents to reduce them are effectual; but they say to their parents, *We shall not return to you; 'Tis time for you to come over to us!* This German divine sees happy auspices in this rare occurrence.

We are at last blessed with the arrival of a new governor, who appears to be of a very easy, candid, gentlemanly temper. Of what principles, you shall guess when you see shortly a sermon which was preached in his audience by one chosen to entertain him in the pulpit at his first arrival.

And now, Sir, give me leave to impose a further trouble upon you.

There is a famous plant in your vicinity at Lebanon, known by the name of Culver's Root—famous for the cure of consumptions. My eldest daughter has been for above six months languishing in what appears to us a consumption, but with odd circumstances which our physicians know not what to make of. I have a strong disposition to become furnished, as soon as ever I can, I say *as soon as ever I can*, with a little quantity of Culver's Root. I know no such likely and speedy way to obtain my desires as to make use of your friendly mediation. You that relieve all the world, and carry on the glory of a family sent into the world on purpose to heal and help its maladies, will, I know, apply yourself to forward the relief of your Mather, with as much alacrity as any in the world. [Close]

Sir, Your most affectionate friend and servant,

To Henry Walrond

DII/AAS draft   October 31, 1716

My dear and most valuable Brother,

[Has no news to report.]

The church which I serve has met in an edifice no less than seventy feet long, sixty-six feet wide, and three tiers of galleries one over another; but yet made so thronged an auditory, that they proposed a swarm. I approved and assisted their motion, helped them to build another meeting-house, and in gathering their church, and ordaining their minister. So I have a flourishing society drawn off from me, but subsisting in the very midst of my own, and such a strange blessing on my own that our congregation hardly misses any of its numbers, and the Lord's-day collections (which in this city bear all our ecclesiastical expenses) are larger than they were before the secession. Within a month or two, another new church will be formed in the south part of our city. And then we shall have seven churches of our United Brethren belonging to this town, besides a synagogue of High Church, and another of the Baptists, and another of the French, with whom we live in all decent agreement.

[Repeats familiar charges against the Society for the Propagation of the Gospel, and his distress over the *Biblia*.]

Among the composures in a packet which now visits you, there is a very little thing entitled *Lapis* etc., which is of greater expectation with me than anything that I have ever yet been concerned in. [Close]

Your most affectionate brother,

To Sir William Ashurst

DII (but with last two   [Probably November, 1716]
paragraphs omitted)/AAS draft

Sir,

[Notes having written to Ashurst recently.]

Three or four of the Representatives (those particularly that act for the city of Boston) have been extremely disaffected unto our agent Mr. D——r and better affected than they should have been unto one whom he had made his enemy by his doing for us the greatest of services. These gentlemen being sufficiently noisy and subtile, and masters of all the arts which were necessary on such an occasion, caused much distemper in the General Assembly at their first coming together.

About nineteen or twenty principal members of the House together did me the honor of a visit, before three days of their session had passed over. At what time I had an agreeable opportunity, first of all, to expatiate on the excellent character of our Governor, and our vast obligations unto you particularly for the share you had in obtaining so rich a blessing for us. And then, I set before them, in as engaging a manner as I could, what reasons there were for our public respects to be still continued unto Mr. D——r. How amply and fully he had been vindicated from aspersions, and how copiously he had been recommended unto us by our best friends with you, for his fidelity and assiduity in our service.

The effect of this conference was beyond what I could have had the vanity to have looked for; a conspicuous change in the tempers and measures of the House ensued. And the House quickly came to very much of what was desired from them. If they do not in the present session come up to all that should be done, it is expected that the men who have been so troublesome will be dropped in the next election, and then the spirit of the people, which appears full of zeal for our Governor and for our agent, will doubtless more fully exert itself.

Our Governor is a person of such candor and goodness, that it is impossible for us to be thankful enough unto our gracious God for him, and unto our good King, and unto the happy instruments of his coming unto us.

Our agent, Mr. D——r, will be animated by the strong passion which his country has discovered for him, to watch all opportunities of being useful to it, in which we are happy that we have Your Honor to be so ready with your suggestions and assistances. His honorable brother will grow continually in the esteem of our people, being a gentleman of right principles and one who by joining lately to one of our churches, has added a strength to the other obligations of a virtuous life, lying upon him. [Close]   Your Honor's most hearty servant,

To Oliver Noyes

DII/AAS draft   [November, 1716]

My honored Friend,

When some gentlemen of your honorable House lately (that is to say, the last Thursday evening) obliged me with a visit, I did offer my present sentiments on two articles, after which there was made some inquiry.

First, concerning our Governor, I declared that I took his candor and goodness to be such that we may be happy in him, and should be thankful for him, and that we shall do well to do everything that may have a tendency to make his government an easy station to him. To this purpose, I read certain passages in letters from our friends abroad. And added my hopes that the faithful methods used continually to rescue His Excellency from some dangers our people were afraid of, would not be ineffectual. And I intimated that I also hoped all wise men would avoid everything that should give the least occasion of suspicion, that they could prefer before him a person of a much less agreeable character for us.

Secondly, concerning our agent, I declared that I was most inclinable to the opinion that we should not be too sudden in laying aside Mr. D——r from his agency with any indignities, inasmuch as all our powerful and more distinguished friends at home were his, and had copiously and vehemently recommended him unto us; and I feared a contempt cast upon him would be such an affront and offense unto them all, as would be greatly to our damage. And though that business of Brand had a very odd aspect, yet there were come over such legal vindications of Mr. D——r, under the seal of the Lord Mayor, and otherwise that it [word illegible] not at all proper publicly to insist upon it. So that some remarkable indiscretion or unfaithfulness in his management seemed the only just cause, at this time, to lay him aside, which, if it were found, there could not one word be spoken for his continuance. But in the meantime, so very great a number of considerable persons in the place were so strongly possessed of his being a great sufferer for his doing a great service for us, they would espouse his cause to such a degree as to make a very uncomfortable clash, which would be attended with much iniquity among us. For which reasons, I could not but think such a matter ought very deliberately to be proceeded in.

This was the sum of my discourse, in all which, as I spoke, *ut qui suum Dominum* [a word illegible], so I wish you could have heard it all. I don't remember that one disrespectful word was uttered of the gentlemen who might have other sentiments, but all possible deference paid unto their merits (tho' no persons particularly mentioned).

Our late Lt. Governor's name did not once occur that I remember in all our conference.

And whereas you have had intimations as if I declared some relinquishment of my former thoughts about our private bank—'tis *cujus contrarium*. I have never done so, to any one man in the world. And at this time I expressly said, 'I may be as qualified as another man to say what I am going to speak, because I suppose I differ from the generality of the gentlemen present in the matter of the bank. I cannot but hope the different views of wise men about that matter will be so temporarily maintained, as not to affect the public tranquillity.'

[Now he will speak more particularly out of friendship to Noyes.]

First, I beseech you to do nothing which they that are most of all jealous of you may have any pretense to construe as a design to give any uneasiness unto our sweet-spirited Governor, and provoke his return, that we may be unhappy in an unknown successor. As His Excellency's interest at home is not easily to be abated, so it will grow among ourselves. And they that shall be thought his enemies will mightily hurt themselves. I much desire that your valuable accomplishments may be ever improved for the benefit of your country.

Secondly, I entreat you to keep your stops in your opposition to what may be the prevailing inclination for Mr. D——r. I take not Mr. D——r to be a personal friend of mine. He has given me cause enough to reckon him very much otherwise. It is very seldom that he has written to me of late years, and when he has done it, I think, it has always been with an acrimony that I take little pleasure in. But I cannot imagine an outrage upon him just now to be seasonable. You sufficiently discharge your conscience in a moderate manifestation of your judgment, and so leaving of it. If the wrath go on, you sacrifice to his numerous friends what your usual prudence in other cases would not so liberally throw away. *Sic causeo.* [Close]

Sir, your most sincere friend and servant,

To John Winthrop

IV Coll 8/MHS   November 19, 1716

Sir,

[Thanks him for his letter.]

The poor damsel is languishing, but has begun the use of the root, whereof the success is with God. May He prepare us for, and carry us through, the sacrifice to which we are called on this occasion.

I comfort myself with hopes of having the honor of that mediation by which there will be conveyed from you, with due acknowledgments of your name and character and family, many valuable communications to our masters in London.

Among these things, when your leisure shall allow it, a full account of the frequent earthquakes about your Hadham (which of late years, they say, have ceased) would be acceptable. [Sends along his sermon preached before the new Governor.]   Your most hearty servant,

To Joseph Parsons

DII (with the long P.S.   January 22, 1717
omitted)/AAS draft

Sir,

Since it is a critical time with you, it appears unto me the best thing that I can do for your service at this time to set before you in as true a light as I can, the true cause of those dark difficulties and encumbrances which attend your proposed settlement in the service of the church now forming in the south part of Boston.

While the ministers of the town are so generally prejudiced, as at present they seem to be, against your being taken into their number, such a settlement seems unto me for a thousand reasons to be despaired of.

But what shall be done for the removal of that prejudice? 'Tis fit you should first of all know the reasons why those faithful servants of God have entertained it.

They seem to fear that you are a person who have sometimes indulged yourself in a *way of lying*, and invented very black slanders of innocent and virtuous men, which is the worst sort of lying, and therewithal improved the arts of insinuation for the sowing of *dangerous discords*.

Upon this fear, tho' their charity be such that they wish well to a good improvement of your talents, yet their conscience of duty to God, and His churches, will not suffer them to recommend you to a flock of such importance, as what is now to be provided for.

The things that have produced a *terror of God* upon their minds about you, are such as these:

You did once and again assert very horrid things concerning Mr. Bulkely, and concerning Mr. Whiting. But the papers lodged in the hands of one of the ministers in this town will doubtless compel all of them, and any others that shall see them, to believe that there was no truth in your assertions.

It is affirmed that you uttered scandals of the same tendency concerning Mr. Woodward, while it was thought he did not favor your interests at Lebanon. But afterwards Mr. Woodward was a better man.

You did report several things much to the defamation of some candidates of the ministry, which were very false; and you never could produce any author for them.

While you pretended the greatest respect unto the two ministers of the North Church, and received nothing but such from them, you did (hoping thereby to ingratiate yourself) at the table of a minister of the South, bestow indecent flings and flouts upon them, for which the mistress of the table severely rebuked you, and told you that you took the wrong way to be ingratiated there. You also know what you said of that gentlewoman when you were afterwards told of this.

You may remember some other mischievous tale-bearings, wherein you were, about that time, detected.

My father then wrote unto you his dissatisfactions. And you never answered his letter.

It is very certain you went into families in our neighborhood and there set yourself to poison them with all possible disaffection to their two ministers. Your practise raised an uncomfortable discord between husband and wife. They that loved us and our ministry found their souls hurt unto such a degree that they desired never to see you more, and obliged your withdraw [sic] from them.

I know something of your way to speak unto my disadvantage, which exposed you to the resentments of some serious people more than you were aware of. All that while, and in all my life, never had I done you any wrong or harm. I now also overcame the evil so far that I discouraged not our private meetings from using of you, tho' one word of mine would have done it. And I now perfectly forgive it all, judging myself obliged, above others, to do you good.

You associated yourself with some of our brethren to form a new church at the north, upon the foundation of an aversion for the two ministers. The defamations with which you fly-blowed the minds of those brethren have not unto this hour worn off their ill impressions. But you know what passed between you and Mr. Gee on that occasion. And if Mr. Gee be compelled now to exhibit the particulars of that story, which he can in part justify (tho' Deacon Atwood be dead), it will make some impression on many that hear it. The design of our New North was delayed a year upon the defeat of your making yourself an interest in such a way.

It is greatly suspected that the troubles in the old church were much owing to your blowing of the coals on the intention of having a new meeting-house built for you.

[Confesses himself unable to offer any advice on how Parsons can clear his name.]

I can only say that if your case were my own, I should not have courage enough to try whether a way could be forced for me into a church in this town with a dislike of it in the most of the ministers, and with a division and contention raised in the place, and a fire, in which I should undergo the utmost hazard of being incinerated. I would much rather accept of opportunities to do good where I should meet with—*Rixae multo minus, invidiaeque;* which you may have the offer of, and which, being offered, such is the tenderness of the ministers for you after all, that they would leave you undisturbed in them.

For my own part, were my assurances of your integrity equal to my dispositions of doing you no hurt, yet I should not think myself strong enough, or bound at all, to engage in any wars to bring about by force of arms your establishment in an uneasy station, and fight the way through an army of contradictions for it.

It may not be amiss for me to add that some eminent persons in the place are of the opinion that you have been so far from having, in your abilities and performances, your profiting appear unto all men, since your first coming hither so many years ago, as to lay them under much discouragement in their hopes of your shining with such a luster as ought to be for a city set upon a hill, the capital city of these colonies. [Close]   Sir, Your thoughtful friend and servant,

Sir,

After I had written the forgoing letter I had many conflicts in my mind whether I should send it unto you or no.

But if you saw my heart, you would see working in it so sincere and so tender a desire to see you in a serviceable and a comfortable condition, and such is the tendency of what I have written, to procure such condition for you, that I send it.

I am still of the opinion that it will be your duty as well as your wisdom to prefer other fields to work in, unto one where unknown and endless humiliations will attend you, and not think of breaking through the bars of a castle.

And it will be a thousand times more honorable for your choice to lead in such a thing, rather than have it owing to a force that it may come to.

One of the most valuable friends which you have, and the most valuable that I have, in the world, seems to be much of the opinion that it would be an unaccountable weakness in you to desire a station where you must have so many, and of such quality, so disaffected.

To Joseph Parsons

U/Scheide   February 4, 1717

Sir,

It is a matter of some concern to me that you should apprehend yourself so much hurt by me as I have heard. I am sure it is quite beside my intention if you have suffered any wrong by anything wherein I have been concerned. And I have declined everything that might have any tendency to raise any prejudice against you, or dislodge you of what esteem you have anywhere enjoyed.

I am freely willing to declare, and I have often declared it, that as to all apprehended personal injuries, they are past and gone, and forgiven, and forgotten, and buried, and you are to me entirely as if they had never been at all. And as to the dissatisfactions of a less personal importance, you have expressed yourself to me so much in the language of a Christian, that I ought to take a kind and a due and a brotherly notice of it.

For which cause, as I ought to leave the flock of the New South unto the direction and government of Heaven in their choice of their minister [crossed out: without interposing any sense of mine to forestall] so, if their choice fall upon you, you will not only find in me all the offices of a candid neighbor, but also I have heard the other servants of God express the like dispositions and resolutions, tho' they do not see light to appear in activities to promote anything which they may fear will prove an occasion of contention. [Close]

Sir, Your friend and servant,

The copy of my letter to you I have never shown to any, but only [crossed out: two or three] some of the ministers of the town, who were before well apprised of the matters in it. I have never spoke of it a syllable to any person of the New South, nor given any copy to any person in the world.

To Joseph Parsons

DII/AAS draft   March 21, 1717

Sir,

[Renews his plea that Parsons and his friends not press for his settlement as pastor of the New South Church.]

Be sure, if you have solicited the votes of any, or importuned them to act for you (which, I am told, you say you never did) this would be so unevangelical a thing that it were alone enough utterly to disqualify the election of a minister.

Instead of this, I find that in the primitive times, when there was a division among a people about the election of a minister, some excellent men of God, whom the votes of many ran upon, cried out, *O people of God, we will throw ourselves overboard rather than the church of the Lord shall suffer any storms for our sakes.* This was the true spirit of the Gospel, well worthy of a Nazianzen and a Chrysostom!

[Says that Parson's settlement in the New South can only be accomplished at the cost of terrible contention, even the dissolution of the church.]

You did upon this [Mather's first letter] address me with many expressions of repentance for the wrong steps you had taken. And tho' they were only in general terms, yet I was willing to declare that so far as they went they were in the language of a Christian, and at the same time I was, yea, ever have been, willing to do the part of a Christian in entirely forgiving and forgetting all personal injuries.

In the short letter wherein I declared this, tho' I intimated that I should leave the South Church to the direction of God, and acquiesce in it, there is no intimation that I could recommend you to their choice, much less that the other ministers could do so, tho' being men of peaceable spirits they have not been ready to appear against you. And the letter has been improved beyond its intention, when this construction has been made of it, for it expressly renounces all *activities* for you.

But while a number of people distinguish themselves by their zeal for your being here, they run you into the hazard of a ruin, which I am now to inform you of. One of them, whose name is Dorby, has lately written a letter to my aged parent, requiring of him an account of the dissatisfactions which have hindered him from recommending you unto that service. And under this compulsion he has prepared an answer to it, which, if it be sent, will be very little to your advantage. When you wronged me t'other day with a false report that I had communicated unto the people of the New South my letter to you, you were pleased to distress a very valuable friend with saying, *That I had utterly ruined you.* To obviate which, and because I desired nothing but your good, that other letter was drawn from me of which a use has been made that good men are troubled at. If the letter which your friends do force the Doctor to, should be sent, all the damage that you feared from what I sent unto you, and what I have been so desirous to save you from, will be unavoidable. But the servant of God, out of tenderness to you, suspends the sending of his letter until the man who addressed him has first spoken with you.

[Warns him against pressing the matter to a formal hearing.]

I earnestly protest unto you, that if you were my own brother I would now persuade you to drop all pretensions here, and be humbly thankful to God that He mercifully opens to you doors of service where you may have more undisturbed opportunities to spend your latter days, in a correction of those errors which have created you so much trouble in all the former stages of your action.

I am, Sir, one that wishes you very well,

To John Winthrop

IV Coll 8/MHS April 8, 1717

Sir,

'Tis with great concern that I have heard of the loss which you and your honorable family have sustained in the death of [your] only son.

A loss to be repaired by none but Him who inflicted it. And may it be so, in the way that He shall choose!

To entertain, and if it may be, to edify your excellent consort in the sadness which this death may give unto her, I make her a humble tender of my *Victorina*. God will have us dead unto the world, and therefore He kills our dearest enjoyments in it. A death so exemplified in the case of my dear *Victorina*, that I hope it may be not unserviceable.

[Asks him to gather "communications" for the Royal Society.]

Sir, Your most hearty servant,

To Robert Wodrow

WII/NLS April 29, 1717

My very dear Friend,

[Sends along his *Zelotes* and *Menachem*.]

The communication between Glasgow and Boston is indeed so seldom (and it has been the more interrupted by the miscarriage of a vessel bound from Glasgow hither above half a year ago, which is not yet arrived), that we are kept in too much ignorance of the circumstances attending the dear Church of Scotland in these days of shaking dispensations, a people of God whose condition the churches of New England have more at heart than any upon earth. [Comforts himself that God will aid the Church of Scotland.]

The last letter wherein I received your favors, was by the hand of young Mr. Erskine, whom, for your sake, as well as that of his excellent father, of whom you gave me so great a character, I treated with all the affection and civility that was possible. I invited and entreated him to let me see him as often as he could; and made as handsome a treat at my table as I could for him, that I might express my regards for his honorable family, and for his patron Mr. Wodrow, and that I might also drop upon him with as much art and love as I could, such admonitions as might be his preservatives. Indeed, he then obliged me with his company; but he was ever after unaccountably shy of giving me the visits which I desired of him. Anon, to my surprise, I was informed that the lad was married! But the plot was carried on with such privacy, that tho' he lives in the same city with me, and not half a mile from me, I never heard one word of the matter until some time after that it was accomplished. Here my story must end!

The lad has never seen me since. The minister who was betrayed and surprised into the doing of his part about the matrimony, is a worthy and a faithful man. And the child having chosen to sit under his ministry, I sent unto him your letter about him, that I might engage his particular care for the future welfare of a youth whose friends are so deeply concerned for his doing well, and so worthy of our doing our best for them. That valuable brother of mine sent me a short note on that occasion, which has in it those emollient passages that may be of some service to the youth with his displeased parent. And for that cause I have here enclosed it. *Valeat quantum valere potest!* [Close]   Sir, Your most affectionate brother and servant,

To John Stirling

U/NLS   [date torn, seemingly
                                              April 29, 1717]

Most reverend Sir,

. . . I can truly say that no part of my correspondence [torn] more grateful than what I have the happiness to [torn] with my most valuable friends in Glasgow, and my o[ther] brethren in the venerable Church of Scotland; and a [torn] with my most honored Stirling, of whom the least I can say is, that of my friends on that island, he is the principal.

[Repeats familiar charges against the Church of England missionaries.]

. . . of the near three hundred publications which have been surprised from this hand, I will freely confess to you that none has had more of my heart, nor is there any that I have been more desirous to see come into operation, than that of the *Lapis è Monte Excisus* which is among those that I now humbly tender to your acceptance. Behold, Sir, a brief system of religion, consisting of, and confined to, such articles as all good men (for the most part at least) are united in; articles which afford a sufficient basis for a union among all the good men in the world; the articles of their goodness; the choice grain of the purged floor. All the controversies agitated upon any point of religion in the world, pretend forever to serve one or other of these maxims. The treatise ostentates very little of learning, but it is the effect of more than a little study. *Intermi, sed non tenuis labor.* . . .

I pray my most affectionate remembrances may be made unto the excellent professors in your University, unto whom I also present the *Lapis è Monte Excisus,* which begins to be recited in our schools. Next unto the felicity I have seen in the favorable aspect which that illustrious body have cast on this unworthy American, I have looked on myself as most highly favored in what I have received from the famous and flourishing Frederician University in the Lower Saxony, whereof the continuation of the *Pietas Hallensis* (as well as diverse other effects of it) has given some very public testimonies. [Close]

Sir, Your most obliged friend and servant,

Sir,

The Indian packet you may, if you please, lodge in the library of your University.

To Dr. John Woodward

U/MHS draft   July 25, 1717

My most honored Friend,

The communications with which I have endeavored some entertainments for you, since I have had the honor to be related unto your illustrious society, have been so many that my letters have pretty near, as I suppose, equalled the number of months that has passed over me, besides what I might say of other performances and remittances. But for these two or three last years I have never been so happy as to know that my packets have not miscarried, and particularly whether what I addressed unto you near a year ago, and the *Hortus siccus* of plants peculiar to America, which I addressed unto Mr. Petiver have reached you. [Says he will double his efforts.]

But I could not let this opportunity pass without beginning to make some amends for my delay to answer your desire to be furnished with some collection of our fossils. The truth is, the load of my various employments obliges me to wish and wait for the assistances of a young gentleman whose name is Mr. John Winthrop, and whose grand-father (the governor of one of our colonies) was a virtuoso in the very beginning of the Royal Society. This ingenious gentleman has promised me his assistances to accomplish what you have desired of me, and as a specimen of more to follow, he enables me now by the hand of one Captain [Ventu?] to transmit unto you a box, which contains between twenty and thirty of such things as you have asked for. I am then to give you his most hearty services, and add that if you please to take some notice of him, when your pen shall again command the leisure of writing for New England, it may still more encourage his industry to help me in executing from time to time all the commands you may lay upon me. He is a man of honor and erudition. [Looks forward to reading Woodward's latest work.]

Your most hearty friend and humble servant,

To Sir William Ashurst

U/Hunt (HM 22312)   August 1, 1717

Honorable Sir,

It is not only my own inclination (tho' heartily and extremely so) but also a command from the ministers of the province, at a late General Convention, that I should render the public thanks to you for all the paternal regards you have expressed for our country, which from no consideration but a generous inclination to do good unto an honest people, you have taken under your auspicious patronage. But they direct me to inform you that they are more particularly thankful for the vast and most comprehensive benefit you have done us in procuring for us a *Governor* who renders us as happy a people as any upon earth; a Governor who will compel us to love him, and love all that have helped us to him; and whose goodness and wisdom will soon triumph over it if any little faction should retain the least uneasiness or disaffection.

[Sends along some "little American entertainments."]

Your Honor's most affectionate friend and obedient servant,

To Dr. Edmund Halley

U/MHS draft   October 1, 1717
(An Eclipse Observed)

Sir,

The services you have done the world by the vast improvements and advancements you have made, especially in the mathematical sciences, which have that peculiar property of certainty to recommend them unto the more polished sort of men, will render your memory as glorious and as lasting as the stars which you touch in your attainments.

Your communications in the *Philosophical Transactions* oblige the curious part of mankind. And those of us who are at a mighty distance below you for skill in the mathematics, are yet more sensibly obliged, when you favor us with points, as you sometimes also do, which are more within the reach of our lower capacities. I am getting ready for you some select and more curious passages, from a manuscript journal of a late voyage round our globe, which I hope to transmit by the next opportunity. In the meantime, something relating to one that every day visits every part of it, shall entertain you. [Praises Halley.]

I could not think of any more agreeable entertainment for you than an observation of a late eclipse, wherein the principal manager was my worthy friend Mr. Thomas Robie, an ingenious young gentleman, and the greatest proficient in astronomical studies which I know in these parts of the world.

Some haziness of the heavens was a little disadvantage to the accuracy of our observation. But yet such as it was, the new astronomical tables which we call Whistonian received a good confirmation from it.

Observations of the sun's eclipse, Sept. 23, 1717, at Cambridge
New England. Lat. 42-25.

Beginning at

Eclipse sensibly decrease,	12ʰ—23¹—00	
a haze being in the atmosphere	1—47—00	
A spot in the eastern limb of the		P.M.
⊙ [symbol for the sun] emery.	3—02—23	
Eclipse ended	3—05—10	

At the beg. of the eclipse,   43—21
the ⊙ altitude

And zenith distance   46—39

At the end, the ⊙ altitude   27—44

And zenith distance   62—16

I have nothing to add but a *serus in coelum redeas*, and that I am, with very great respect, Sir,

Your most affectionate friend and servant,

To Thomas Prince

DII/MHS   October 26, 1717

Sir,

Having first repeated my thanks to you for your goodness in the hopes you have given us of your assistance for the public sacrifices in our church on the morrow in the forenoon, I take the freedom to request that it may be rather before than after nine o'clock in the morning that you let our patriarch have the sight of you; and this (not only because *Aspectus viri boni delectat,* but also) because I would have him to be wholly out of the pain which my absence always gives him. [Brief gossip about an unidentified minister.]

Your brother and servant,

To Wait-Still Winthrop

U/AAS draft   November 11, 1717

My dear and most valuable Friend,

Your pious gratitude unto Heaven disposed you diverse months ago to make an offer of so expensive an action as the publishing of something to serve the glorious cause of piety, and answer the end of the new life which the prayer-hearing Lord has given you.

For diverse reasons I chose both to alter and abate what you proposed in that grateful offer, and instead thereof I prayed the favor of your assistance as far as forty or fifty shillings might go, to an essay upon which my heart is as much set as any that I have ever been concerned in.

'Tis now finished at the shop of the bookseller near our New North Church, to whom I have said that I believed a gentleman would take off a number of the books to the value aforesaid.

But, if there be the least inconvenience or difficulty arisen to divert what was projected——

However, one of them is now humbly tendered unto your acceptance by, Sir, Your most sincere friend and servant,

To John Winthrop

IV Coll 8/MHS   November 15, [1717]

Sir,

The providence of our God most sensibly interposing has again put upon me the honor of doing justice to a family to which I have always had a strong attachment.

I could not have a more candid and constant friend than your honorable father; and I shall be ever proud of paying my due acknowledgments unto his merit in the most public manner that is possible.

I find that elogies [sic] go down best, and have the most kindly operation, when they are concise, and comprehend much in a little, and speak but what everyone felt the truth of.

If you do this poor sermon the honor of passing thro' the press, the sooner the better. (Perhaps Mr. Philips might order the press which he is more particularly master of, to do it out of hand.) Because the season of such things adds unto the beauty of them, and you know Tiberius's compliment unto the Trojans. [Close]

Sir, Your most hearty friend and servant,

This minute, Crump (who is Mr. Philips's printer) happens to come unto me upon an errand. And he tells me that if you think fit to have the work done, in a large, fair, decent character (which is all he has unemployed) he will with all his heart immediately go on the service proposed.

But I entirely leave all to your discretion.

III

LATE in 1717, Cotton Mather began to raise money and goods toward founding a new college in Connecticut. He wrote to one likely sponsor, ELIHU YALE (1649–1721), a New Englander by birth but now a wealthy London diamond trader, official of the East India Company, and philanthropist. Yale had been contributing to the young collegiate school at Saybrook as early as 1714, when he sent about a thousand books for its library. When a new building was begun at New Haven, Mather wrote to GOVERNOR GURDON SALTONSTALL (1666–1724), the great-grandson of Nathaniel Ward, hinting broadly that Yale could be persuaded to contribute handsomely if the school were named after him. He was right: in June, 1718, Yale sent over books, three bales of goods, and an expensive portrait by Kneller—the largest private contribution made to the school before the mid-nineteenth century. At the September commencement both the building and the school received Yale's name. (In the same month, Yale was sued by the Exchequer when a goldsmith for whom he stood surety absconded with 14,000 pounds, which Yale paid.)

Mather knew that Yale's munificence was largely the product of Jeremiah Dummer's salesmanship. In 1712 Dummer had been appointed colonial agent for Connecticut. It was Dummer who first interested Yale in the college and later managed to divert the beneficence of the wealthy Hollises from Harvard to Yale. He also persuaded Newton to send some of his works to Yale, and Steele to send complete sets of the *Tatler* and *Spectator*. Whatever reservations Mather had about Dummer's character were dwarfed by his awareness of the influence Dummer could wield in London. Dummer's fruitful efforts on behalf of Yale College were probably driven in part by the fact that, despite his considerable academic attainments, he had been turned down for a teaching post at Harvard: Samuel Sewall and others (Mather at times included) distrusted Dummer's Europeanized theology and manners.

Mather's own efforts for Yale stemmed from his wish to see established another nursery for New England's ministry; but, like Dummer's, they also took a special enthusiasm from his quarrels with Harvard. Like Dummer, he persuaded Yale and the Hollis family to turn their benefactions from Harvard to Yale. His diary for the period erupts into sneers at "the senseless diversions which they call the Commencement at Cambridge," and into cries of nearly uncontainable resentment: "Oh! for a wise, a meek, a humble, and a patient conduct under the venom and malice which the disaffected rulers of our College treat me withal!" The growth of Yale delighted Mather in proportion to how much indifference the Harvard Corporation showed to his talents. He prayed that "our College might be rescued into a better condition" and believed Harvard to be in a serious decline. Others shared his belief. In November, 1718, Samuel Sewall stood up at a meeting of the overseers and complained, against President Leverett, that the exposition of scripture in the College Hall was not being carried out.

Another indication of decline was the fracas involving Ebenezer Pierpoint, to whom in 1718 the college refused an M.A. on grounds of incompetence, and because Pierpoint used disrespectful language to the academic authorities. In an unprecedented action, Pierpoint sued in the civil courts, prosecuting, for slander, the tutor who had reported his supposed offenses. For his defense he mustered the Dudleys, the Council, and of course the anti-Harvard Mathers. The suit was dismissed in court, but it threatened the breakup of the college and began a campaign of criticism against it that lasted for five years. Mather expected, as his letters reveal, to capitalize on the Pierpoint episode by pressing Samuel Shute to bring the college further under the jurisdiction of the governor and the civil courts. Shute owed him some favors: Mather had written several fulsome panegyrics on him and constantly wrote to England to anticipate and forestall any charges that might be brought against him from his opponents in Massachusetts. Despite his involvement Mather did not relish the hubbub, and wrote in his diary that he wished to see an end to party spirit in Boston.

At the same time a unique opportunity arrived for Mather to Do Good to his dearest friend, John Winthrop. Mather did all he could to relieve Winthrop in what finally made Connecticut un-livable for him—the protracted turmoil created by disputed titles to Indian lands in the colony. In 1684, a drunkard son of Uncas, sachem of the Mohegan Indians, deeded a vast tract of land to Capt. James Fitch, a magistrate, who began selling the lands throughout eastern Connecticut. The Winthrops regarded Fitch as an upstart. Soon both parties prosecuted the others' tenants as trespassers. The Winthrops and their adherents, Fitch and his, became warring factions. The land dispute engaged Connecticut politics, for the judges who decided the validity of the titles were political appointees of the Assembly. The hundreds of landowners who comprised each faction struggled to elect their own men, on whom their property rights ultimately depended. The dispute merely simmered between 1705 and 1717, when a "native right" party arose and a series of land battles ensued, lasting into the 1720's. These sometimes ended in riots and, so Governor Saltonstall and others complained, in an erosion of law and authority in Con-necticut.

John Winthrop suffered from being at the center of the dispute. The tenants on his father's land used the uncertainty of the land titles as an excuse for withholding their rent. Winthrop had other gripes against Connecticut, where he felt he had never received the respect due to a Winthrop. He disliked Governor Saltonstall be-cause he believed both that he, a Winthrop, should be governor, and that Saltonstall connived in turning his tenants against him. After preaching very successfully in New London, Saltonstall had been chosen in 1707 to succeed Fitz-John Winthrop as governor, and he was annually reelected for as long as he lived. (A wealthy, orthodox, and somewhat pompous man, he would have been pleased by Cotton Mather's description of him as "a constellation of the most fulgid endowments.") Seeing Winthrop, his dearest friend, disgruntled and uncomfortable, Mather tried to relieve him, even while a new fever epidemic raged in Boston, carrying away many noted people and many members of Mather's congregation. He wrote on Winthrop's behalf to Increase Mather, to Governor Hunter of New York, and to Governor Saltonstall.

Mather's intercession for Winthrop gave him the delicate task of Doing Good for his friend through the governor, his friend's enemy. The task was made even more difficult by Mather's own dissatisfaction with Winthrop, which often broke through the usually cordial tone of his letters to Winthrop as muted admonitions. In the interesting letter of August 25, 1718, for instance, Mather urges Winthrop to leave Connecticut and come to live in Boston, as a last resort (Winthrop actually was thinking of migrating to England). In Boston Winthrop could be "serviceable, as they have been from whom you are descended." Mather was telling Winthrop not only that he could live more peacefully in Boston, but that the change might help him to conquer his well-known inactivity and, by enlisting his presumed gifts, lead him to recover his failure to live up to the family's achievements. Mather came close to sharing Sibley's sentiment that John Winthrop "inherited the Winthrop name without an ability to maintain the Winthrop character."

Mather's concern for Winthrop was not selfless. He had reason to feel indebted to Winthrop. Mather's *Curiosa Americana* dated December 10, 1717 ("A Horrid Snow") is followed in this section by a letter which Winthrop sent to Mather three months earlier. For whole paragraphs Winthrop's letter is identical to Mather's and raises questions about Mather's honesty. Much material in the *Curiosa* came to Mather from his friends and correspondents. Yet he very rarely mentioned their names in his communications to the society, and almost never as the sources of his information. In September, 1712, for instance, he asked his friend Samuel Penhallow for an account of some trees found far underground. We do not have Penhallow's reply, but we do have the letter on this oddity which Mather sent to the society; nowhere in it does he hint at Penhallow's aid. Again in December, 1713, Mather wrote asking Penhallow for an account of "two very sympathizing sisters at Hampton," which also became the subject of a communication, again without Penhallow's name. Mather also got reports from his friend Thomas Prince, to whom he wrote asking for news of birds "rained" at Newtown, of a leviathan dug up at Virginia, and of a strange birth. All of these became the subjects of separate *Curiosa*.

It is impossible to say how much Mather merely parroted from these informants and from others he used. But a comparison of his letter to the society with Winthrop's letter to him suggests that, even in eighteenth-century terms, it exceeded the borrowing acceptable and necessary within the community of science and scholarship. Another time he got some information about the waterdove from Winthrop, and wrote to tell him that he had given it "a very fair lodging in our *Biblia Americana,* with an honorable mention and character of the generous hand, which . . . sends him forth unto us." In the manuscript of the *Biblia,* Mather wrote in his debt to "my ingenious friend, Mr. John Winthrop, from whom I have this communication"; but later he scratched out and nearly obliterated the words "ingenious" and "Mr. John Winthrop," leaving only "my friend from whom I have this communication." The shabby fact about this "fair lodging" of Winthrop's name is that Winthrop was Mather's best friend, one of the few men he could talk to naturally. Except for the undercurrent of disappointment, Mather's correspondence with him radiates cheery comradery and good wishes. In many letters he promises to boost Winthrop's name in London as a devoted amateur scientist. Yet Winthrop was not elected to membership in the society until 1733, sixteen years after writing his letter on the snowfall for Mather, five years after Mather's death, and apparently on his own merits. Mather could have, and because of Winthrop's help should have, promoted him. But one concludes that he would not allow friendship to detract from his own fame.

Where his own reputation was not at stake, however, Mather was unfailingly generous and charitable. He encouraged another friend, Samuel Sewall, who noted in his diary at the time that John Leverett "had laid out Madam [Rebekah?] Brown for me." In recommending widow Brown to Sewall, Mather saw another opportunity for one of his many puns (see the letter in this section); meanwhile Sewall had begun courting the famed Madam Winthrop, the widow of Mather's friend Wait-Still Winthrop). He also counselled his wife's young nephew, Samuel Bishop, sent money for his wife's relative, Mrs. Anne Wyrly (despite his own straitened circumstances), and attempted as always to play something of the role of a bishop in settling church disputes in other New England congregations.

To Elihu Yale

U/AAS   December 3, 1717

Sir,

When our sacred oracles mention *priests clothed with salvation* we consider them as persons who have nothing but salvation, and what leads to it, conspicuous on them: a most conscientious care to obtain salvation themselves, and assist all that are concerned in them also to obtain it. . . .

We hope this has been the endeavor and the character of those to whom you have lately made a generous present for the clothing of them; and as you have had the satisfaction of being so persuaded on good grounds concerning them, that it is indeed so, and that your civility has not been misplaced, so we would now add unto it by informing you that your present is arrived, and we return you our humble thanks for your favor in it.

Your own goodness in dispensing as well as that of your worthy kinsman Col. Tayler in proposing, such a testimony of your esteem for us, is what we acknowledge with the gratitude which becomes us. And we make no doubt that the more you are truly apprised of what we are and what we mean, you will be but the more confirmed in your opinion that a variety of sentiments in matters of doubtful disputation is very consistent with all possible exercises and expressions of charity in good men towards one another, under their various illuminations. In short, Sir, the ministers of Boston are those genuine Protestants who maintain that the sacred Scriptures are a sufficient rule for belief and practise in the church of God; and that for the interpretation of the sacred Scriptures, every Christian has the right of judging for himself. As they exert no ecclesiastical tyranny on their people, and expect them to receive nothing from them in their ministry but from an evidence wherewith conscience is convinced, so they impose no terms of communion but those which are the plain terms of salvation, and with an equal brotherly love they embrace all that have a true piety appearing in them, whatever different forms may distinguish them in lesser matters. [Florid close]

Your truly grateful friends and servants,

To James Clark

U/AAS draft   December 4, 1717

Sir,

[Thanks him for his letters.]

I sympathize with you in the troubles which the building of new kirks occasions among you. But from our city of Boston you will have little testimony against the irregularities of such motions in the city of Glasgow. We have no parishes. Our people do live strangely intermixed. Several times within these few years the zeal of pews and seats has produced new meeting-houses. The ministers of the city generously give way to the inclinations of the people: assist them in their first embodying, dismiss any of their flocks that go from them, keep up a spirit of charity, of communion, of self-denial, entirely leave it unto the Lord of Hosts by His work on the hearts of the people to determine their auditories for them. And it marvellously comes to pass that they still have sufficient and very numerous auditories, and their subsistence, which is in that uncommon way of the Lord's-day collections, is not abated by the swarms which we part withal. Thus we jog on lovingly and peaceably, and gain all good ends better than if we made our too-just remonstrances against the fault of their being too insensible of their strong obligations unto their pastors. There will on these occasions be many crooked things that cannot be made straight, and I have told you our poor way of dealing with them.

[Has little else to report.]

Sir, Your most affectionate brother and servant,

To Sir William Ashurst

U/AAS draft   December 10, 1717

Sir,

[No news to report.]

I am troubled that a country so much indebted, and I think I may say, so well-affected, unto so excellent a Governor, does not rise to higher expressions of their gratitude unto him. The Massachusetts province, imagining a thousand a year to be a pretty tolerable advance for their part of a salary, are not yet sensible that by the iniquity and confusion in our trade, what is called a thousand is not really so. But I am in hopes they will shortly grow into a better sense, and let so good a Governor see how desirous they are to keep him.

[Sends along some recent publications.]

Your servants in the Indian commission get on as well as we can. And there are especially two things which we have now in view for our encouragement. First, we are getting into a hopeful way to have young Indians under an education that may qualify them to be instructors unto their countrymen. And, secondly, we have a comfortable prospect of having a considerable number of our eastern savages brought over from the popish to the Protestant religion.

I will only add that among your commissioners, we have so singular a blessing in the discretion, fidelity, and activity of Col. Winthrop that we cannot but wish that whatever you can allow to him of the conveniency he desires in the remittances hither, may be allowed him.

Death has lately deprived us of his honorable kinsman Major General Winthrop. . . . [Close]

I am, Your Honor's most sincere and humble servant,

To John Stirling

U/NLS (draft at AAS)   December 10, 1717

Most honored Sir,

[His *Biblia* remains unpublished; sends along *Malachi*.]

You exceedingly revived me with one word you let fall, which intimated as if there might be a possibility of our *Testimonium Glascuense* being published with you. The copy I sent unto London, which was honored with a preface of the famous Dr. Edwards unto it, was unaccountably lost in the death of the bookseller, and sometime after, in the death of the Doctor himself. So I buried it. But an eminent person in the west of England lately wrote me bitter lamentations that the Whistonian Arianism had begun to infect not only the Church of England, but also the young Dissenting ministers in those parts of the country; and this renewed my thoughts that a testimony against that pernicious heresy may be seasonable. If ours may be thought of any use at all, I shall very much rejoice in your giving what countenance you think fit unto it. I only request that it may still be dated for the year 1713, when it was written, and that you lay aside the name of the writer, any further than as he may pass for a *Glascuensian*; and that an expression within the four first pages, of *The Father be the Fountain of the Deity* be changed into *The Father be the Fountain in the Deity*; and that the press-work be carefully inspected and faithfully corrected; and, finally, that my most honored Principal Stirling will please to alter, omit, supply, do everything in it, as his great judgment, unto which I entirely leave it, shall see cause to direct. [Close]

With utmost regards, Your sincere servant,

To Dr. John Woodward

Murdock/MHS   December 10, 1717
(A Horrid Snow)

Sir,

Tho' we are got so far onward as the beginning of another winter, yet we have not forgot the last, which at the latter end whereof, we were entertained and overwhelmed with a snow which was attended with some things that were uncommon enough to afford matter for a letter from us.

[Mentions various unusual snows described by Tacitus, Boethius and others.]

On the twentieth of the last February, there came on a snow which being added unto what had covered the ground a few days before, made a thicker mantle for our mother than what was usual; and the storm with it was for the following day so violent, as to make all communication between the neighbors everywhere to cease. People for some hours could not pass from one side of a street unto another, and the poor women who happened at this critical time to fall into travail, were put unto hardships which anon produced many odd stories for us. But on the twenty-fourth day of the month comes Pelion upon Ossa. Another snow came on which almost buried the memory of the former, with a storm so furious that Heaven laid an interdict on the religious assemblies throughout the country on this Lord's-day, the like whereunto had never been seen before. The Indians near a hundred years old affirm that their fathers never told them of anything that equalled it. Vast numbers of cattle were destroyed in this calamity, whereof some that were of the stronger sort were found standing dead on their legs, as if they had been alive, many weeks after, when the snow melted away; and others had their eyes glazed over with ice at such a rate, that being not far from the sea, their mistake of their way drowned them there.

One gentleman, on whose farms there were now lost above eleven hundred sheep, which with other cattle were interred (shall I say, or inniced) in the snow, writes me that there were two sheep very singularly circumstanced. For no less than eight and twenty days after the storm, the people pulling out the ruins of above a hundred sheep, out of a snow bank which lay sixteen foot high drifted over them, there were two found alive, which had been there all this time, and kept themselves alive by eating the wool of their dead companions. When they were taken out, they shed their own fleeces, but soon got into good case again.

[Mentions the fate of other creatures: two swine buried for twenty-seven days and found alive, hens and turkeys found alive after a week.]

These carnivorous sharpers, and especially the foxes, would make their nocturnal visits to the pens where the people had their sheep defended from them. The poor ewes big with young were so terrified with the frequent approaches of the foxes, and the terror had such impression on them, that most of the lambs brought forth in the spring following, were of Monsieur Reynard's complexion, when the dams were all either white or black.

[After the snowfall, an "infinite multitude" of sparrows appeared.]

It is incredible how much damage was done to the orchards; for the snow freezing to a crust, as high as the boughs of the trees, anon split them to pieces. The cattle also, walking on the crusted snow, a dozen foot from the ground, so fed upon the trees as very much to damnify them.

The ocean was in a prodigious ferment, and after it was over, vast heaps of little shells were driven ashore, where they were never seen before. Mighty shoals of porpoises also kept a play-day in the disturbed waves of our harbors.

[Whole houses were covered with snow.]

And now, I am *satis terris nivis*. And here is enough of my winter-tale. If it serve to no other purpose, yet it will give me an opportunity to tell you that nine months ago I did a thousand times wish myself with you in Gresham College, which is never so horribly snowed upon. But instead of so great a satisfaction, all I can attain to is the pleasure of talking with you in this epistolary way, and subscribing myself, Sir,   Yours with an affection that knows no winter,

JOHN WINTHROP TO COTTON MATHER
IV Coll 8/MHS   September 12, 1717

Sir,

. . . among the small flock of sheep that I daily fold in this distant part of the wilderness (for I am a poor shepherd) to secure them from the wild rapacious quadrupeds of the forest, that after the unusual and unheard of snows, the aforesaid animals, from the upland parts of the country, was in great numbers forced down to the seaside among us for subsistence, where they nested, kenneled, and burrowed in the thick swamps of these ample pastures, nightly visiting our pens and yards for their necessity etc., and the ewes big with young being often terrified and surprised, more especially with the foxes, during the deep snows. It had such impression on them that the biggest part of the lambs they brought forth in the spring are of Monsieur Reynard's complexion and color, when their dams were all either white or black. The storm continued so long and severe that multitudes of all sorts of creatures perished in the snow drifts. Lost at our island and farms above eleven hundred sheep, besides some cattle and horses interred in the snow; and it was very strange that twenty-eight days after the storm, our tenants at Fishers Island, pulling out the ruins of one hundred sheep out of one snow bank in a valley where the snow had drifted over them sixteen foot, found two of them alive in the drift, which had lain there all that time, and kept themselves alive by eating the wool off the others that lay dead by them; as soon as they were taken out of the drift they shed their own fleeces, and are now alive and fat, and I saw them at the Island the last week, and are at your service.

The storm had its effects also on the ocean. The sea was in a mighty ferment and, after it was over, vast heaps of the enclosed shells came ashore, in places where there never had been any of the sort near before. Neptune with his trident also drove in great schools of porpoises, that our harbor and river seemed to be full of them; but none of these came on shore, but kept a play day among the disturbed waves. . . .

To Governor Saltonstall

U/AAS draft   December 23, 1717

Sir,

[No news to report.]

We have had your sympathy with us in the dark time that we have lately had passing over us, wherein we have lost very many of our more pious and elder people, besides the men of station. But our city, whereof the bill of mortality for the month of November made eighty-four, is now in a better state of health, and the inhabitant says not, I am sick, as formerly.

In our nation there seems to be an admirable tranquillity, and the building of two new houses in the capital city, within these few months, is brought as one demonstration of the growing satisfaction. But a tremendous growth of immorality, and a taint little short of universal, on the morals of the nation, has an aspect which wise and good men can do no other than tremble at.

Concerning our present King, I will observe two things remarkable.

The first remark is old Mr. Boldes'—that our King has not one enemy in the world, but what is an enemy to the Kingdom of our Saviour, but what maintains principles and pursues interests inimical to the Kingdom of our Saviour.

The second is another's. That our King is the only King upon earth who has declared himself willing that our Lord Jesus Christ should be restored unto His Throne, which is by persecution everywhere denied unto Him. There is not another King upon the earth but what usurps upon the Throne of God in the conscience of man. Ours would have our Lord Jesus Christ reign there, if his own froward, foolish, and unjust subjects did not hinder him.

[Notes the progress of Reformation in France.]

All that I shall add is to request a favor. We have had written to us an odd story from Saybrook, of some diabolical occurrences relating to a fellow who was in pursuit of Kidd's hidden treasures. To have such things well-attested, or well-confuted, is a thing of some good consequence. To get all real proofs of an invisible world thoroughly confirmed is a thing well worthy of a gentleman, and even of a governor. Don't think every honest man to be relied on as worthy to be ranked among the *wise men of inquiry* (as the Jews call their philosophers) on such occasions. I humbly request Your Honor to take that Saybrook affair under your cognisance and let your more exquisite sense thereof determine what is to be received. [Close]

To John Ruck and John Frizzel

U/AAS draft   [late 1717?]

My constant Friends,

Since the kindness of an obliging flock (to whom I owe my all) has allowed my removal to a habitation in which I count myself as happy as this world can make me, my old cottage so spends its rents in repairs, and is so occupied by tenants who think it best for them to pay no rents at all, that everyone advises my exposing it unto sale.

You are sensible that I am a very unskilful and unactive sort of a man in matters of buying and selling (my trade being always confined unto one commodity—that is, books). And you don't like me the worse for that.

Now I must either be a man something for this world (which you won't approve) or else I must fly to you, whose constant friendship I often tried but never tired.

Pardon me, that I am so rude as to entreat this favor of you; that you would examine the house and land, state a good, stout, sufficient price for it, and put me into the best way for the sale of it.

The truth is, as times go, a very noble salary from a liberal and generous people will need such an accession as the interest of that money to support unavoidable expenses.

I can plead this for my own excuse in this troubling of you: I never ask anything from the best friend in the world, but what I should myself be ready to do, and with all imaginable pleasure do, for every man in the world.

A multitude of blessings from above is always wished you, by, Your most hearty servant,

Unaddressed

U/AAS draft   January 6, 1718

Reverend Sir,

Your funeral sermon on our departed friend I have perused with much satisfaction in the solid, proper, lively thoughts with which it has entertained me. I am greatly gratified with the composure, both for the matter and manner of it; and above all, for the faithful warnings to an unfruitful people given in it. I am so much a well-willer to the design of publishing it, that if any pecuniary assistance towards it be necessary, my mite shall be contributed among the rest. [Crossed out in the margin: which I can't forbear saying in a parenthesis, is more than the chief subject of your generous elogy [sic] would have offered you on a much more just occasion.] And, if an expression of my esteem for Mr. Shepard and his performance were all that would be expected in a preface unto it, I should count my mean hand honored in a leave to write one. But some weighty reasons, wherein mere conscience, and a concern for the honor of our holy religion (which has been deeply wounded) and which I may more fully explain to you if I should live to have the pleasure of seeing you, oblige me to decline the office of giving a character. Especially, having been so warned as I was in a very odd preface to a funeral sermon on Mr. Green, by a javelin thrown, as it was thought, with a particular aim at me, for the honorable testimony I bore to some servants of God much superior to either the writer or the written of. According to your desire I return your M.S.S. with my hearty thanks for the communication.

[The rest of the letter deals with troubles in the church in Brookline.]

To Elihu Yale
Quincy (with many errors)/AAS draft   January 14, 1718

Sir,

[Describes the piety and liberality of the New England way of worship.]

The people for whom I bespeak your favors, are such true, sound, generous Christians and Protestants, that their not observing some disputable rites (which no act of Parliament has imposed on these plantations) ought by no means to exclude them from the respects of all that are indeed such, and from the good will which we all owe to the rest of the reformed churches, all of which have their little varieties.

You have, Sir, been therefore most kindly inquisitive what you may do for such a people. And I will presume upon so much of an answer to your noble inquiries as to suggest not what you may do, but whom you have to do for.

The colony of Connecticut, having for some years had a college at Saybrook, without a collegiate way of living for it, have lately begun to erect a large edifice for it in the town of New Haven. The charge of that expensive building is not yet all paid, nor are there yet any funds, of revenues, for salaries to the professors and instructors of the society.

Sir, tho' you have your felicities in your family, which I pray God continue and multiply, yet certainly, if what is forming at New Haven might wear the name of *Yale College*, it would be better than a *name of sons and of daughters*. And your munificence might easily obtain for you such a commemoration and perpetuation of your valuable name, which would indeed be much better than an Egyptian pyramid.

We have an excellent friend, our agent Mr. Jeremiah Dummer, who has been a tender, prudent, active and useful patron to the infant college of Connecticut, as well as many other good interests; and will have his memory precious with a good people, and among them that survive him, for his having so signally befriended it on all occasions. He will doubtless wait upon you and propose to you, and concert with you, the methods in which your benignity to New Haven may be best expressed.

Nor will it be any disadvantage unto your person or family for a good people to make mention of you in their prayers unto the glorious Lord, as one who has loved their nation and supported and strengthened the seminary from whence they expect the supply of all their synagogues. [Close]   Your most sincere friend and servant,

To Increase Mather

U/AAS draft   [Probably February
                                                or March, 1718]

Sir,

My very high esteem for Col. Winthrop, and my perpetual and even passionate regard for the welfare of him and his, is well known unto you.

I was lately informed that the Governor had entertained some displeasure at him, which might issue in his being removed from a station which I always think with pleasure of his being in.

I know not that ever I once visited the Governor in my life, but under the influence of a thought which I doubt comes but seldom into the souls of those who are with bitter hatred raging and railing at me, for the little acquaintance I have maintained with him; that is to say, *what good may I do? what service is to be done for CHRIST, or for some whom He would have to be served?*

Under the influence of this thought I went this week unto the Governor, and finding to be true what I had heard, I remonstrated unto him with all the importunity that I could use for my life, that Col. Winthrop was 'a gentleman of excellent piety and of bright abilities, and of a fine education, and of a worthy family, and (if that would weigh anything) so much my friend that I felt all that was done to him, and therefore—'

The Governor's answer to me was to this effect, 'that his dissatisfaction at Mr. Winthrop was Mr. Winthrop's being evidently and violently attached unto Noyes's party and designs and interests, the whole aim whereof was not merely to treat him with continual indignities, and render him uneasy, but also to embroil and undo the country. And that Noyes's disciples did very much disqualify themselves for any good aspect of his upon them.'

I don't remember that the Governor mentioned particulars upon this head. But he particularly told me he took it very ill, that when the 'Council-board had with so much unanimity directed the court to take some cognisance of Colman's arraigning the legislature as *establishing iniquity by a law*, Col. Winthrop openly went off the bench, in such a manner as had a tendency to animate a mutinous mob against the government.'

He added that Col. Winthrop was become so incurable in his adherence to a very ill party of men, that his best friends and relatives were——

I let him know that I still insisted on my petition, because I certainly knew he was a man of so strict virtue and honor, it was by pure mistake if any wrong step were ever taken by him.

At last the Governor told me he would put off till Friday some things he intended for Tuesday. And the least signification that Col. Winthrop was at all sensible that his measures had not been so well-considered and disposed to endeavor what he should apprehend most for the public welfare, without being biased by the private views of them who aim at hurting and wounding a Governor that intends no harm to any of them—should incline him to the favorable side.

Now, Sir, I have many reasons to think it will be to no purpose for me to confer with Col. Winthrop on this occasion. The opinion which is entertained of me in the town with some where I little deserve it, I am well aware of. Nor am I willing to meddle with their civil affairs.

But nothing shall forbid my concern for Col. Winthrop's prosperity.

And his veneration for you will oblige him to take much notice of what you shall say to him.

I do therefore entreat you to procure an interview this day with my dear friend, and lay all these things before him, which I choose to give you in writing that so (having so very many things to think of) your memory (which holds to a wonderment) may not lose one punctilio in the recitation. I am, Sir,   Your son,

[To Samuel Sewall]

U/AAS draft   [March 17, 1718]

Sir,

You have so much answered the character of the Arabian judges in doing of justice, and loving of mercy, for the widow, that I cannot but believe my poor *Marah* will be welcome to you.

But Your Honor will allow me now at length to offer you my

opinion that all the regards are not yet paid which you owe unto the widow, and which are expected from you.

I know not whether Keturah was a widow or no; but I know that the patriarch Abraham, whose name is more diffused and perfumed than any man's that ever was upon the earth, was a widower, and you know the rest.

In short, if once you could be thrown into a *Brown*-study upon the matter, I believe you would soon see yourself in a way of making the remainder of your pilgrimage as happy as it can be in this present evil world. [Close]   Your Honor's most hearty servant,

[To Governor Saltonstall]

U/AAS draft   March 25, 1718

Sir,

[Opens with rather florid praise of the governor's character.]

I confess Mr. Winthrop to have been very much recommended unto my tenderest, and I will ask leave to say, paternal regards: by his original, by his education, by his capacities to do good in the world, and by a thousand civilities I have received from him. At the same time I cannot conceal it that I have with trouble more than once heard it, not only that many people in Connecticut use him coarsely, rudely, with much rusticity and expression of aversion, but also that in some law-suits he has been in danger of meeting with very evident injustice and oppression. I have heard it that he has apprehended himself so oppressed as to be under strong temptations of resolving to pluck up stakes and throw himself upon such methods as use to be the effects of strong resentments. Not one word of all this have I heard, that I remember, from himself. 'Tis the report of which others have occasionally made me sensible. And the distress it gives me compels me to solicit Your Honor, on the behalf of this my friend and son, that you would please, with your usual wisdom and goodness, to advise him if there be any part or step of his conduct which it may be necessary for him to take, that he may more oblige a people whom we may by some small thing or other which we ourselves are not so well aware of, greatly indispose unto us. And my solicitations go on, with my petition that you would kindly take him as far as may be under your protection and patronage, and as far as your discretion shall allow of it, make your influences useful to him among your people. 'Tis pity, his talents, of more sorts than one, should be rendered useless to the colony; pity, his neighborhood should lose the benefits of his presence with you; pity, one of such accomplishments and other circumstances that speak for him, should sink under discouragements. I am assured I need say no more. I am certain Your Honor wishes exceeding well unto my *Ascanius*. I am satisfied, your first thoughts on the subject I have written of will suggest something beyond all that I can write; and my son will soon feel the cherishing rays of your favor upon him.

I have nothing to add. . . .

Your Honor's most affectionate servant,

P.S. *Nothing to add!* I must add something because I blush to address you without some ultramarine communications. And yet I can think of nothing worthy to be called anything more than nothing. Such a thing is a copy of what I have just now written to the East Indies, by which you will perceive two things: first, what is a-doing there, about which your extensive genius is, I know, inquisitive; and, secondly, what my poor thoughts are about what is now daily to be looked for, wherein, ever since last February was a twelvemonth, I know not that there is one minister in the country of the same opinion with me. When it has answered these two ends, Your Honor will permit the return of it, and pity me under the encumbrances of so many correspondences; but yet rejoice with me that when the envy and contempt which my own country continually treats me, and even tires me withal, does greatly cripple my opportunities at home, and leave me none but what the providence of Heaven strangely preserves and reserves for me, my opportunities to do good in any other countries do so grow upon me. [Sends along one of his recent treatises.]

Unaddressed

U/AAS draft   April 29, 1718

Sir,

A very few words may serve to answer your two inquiries.

You inquire, first, whether Judas partook in the sacrament of the Lord's Supper with the rest of the disciples.

It appears at the least very questionable whether he did or no; or, 'tis rather past question, that he *did not*. For this decision, waiving the opinion of the ancients, which lies that way, it is enough to observe that it is said, *Having received the sop, he went out immediately*. The sop was a part of a rite belonging to the paschal lamb. If he then went *out immediately* he did not stay for what was to be done after this. The institution of our eucharist was after this. And the season was now such, that Judas apprehended the affair he was now upon, to require a dispatch that would not allow him to stay until our Saviour had finished what he had now to do at this interview with his disciples. Most certainly, our Saviour, who expected that son of perdition in His prayers for those who were to enjoy the benefits of His approaching death, would not admit him to enjoy the symbols of those benefits.

You inquire next:

Whether a man whose wife obtains a legal divorce from him upon a conviction of an adultery, may afterwards marry the woman with whom he had committed it.

The most illustrious divines among the Protestants have generally concurred unto it, that a divorced adulterer may be permitted another marriage, for the same reason that marriage is directed as the remedy and prevention of impurities. The government of the place not inflicting the just punishment of death on the criminal, and the divorce having dissolved the former marriage as death would have done, what shall he do in the unhappy case of burning, but use the course which the compassion of Heaven has prescribed for it! But tho' the law of man should allow another marriage unto an adulterer, yet there are some circumstances which the everlasting law of the Holy God will require to be complied withal; and more especially if the adulteress be the person with whom the marriage is proposed. The man may do nothing that shall be inconsistent with a true repentance for the crime with which he has proclaimed his lack of understanding, and has destroyed his own soul!

A famous divine judges that the return of a divorced adulterer unto a marriage will require, at least, these four conditions. That all possible endeavors be first used for a reconciliation unto his injured wife, and be rendered hopeless. That the man use all possible endeavors in the ways of piety and austerity and mortification to preserve his [contruency?] in a single state. That he have the countenance of lawful authority for what he does. And, finally, that there be such a removal to distant habitations as may not leave the wronged person too near unto him who was done the wrong; as also, that the new marriage have nothing of pomp in the celebration of it.

How much more will such conditions be the least that can be required in the sad case now before us, that the adulteress herself must be the espoused person!

Yea, tho' the thing done by David be thrown into one of the scales, yet it must be considered how far the adulterer can pretend unto the repentance which must be found in him if he would be qualified for the pardoning mercies of God.

Will such a conduct in the adulterer be found consistent with the restitution, and the reparation, which repentance will oblige him to make unto the wife whom he hath injured!

Will it look like repentance for him to marry a woman which ought to be more bitter than death unto him?

Would it not better express repentance for him to inflict upon himself the penance of continual prayers and tears, and self-denial, and the same restraint upon his appetites which a captivity wherein marriage would be denied unto him, would have compelled him to!

And certainly, the laws which permit such a marriage as has a tendency to invite consorts that are weary of one another to betake themselves unto adulteries, that they may thereby qualify themselves for what they esteem their privileges, have not made a due provision for the safety of the commonwealth. Now, let it be considered whether it would not be a scandalous action, and inconsistent with the true spirit of repentance, for a man to do what the laws would, if they were what they should be, forbid his doing of!

It appears that this marriage is liable to exceptions, which must render it by no means to be countenanced.

To Governor Saltonstall

U/AAS draft   June 30, 1718

Sir,

It was a very strong animation and encouragement unto my poor essay upon the *Psalter*, when I found Your Honor to cast a favorable aspect upon it.

Our excellent Governor, by subscribing to it, has given an example which, no doubt, some others will follow. But your generous offer to bring some numbers of the good people which are under [your] happy government into the subscriptions, has emboldened me to trouble you with half a hundred of the proposals. I am truly ashamed of my rude boldness; but we authors are a bold sort of creatures, and fancy that all the world allows us as much a liberty to address men of quality for their smiles upon our undertakings, as to get what of the sun we can to shine upon us. And Your Honor has always allowed me a singular share of liberty this way, beyond what others durst presume upon.

We have little foreign intelligence but what Your Honor is well-apprised of.

The famous action of the Czar in disinheriting and abdicating the Czarowitz for *keeping of bad company,* I have rarely told unto any people who have not presently had their wits a-wool-gathering.

They flatter us that the discord [crossed out: between a father and son] in another country is pretty hopefully accommodated.

The Doctors of the Sorbonne have lately published instruments decrying and condemning of episcopacy, declaring it a usurpation and asserting in strong terms the old Arian heresy, and all that Jerom [*sic*] writes upon it. The translators dedicate these things to the Archbishop of Canterbury, telling him that they believe His Grace to have the same sentiments which they assure him a great part of his clergy are come into; and that it is amazing to see those in France who are yet called Roman Catholics to be better Protestants than a great part of the Church of England after a struggle of two hundred years to get rid of popery; and that France is in a violent pang, which must needs quickly produce a more glorious and established reformation than has yet been in the world.

These things look a little 1716-ish.

But the issue of these things, and of the peace between Spain and Emperor and Turk must be waited for. [Close]

Your Honor's most sincere and humble servant,

To John Stirling

U/NLS (draft at AAS)   July 10, 1718

Sir,

Ever since I have been in any measure capable of making a judgment upon so great a subject, the Church of Scotland has appeared unto me the most illustrious that is to be seen upon the face of the earth.

'Tis a church which made a more thorough work in the Reformation at the entrance of Antichrist into his last half-time, than the rest of Europe, and more thoroughly came out of the Romish Babylon, and has ever since been in struggles above any, to hold fast that which it has received and let no man take away its crown.

'Tis a church towards which the dispensations of her glorious Lord have had in them all along something remarkable, beyond what He has dispensed unto others, none affording such marvellous materials and memorials for a history!

'Tis a church which has been persecuted with more barbarous and inhuman cruelties, especially in the days of [crossed out but clearly legible and intended to be read: a perfidious and infamous tyrant] one whom the oath of God obliged for to have been a protector unto it; and under its persecutions it has afforded as brave an army of martyrs as ever were seen among the spectacles beheld and admired by the angels of God.

[Praises the ministry and discipline of the Church of Scotland.]

A church which, that so nothing that may render it lovely may be wanting to it, improves continually in a spirit of kind forbearance and sweet charity, and brotherly affection towards dissenters in lesser matters, while genuine *piety* is conspicuous in them, and proceeds the furthest of any upon that Golden Rule, To receive all that *Christ* receives to the Glory of God, and presses on towards more and more conformity unto the maxims of the Everlasting Gospel.

[It is a glory to be a member or servant of such a church.]

It is an exceeding trouble unto your friends afar off, that so many pious men should so easily withdraw from your communion, and raise disturbances upon dissatisfactions of a political original. The churches of New England enjoy much tranquillity by their endeavors to make the terms of communion run as parallel as may be with the terms of salvation, and make only the *piety* which qualifies for the Kingdom of God the basis of union among them. It may be, the Holy One may permit these, and some other troubles, to afflict the dearly beloved of His Soul, on purpose that He may awaken an inquiry, how far this golden reed alone is employed for the measures of her sanctuary. If it should be found (which I know not) that human prudence operates too far in taking the measures of the church-state from any other limitations, the dropping of it may be so acceptable unto Heaven as to put an end unto the chastisements.

[Has not heard from Stirling for six months.]

I have often thought it a loss unto the world that the incomparable

259

ministers in the Church of Scotland have their pastoral employments lying so hard upon them that they have no time for the writing of books, for which there are so many of them whose talents would be found beyond what is common among the children of men. Certainly, it would be worth the while for ways to be invented that more of your pens may be employed for the instructing of the world.

But we in these American churches labor under the same disadvantages, which yet hinders not, but that now and then some small things are published among us, whereof those (of mine) that are come abroad since my last packets half a year ago, are here humbly tendered unto your acceptance. One of them, on *Good Men United*, will it may be surprise you, when you find in the inscription that it was preached at the ordination of an Anabaptist. Yet you may be assured that I myself am as little of an Anabaptist as any man in Scotland. But I cheerfully took this occasion to bear my testimony unto the terms which I apprehend the only foundation for union among the people of God, and those principles and proposals, upon the obtaining whereof I apprehend the Kingdom of God will ere long more than ever arrive unto us. [Close]

> Sir, Your most affectionate friend and servant,

[Asks Stirling to show the letter to Wodrow.]

To Anthony William Boehm

U/AAS draft   July 15, 1718

My most honored Friend,

[Asks his help in making the *Lapis è Monte Excisus* "as operative as you can."]

But what I have now principally to request of you, is that by your mediation there may be again conveyed a small testimony of an American remembrance for the orphan house at Glaucha. Tho' I have had no letters from our excellent friends in the Frederician University ever since that rich and long one, which highly to my satisfaction you have translated and published, yet I take it for granted that our small civilities may still be seasonable and acceptable to them. I am now got into the way of doing what little I can do for the children of God and His Kingdom there, by bills of exchange. And such a bill I now send unto Mr. Henry Newman for the sum of ten pounds sterling, with my directions that he wait upon you and that by your methods in concert with him, it may be transmitted in what specie and manner you think fit unto our dear Dr. Franckius, for the use of his orphan house. [Close]   Sir, Your most affectionate brother and servant,

To John Winthrop

IV Coll 8/MHS (draft at AAS)   August 25, 1718

My very dear Friend,

It is with unspeakable dissatisfaction that I have heard something of the uncivil and barbarous usages which you suffer from your *Connecticutians*. I hoped that my strong applications and large remonstrances to your Governor some while ago might have put a period unto them; and he gave me cause to think that there will be nothing wanting in him of a true zeal to do you all possible service. But since your uneasy circumstances do (as I am told) still continue, you must give me leave earnestly to recommend unto you, A *removal into this capital city of our province.*

Here you will have the most valuable opportunity of a conversation with friends who love you most affectionately, and whom you love above all the men in the world, and such as will soon make way for your being serviceable, as they have been from whom you are descended.

Here you will soon be apprised of methods and people whereby your plentiful estate may soon be brought unto improvements that will render it yet much more considerable.

Here you will be accommodated with all the enjoyments which a Christian, a gentleman, and a philosopher can wish for.

And as you have a singular inclination to see and make *me* happy, I will add, your coming to this town will be a vast addition to *my* happiness.

I conjure you to show this letter to Madam your consort, that so she, who is one of the best of women, and one to whom you can deny nothing, may lay hold on the occasion to urge a matter so highly agreeable to, Sir,   Your hearty friend and servant,

. . . If you please, to send the proposals about the *Psalterium Americanum* to Governor Hunter. It may be he will do as four governors have already done.

To Governor Saltonstall

Quincy (mangled version)/   August 25, 1718
AAS draft

Sir,

'Tis an unspeakable pleasure unto me that I have been in any measure capable of serving so precious a thing as your college at New Haven. Governor Yale now gives you a sensible proof that he has begun to take it under his patronage and protection. But I am informed that what he now does is very little in proportion to what he will do when once he finds by the name of it, that it may claim an adoption with him. *Yale College* cannot fail of Mr. Yale's generous and growing bounties. I confess, it was a great and inexcusable presumption in me to make myself so far the godfather of the beloved infant, as to propose a name for it. But I assured myself that if a succession of solid and lasting benefits might be entailed upon it, Your Honor, and the honorable trustees, would pardon me, and the proposal would be complied withal. It is a thousand pities that the dear infant should be in danger of being strangled in the birth by a dissension of your good people about the place where it shall be nourished in the wilderness. But probably the *Yalean* assistance to New Haven will prove a decisive circumstance, which will dispose all to an acquiescence there.

[Sends along a copy of his letter to La Pillonnière.]

Your worthy ministers will go before their people in giving thanks to God our Saviour for the deliverance of all the glorious confessors in the French galleys, obtained by our King's interposition on their behalf, I suppose on the occasion of the noise which the martyrdom of Mr. Arnaud made the last winter.

When the servants of God meet at your commencement I make no doubt that under Your Honor's influences and encouragements, they will make it an opportunity in the most serious and mature manner to deliberate upon projections to serve the great interest of education, and so of religion, both in your college and throughout your colony, as well as whatever else may advance the Kingdom of God; and not suffer an interview of your best men to evaporate such a senseless, useless, noisy impertinency as it used to do with us at Cambridge. [Close]   Your Honor's most sincere servant,

262

IV

AT the first signs of success in converting the Mohegan Indians in Connecticut, Mather wrote with pleasure to the General Assembly of Connecticut. His hopes for reforming the eastern Indians were also lifted by JAMES WOODSIDE (fl. 1720) one of the many ministers from the north of Ireland who had begun to migrate to New England. Woodside and his wife settled in Brunswick, Maine. Like other missionaries they entertained the Indians in their home and, like the others, soon discovered that they had to spend their own funds doing so. Mather's letter to Woodside speaks for his inside knowledge of the missionary work and his sensitivity to its problems, such as the intense cold. Indeed, only a year later the health of Woodside and his wife failed, and they were relieved of their commission. Shortly after, Mather wrote a testimonial to Woodside's pious character.

Still determined to see *Biblia Americana* published, Mather wrote for help to Mrs. Gurdon Saltonstall's brother in England, RICHARD WHITTINGHAM (c. 1665–1730), and to ROBERT HACKSHAW (d. 1738), a London paper merchant who helped publish the *Magnalia*. Also, while chiding Jeremiah Dummer for his loose religion, he implied—in the very act of naming, then denying, the implication—that Dummer could redeem himself by finding the book a publisher. Meanwhile he wrote and published one work after another. He sent to Saltonstall his expanded and now printed letter to Ziegenbalgh, *India Christiana*. The book he most hoped to see in print was his translation of the psalms, *Psalterium Americanum*. In a letter to the attorney general of Massachusetts in May, 1718, he announced that he intended merely to "do something to help devout men in their more private fruitions of the most glorious Book of Devotions that ever was upon earth"; he stressed that he was "not so vain and eke so presumptuous as to propose the dethroning of our public rhymes. . . ." (The publication of the *Psalterium* was partly financed by Gurdon Saltonstall.) His "Letter to La Pillonnière" (a French Jesuit who had converted to Protestantism) was well received after appearing in the *Occasional Paper* of SIMON BROWNE (1680–1732), pastor of the important congregation in the Old Jewry, London. This tract, Mather confided happily in his diary, became "a celebrated letter, and was much talked of." In addition he submitted his *Religio Generosi* to THOMAS BRADBURY (1677–1759), a Congregational minister in London and a political polemicist noted for his violent harangues. Browne and Bradbury would soon command attention in the now-brewing controversy over Arianism, which began to worry Mather seriously.

Although his letters only hint at it, Mather's private affairs remained distressing. His troubles with Cressy did not relent, even though Cressy at this time seems temporarily to have settled down in Boston as a bookkeeper. The anguished but unexplained cries of "My GOD! My GOD!" in Mather's diary entry for August, 1718, could represent the birth of Cressy's illegitimate child. More ominous were the first signs in late 1717 and throughout 1718 of mental instability in Lydia. The diary talks darkly of "pollutions" and intimates that Mather had stopped sharing his bed with her. The one suggestion of these burdens in Mather's letters is his statement that things look "1716-ish"—preparing, that is, for the imminent collapse of Catholicism and for an apocalyptic release from his cares. This rising interest in prophecy made him curious about the work of JOHN LACY (b. 1664), a wealthy member of Dr. Calamy's congregation at Westminster who had come under the influence of the so-called French prophets. In 1717 Lacy issued a collection of his prophecies and some works written while in a trance. Calamy and others witnessed his demonstrations of healing and his ecstasies accompanied by hiccuping and gasping. When Calamy publicly censured him for these displays, Lacy went into another ecstasy. William Whiston tried to rescue Lacy from his delusions, but Lacy was at last committed to Bridewell in 1737.

To the General Assembly of Connecticut

U/AAS draft   October 8, 1718

Honorable and Much Honored,

It is with a very great satisfaction that the commissioners for the evangelical affairs among our Indians have heard of the purpose you have had, and the progress you have made, for evangelizing the remnant of Indians in your colony who still continue in their pagan impieties.

The truth is, it has appeared a matter of no little grief and shame unto many considerate minds, among us as well as among yourselves, that in the very heart of a colony renowned for the profession of Christianity, there should for fourscore years together be a body of the aboriginals persisting in the darkest and most horrid paganism.

We are sensible of some noble essays which have been formerly made by some excellent persons in your colony, for the Christianizing of this foolish nation. But tho' what has been essayed has not been hitherto accomplished, we must not be discouraged. A persevering and unwearied zeal may do wonders at the last, when the time to favor, the set-time, is come.

Your friends here take the liberty to encourage, as far as we can, your proceeding upon the good work which you have begun. Yea, we do importunately beseech you, that no private views may prevent your doing all that may be expected from a righteous and a generous people to quiet the minds of your Indians, with all possible security for their peaceable enjoyment of that small portion of lands which has been reserved for them. We importunately beseech you that all due provision being speedily made for a clear, firm, lasting settlement of claims, what of the Indian lands will be proper to be reserved for that intention may be presently put into a condition of improvement for their benefit.

[Pledges the assistance of the commissioners in Boston.]

We long to see the reproach of *Mohegin* [*sic*] rolled away from us, by some very vigorous and laudable action done towards bringing the people whose land we possess into the Kingdom of God.

And no doubt it might contribute unto the success of our endeavors if when a day of prayer is to be observed through your colony, *A good success of endeavors to bring the Indians unto the knowledge of service of our great Saviour* were one article in the order for it.

[Close]   Your most affectionate servant,

To Samuel Bishop

U/AAS draft   October 13, 1718

My dear Child,
   [Thanks him for the present to Lydia Mather.]

'Tis not easy for me to express how intense my desires and prayers for you are, that you may be preserved from the snares of death, which young men too generally fall into; and that you may embrace those ways of early piety which may render you happy in both worlds, and enroll you among the children of wisdom.

Were your admirable grandfather now living, he would pursue you with incessant admonitions to know and serve the God of your fathers, and betimes remember your Creator and Redeemer, and begin to answer the end of your life, in living to Him that made you.

In a book of *Morning-Exercises* you may find a sermon of his about secret prayer, which is well worthy of your perusal. But now, you must from an uncle suffer the same inculcations, which, because they must be very many and very urgent, I must employ now and then a book upon that intention. I now single out a few of the many treatises which I have published, for the directing and quickening of serious godliness in such as are coming into the world, and earnestly request it of you to bestow a serious perusal upon them, as having in them the sum of what I would write or speak unto you if I had the fullest opportunity of the largest conversation with you. [Close]

Your affectionate uncle,

To Thomas Bradbury

U/AAS draft   October 13, 1718

My most honored Brother,

[Sends along some recent works.]

I am glad that our invaluable Barrington has committed my *Religio Generosi* unto your perusal, and, as I perceive, in some degree unto your disposal. I hope you find it the richest and yet plainest collection of the works which men behold, and for which our glorious God is to be magnified, that you have met withal. I must confess that I shall count it a very great happiness, if my glorious Lord will accept me among the priests of His creation, and employ me to bespeak and procure His praises from the spectators of His workmanship. If He reject my sacrifices, I humbly submit unto His infinite justice and wisdom, and herein also I would become yet more a sacrificer. Tho' he has caused a considerable number of my more elaborate composures (even such as this) to lie buried in obscurity, yet he has permitted me near three hundred times to serve Him in the way of the press, with such things as have had least of my design and study for them;

and his Grace therein ought to be sufficient for me. But I cry to Him for His favorable aspect upon these offerings also; and if you may be the instrument of bringing forward this publication, my obligations unto you, and unto God for you, will be inexpressible. I entreat you, my brother, I entreat you to oblige me in this particular. I leave to you the formation of the title, according to your pleasure. Your orders for the character and the correction I shall rely upon. A preface of yours to it I should count an honor unto me, and it. You may assure the bookseller that I shall immediately myself take off five pounds worth (in our money) of the copies, at a just price, if he risk them to me. Our colleges will, I suppose, also in time take off great numbers, by the book's coming to be read in them for their philosophy.
[Close]   Your most affectionate brother and servant,

To Jeremiah Dummer

U/AAS draft   October 22, 1718

Sir,

The many good offices you have done me will never be forgotten with me, nor will the sentiments of gratitude which they have produced in me ever be extinguished.

The incomparable Governor whom you underwent so much trouble and expense to obtain for us, is that for which not I only, but all New England, is insolvently in debt unto you. Nothing but the immense pleasure of having done so much good can be an adequate recompense for so rare and vast and general a benefit.

It were impossible to do a greater disservice unto the best of Kings, or a greater prejudice unto the most loyal people in his dominions, than for a small party of men, whose designs against both deserve all possible discountenance, to procure his removal.

The next kindness you have done for us has been in our Lieutenant-Governor, whose conduct is perpetually good and just and wise, and such as has procured him a very great esteem and [yields?] a universal satisfaction. Your managements for the *Collegium Yalense* will eternize you, and, if statues had ever been seen on the western side of the Atlantic, you could not be long without one. In the meantime, 'tis one to have it asked *why hasn't he one!*

[Thanks Dummer for putting him in touch with Sir Richard Blackmore and Simon Browne.]   Your affectionate friend and servant,

To Simon Browne

U/AAS draft   October 22, 1718

Sir,

Your *Occasional Paper,* I hope, will prove more than a mere *occasion,* even a very operative cause, of more than a little good in the world.

It will be a great satisfaction to me if any communications from hence [crossed out: of mine] may contribute unto the stores which furnish you for the noble service of asserting the cause of piety and liberty wherein you have engaged. Some small ones from a far country now wait upon you.

There needs nothing to give you triumphs over the Church-tyranny which you are bravely combating, but only for mankind once to deserve the name of a *reasonable creature.*

[Wishes Browne's *Paper* success.]

Your unknown friend and servant,

To Governor Shute

Quincy/AAS draft   October 31, 1718

Sir,

As in duty forever bound, I repeat my humble offers of service to Your Excellency, that if in the present sessions of the General Assembly there may be anything within the small sphere of my activity to be done for the public (for I perceive Your Excellency knows no other) interests, your commands may be laid upon me.

At the same time I will humbly tender to Your Excellency my poor sentiments concerning some affairs of the College, because I am informed, a meeting of (those unaccountably called) *the overseers of the College* is this day expected.

It appears unto your servant a very strange thing that when the life and soul of that society (in its present feeble circumstances) in Your Excellency's favorably looking upon it, and breathing into it, there should be so little acknowledgment of the dependence, as I am informed there was when Pierpont carried a message from Your Excellency.

It appears a very strange thing that when King William and Queen Mary and my Lord Bellomont, and our General Assembly (many times over) and Governor Dudley, and all the world besides, declared for near twenty years together that the College had not a sufficient charter to animate it, they should now by unseasonable challenges and presumptions to act as upon such a one, make their precarious condition to be inquired into. It appears a very strange thing that, supposing they had all the charter they pretend unto, they should expect that the members of that society should be exempted from the reach of the laws of the province and the common law of the nation. Which point, if it be this day given to those who know very well that when the utmost punishments of the College have been inflicted formerly, the civil courts have taken after all a cognisance of the crimes—it will certainly bring the state of the College into the General Assembly, and then!—clamor enough, be sure on't!

For the abused and oppressed Pierpont, when he has been done what Your Excellency may order him, to have his degree ordered for him, and so the *Batrachomyomachia* between him and the (pretended) President brought unto a period, seems to be as compendious a way as any to quiet these academical commotions.

Tho' the College be under a very unhappy government, yet for my own part I earnestly desire that we may go on as easily and as quietly as 'tis possible; and Your Excellency's incomparable goodness and wisdom will easily discern and approve the intentions of the freedom used in this letter, and leave it, and its writer, covered under the darkest concealment; and the rather because (for some reasons) I desire to keep at the greatest distance imaginable from all the affairs of Harvard.
[Close]   Your Excellency's Most faithful and obedient servant,
My aged parent, Your Excellency's most sincere servant, allows me to write after this manner with his most humble service.

To John Winthrop

IV Coll 8/MHS (draft at AAS)   January 11, 1719

Sir,

A small accident last night, which yet had no harm in it any further than that it gives occasion for this little schedule, will detain me this day from the satisfactions I proposed with you, in dining with the best of governors, and the most sincere and candid friend in the world.

I will submit (even with an Indian patience) unto any punishment that may be ordered me for this desertion, tho' it be a most involuntary action, or what rather my passivity in it will not allow to be called an action, it being the effect of a very kidnapry.

If you judge that good manners require it, I request that His Excellency may this morning be informed of my crime, who perhaps may then fill his hospitable table with better (tho' 'twill be impossible for him to do it with better-affected) company.

'Tis a thought that sometimes visits me: if our dear Governor be a *man* so lovely in many excellent qualities, what is that MAN who is GOD, and the Governor of all worlds! My dear child, think as often and as highly of *Him* as thou canst.

I am, His Excellency's hearty servant and, Sir, Your most constant friend,

Sir, I have begun with sending you that piece of my dear Sir Richard which will prepare you for the rest. You and he make a great figure in my *Album Amicorum.*

To John Lacy

U/AAS draft   January 17, 1719

Sir,

You are unknown to me any otherwise than as the knowledge of you, and of your extraordinary circumstances, has arrived unto the rest of the nation. And I am like to continue much more unknown to you, even after this address of mine has reached you.

When so astonishing a descent from the invisible world was made upon ours, as what there was in the case of those whom we called the Ecstatics, I always thought our common way of treating it was foolish, brutish, barbarous, and equally full of ignorance and of iniquity. And it is with much pleasure that I read the detection of our delusion by the nameless and modest gentleman, who five years ago published a treatise full of wisdom and candor on *The Ways of God's Revealing Himself to and by the Prophets.*

Long, long have I been of the opinion that the revival of Christianity, and the arrival of the Kingdom of God, must be by the return of the prophetic spirit unto us, in such angelical possessions as carried on the work of the Gospel in the primitive times, when our ascended Lord gave such gifts unto men, gifts which continued in the Church till towards the coming on of the dark three years and a half, for which long period it has not rained. And I know such in the world as do send up from the dust importunate cries unto Heaven, that the multitude of the Heavenly Host may come down upon us with their influences to accomplish what [appears?] otherwise to be despaired of.

It was not without apprehension that in the extraordinary occurrences of your case, there might be some drops falling before a mighty shower that is intended, and a trial made how the world would entertain the only means of its cure.

I extremely approved the sentiments of religion, even of that real and vital piety, which were expressed in the exhortations that passed through you unto us, and the disclaim which the Spirit made of all our parties.

But then, I have not been able to get over the stumbling-blocks which have so clogged the reception of your prophecies, in the evident miscarriage of so many of your predictions, which creates a suspicion that the evil spirits foreseeing what is ere long to be done by the good ones, have got liberty to anticipate them with counterfeits that may raise wonderful prejudices in the minds of a wretched world against that work of God which is coming on. The matters uttered in the prophecies also appeared often too low, too mean, too trivial and jejune for such an Author as had His Name used in them.

In this dark suspense, I keep waiting to see what our glorious Lord will please to do; for when that Sun of Righteousness appears, He will dispel our darkness; the beasts will then also gather themselves together and lay them down in their dens.

In the meantime, whether the Sovereign Lord has permitted you to be assaulted by a *Satan transformed*, or no,—I cannot but love the excellent piety which I suppose working in you. [Close]

Sir, Your friend and servant,

To Jeremiah Dummer

U/AAS draft

January 19, 1719

My very dear Friend,

[Asserts his friendship for Dummer, who "never had a more constant, a more faithful, a more grateful friend in the world."]

Our dear Governor is pestered with a disaffected crew, which yet he keeps under with an incomparable conduct. Some of his worst enemies are a pack of wretched Jacobites (the only ones in the country I can [word unclear] say of it) of the church which on the Lord's-days he gives his perpetual attendance to. His ordering the removal of a scandalous crucifix, which their church-wardens had put up in the front of their pulpit, has thrown a number of the bigots into a rage that reaches to the heavens. Their indiscretion in thus exposing the Church, to a country where the Governor would have commended it, is a little wondered at.

[Urges Dummer to be patient in the face of abuse from home.]

My dear child: Thou art generously full of good offices to mankind. But, oh! that thou wouldest entertain right sentiments concerning the Kingdom of God, the advancement whereof does for mankind the best of offices; and study what noble things it may lie within thy reach to do, that the Kingdom of God may be served in the world. The rewards in the future state for all such services will be glorious.

I do not mention this with any eye to our *Biblia Americana*, for I have entirely buried it. But you have bright faculties, that being exerted upon the best intentions, would soon do wondrously. [Close]

Yours most affectionately,

I hope you and Mr. Newman have received what I brewed for you in October. You'll excuse the enclosed—I never heard of any premium for squaring the circle. But this is our Indian, mendicant, way. I can't help it.

To Robert Hackshaw

U/AAS draft   January 27, 1719

My much honored, and never forgotten, Friend,

Tho' many years are passed since our treating one another in the way of an epistolary correspondence, yet in all this time I have not lost at all my sense of the vast obligations which you laid upon me in your generous disbursements for the bringing forth of our *Magnalia*; nor have I abated of my value for the exemplary piety which forever gives you an excellent character.

[Regrets the fewness of their correspondences.]

I am sensible that our church-history meets with a various reception. It is decried with you in London, where your critics are sufficiently humorsome and generally full of aversion for that sort of piety which this book designs to propagate. In several other parts of England, and much more in Scotland and in Ireland, it is cried up; yea, hyperbolically spoken of, and has its desired operation. In my own country, which yet is not without a party of malignant people in it, it grows more and more into respect. A quantity of them sent over at a moderate price would be very vendible. [Laments that several of his most important works lie unpublished.]

Our *Biblia Americana* particularly. 'Tis a wonder to see how oddly and how weakly, and with what unaccountable contempt the Dissenters in your city have treated the offer of a work which many have thought would have been a little reputable to themselves, as well as more than a little serviceable to the best of interests. [But he leaves affairs in God's care.]

Your grateful, faithful, hearty friend, and humble servant,

TO RICHARD WHITTINGAM

U/AAS draft   January 29, 1719

Sir,

How many sevens of years (I think, about three) are now rolled away since I enjoyed those agreeable interviews with you which made some of the most grateful moments in my life! And what shall we render to that glorious Lord, from whom, having obtained help, we continue to this day!

In this time we have both of us had many changes passing over us, especially in some of our domestic circumstances.

I could not but sensibly sympathize with you in your loss of your valuable consort, having myself some while before lost the amiable [crossed out: lovely] consort that I enjoyed in your memorable kinswoman, who has left me an Elizabeth, now fourteen years of age, a daughter not the meannest for sense and beauty, and a Samuel, now twelve years of age, one likely to prove an uncommon scholar and blessing, and already ripe for admission into the College.

[Has from time to time sent Whittingam some of his publications.]

Tho' our *Confirmed Christian* falling into the odd, covetous, deceitful hands of Sir Henry Ashurst were destroyed by a particular baseness in his way of treating it, yet a gracious God has accepted me, and allowed me to serve Him, with near three hundred publications. [Repeats familiar story that his best works lie unpublished.] Among these, our *Biblia Americana* makes the greatest figure, a work which my brethren in England think it not as yet worth their while to give reception to.

My dear friend, I assure myself that you retain in a full, a strong, a growing vigour, those impressions of piety which you had when we were together here engaged in the service of our GOD. [Close]

Your most constant friend and hearty servant,

To James Woodside

U/AAS draft   February 3, 1719

Sir,

'Tis more than time that your brethren here should bid you welcome to the western side of the Atlantic, and make you a tender of all the brotherly assistances that we are capable of giving you, especially under the difficulties which at your first arrival you cannot but meet withal.

The glorious providence of God our Saviour, which has been at work in the removal of so many people, who are of so desirable a character, as we see come and coming from the north of Ireland unto the north of New England, has doubtless very great intentions in it; and, *what He does, we know not now, but we shall know hereafter.*

He who defeated the purposes of such a removal attempted by some excellent persons of your nation and spirit, more than fourscore years ago, now seems to favor them. Is it not because He has a work to do which we are not yet aware of! Happy, and honored, these instruments by whom our glorious Lord comes to have these ends of the earth for His possession!

The people who are upon this transportation are of such principles, and so laudable for their sobriety, their honesty, their industry, that we cannot but embrace them with a most fervent charity, and cherish hopes of noble settlements to be quickly made in a region which has hitherto been a repeated *Aceldama.* The people who were formerly taking root there carried not the ministry of the Gospel with them, and were once and again suddenly cursed of God. The Indians there have never yet been permitted of Heaven to break up a town that had a minister of the Gospel in it. [Hopes that other ministers like Woodside will emigrate.]

I make no doubt that the last month you have passed through has been the coldest and hardest that ever you saw in your life. And if you are in any tolerable manner got through it, we shall never be afraid of you.

Many services of no small consequence have you to do among the people who constantly attend upon you. But, Sir, you shall give me leave to solicit your attendance on a people who are not a people. Our neglect of Christianizing the eastern savages has been punished, as was that of the Britons to Christianize the Saxons in the days of Gildas. I beseech you, Sir, to set your hand as far as you can unto this work of God. Study, and contrive, and pursue as many ways as you can to convey right sentiments of Christianity unto those barbarous proselytes of idolatry. You are many ways qualified for it; you have interpreters near you; and you are so expert in the Latin tongue, as well as in polemic theology, that you need not be shy of encountering the *poor priest* that poisons them.

[Promises Woodside that he will be paid for his efforts.]

Your most hearty brother and servant,

CHAPTER FOUR

1719–1723

The revival of Arianism; the Salters Hall Conference; criticism of New England by English Dissenters; deteriorating marriage to Lydia; the Howell estate; disappointment over *Biblia Americana* and *Curiosa Americana*; conflict with Elisha Cooke's "popular party"; church disputes in neighboring towns; Thomas Prince; the Brick Meeting House; attempts to improve Increase, Jr.; the smallpox crisis; revived Indian fighting; withdrawal of Governor Shute.

I

For a long time Cotton Mather had foreseen a revival of Arianism clamorous enough to challenge Reformed Christianity. As early as 1712 he had urged William Jameson, his blind correspondent in Scotland, to confute the Arians by writing a history of ante-Nicene opinions on the eternal deity of Christ. By 1719 the Arian movement became a force to reckon with and to crush.

The Arian heresy arose during the earliest period of Christianity from the attempt to reconcile the unity of the godhead with the distinction of personality in the trinity. Arius, writing in the fourth century, maintained a complete distinction between the Father and the Son. He endowed the Son with free will and a capacity for change, and depicted the Father as a Hellenic first cause. In his scheme, God was unknowable, Christ a creature detached from Him and neither divine nor eternal. Neither mediator nor saviour, Christ could not bring man to God. The result was a step toward unitarianism, a threat to scriptural revelation and, many felt, a subversion of Christianity itself.

As an institution Arianism formed the religion of the eastern half of the Roman empire until late in the fourth century. As a doctrine, it figured in later Christian disputes as well. In eighteenth-century England it equipped rationalistic theologians in their attack on Puritanism. The two outstanding English Arians were Dr. Samuel Clarke and William Whiston—Mather's "two grand satanic tools." Clarke, a disciple of Newton and a famous metaphysician, was Rector of St. James, Piccadilly. He deduced the moral law from logical necessity rather than from Scripture, and became popular with the rationalists, while orthodox ministers accused him of preaching a disguised deism. He carried on a famous controversy and correspondence with Leibnitz, won the praise of Addison, and in 1712 published his *Scripture Doctrine of the Trinity*, declaring the Father alone supreme. William Whiston was the successor to Newton as professor of mathematics at Cambridge. Mather admired him and had a correspondence with him, which has not survived. In 1712 Whiston reprinted in England Mather's *Old Paths Restored* (1711), with a preface in which he explained that as a rationalist he could not accept Mather's doctrine, although in it he found excellent things (his exposition of them, however, is overlaid with an arch irony). Continuing to respect Whiston as a scientist, whatever his religious views, Mather sent to Thomas Prince for Whiston's *Speculations*, which he hoped might account for the "aurora borealis" that appeared in Massachusetts in December, 1719, and produced some panic. Clarke's views engendered a long pamphlet war; Whiston's lost him his professorship.

To combat the heresy a group of English Nonconformists— Presbyterians, Baptists, and Congregationalists—met in Salters Hall in London in 1719. Mather kept a close watch on the conference, not only because he regarded Arianism as a serious threat, but also because many of his correspondents attended it; later he contributed to the exchange of pamphlets that grew out of the conference. The leader of the conservative group at the Hall was Thomas Bradbury; the opposition was represented by the Whig politician John Shute Barrington, a now-alienated member of Bradbury's congregation, and a brother of the governor of Massachusetts. Of Mather's other correspondents at the conference, both Simon Browne and Isaac Watts voted with the minority, who refused to impose acceptance of the doctrine of the trinity on the Independent ministers. (This led Browne into a later controversy with another of Mather's correspondents Thomas Reinolds, who Mather distrusted.)

Arianism and the results of the Salters Hall conference are the chief, passionate concerns of Mather's many unpublished letters of the early 1720's. He tried to explain his convictions to "Mr. Andrews," among others, probably JEDEDIAH ANDREWS (1674–1717), a Presbyterian minister in Philadelphia. (Andrews died before the date of Mather's letter to him; but Mather more than once unknowingly addressed correspondents who had died.) Andrews had written to Mather in 1713 urging him to do something to combat antinomianism in the southern colonies; Mather's response was the anti-antinomian tract, *Adversus Libertinos* (1713). His letter to Andrews stands on two essential principles: that God and Christ are and must be regarded as co-eternal, else Christ is mortal, changeable, and no Saviour; and that more is required for admission to communion than professing belief in Scripture which, Mather said, "all the heretics upon earth are willing to do." Mather's correspondence with Isaac Watts became strained as Mather's rather envious admiration of him made capital of the heretical tendencies Watts displayed at Salters Hall. Mather had asked Jeremiah Dummer not to show Watts his *Psalterium Americanum* because, as he explained in a later letter to Watts, he thought the work too shallow. His reticence, however, had less to do with modesty than with the suspicion that Watts was an Arian himself. At the conference, as noted, Watts voted with those who refused to impose a subscription to the doctrine of the trinity. In fact Watts was a liberal Calvinist, perplexed by points of doctrine, with unitarian leanings that became pronounced toward the end of his life. Self-defensively he wrote to Mather on February 11, 1720, to assure him that very few in London sided with Clarke's theology, and that the eighty ministers who refused to sign the majority platform did so not on doctrinal grounds but because the subscription proceeded in a disorderly way.

Mather seems to have been unconvinced: in his letter of July 5, 1720, he reminded Watts that because Arianism struck at the heart of Christianity itself, Arians should be excluded even from the very broad terms of communion and salvation he had proposed in *Lapis è Monte Excisus*. He added bluntly that in his view Watts's poems were already poisoned by the heresy. Behind this thrust at Watts, the letter makes plain, was Mather's outrage at the criticism of the style of his own *Magnalia* by John Oldmixon and others in England. Identifying criticism of the *Magnalia* with attacks on the Reformation, he made no distinction between Arians and literary critics who mocked him. Mather is thus an early case in the long line of American writers resentfully smoldering under their treatment by prejudiced, haughty Europeans.

Mather did not merely keep informed on Arianism abroad. He fought back through his own writings. His correspondence in this period reveals his determined but unsuccessful efforts to publish an anti-Whistonian tract, *Religio Generosi*. How an interplay of religious and political enmities at home and abroad prevented its publication becomes clear only in the later letter, included here, which Mather wrote to Benjamin Colman in September 1722. Mather had dedicated *Religio Generosi* to Jeremiah Dummer and John Shute Barrington, the brother of Governor Shute. But Barrington had left the congregation of Mather's friend and correspondent Thomas Bradbury, and become Bradbury's chief opponent in the Salters Hall Conference. And it was to Bradbury that Mather had sent the *Religio* for publication. Barrington apparently dropped his patronage of the work because of Mather's friendship for Bradbury and because he believed that Mather had represented him as an Arian. Anxious to patch up the quarrel, Mather denied having called Barrington an Arian, or ever thinking him one. In this way he hoped not only to salvage the *Religio*; he also wished passionately not to offend Governor Shute by offending, or having people think he offended, Shute's brother. Barrington did not forgive Mather for the real or imagined insult. Bradbury later wrote to Mather that Barrington denounced his "mercenary pen" and considered him a menace to the Dissenting interest by his "Arian tricks" and by "making a devil of God." Mather proposed dropping the dedication to Barrington and dedicating the work to Dummer alone, but it apparently was never published. He wrote another anti-Whistonian tract, *Goliathus Detruncatus*, to show, contra-Whiston, that the ante-Nicene fathers were not

Arians. This work also became lost in England when Dr. John Edwards died while preparing it for press.

One of Mather's anti-Arian works did get published, however. *Some American Sentiments on the Great Controversy of the Time* is a formal epistle dated July 1, 1720, and addressed to four ministers in London, including Thomas Reinolds. It is worth summarizing here as the fullest statement of Mather's views on the controversy and as a commentary on his correspondence. Mather begins the epistle by identifying Oldmixon's attacks on the *Magnalia*, once again, with attacks on Christianity: "We should not be insensible (having been very publicly informed of it) *That the style of manner of the New-England writers does not equal that of the Europeans*." After this initial and by now compulsive barb, Mather's tone is moderate and, above all, conciliatory. He makes a show of inviting controversy among the well-meaning: "In very many disputed points of religion, they who pull the saw may by-and-by shake hands with one another as Brethren in Christ." Mather sees the Arian controversy as another expression of the central dilemma of Protestantism: how to grant the individual considerable freedom of worship while drawing the line on aberration. Thus he tries to reconcile "two very glorious truths": first, that "no man is to be forced with civil penalties to profess and perform anything in religion whereof he is not convinced in his conscience that God requires it of him"; and second, "that there are certain maxims of piety which all who truly live unto God are united in. . . ." He disputes both the overscrupulous who would omit from communion those differing with them on minor points of doctrine and, equally, those who would admit the holders of "damnable heresies." Basically he sides with the Salters Hall majority, that a mere subscription to the word of Scripture is an insufficient basis for communion. Every heretic, even a papist, will so subscribe, freeing himself to perpetrate damnable heresies under an official but corrupt orthodoxy. Mather would require for communion a trinitarian belief: "That the One God, who is the Father, and the Son, and the Holy Spirit, is for ever to be adored as our God, and acknowledged in all our ways; that a Glorious Christ, who is the Eternal and Almighty Son of God Incarnate, and enthroned in our Jesus, is the Redeemer, who has made himself a Sacrifice for us, and on whom we are to trust for our deliverance from all the miseries which our fall from God has brought upon us." Whatever other leeway can be granted for personal interpretation of Scripture, none can be allowed on this point as a basis of communion and salvation.

Mather was simply addressing the old Augustinian problem of love versus knowledge as a means of faith. Must love precede knowledge? Can one ever know what he does not want to know? That problem always manifested itself in New England as a question of whether to retain, and in what form, the only rites left to Puritanism, namely baptism and communion. For Mather, the doctrine of the trinity also terminated the distance he was willing to go in having Puritanism adapt itself to the mainstream of European culture, especially its increasingly fashionable rationalism. He was fighting the battle which New England ministers had fought from the beginning, and which was not abandoned until around the death of Thomas Jefferson. He wanted to keep alive within Congregationalism a sense of man's dependence on Christ for salvation, and through that the need for an educated ministry to explain difficult points of salvation, and through that the existence of the institution of the church itself.

Given Mather's messianic sense of himself it was inevitable that he take the Arian heresy as a slap in his own face. It seemed to him an attack particularly on New England as the vanguard of the Reformation, and more particularly on himself as its commander. The linkage in Mather's mind of Reformed Christianity, New England, and his own works, explains his reaction to the publication in 1719 of a *History of New England* by DANIEL NEAL (or NEIL; 1678–1743), an English historian and minister who had studied at Utrecht and Leyden. Enthusiastically received in New England, Neal's history eventually won him an honorary M.A. from Harvard, although Mather did what he could to prevent it. Mather praised the book in his letter to Isaac Watts, Neal's close friend, on July 5, 1720; but on the same day he wrote to Harvard and slashed it. It was, he said, merely a paraphrase of the *Magnalia* from a secular point of view, with a grossly distorted narrative of the witchcraft proceedings taken from Calef. Still indignant at English aspersions on his own work, he took to heart Neal's derogatory comments about the cultural climate of New England, "as if none brought up there knew how to write modern English." Because he equated attacks on his style with attacks on Christianity, he suspected that the notion of awarding a degree to Neal originated from English Arians, probably *"Timeo Danaus"* (Timothy Cutler?; actually, Neal had remained neutral during the Salters Hall conference). Mather could not have been pleased when Neal later published in England a defense of the smallpox inoculation with a preface by Benjamin Colman.

Dangerous and absorbing as Mather found it, the Arian controversy could not take his mind off his deteriorating marriage. The ever more numerous fits of temper in Lydia became definite signs of mental breakdown. He tried to overcome the "grievous outbreakings of her proud passions," he wrote in his diary, with love and meekness; but her rages made the year past, 1718, "a year of such distresses with me as I have never seen in my life before." Clinically he could make out a pattern in her behavior: when her paroxysms passed she treated him over-fondly; he suspected either a hereditary "distraction" or a "possession." Taking an aversion to his diary, she began "rummaging" in it, destroying parts of it. He began to hide it. In February, 1719, he lamented that this "furious and froward stepmother" had begun abusing his children. And by "exposing her madness," he foresaw, Lydia would "bring ruin on my ministry."

Lydia and her family were also exhausting Mather's already flat pocketbook. The pathetic story of his attempt to supervise the Howell estate can only partly be told from the remaining evidence. We know that Lydia's daughter Katharine had been married to a profligate Boston merchant named Nathan Howell, who died on May 2, 1716. A month later Mather told Lydia's sister, Mrs. Anne Wyrly, that Howell had been "the worst husband upon earth. Had he lived he had soon brought a noble to nine-pence. . . ." That same month Mather had letters of administration granted to him and legally began to oversee Howell's estate, although well aware of his hereditary naiveté in financial matters. In 1717 he performed the marriage of Katharine Howell, the widow, to the Boston merchant Samuel Sewall, the diarist's nephew and the son of Major Stephen Sewall of Salem. Later that year he relieved Pelatiah Whittemore of his attorneyship in the estate and transferred it to one of the Sewalls, which one is uncertain. His diary for the next few years contains only occasional references to the estate, but they all point to his difficulty in managing it. He seems to have let it slide. According to the arrangement, he was obliged to return an inventory on or before June 4, 1717. He failed to do so, as he failed to give the Probate Office an account of his receipts and expenses in the administration. (It is hard to avoid the suspicion, which is no more than a suspicion, that Mather was using some of the funds.) The difficulties were burdensome enough to serve as proof of his self-glorifying imitation of Christ: "My wife, in her froward pangs," he wrote in his diary on January 27, 1719, "having happily thrown the administration into my hands, I gladly take it."

For all this masochistically welcoming tone, Mather had never been in such serious trouble before. By 1720, four years after assuming the administration, he still was not free of it. The money from the estate had not been released, consequently none was coming to Katharine Howell's orphaned children, George and Nathan Howell. (The children died in January, 1728, shortly before Mather, while skating on the Common.) Mather was forced to support them out of his own pocket. On top of this, the depreciation of the currency proved particularly hard on the clergy and on other salaried people; many widows and orphans, whose estates consisted of money on interest, found themselves suddenly impoverished. The result was that Katharine's husband, Samuel Sewall, threatened Mather with arrest.

Mather's reaction can be gathered from a letter written on his behalf to Samuel Sewall in April, 1720. Urging Sewall to call off his nephew, the writer (who may have been Mather himself, although the letter is not in his hand) describes visiting Mather recently and finding him overwhelmed with the administration of the estate, oppressed with such "heavy and many troubles" that "we shall quickly lose him." Because Sewall's nephew stirs people up to arrest him for maladministration, at every knock at his door Mather's "heart dies within him, as he says, fearing there is an arrest to be served on him." The writer warned Sewall that a failure to relieve Mather would result "either in the death, or in something worse than that soon coming on the distressed gentleman." Already Mather had had to call off his lecture because "this wretched administration undoes him. . . ." Lydia did her part by siding with her daughter against Mather. Mather apparently had made an inventory of the estate that was, by innocence or design, greatly overvalued, and Lydia insisted on taking it for a true account. Mather's "terrible wife," the writer told Sewall, "will have a great estate whether there be one or no." In October, seemingly in the hope of ridding himself of the whole problem, Mather signed over the administration to John Briggs (the "Irish attorney"), Daniel Willard, and Pelatiah Whittemore.

In desperation Mather began taking handouts from everyone. He seems to have borrowed even from his son Cressy, whose business sense, at least, he respected and leaned on. His financial straits and Lydia's abuse of his children probably decided him on sending his daughter Elizabeth, "Liza," to live with the Boston physician and politician DR. JOHN CLARK (1667–1728), the brother of his second wife. The decision was difficult to make. As he felt more and more estranged from Lydia, Mather increasingly took to noting that Liza was the image of her mother and namesake, a living reminder of his second wife Elizabeth, and of a happier past. Another difficult decision must have been involved in what was surely one of the most painful letters he ever had to write—the one included here to THOMAS HOLLIS (1659–1731), dated August, 1720. Hollis, a Baptist merchant in London to whom Mather dedicated his *Christian Philosopher* (1721), was the first of three Hollises who were substantial benefactors to Harvard. He sent books, provided money for the president and fellows, and founded professorships in divinity, mathematics, and experimental philosophy. Earlier Mather had tried to divert Hollis' benefactions from Harvard to Yale. Now he had to plead with Hollis directly for a scholarship that would enable him to send to Harvard his son Samuel, in whom he invested much of his long-defunct hopes that

Cressy might follow in the Mather line. No less painful was the letter he wrote to President John Leverett on July 31, 1719. Its forced cordiality is the result of trying to wring a scholarship for Samuel out of the man he privately called an "infamous drone." Whether from Hollis directly, or from Hollis money already at Harvard, Samuel was granted an allowance. Mather wrote out a set of directions for him to observe while at school, and sent him to board at Cambridge with a Captain Bowman. In Mather's view, Samuel's attendance at Harvard was a birthright. But now it could be obtained only by begging for it. Young Benjamin Franklin could hardly have known the inner meaning of the advice which he received at Mather's study door: "Stoop."

By courting success on so many fields, Mather opened himself to an equal number of disappointments. As he began to work afresh on his still unpublished *Biblia Americana,* his *Curiosa* became a source of new frustration as the Royal Society failed to print them as well. Of his nearly fifty lengthy reports, enough for a large volume, there appeared in the Society's *Transactions* only a nine-page, bare-bones summary of his *Curiosa* for 1712 (in *Transactions* no. 339), stripped of the good humor and stylistic graces of the originals. Mather surmised that either his communications to the society had failed to reach London, or that Dr. John Woodward, to whom he addressed most of them, had died. To make sure that his reports reached the society he now sent them via HENRY NEWMAN (1670–1743), Secretary of the Society for Promoting Christian Knowledge and New Hampshire agent in London. Woodward, however, was alive. Relieved, Mather wrote to him the interesting letter of July 27, 1720. His commiseration for Woodward's difficulties betrays a transparent self-pity, and through the notes of comfort for Woodward one hears him resolutely beating his own breast. With Woodward alive and assuring him that most of his communications had reached the society, Mather sought other explanations for the neglect of his *Curiosa.* He wrote to Robert Wodrow that the Royal Society was now wholly swallowed up in mathematics to the exclusion of natural history. Privately he assigned his neglect to the typical English contempt for Americans and to the formula, Do Good and Be Abused. Perhaps because of his coaxing letters to the society at this time, his "Way of Proceeding in the Smallpox Inoculated" did appear in the *Transactions* for 1722. But, on the whole, his *Curiosa* in these years are shorter and hastier than the earlier ones, indeed they are sloppy and uninspired. Given the spirit of high public purpose in which he wrote them, not to mention his mania for publication, the society's failure to publish and flatter his communications must have made a dismal and discouraging addition to the burdens of a seriously ill wife and the threat of jail.

To make Mather's cares all but insupportable, in his political activities he began to pay a price for his loyalty to Governor Shute. He supported Shute vigorously because of Shute's piety and favor to Dissenters. His letter to the governor in October, 1719, epitomizes the intimacy and cordiality of their relationship and Mather's obsequiousness in trying to maintain it. A year earlier, wishing to ingratiate himself, Mather had addressed a long letter to Shute's brother, Lord Barrington, which was printed in the London *Flying-Post*—a florid panegyric on Shute aimed at forestalling any complaints against him which might reach London from Boston and threaten his removal. "His Majesty could not," Mather wrote of Shute, "among the many millions of his good subjects, find a more faithful steward of his interests." As a result of this published letter and his other good works for the governor he began to get, as he wrote to Jeremiah Dummer, the "fury and outrage of our venomous malcontents." All of Shute's opponents became his.

And opposition to Shute was widespread and venomous indeed. A new Indian war was expected; the trade was badly depreciated. The antagonism to Shute found an issue in the choice of Elisha Cooke as Speaker of the House. At first Shute refused to approve Cooke as Speaker. Many people felt that in negativing Cooke, Shute was attacking their cherished privileges. By May, 1720, Shute gave in, but he insisted on negativing the House's choice of Nathaniel Byfield and Dr. John Clark, Cooke's friends, as councillors. The Assembly defeated Shute on the issuance of paper money and rejected his wish to provide fortifications for the northern frontier. The House reduced his salary. Quickly drawn into the dispute, Mather was charged with persuading Shute to negative the choice of Dr. Clark. In the undated draft letter in this section, probably to Clark's wife, Mather swore that he had not done so, but in fact had always praised Clark. In this case, a note written at the same time to Shute, preserved at the American Antiquarian Society, shows that Mather was lying. In the note he advises Shute to put the matter before the authorities in England and to justify his right to negative Clark by arguing that "the honor of the Crown, as well as of the chair, was concerned in it." Mather's political duplicity stemmed from his domestic trials. Clark, who had been Speaker of the House in 1709–1710, supported Elisha Cooke's "popular party." On the other hand, he was also Mather's former brother-in-law and as a physician attended Elizabeth Mather during her final illness. What made Mather wish to keep Clark's friendship, however, was that Clark was now caring for Mather's beloved daughter "Liza."

As Mather's tactics became more questionable the more he worked for Shute and against Cooke, he got the name of a double-dealer. The charge that he gave his acquaintances one reputation to their faces and an opposite one privately was, as his letters show, deserved. A further, murky case involved Cooke's friend John Plaisted. Mather, Plaisted complained, had been heard to call Elisha Cooke a drunkard, on the word of Governor Shute. When Shute heard this tale, Plaisted said, he denied telling Mather anything of the kind. What he *had* told Mather, Shute reportedly said, was that John Plaisted was a drunkard. Plaisted resentfully asked Mather to clear up the affair. Mather wrote to Samuel Penhallow to disavow having called Plaisted a drunkard (the "credible gentleman" of this letter is probably Cooke). But in a memorandum, also preserved at the American Antiquarian Society, Mather deposed that he had been made to believe that Cooke went on a drunken jag for a few days at Piscataqua; discovering that the report was false, he deposed, he went to everyone to whom he had mentioned Cooke's drunkenness, and retracted his story. By self-righteously denying that he ever called Plaisted a drunkard, Mather's letter to Penhallow makes it seem that he had no part in the affair at all. Actually he had spread and then retracted a story that Cooke, if not Plaisted, had been drunk at Piscataqua. Mather's underhanded attempts to embarrass Shute's opponents, inept and certain to boomerang, made Samuel Sewall fear that Parliament would revoke the charter.

It is worth adding that in these complex, shifting political alignments Mather's former foe, Judge PAUL DUDLEY (1675–1751), now became his ally. In his momentous blast at Dudley's father Joseph in 1708, Mather had included the son with the father in his charges of bribery. He had also accused Paul Dudley of championing the claims of the crown against the interests of the people, and of publicly hoping aloud that the charter would be vacated. Mather made up with Dudley when Governor Shute, anxious for Dudley's support, appointed him a judge of the Superior Court in 1718. Dudley joined Mather in attacking Leverett as president of Harvard. Some social and intellectual ties helped ease them into the alliance. Dudley was the brother-in-law of Mather's friend John Winthrop and a Fellow of the Royal Society, to which he contributed several papers on Indian languages, rattlesnakes, and maple sugar. But in the last analysis it is hard to decide whether Dudley played in with Mather for political insurance, or Mather with him. (In 1720 Dudley moved to Roxbury, where he was very unpopular with the radicals. It is to Roxbury that Mather writes him.)

Somehow, Mather found time to encoil himself in ecclesiastical disputes as well. His letters to SAMUEL DANFORTH (1666–1727), minister at Taunton, almanac writer, poet, and friend of John Cotton of Plymouth, and to JOSEPH GERRISH (1650–1720), minister at Wenham, are only two of very many letters Mather wrote during 1719 and 1720 to resolve church difficulties in neighboring towns. His letter to Gerrish concerns a wrangle between the churches of Wenham and Chebacco that rested on seven pence. In May, 1719, Gerrish met with four Boston ministers to settle the dispute. The ministers advised one Rogers to confess that he had misrepresented Gerrish, but Rogers refused.

To Governor Saltonstall

U/AAS draft

June 29, 1719

Sir,

[Regrets not having written to Saltonstall for a while.]

Doubtless you do with pleasure consider the great and strange things done for poor Sweden in the late revolution there, which has at once restored unto them all the Gothic liberties which their two tyrants had ravished from them. Nor can you without wonder consider the immediate hand of Heaven, defeating an invasion upon the British Islands; which, if it had proceeded, must have been attended with tremendous consequences, and where the Jacobite-party is yet so very numerous, that many are not without thoughts of the clouds returning after the rain.

In the midst of these things, Your Honor will with no little astonishment consider the most grievous tidings that ever came over the Atlantic unto us. In the west of England, the Arian heresy broke in among the Dissenters, and infected many of their ministers (and some of chief note among them) to such a degree that the people shut the doors of their meeting-houses upon them. A horrid flame was enkindled, the smoke whereof was perceived on this side of the ocean. They wrote unto London to be advised upon question [sic] of that importance—whether to require a subscription to anything of a mere [human] composition were not an imposition. In a great convention of ministers now met at Salters-Hall, there were sixty-three ministers who signed the first of our thirty-nine articles, and the fifth and sixth answers in the Assembly's catechism. Fifty-three refused, on the pretense in the question but now mentioned. Your Honor has too much of sagacity to be insensible that these things have a terrible and an amazing tendency. Mr. Whiston and Clark have been the two grand satanic tools of this mischief, and multitudes of their own church ('tis said, the generality of the gentry) are gone into their heresy; but of that, there is less notice taken. I break off with my old Polycarp—*Good God, unto what times hast thou reserved us!* [Close]

To "Capt. Bowman"

U/AAS draft   July 14, 1719

Sir,

The desirable and extraordinary growth of the College puts many of the students upon a necessity of living, as all the students of some famous universities in Europe do (not in a collegiate way, but) scattered as boarders in private families.

The good people of Cambridge do with a public spirit, and with an eye to the general good, wish well to the College, and they also find the growth of it so much for their own personal interest, that we cannot but hope all the private families in Cambridge will be ready to give their best assistances.

Besides those considerations, I promise myself a good success of the request I am now going to make, from the very great respect which I know you have to the venerable grandfather of the lad for whom I make it.

What I request (and I have my worthy neighbor, Mr. Gee concurring with me in it), is that you would accept my little son Samuel Mather, with Ebenezer Gee, to the benefits of a chamber and a table in your hospitable and religious family, upon such terms as you shall judge convenient.

While you shall in such a way serve the churches of God, unto which I hope these children will anon be valuable presents, I shall be very particularly sensible of the obligations which your kindness will therein lay upon, Sir,   Your most hearty friend and servant,

To Jeremiah Dummer

U/AAS draft   July 15, 1719

Sir,

Doubtless you are informed from other hands what is a-doing on this side the water, and by what arts our foolish and froward party of malcontents got a few of their number into the Assembly, and how much they have been disappointed of doing the mischiefs they intended; and yet how much good they have given obstruction to.

You seemed among you to grow weary of my *eusebii chronicon* and so I dropped it.

It is also some discouragement unto my writing, in that so many of my silly letters come over in the public prints, as much unto my disadvantage as beyond my expectation.

If the publication of my *Religio Generosi* had been favored, it would have made me some recompense for the fury and outrage which I suffer from our venomous malcontents for the letter which the *Flying-Post* sent over to them.

[Again asserts that Dummer deserves a statue for his services to the country.]

I would not have given you the trouble of the enclosed pamphlet if it had not been to let you see some of our public circumstances. Col. Tailor (who did not hear the sermon) and Dr. Clark (the tool of the trumpeter you wot of) mightily opposed the publication of it, when the Governor and Council were proposing it.

I tender my *Psalterium* to your acceptance, with my request that you would make a present of it (or show it at least) where you think it will be most acceptable. I have so mean an opinion of the performance, that I durst not offer it unto Sir Richard Blackmore's Lady, nor let my friend Mr. Watts have the sight of it. And yet, I am willing that you should peruse the preface.

I congratulate unto the honorable Governor Yale the restored peace at Connecticut, by which his College is likely to triumph and flourish. I never had the vanity to flatter myself with any thought of an interest in his esteem or affection. But I am sure I wish him very well.

The greatest kindness that my Pamphilus can do for his old, crazy, dying friend, is to bring into their operation, if it be possible, my poor *Essays to Do Good* in a world which I am going out of. [Close]

Your most affectionate friend and servant,

To Judge Paul Dudley

U/AAS draft

July 15, 1719

Sir,

When my affection to the Governor and fidelity to the government has exposed me to the fiercest outrages of a fiery crew, and they are every hour loading me with expressions of their malice and fury, I perceive 'tis a surprise to some that neither the Governor nor government seem to take the least notice of it.

The party have often told me odd things of the derision and indignity wherewith some who have urged me to serve them have treated me, after that I have done so. But those things I must believe with discretion.

However, I cannot but ask it, as a justice, that His Excellency, with some who are his friends (tho' perhaps they durst not appear so as I have done) would oblige me so far as to appoint me a time and place wherein I may enjoy an interview with them, and at least receive their direction for my conduct under the storms raised upon me.

I am told, the honor of His Excellency is a little concerned in my being treated somewhat civilly (I will not say, gratefully) on this occasion. Some are of opinion that for his friends to publish a third edition of the wicked letter, with an introduction that shall be of some such tendency as the rough draught enclosed, may be an uncommon service to him, and all the country, and a sore contusion and confusion to the adversary. [Close]   Your Honor's most hearty servant,

To Joseph Gerrish

U/AAS draft   July 26, 1719

Sir,

The church whereof I am the servant had your letter yesterday read unto them; whereupon, tho' the brethren expressed all possible readiness to serve a church in distress, and a particular compassion for yours, yet they did not agree to send their delegates unto you on the present occasion.

They hoped that the nearer churches, and those of your next neighborhood, unto whom you have wisely applied yourselves, will be enough to answer your just intentions, and sufficiently direct, and (if need be) defend your proceedings.

But that which they seemed principally to insist upon, is that their two pastors had already heard your case and given our judgment upon it, in an instrument which you have under our hands. This they thought would be improved by those whom you have to contend withal, as an exception against our now appearing as judges, which they would have me by no means exposed unto.

Perhaps, if that instrument be offered unto the Council, it may do very near as much good as could have been done by one of my weak abilities, if I were actually present with you.

It is possible that when the delegates of the churches which attend upon the desires of Chebacco understand that the Church of Wenham has in pursuance of a vote passed several months ago, desired a council of other churches to take the cognizance of your affairs, they will not think it their duty to interpose any further.

If they do, I yet make no doubt that they are all (except Chebacco) so wise and just and good, and unprejudiced, that you might even venture them to be your judges. 'Tis very unlikely that they should so degrade themselves as to let the trouble which is given them from some froward and haughty offender, drawing into his interests a minister who has once publicly condemned him, go unrebuked.

And much more, if the churches that you have called, should act in conjunction with them.

You have doubtless reason to complain of the letters from Chebacco to the churches which have so publicly heaped reproaches upon you and your flock. Churches ought not certainly to be so infamously treated upon so little evidence as Chebacco has gone upon.

All the delegates of the churches with you, will doubtless bear their testimony against such rash tendencies to throw all the churches into combustion and confusion, as often as one or two unadvisable men shall think the peace of them all worth no more than *seven pence. A goodly price is it valued at!* And the least satisfaction that you can demand, will be that if the Council vindicate your proceedings, the vindication be read, as publicly, to the churches where you have been defamed. However, in this also, even in demanding of right, *let your moderation be known unto all men.*

But if the church which I serve had thought it proper to send me unto you, yet the holy providence of God would have stopped me, by the condition of the aged Doctor, whom I must not leave a day, at the time when he has been for now six days together laboring and languishing under an unconquerable hiccup, which threatens to terminate within a few more days (if it can't be stopped) in a general convulsion, of an apoplectic aspect. As the aged servant of God is with much presence of mind looking into the Glorious World and rejoicing in the hope of the glory there, so he much laments the troubles which have lately as well as formerly, through the managements at Chebacco, been given to so many churches, and wishes that there may be due rebukes given to them. Nor can it be any other than a lamentation with him, that so contentious a spirit should prevail, as has appeared in the long strife which has been continued among your people upon so small an original. [Close]

Your brother and servant,

To John Leverett

U/AAS draft July 31, 1719

Sir,

My Ascanius waits upon you with our full persuasion that you will be a father to him.

Near thirty years ago, I gave a madwoman at Charlestown a splendid shilling, for this: that having a little daughter of my own in my hand, and asking her whether this were not a very pretty and comely creature, she wisely and with a very instructive satire turned upon me, *The crow thinks so, Sir.*

I should have made this report of the lad who is now proud of becoming your charge, that he is of capacity good enough, presently conquers what is to be assailed, is of a temper singularly sweet and sociable, is of unspotted morals, not without a tincture and a tendency of the more vital piety, has the manly prudence and reserve in which his years are somewhat anticipated, and comforts himself in the prospect which he has of your being not only his president and governor, but also his tutor, and so his father. I was going on, but I shall never forget, *The crow thinks so, Sir.*

Wherefore, all that remains for me is to recommend him unto your wise, and kind, and paternal tuition, adding my humble request unto you, and unto the honorable Corporation, that his grandfather's request of your civilities and benignities toward a child of so much good expectation (if the crow may say so) may meet with a favorable consideration. Wherewith I subscribe, Sir,

Your most affectionate friend and servant,

To [Jedediah?] Andrews

U/AAS draft August 10, 1719

Sir,

[Laments the revival of Arianism among the Dissenters, splitting them into two camps, one subscribing to the thirty-nine articles, the other, a great number, refusing such subcription on the ground that] nothing is to be urged for to be signed but the express words of the Scripture, which all the heretics upon earth are willing to do; of these, we must not suppose all to be Arians; but I have seen them too justly called Laodiceans. And the conduct of these gentlemen, who every one of them t'other day signed the article aforesaid, that they might qualify themselves for their places, appears very unaccountable. The grand poisoner has been Dr. Clark, who has refined upon Arianism so far as to decry the Arians; and yet his whole (pretended) New Scheme is in the very words of it, the vomit of the infamous Valentinus Gentilis, whom the Switzers beheaded for his blasphemies about the middle of the sixteenth century. Tho' we are for the communion of all good men on the terms of that substantial piety which has united them, yet it is very weakly done to call it a persecution, when we refuse communion with such as profess heresies destructive of all piety. But upon the principles of these gentlemen, there are no heretics whatsoever but what we must receive to our communion if they will but say, *we believe the Scriptures.* There never came worse tidings over the Atlantic than what we now hear of this fearful apostasy, this dreadful division, which a lamentable decay of piety among our brethren has been an introduction to.

I am sorry that any of the poor ecstatics are come hither also. Their false prophecies, the mean things delivered in their inspirations, and the total denial of all success to their ministry, argues a satanic energy to have been upon the most of those poor people. But I doubt whether the strange descent from the invisible world upon ours, in the whole affair, have been treated with so wise a consideration as it has called for. God graciously preserve His people from delusions.

To Samuel Penhallow

U/AAS draft   [Probably August 20, 1719]

Sir,

Just now I was assaulted with a threatening letter from one who subscribes himself John Plaisted, and charges me with saying *That Govr Shoot said, I tould yew that Cors John Plaisted was a drunkard, and had been so several times:* and he says, *I am informed of this by a credebell gentelmn.* You'll excuse me that I transcribe with utmost exactness.

If this be the Mr. Plaisted that formerly I had the honor and pleasure of being acquainted withal (which I never was with more than one) you will oblige me with informing him, that you have it under my hand that I never spoke one diminutive or disadvantageous or disreputable word of him to any man living in all my life, much less any such scandal as he mentions. Nor did I ever hear His Excellency Governor Shute, or any man else in the world, speak such a thing of him. As for the *credible gentleman* that was his informer, I am suspicious it might be one who is generally esteemed very faulty and vicious in the character aforesaid. I am sure he was too much of a liar to be deserving the character of a *credible gentleman.*

This is all I have to offer. But whereas the gentleman demands of me *I pray you woold write me the hole of it fully*—I shall at present rather discharge my duty by writing the whole of it fully to you, my cordial and constant friend, that he may be informed by one whom I take to be a *credible gentleman,* of all that I think proper to say unto him, having many reasons, besides one to be found in the XXVI chapter of the Proverbs, to decline answering his letter in any other way. As I never did him the least injury in my life, I wish all possible prosperity to him and his. . . . Sir,

To Jeremiah Dummer

U/AAS draft   August 25, 1719

[Notes having received a letter from Lord Barrington.]

I prepared for the public a composure wherein all persons of erudition must own they have some entertainment, something that must be agreeable, a composure wherein I have endeavored a part in the royal priesthood. The title of it is *Religio Generosi.* I made a dedication of it unto Mr. Barrington, and therein I made use of your name also, being willing to testify unto the whole world my esteem for you.

[Describes to Dummer his arrangement with Thomas Bradbury, as in the letter of 13 October, 1718.] I have had no answer [from Bradbury]; but just now, Mr. Barrington lets me know that Mr. Bradbury is very much fallen under his displeasure, and speaks of the manuscript aforesaid with such an air as makes me think he is not fond of hearing any more about it. Now, my friend; if you will please to visit Mr. Bradbury, and either in concert with him, or wholly in your own way, procure the publication of this treatise, I subtreat you that the former dedication being laid aside, you would accept and allow of the enclosed instead of it. Or, if you, and my worthy friend, think the work unworthy of the light, I earnestly ask that you would be so good as to take the manuscript into your hands, and send it back to New England by the first convenient opportunity. [Close]   Yours forever,

To Judge Paul Dudley

U/AAS draft   August 31, 1719

Sir,

[Claims to share Dudley's affection for the governor.]

In the exercise of this disposition, I cannot but offer you my sentiments, that His Excellency's resolution (if he has one) to continue Giles in his command at Brunswick, is as likely as any one thing to give our diminutive and calumnious crew a handle to hurt him, as anything that has yet happened. Hitherto, his incomparable prudence and patience has left 'em without any real matter to work upon. But now they have evidences that this officer makes it his business to debauch both the English and Indians, whereby His Majesty's interest in the eastern parts is in evident hazard of ruin. Yea, there are such proofs of his vile practises to divert the Indians from the reception of the Gospel, that the commissioners will doubtless at their next meeting, with earnest remonstrances, beseech His Excellency to remove him, which had much better be done before. His Excellency's known virtue, and his noble and constant concern for the countenancing of piety, is a more powerful orator with him than we can be, for his putting a better man (who stands ready, and will *see when good cometh*) in the place of one who does corrupt the earth. And upon second thoughts he will doubtless think that an aversion to gratify a blockhead, who happens to be in ill-terms with the man aforesaid, as well as we, will not be a sufficient reason for him to do what may arm that blockhead and company with clamors against him.

[Asks Dudley to urge the governor to remove the "obnoxious man."]

I would myself do my part in it, but I am loath to meddle too far in political matters, tho' indeed this being a religious one, I must think of some other excuse; and can find none, but that my merits are not such as to entitle me to any influences. [Close]

Your Honor's most sincere and faithful servant,

To Isaac Watts

U/AAS draft   September 7, 1719

Sir,

Your very charming version of the Psalms has arrived unto me, and

I rejoice in the favor which the glorious Hearer of Prayer has granted you, in his restoring your health and strength so far that you can at all resume your studies. [Says that Watts has many friends in New England.]

But while you do so admirably accommodate the songs of the Old Church unto the plainest intentions of Christianity in our days, you will not wonder if some are fond of retaining all the very words of the ancient inspiration, partly because there is a profound sense in every one of them, and every syllable is full of instruction to them who are (which, alas, too few are!) so wise as to observe it; and partly because the spirit of prophecy has therein described unto us the condition of the church, both in our days and in those which are to come, with intimations that carry a vast pleasure and wonder in them. For this cause, one in this country, who has always a very great and just value for your performances, a while since published a *Psalterium Americanum*, with which he would have presented you if his mean opinion of the work had not rendered him ashamed of thinking to treat so critical a master in poetry with what can deserve little other than censure from him.

[Laments the growth of Arianism and schism among the English Dissenters.]

To Samuel Danforth

U/AAS draft   September 28, 1719

Sir,

[Expresses his distress over Danforth's recent illness.]

We are further distressed by the advice we have of ecclesiastical troubles arising in your neighborhood. And on how trivial an occasion, of how criminal an original!

'Tis very strange to find a silential vote counted invalid in cases wherein most of our churches have used it, and where they that make a strife about it, have till now been in the use of it. If they are now dissatisfied, it must not be upon what is past; but they may for the future agree, as every society may, upon what way of voting they will take satisfaction in.

A negative vote doubtless is not universally and perpetually to be called for, but only in such cases as the society under a good conduct may judge proper for it. That question, whether a church are to be carried by the number of voices, without regard to strength of reason and argument, I don't know whether I am acute enough to understand it. Be sure, the major vote must carry a matter. For every man thinks his own reason and argument the strongest; and, I pray, who shall be judge?

Notwithstanding the power of a particular church to order its own affairs, yet when baptism has been administered, according to the direction of a general council of all the churches, and a church has gone on for years together in such an administration, it seems a very unaccountable thing for such a church to alter it. And if the pastor be for continuing of the administration, the vote for innovations will have his negative upon it. So he may go on in the right ways of the Lord.

In the church that I serve, we are so far from calling for the manual vote of all the baptized on this occasion, that we don't ask it from the brethren of the communion themselves. But having propounded the candidate, a week before, he is received into the covenant (if no objection has been offered) without any more ado. [Close]

Your affectionate,

To Governor Shute

U/AAS draft

October [16?], 1719

Sir,

A preacher upon Joh[n] II 3, *They have no wine*, divided his text (as the fashion then was) into two parts. First, here is *Liquor optimus*, that is, *Vinum*. Secondly, here is *Rumor pessimus*; that is, *Non habent*. This was no doubt in Queen Elizabeth's days, when sermons were so filled with latinities, that a grave alderman, who was yet a Roman Catholic but understood not a word of Latin, told a preacher after sermon, that he was much edified and gratified by his worthy sermon, in the hopes it gave him that the Latin service would return again.

[Is happy that Shute has returned from New Hampshire.]

But I should be guilty of an inexcusable negligence and ingratitude if I should forget the orders Your Excellency left with me, to send my servant unto your cellar with what the chemists call a *receiver*, by the arrival whereof Your Excellency proposed with the *Liquor optimus* to prevent one *Rumor pessimus*, which indeed is the only one that ever Your Excellency found me the author of.

Thus I do instead of praying for a pardon, endeavor to avoid the want of one, and at the same time render myself a subject of a favor from one whose wine has never any relish to him, except his friends take more of it than he does himself. [Florid close]

Your Excellency's most obliged and obedient servant,

To John Winthrop

IV Coll 8/MHS   November 30, 1719

My dear Friend,

Your late illness has very sensibly indisposed me, put me and kept me in considerable and continual pain. I beseech you to fetch me out of it by giving it me under your hand that you are alive, and that you are better, yea, and that you have got good by your illness.

In the same letter give me as punctual a description as you can of your water-dove, that so my account of it may be authentic as well as punctual, and may have your name (which I would snatch at all occasions to do honor to) incorporated into it. Yea, if you can, let it be written with a quill which the wing of the bird shall afford you.

I hope very quickly to transmit unto you what I remit this winter unto the Royal Society. In the meantime I have nothing to entertain you withal, but the first compliments which were ever paid in our country to the *fifth of November*, which, doubtless, will be whiggish enough to gratify you. [Peace is expected.]

Your most hearty friend and servant,

To Thomas Prince

U/MHS   December 23, 1719

Sir,

It has been told me that you have Mr. Whiston's *Speculations upon the Celestial Explosions*, with which Europe was entertained a while ago.

The accounts which I have received from a considerable distance, both northward and southward, of the fiery glade that surprised us on the eleventh instant, make me wish to see the Whistonian pamphlet. You are always obliging, Sir,   Your brother and servant,

To John Winthrop

IV Coll 8/MHS   January 11, 1720

Sir,

Inasmuch as the favor I received from you the last week (after my forwarding of my last packet) calls for the quickest as well as the deepest acknowledgments, I could not let this post return without my acknowledging that I have received it, and that I have nothing to keep me from starving under the bitter cold of the season, except I sweat under the load of your kindnesses, whereof I am extremely and forever sensible; and that I have assigned our dear Soogelande † a very fair lodging in our *Biblia Americana*, with an honorable mention and character of the generous hand which like another Noah, sends him forth unto us.

[Asks him to write.]

'Tis dreadful cold. My ink-glass in my standish [inkstand] is froze and split, in my very stove. My ink in my very pen suffers a congelation, but my wit much more. For it serves only to tell you that by the next post you may (if we live) hear further from me. [Close]

Your affectionate friend and servant,

My dear—hast thou not yet with thee one of Sir Richard's [Blackmore's] volumes, his *Essays*, in prose? Examine thy library.

To Henry Newman

U/AAS draft   February 17, 1720

Sir,

[Thanks him for passing along letters from Tranquebar.]

I have thought it my duty to present unto my masters in the Royal Society such *Curiosa Americana* as I could get the time and skill to become the owner of. Several worthy members of that illustrious body which I have had the honor of corresponding withal, have been taken off by death, and left me the faster dying behind them. And after the rest, I have had some intimations that my most learned friend Dr. Woodward is also dead, which my not hearing from him all this last

† The water-dove. In *Biblia Americana* Mather writes that the Indians call the bird "*Coecoe-on-Sogelande* [*sic*]; which is as much to say, *The Messenger of the Great Rain.*"

year confirms me in my fear of its being true. Considering with myself hereupon to what gentleman of the Royal Society I should apply myself with my little stores, I could think of none more inviting than the incomparable Dr. Chamberlain, of whose uncommon and universal erudition I have seen convincing demonstrations, and of whose excellent candor I have received such an account (especially from our friends Judge Dudley and Mr. Belcher) that I cannot but presume upon his favorable reception of what an American stranger has addressed unto him. I do therefore entreat of you that thro' your hands these mean collections may pass into his, and that you, who know my small capacity, joined with a variety of employments which does not fall to everybody's share, would make on my behalf the apology necessary for the meanness of them. [Close]

Your most obliged friend and servant,

Unaddressed

U/AAS draft [Probably early 1720]

Sir,

Through the wrath of the Lord of Hosts, how much the land is darkened! What is it our brethren would be at, when they insist on a subscription to the express words of the Scripture as a sufficient basis for communion, and reproach all demands of explication in others, as if it charged the Scriptures with insufficiency!

These very weak men! Do they maintain, that we must embrace as our brethren in Christ, and admit unto the Christian communion and ministry with us, all those whom it would be a fault in us to persecute! No difference between toleration and coalition—what fusion this! What sophistry!

Or, do they really think that there are no damnable heresies! That Socinians, for instance, are our brethren in Christ! Or Quakers, both of whom have no Christ, but One who is much an idol as that on the plain of Dura! Are there any heretics in the world who do not subscribe the express words of the Scripture! Hold they that if a man be not a bad liver, he may hold what heresies he will, and yet be accepted with God! What notion have they of living to God, without the faith of a CHRIST who is One God with His Eternal Father!

Dissenters, who hath bewitched you! Nothing but a fearful decay of piety could have produced what we have seen in our brethren! What resentments would a Baxter, an Owen, a Bates, and the men of the former generation, express if they should see the ignorance and the treachery of our woeful day! No; my poor letter, which they have published, is all right, all just. Not a syllable to be retracted.

And the folly, I say the folly, of those men who represent as not consisting well with my zealous profession for a union on the terms of piety—is to be pitied rather than answered. [The letter breaks off in the middle of the next sentence.]

To John Leverett

U/AAS draft

March 10, 1720

Sir,

With my humble thanks to you for your favors to the son and hope of my family, and prayers for the continuance thereof, he now, with all possible alacrity, flies back unto your tender wing, where he assures himself of his being very happy, as I do myself of his proving no ungrateful soil to your instruction.

I am, with great respect, Sir, Your most obliged friend and servant,

To John Nicols

U/AAS draft

April 18, 1720

Brethren,

[Grieves over the "encumbrances under which your evangelical affairs are laboring."]

It has been a trouble to us that we have been able to do no more among our people for your assistance in your laudable design of erecting an edifice for the worship of God. But you will very much excuse us, when you shall understand how much the people of this town have been of late set upon the building [torn: apparently "of meeting-houses"], even of needless ones; and of such as have only a tendency to bring heavy burdens on the neighborhood. The corruption that has lain at the bottom of these proceedings, and the sad things which have been improved as temptations for them, would be a story which you will expect from other hands rather than ours. But these follies among us, wherein we are doing of hurt under a show of good unto ourselves, have disabled us for doing of that good unto others which we could have wished for. And then, the necessary assistance which is demanded from us, for our own infant and nearer plantations, adds to our incapacity of doing for others at a greater distance from us. We find here that when a few people are under [provocation?] set upon it, they can raise three or four thousand pounds for a meeting-house, and the fine pews will pay very much of the charge. But, alas, a zeal of God will not so often provoke to good works, as a more inferior principle.

The advice which you desire from us, concerning an address from you to our General Assembly, which meets not before the latter end of the next May, must be, that we cannot as yet find it advisable. Because we have so many towns wherein a few people may find occasion to declare for the Church of England (which are the Dissenters in this country) and may then take occasion to solicit the General Assembly for a contribution to build for them (which would marvellously involve us and perplex us) therefore, and for some other causes, we find our friends in the government here incline rather to study some other way of serving you. . . . [Close]   Your brethren and servants,

[Probably to Mrs. John Clark]

U/AAS draft   [c. May, 1720]

Madam,

Having been informed that the gentleman your husband (as well as his brother) have taken up an aversion for me, and given very public discovery of it, on the account of my having advised the Governor to put his negative on the Assembly's choice of Dr. Clark as a councillor, I take this occasion to declare unto you the utter and entire falsehood of it.

I write not unto either of the two brothers because I am not altogether unapprehensive of the sentiments they have of me. But I write unto you, because I am under many obligations to you, and obliged particularly to give you satisfaction, and you will believe me, at least, when I declare with such a solemnity as I am now using on this occasion.

I do then here declare under my hand, and as before the glorious God, that I never once in my life advised the Governor to put his negative on Dr. Clark; but instead of advising to it, I have ever done what is directly the reverse of it. Above a year ago, my intercessions were they that prevailed with the Governor to defer and forbear that expression of the uneasiness, which his apprehensions of Dr. Clark's disaffection to him had given him. And on this election, I again prayed that no such thing might be done. I begged for the leaving of it undone, as a thing which I always thought would be attended with uneasy consequences. The men who have charged me with being any way directly or indirectly accessory or instrumental to this negative, I do here under my hand affirm to every one of them [a one-line parenthesis torn] *There is no such thing as thou sayest, but thou fainest them out of thy own heart.* (Tho' 'tis as true as that I am the author [of] a pamphlet lately published, by *An American.*) Yea, I affirm that some other gentlemen also, who have been thought the persuaders of this matter, were far enough from being so.

I have ever spoken of Dr. Clark as a pious, learned, useful gentleman, and one of a singular goodness in his temper. And if I have at any time lamented the misunderstanding between the Governor and him, this is all that the most malicious talebearer in the world can say I have ever let fall, that the worst aggravations of malice could call disrespectful. If any such discord-sowers have put a dress of their own upon anything I have said, and make it carry a defamatory aspect on him, all I shall say is *I know who is their father.* As for me, the leasing-makers dare not look me in the face!

[Denies that he has ever said anything injurious about her husband.] I court no man's favor. I give thanks unto him, and unto you, for your parental goodness to dear Liza, the lively image of her lovely mother, of whom I never spoke anything in my life of such a disreputable tendency as the lying talebearers invented (for the disturbance of surviving relatives) five years ago. But, because I am sensible my character must lie much at the mercy of lying and loathsome talebearers, I only ask that according to the ancient law, the child may not suffer for the crimes of the father, and that dear Liza may not lose her esteem with her uncle, whatever her father may do for his. . . .

To John Winthrop

IV Coll 8/MHS

May 9, 1720

My dear Friend,

This day sennight I received by the hand of a post (whom I never saw before) a packet with two letters from you, for which he makes me pay (tho' more than you designed) no more than I shall always count well spent for the least line of yours which I ever set a value upon.

In one of your letters, which is dated Jan. 13, you say *I now enclose to you for a safe conveyance, a small box directed to Dr. Woodward.* Alas, this box never came to me, was never delivered, nor did I ever hear of it until (as I said) *this day sennight.* So ill do our people serve us!

I would gladly entertain you, even with packets of new things. But at this time I go not beyond the bulk of a single letter, because I would not put you to I know-not-what expense; but first request you over again so to settle the method of our correspondence as (these hard times!) may be least expensive.

[Tells of the outbreak of Arianism.]

The Holy One has ordered it that a letter of mine, written the last fall upon that subject, has been published and scattered through the nation, and has proved an incredible service to the cause of truth, which was laboring. And the compliments upon me for it are contrivances to fetch over thither the meanest man in our country.

Peace is the word among the nations of Europe. Only the Russian leviathan wants a hook in his jaws. I hear the King of Prussia has one (of a hundred thousand men) ready for him. [Close]

Your assured friend and servant,

My friend, can't you recover the missing volume of Sir Richard Blackmore's essays? Have you thought yet what special oblation to make for the life of your son?

To Jacob Wendel

U/AAS draft   May 10, 1720

Sir,

Your known disposition to do good endears you to all good men, as well as to me; and you will take it well if I suggest unto you one agreeable opportunity for it.

A late author, whose name is Dr. Mastricht, has published in Holland a work, in two quarto volumes, entitled *Theoretica-practica Theologia.*

The world has never yet seen so valuable a system of divinity and of church history. 'Tis orthodox, 'tis concise, 'tis complete. In one word, it is everything. The sun shines not [on] any human composure that equals it. In these two volumes, our young ministers would have a rich library; 'twould set them up for the discharge of their ministry, more than a library of more scores of pounds otherwise placed, than they are able to lay out and furnish them for every good work! Happy would our churches be, if they were fed from the stores, and with the admirable spirit of the most real and vital piety, all along breathing therein, which are to be found in Dr. Mastricht.

Now, Sir, for the sake of our young ministers, and of the churches that expect service from them, I address you with a request that you would obtain from Holland, a number . . . of these books, at as low a rate as you can, which your correspondents will find in the shop of every noted bookseller, and run the hazard of selling them at their arrival here.

If I am living at the time, I shall do more than the duty of a very zealous hawker for you. I will employ all the force I have to get the books advantageously disposed of. If I am not (as I suppose I shall not be) so many months hence alive, do you publish this letter and advice of mine as far as you please, to render my design effectual.

Thus let us do all the good we can, and as fast as we can. The time is short. Your affectionate friend and servant,

Unaddressed

U/AAS draft

[1720]

Sir,

My domestic circumstances oblige me to draw off one hundred pounds of the three in your hands, and to transfer it into the more immediate possession and disposal of a child, unto whose share it falls.

At the same time, the interest for the last year now become due, is what the domestic necessities do also compel me to entreat of you that it may accompany it.

If you please therefore to deliver one hundred and eighteen pounds unto the bearer, Mr. Dan. W. (who acts in the quality of my attorney) it will very sensibly gratify one to whom I know you always take delight in doing what shall be acceptable, and who is, Sir,

Your hearty friend and servant,

To John Briggs
U/AAS draft   [1720]

My dear Friend,

When I think on the favor of God which I have received and enjoyed in your friendship, and in the kindness which you have done me, when all men forsook me, and those on whom I had most reliance proved broken reeds, I find myself unable to express the sentiments of gratitude which I am filled withal, first unto our gracious God, and then unto you, His instrument.

I shall be forever studying how to answer my strong obligations to you. Besides the demands which you may in justice make on the estate that you have served (which you will represent unto the judge), I must personally consider what returns I may be capable of making to you.

Now, as a sort of pawn or pledge ('tis not the first time, a staff has been made one) with which in your hand you may at all times irresistibly demand of me all the services that I am capable of rendering you, I present you with a staff which has never yet been in any hand, but what you have a value for. Take it, and keep it, and use it, and remember me with it. A staff has before now had such marvellous efficacies as this will by no means pretend unto. The only point in which this mean staff hopes and begs to be efficacious is that of being accepted as a small testimony of my love to one who has proved a strong rod unto me, when I was just sinking; and of my being, Sir,

Yours, under perpetual and adamantine obligations,

[Probably to Increase Mather, Jr.]
U/AAS draft   [1720?]

Child,

What in the world shall I do!

But having such a son in my quiver I shall not be afraid of my adversary in the gate.

[Chewte?] going to live out of town duns me today with a horrible bill of 14£, which must be paid before he can make up with his creditors, and get leave to go.

I know of no way to discharge my debts but by the rent and (anon)

sale of my house and land—and if once I get out of debt, I promise myself never to get in again.

In the view of that, you have already delivered me from one much greater encumbrance. If you can in the same view deliver me from this lesser one, I think I have no more to afflict and humble me.

However, you have a mind as ingenious and projecting on such occasions as mine is beyond all expression awkward, as being wholly swallowed up in what is for the good of others, to which I have been all my days entirely devoted.

I request your advice to me, and if it may be without any disadvantage to you, your interposition in the present difficulties, which, I hope, are the last in which you will find involved,

One who loves you as well as yours,

To Robert Wodrow

U/NLS   June 10, 1720

Sir,

[Sends along some "American composures."]

I long for your history of Scotland, and hope that it will find a better acceptance than the history of New England which one Mr. Neil has lately [word illegible] of the religion in it, and of everything that most embellished it (and added some things from some very lying authors) and so recommended it unto an age which has a relish for such things as may least serve the cause of piety. But yet the gentleman has expressed so much good affection to my poor country that I cannot but wish a good reception for his performance. You will not wonder at it if a work of such a noble and holy design as yours meet with some envious enemies. [Claims that God preserves New England from Arianism and Gentilism although "we have our share in the epidemical decay of piety in which the churches of the Reformation are languishing." From here on the margin of the letter-book is tightly bound, concealing the final letters of the line.]

You were pleased once to touch upon someth[ing of] a philosophical consideration in the letters w[ith which] you obliged me. The present Secretary of [the] Royal Society so confines himself to mathem[atical] matters in the *Philosophical Transactions* wh[ich he] publishes, that natural history is almost for[gotten?] in them; so that the annual remittances [which] I make unto my masters, and are usually as m[any] as there be months in the year, lie buried in [obscurity?]. However, I am informed that there is now [at?] press at London a very large collection of t[he?] discoveries and curiosities whereto our age is [?], interspersed with the devotionary strains of [the] *Philosophical Religion,* but so evangelical[ly?] such claims are entered for a glorious [Christian?] philosophy, as were never yet made in th[e world?]. I know not whether the publishers have [cal?]led this work *Religio Generosi* or *Philosophia,* having left it unto them to determine. But I shall direct them to send it unto Gl[asgow] when it is come out of the press. [Close]

Your most affectionate brother and servant,

To John Winthrop

IV Coll 8/MHS (draft at AAS)   July 4, 1720

My very dear Friend,

Your very kind present, behold, I have consecrated unto a service which I am sure you will be pleased withal. And this I did not because I abound in riches, for I encounter with many straits and wants, and *Res augusta domi* exposes me to many difficulties; but for this very reason, because I thought it a service that you would be pleased withal.

In this publication I have had the experiment of my dear Franckius renewed unto me. For, having prepared the treatise, but being at an utter loss how to publish it, *just then* your bounty arrived, by which it comes abroad for the service of the most substantial piety.

I propose to lodge your *Coheleth* (for 'tis *yours*) in such hands as it may be most useful to, especially the colleges here and in the Lower Saxony. And I pray that you would give me your direction how to send you a dozen or two to pass through your hands to yours at New Haven.

But in a singular manner next unto my own son, I intend these instructions for yours (whom you shall give me leave also to adopt for mine) who, I hope, will begin to read before he is two years old, and begin to LIVE before he is four, and give you the heart of a glad father with his wisdom. [Close]   Your most obliged friend and servant,

[Adds that he expects to hear shortly from the Royal Society.]

To Isaac Watts

U/AAS draft   July 5, 1720

My very dear Brother,

[Urges him to combat Arianism.]

I continue my poor zeal for a civil indulgence to all good subjects and good neighbors, and for a sacred communion with all that under various forms by adhering unto the maxims of piety, oblige us to esteem them our brethren in CHRIST. But I should sin against a glorious Christ if I should not count them His enemies, who deny the eternal power and godhead of Him, who is my Creator as well as my Redeemer, and who will have Him to be in His nature inferior (and if He be *at all*, He must be *infinitely* inferior) unto His Eternal Father. These men, by setting up an idol for a Christ, and hastening after another God, go to rob us of the faith which is the life of our souls; 'tis impossible for us to live by the faith of the SON of GOD if we hearken to them. Such traitors to the King of Heaven we must beware of coming into the least misprision of their treason. You must pardon me, my dear Isaac, if I do not repent of my excluding the Arians out of all my projections for the uniting of all good men in a syncretism of piety, which you have blamed me for. I must and will do all I can, that all good men may exclude them and shun a fellowship with such idolaters; and I shall mourn that any dear children of God should so patiently bear with them that are evil, so patiently see His Eternal Son, and their Beloved Saviour, pulled down from the throne of His Glory. The zeal of God was made for this, if any occasion. I am loath to say unto a brother so unspeakably precious to me, anything that may be grievous to him; and yet I will tell him that I have heard some of our best people wish that a passage in his *Lyric Poems* (which are passionately esteemed and admired with us) which compliments one who finds a CHRIST in the Heavens, another than what he took him to be—before His going thither—had been omitted.

[Says he has fully expressed his views on Arianism in a recent letter to Reinolds.]

I have written to our brother Neil, my thanks for the good affection he has expressed unto our poor country in his History.

And I have nothing more at this time to add, but only to pray your acceptance of a few more small American treatises, which are our latest publications. If our *style and manner of writing* be, as the historian tells us, inferior to that of you Europeans, yet the piety inculcated in what we write is as necessary for them, as for us who are so much inferior to them. [Close]   I am, in Him, Your brother and servant,

To Daniel Neil

DII/AAS draft   July 5, 1720

Sir,

The *History of New England* whereof you have made a kind present unto me, obliges me to render you my thanks for the favor you have done unto me, and for the honor that you have done in many points unto my country.

Your performance is the reverse of what was done by the malicious and satanic pen of one *Oldnixson* (some such name) in his account of the *English Empire in America*, whose history of New England has far more lies than pages in it, and the more unpardonable because contradicted in the very book which he was at the very same time living on, and railing at.

No doubt some of our people may inform you of certain passages in your well-penned History which might call for a little further elucidation, a thing which is incident unto all human composures, and which must not be wondered at. But I hope they will be all sensible of the candor which you generally express towards the country, and of the good wishes which you have to the welfare of it.

We ought certainly to have a grateful sense of it, that any men of worth should count such a poor, despised, maligned country as ours worthy of their cognizance; and much more of such pains as you have taken to represent us under an advantageous character unto the world.

But I must confess to you that my poor country was never famous for gratitude unto its benefactors. Nay, we have greatly dishonored our profession by our defect in that virtue. They that serve New England expect the recompense at the Resurrection of the Just. So that, if you hear little from us that may appear a just consideration of your merits, you must not be surprised at it. However, some of our best men are considering of the most proper way to testify their friendly construction and thankful reception of what you have done for us. And our excellent Governor is not wanting to prompt them unto their duty in it.

[Sends along some of his works.]

                        Your obliged friend, brother, and servant,

Unaddressed

[Probably July, 1720]

My dear Brethren,

There is (as you know, no doubt, better than I) a meeting of some gentlemen tomorrow upon an intention to obtain from the College some singular testimonies of respect and honor to Mr. Neil for his History of New England.

A strong (and well-grounded) aversion in me, for having the least hand in any affairs relating to the government of the College (to which, and to the present government whereof, I wish infinitely well) will not allow my being with you. And yet I will take leave to offer my sentiments unto you, my two brethren, who are willing at all times to hear me with candor, and bear with my many infirmities.

Tho' I do abroad speak with all due tenderness of Mr. Neil's performance, and I do really think the esteem he sometimes professes for the country deserves to be thankfully acknowledged, yet I will to you in private more freely explain my most inward thoughts, which the law of goodness will release me from uttering unto others.

The poor Church History of New England was written with no design so much as to serve all the interests of real and vital piety, for which it lays hold on all occasions. And greater men than any that have treated it with a contempt (whereof I am very patient) have written to me that if it has met with any contempt, it has been because a disservice to the most glorious piety was not pursued in it.

All that my brother Neil has done has been to put the Church History into the order of annals, and entirely to divest it of, and to divert it from, the service principally intended in it, and make it a dry political story; and also strip it of those embellishments which, however the modern gust cares not for, the famous Alsop (discouraging the ministers in his time from attempting an abridgment) had such a relish for, that he said in an assembly of them, *'Twas a weak proposal to abridge that work, for there was nothing superfluous in it; but instead of abridging it, they should all read it all twice over, as he had done.*

But I would with an equal indifference entertain the invectives which that poor work has undergone, and the compliments (very excessive ones) which I have received from eminent persons in more than three nations upon it.

If Mr. Neil had stopped here, all might have been well enough. But there are many points wherein he has done very indiscreetly and very injuriously.

His taking his materials for the story of the troubles from the invisible world from such a senseless, lying, malicious wretch as Calef, when he had (besides others) Mr. Hales's before him; and the gross falsehoods which he inserts thereupon (particularly a base lie concerning a gentlewoman, that never had the least foundation of truth in it), and the Sadducean folly which he discovers—is no mighty recommendation for his performance.

But then, his living upon the Quakers' Martyrology as an authentic relation; and after he had been forced, with Mr. Colman's words (which I was always glad of) to confute and confound his own endeavors to blacken the country, to publish in his appendix an abstract of the country's laws, whereof not one has been in force for near this forty years, as if they were our present laws, and conceal the present laws, and all the public rescission which we have made (and was the first thing we did in a convention after the Revolution) of the laws which might infringe a due liberty of conscience, upon which there come over to us this year letters from several quarters, moving for a repeal of those laws—a man must be a very pitiful historian to proceed in such a fashion.

To pass by a thousand other things (which if Mr. Neil had had the sense to have shown his M.SS. unto our valuable friends Mr. D. or Mr. N. would have been expunged) I cannot forgive his indignity to the College. Upon his contemptuous account of our library there he adds, as if none brought up there knew how to write modern English. An eminent person in England complains to me of this passage, as *excessively silly*. The gentlemen to whom I now write are a sufficient contradiction to it. Nor do the President, and some others now residing at Cambridge, want Mr. Neil to instruct them in an English style.

But it is plain that this my Independent brother, is (as too many honest men of that denomination are), a very weak and shallow man. And it will not be much for the reputation of our college to consider him as otherwise.

But as in emetics, at last the green comes up, and so the poor man vomits up all his gall; so I do at last freely show the utmost of my gall on this occasion.

I am not without a suspicion that the original of demands (I mean the ultramarine original) to have some special recompense from hence to Mr. Neil, may be this (*Timeo Danaus*). There is a strong and a deep conspiracy in our very wicked nation at this day to dethrone the eternal SON of GOD. A number of our godly brethren have been so sinful as to be drawn into a very perfidious and criminal silence on this horrid occasion, out of complaisance to ———. Mr. Neil has been one of these unhappy men. Our more faithful brethren write over to us, about *pumping for compliments from hence unto them.* If Mr. Neil had not been one of that Laodicean party, perhaps there would not have been this pumping for him. You see 'tis a time of jealousies.

I leave all to your wisdom and sagacity. I am not willing these impertinencies of mine should be communicated unto any (except unto your honorable President, with my service to him, and condolence in his late and great bereavement).

[In the margin: I have not the least objection to make against the College writing a letter of thanks to Mr. Neil for the pains he has taken in his History.]

To Jeremiah Dummer

U/AAS draft   July 13, 1720

My dear Friend,

[Thanks him effusively for his financial aid to *Religio Generosi.* Says he will already have much of the news from his other correspondents in America.] From them, you will particularly hear what a disturbance our satanic party here have made, and how much trouble our good Governor has had with them, and what a victory is this day obtained over them. 'Tis to be hoped that having thus begun to fall, they will surely fall, and we may anon see better things than what have lately been found among us. There was a time when this poor colony had like to have been utterly broken up through a controversy about a hog. (The gentleman contending with law-suits about a right unto a stray sow, until the case was brought into the General Court, where it raised a contention about the Governor's negative period.) Your friends will inform you to your wonderment how near we have just been to ruin, upon a controversy about an animal, *Epicuri de gregè,* and one oftener fuddled than any hog in the country.

[Expresses his friendship for Judge Paul Dudley and for William Dummer, Jeremiah's brother.]

Our college increases in the number of students; between forty and fifty were admitted the last year, at the head of which numerous class is a very promising little spark ycleped Samuel Mather, the son of a most cordial and zealous friend of yours.

Yale College flourishes very notably, and all differences which threatened the life of that society are most happily composed, especially through the decisive bounty of our honorable friend unto New Haven, whose name will now always be mentioned with honor in our American world. [Asks him to thank Elihu Yale.]

Your most affectionate friend and servant (under the ponderous load of ten thousand obligations),

To Dr. John Woodward

U/AAS draft   July 27, 1720

—And is my dear Doctor yet alive? I heard he was dead. I read what imported his death! I feared that he, as well as the bright stars discovered by Gemma and by Kepler and by Hevelius had wholly disappeared. My fear was confirmed by my not having received one line from him, even for two years together; nor known whether he had received my poor continuations of our *Curiosa Americana.*

—But with the joy of one that upon waking finds himself safe after a very terrifying dream, I find him yet living, and shining with his distinguishing luster among the lesser fires. [Mentions that Woodward's packet, containing his *The State of Physic* never reached him, yet he happened upon it, read it, and was entertained and edified by it. Professes surprise at the book's hostile reception.]

I see that tho' you allow so just and great a share to bile in the animal economy, bile does more operate and is really more powerful than one could have easily imagined. When I see how fiercely and how coarsely they who please to make themselves your adversaries fall upon you, I blush at the sight; I blush for them who are not sensible of what they provoke indifferent spectators to think of them. One would almost suspect that they had eaten of a famous weed growing in our neighborhood, upon the tasting whereof people are seized with folly, and continue in the fancies and actions of natural fools for several days together. That ever so honorable and serviceable an order of men should so expose themselves, and the most valuable science professed by them, and make themselves the diversion and the derision of those that should rely upon them as their oracles! While they take such pains to render one another vile, they do but wound themselves and stab their own reputation, and vilify their profession, and oblige people to reflect, *are these they whom we are to trust our lives withal!* How mean and how sad a thing is it, that instead of observing, *Figulus figulum,* the observation must run, *Medicus medicum.* [Urges Woodward to be patient in the face of attack, and to "shine on."]

A very considerable clerk, handling that problem *An Semper calumniis respondendum* wisely answers, No, by no means. But go on writing of such books as will be of a lasting benefit unto mankind. [Urges him on.] Good Sir, hasten the publication of your long-expected *Natural History of the Earth.* Let us not complain that you'll delay until the conflagration. [Close]   Your most affectionate friend and servant,

To Thomas Hollis

U/AAS draft   August 1, 1720

Sir,

[Thanks him for his "generous bounty" to Harvard College.]

But no person has more cause to celebrate your goodness and acknowledge the hand of a gracious God inspiring you with it, than he who now addresses you. God has blessed me with a son of uncommon hopes, at the age of twelve ripe for admission into the College. A year ago, I was by some singular difficulties reduced into circumstances that rendered me unable to go through the expenses of his academical education. In this distress, and upon the prospect of his being diverted from the service to the Kingdom of God, so much desired and designed for him, we poured out our tears together before the Lord. Just then arrived your noble bounty to the College, with some allowance that the direction of the lad's grandfather should be considered in the disposal of it; who, proposing some assistance from the interest of it for the education of his grandson, while he should be yet an undergraduate in the College, there appeared some compliance with it; and my distress was, as by a most seasonable interposition of Heaven, provided for.

You may wonder perhaps that one in my station here, and not altogether unknown in the world, should need the help of any charity on such an occasion. And an intimation of your wonder at it is improved by the Corporation, for the stopping of that allowance. But, Sir, not to observe that I have known such as for many years have not let one day pass them without being able to say, that they have on that day spent something on pious uses, and have particularly been at annual disbursements toward the [a word blotted] of poor scholars at the College, yet find themselves unable to maintain a son of their own there without some assistance; it will be enough if I inform you more particularly of my own condition. The churches of New England allow salaries to their ministers, like those which have been formerly noted among the French Protestants, among whom the greatest men they had (men whose books I am not worthy to carry after them) were always but very meanly subsisted. A very great part of our ministers have lived very much upon their own personal estates. In Boston, the capital city of these colonies (where the glorious Lord has assigned me my station), the ministers encounter peculiar difficulties, all the charges of living there being above what they are in other parts of the country, and our salaries being paid in bills of credit, which are sunk in value to be but about fourteen shillings in the pound. I have several years very much subsisted on the revenues of my personal estate, which is now so wasted that I can do no more as formerly. And I have during the forty years of my public employment, so entirely devoted myself to serve the Kingdom of God, that I have never allowed myself a moment's time to consult my own temporal interest, but referred myself to the sixth of Matthew, and the thirty-third, which I am sure will never fail of an accomplishment. If one channel fail, the glorious Lord, whose faithfulness does never fail, will open another.

When the gracious providence of God first gave my little son a prospect of some advantage from your beneficence and munificence to the College, some observers of such things were willing to interpret it as a recompense of my public appearance to own the church of the godly Baptists in my neighborhood, when some others refused that communion with them. Whether this advantage be continued or no, I thought it my duty to address you with a very thankful acknowledgment for the benefit of that sum of about nine pounds, which the Treasurer tells me will be the allowance for the year that is now expired.

[Has not enclosed some of his publications because of Hollis' failing sight.]   Your very much obliged servant,

To Dr. John Clark

U/AAS draft   August 13, 1720

Sir,

It was not until this day that I was made sensible of your great kindness to your little kinswoman, and the share you have had in what has been done for our dear Liza's comfortable subsistence and education.

It would be the vilest ingratitude in me if I should not have a very grateful sense of the favors that are shown to that child, and if I should not express it on all occasions.

The relation to, and resemblance of, a never-to-be-forgotten mother, by which that child is recommended unto me, are not the least of her endearing circumstances. And as the Scripture mentions an uncle's taking up an orphan, so I can with delight see a gracious hand of Heaven at work in disposing an uncle to cast a compassionate eye upon an orphan, whose distressed case called for much commiseration.

I thank you for the notice you have taken of her, and ask you to cast a tender eye always on her. . . . [Close]

Your obliged brother and servant,

II

By 1720, disappointed, betrayed, fallen on bad times, Cotton Mather could see his life only as an unalloyed crucifixion and took to calling himself the "man of sorrows." The now passionate, sometimes frenzied tone of his letters, and their crass duplicity and cajolery, tell us much about the corruption and petty hatred that accompanied the transformation of Puritan society in the early eighteenth century. At the same time, their crumbling syntax and changed handwriting—dramatically deteriorated from the earlier neat script into wandering margins, slanting figures, and disconnected loops—graphically convey Mather's faltering self-esteem and over-taxed energies.

Mather lamented to THOMAS PRINCE (1687–1758) that, unable to fight off a long siege of illness in late 1720 and early 1721, he found it difficult to carry out his ministry any longer. Ailing, and increasingly under attack, he seems to have thought of Prince as a successor. Prince, the grandson of Governor Hinckley of Plymouth, now begins to figure prominently among Mather's correspondents although he was twenty-five years Mather's junior. A theologian, scholar, and bibliophile, Prince had returned to Massachusetts in 1717 after travelling in the West Indies and Europe. At Mather's prompting he became an associate with Joseph Sewall at the Old South Church. Charles Chauncy rated him second in learning only to Mather himself; but, pedantic, something of an anglophile, and very nearsighted, he turned out to be an unpopular preacher. As his intimacy with the Mathers grew, he wrote introductions to their works and collected and preserved their papers, a familiar ritual in dynastic New England. His important collection, with his notes, appears in the *Collections of the Massachusetts Historical Society.*

Mather's ministry suffered not only from his failing health but also from a diminished flock. He saw his congregation being drawn off to the new Brick Meeting House. He dealt with the loss in the same contemptuous language he had applied earlier to the Brattle Street Church, and explained it as almost an antitypical fulfillment of the pattern the Brattle group had set, a triumph of the too-refined and ostentatious nouveau-riche, "the religion of pews." In May, 1721, he was forced to preach his flock a farewell sermon. To put a brave face on this latest sacrifice he tried to show, he wrote in his diary, "how easily and cheerfully we endure their departure from us"; but that his church had undergone "a very great abridgement" could not be smiled away. Indeed his congregation almost no longer existed. Too ill to carry out his ministry even though it was reduced, he also wished to resign his Indian commission and for that purpose wrote to Robert Ashurst, who succeeded his father Sir William Ashurst as governor of the New England Company early in 1720. Mather's frequent offers of resignation from the commission usually grew out of irritation as he failed to get his way at the commissioners' meetings; it always gratified him that the Company refused to accept his resignations. They refused his latest proposed withdrawal as well, although this time it grew not out of pique but out of depression and a feeling of uselessness.

Cressy and the Howell estate also went into creating the "man of sorrows." In April, 1721, Cressy took part, Mather wrote, "in a night-riot with some detestable rakes in the town." Overburdened, Mather for once lost his patience. He had always treated Cressy with pious and fatherly concern for his godliness, tempered with appreciation of his good-heartedness. Now he became fed up. By late April "my wicked son Increase" seemed incorrigibly "ungodly, distracted, hard-hearted"; he decided to "chase him out of my sight." In May he sent Cressy off to THOMAS FOXCROFT (1697–1769), a minister of the First Church in Boston, who was about Cressy's age. Partly he once again hoped to improve Cressy by acquaintance with a pious, intelligent, and scholarly young man, slightly liberal in his beliefs; but just as strongly, he simply wanted Cressy out of the way. Still in serious debt, he wrote to Judge Paul Dudley for a loan or gift to pay off his attorney. How desperately he tried to enroll patrons for his work appears in his remarkably self-abasing letter to the merchant John Frizzel. Ethically the letter represents probably the most questionable act of Mather's career, for he now merely uses the moral authority of his faith to fish for and sanctify a handout. He had stooped to forgery with Frizzel once before, when he prepared a letter to be signed by Cressy. The forged letter included here is beyond doubt in Mather's hand. It was definitely written by him to wheedle money out of Frizzel by recommending "this noble work of the Doctor's."

The early 1720's was a difficult time for Massachusetts in general, a period of worsening relations with England and new threats against the charter. By his indiscreet ventures into these cross-currents, Mather was creating and preparing further trouble for himself. Late in 1720 he wrote a defamatory letter against Elisha Cooke and Cooke's political allies. Somehow the letter was delivered over to Cooke, who strongly protested. Mather gives varying accounts of how Cooke got hold of his letter. Apparently he had sent the same letters to Samuel Penhallow and to Lieutenant Governor Wentworth. In one place he blames Wentworth for disclosing the letter, in another he blames Wentworth's wife, in still another he claims that the letter was intercepted en route to Samuel Penhallow; he probably could not explain its detour himself. In the letter he carped at Cooke and his friends as "idiots," "fuddle-caps," "American monsters." He was widely attacked for these remarks, whose disclosure followed hard on his having retracted his charge that Cooke was a drunkard. The disclosure also typifies the air of suspicion and betrayal that now attached itself to everything Mather did. He noted in his diary that he had become afraid of writing openly to his friends.

Mather brought more trouble by trying to defend Jeremiah

Dummer. Dummer was always suspect because of his religious views and because, as Mather insisted, the people of Massachusetts expected their agents to do the impossible. Dummer drew fire when he complained in England about the treatment of Shute at home, and wrote to Massachusetts that as a result the court had officially approved Shute's conduct and frowned on the House. After receiving Dummer's letters, and goaded by Elisha Cooke, the House in September, 1721, ordered Dummer dismissed from his agency, and also dismissed Mather's friend Paul Dudley from his post as councillor. Here Mather saw a chance to savage Cooke and to repay the House for having encouraged people, he believed, to ignore the April, 1721, order for a general fast. He appealed to Jeremiah's brother, Lieutenant Governor WILLIAM DUMMER (1679–1761), who always sympathized with the established ministers and acted for them in the legislature. Jeremiah Dummer was restored to his agency, but in retaliation the House refused to vote him an allowance. Mather's meddling brought him few successes or consolations, unless indirectly it hastened the death by apoplexy on March 16, 1721, of Oliver Noyes, one of the "very wicked party . . . who fill the land with strife and sin."

To John Winthrop

IV Coll 8/MHS (draft at AAS)   August 29, 1720

My invaluable Friend,

My glowing affection to you from your very childhood uninterrupted and inviolable to this day has not been upon those terms—*Amo te, non possum dicere quare.* In your descent, in your temper, in your accomplishments, I have seen a reason. But there have been added hereunto, the obligations which your kindnesses have laid upon me, wherein, oh! may I arrive to the honor of reciprocations!

[Notes having earlier sent *Coheleth* to Winthrop.]

My *True Way of Shaking off a Viper* will be a sufficient and eternal confutation of all that *malice (at the highest!)* can do to hurt a friend for whom you have the kindest regards; a contusion to the serpents, and a confusion to all their sibilations.

It was never dispersed in this country, tho' printed (after a wretched fashion) at London, about nine years ago.

Our patriarch the last week read it. It gratified him! It ravished him! He expressed his desires to have it published. And his venerable hand will write a preface to it. But he asked me how I could get through the charges of the impression. I replied, 'that I had at New London a friend who is better to me than a brother; a friend who never thought that he could overload me with his favors; a friend who had several times helped me through my designs to serve the Kingdom of God and the cause of piety. He does for me as the brave Ambrose (a person of quality thereby made famous) did for his Origen. And his goodness on such occasions is inexhaustible.'

In pursuance of this declaration, tho' you have so lately assisted my *Coheleth*, my ink will not blush at it (tho' I should) if I again grow so very impudent as to solicit for a little of your assistance towards the charges of an impression, which may happen to do some execution among your *Vipers* as well as ours. [Close]

Your most affectionate friend and servant,
[Asks Winthrop for an account of a recent whirlwind.]

To Jonathan Belcher

U/AAS draft   August 29, 1720

Sir,

A while ago, a blundering and beggarly fellow of Newbury addressed me with a request, *That if I had any spare bills I would bestow some of them upon him!*

The excellent advice which Your Honor gave me t'other night (I am sorry I was not in the way the last night, when I might have enjoyed the inculcations of it) has had such a powerful impression upon me, that I will do nothing but keep to my *True Way of Shaking off a Viper*, which I have laid before you.

But see the consequence! The last week our patriarch saw the little treatise. It gratified him; it ravished him! He said, *can you get it published here, and let me write a preface to it!* For it was never published in this country. The venerable old Doctor thought it would be a sufficient and an eternal confutation of all that malice (at the height) could ever do to hurt us, an effectual contusion to the serpents, and confusion to all their sibilations. But, said he, how will you get through the charge of the impression. I replied, Among other friends I have a dear Jonathan, whose love surpasses, and who will rejoice to save me from the javelins—and I will ask him to give me a little (I shall want but a little)

323

assistance. And it may be I shall also contrive into the work two or three more innuendoes, wherein his more particular service will be aimed at.

This is my story, a repetition of my Newbury story. [Close]

Your Honor's most affectionate friend and servant,

To Lieutenant Governor William Dummer and Judge Paul Dudley

U/AAS draft   [c. September, 1720]

Sirs,

Tho' I am in a manner entirely ruined by my constant adherence to a maxim used in a speech to a King of Prussia—*A capacity to do good not only gives a title to it, but makes the doing of it a duty*, a maxim which I have lived upon and for more than forty years let not a day pass me without acting upon it, but been guilty of so much indiscretion in the applying of it that an exasperated world has now scarce one hearty friend left me in it; yet I cannot forbear one touch more at *meddling with state-affairs*, which I intend for the last they shall ever find me in.

I heard it this day complained by one related to the House of Representatives, that the House is entirely under the instruction of those whom I have unpardonably called *American monsters*; and that under their influence the House is coming on to lay aside your invaluable Dummer from his agency, which will be a finishing stroke for the ruin of a country fallen into the hands of men skilful to destroy.

And that the friends of the country in the Council, either through sloth and sleep, or from a judgment of God upon us, utterly neglect all such interviews with numbers [*sic*] of the House, and endeavors to enlighten them, as they have used on some former occasions. I could not but remonstrate unto Your Honors against so great (and give me leave to say, culpable) a negligence; and press you, by all that is dear to us all, that some speedy care be taken, by discourses with the deluded Representatives (for which 'tis easy by Col. Dr's and Ch's help to obtain opportunities) to prevent the mischiefs which three or four sons of malice are bringing upon us.

I now take my leave of all essays to serve a country set upon self-destruction, and forever ungrateful, unrighteous, and barbarous to all that serve it. [Close]   Your Honors' most hearty servant,

To William Dudley

U/AAS draft   October 5, 1720

Sir,

'Tis one who loves you, and values you, and esteems you at a very
high rate that now addresses you. But his merits are so little, that he
must introduce another to give an efficacy to the address which your
present circumstances have procured from him.

The former century had not a more incontestable piece of history belonging to it, than that of the Duke of Buckingham receiving a warning
from the spirit of his dead father, in an apparition to a friend of his,
which cautioned him about the fate near unto him.

Your honorable father, whose bones are laid with Joseph's, yet is in
spirit no doubt concerned for the welfare of a son for whom he had,
while he sojourned here, a tenderness which could be equalled by nothing but what he had for your elder brother. In you two were contracted
the rays of the more than paternal passion which were once diffused
among three or four more, *all which died before their father.*

You shall suppose him now employing of my pen, to bring from him
this advice unto you.

'My dear son: you are in extreme hazards, wherein Heaven will interpose to rescue you if you will with an unprejudiced mind resign and
attend unto the divine direction.

'You have carried on a courtship to a young, I say a young, gentlewoman who expresses a most unaccountable aversion for you. She ac-
knowledges that for your person, your piety, your family, your interest,
and the figure you make in the world, and your superior capacities to be
very serviceable, that the country has not in it a match that equals you.
(And if she did not acknowledge it, yet all of her sex that have any
sense in them do and must.) Nevertheless, the *silly dove that has no
heart,* for what would be for her own prosperity, continues an unaccountable aversion for you. If this aversion proceeds only from her own
childish humor, she forfeits your love, she proclaims herself unworthy of
you, she assures you that you never can be happy in her. But I have
cause to apprehend that the impression is of a higher original. 'Tis the
invisible world that makes it, the invisible world which is more concerned about the marriages transacted among the children of men, than
you that are buried in flesh do commonly imagine. Heaven interposes

325

in the matter. If she should be overcome to let you call her your wife, while she has this aversion remaining uncured in her, she cannot be happy; but you must be thrice and four times miserable. Your life will be embittered with temptations beyond what can as yet come into your imagination. The aversion seems incurable; perhaps it has at some time or other made very sinful imprecations, which are a snare to the soul that makes them. [Quotes Hippocrates.] My advice to you, is that you set apart some convenient portion of time, and with all proper humiliations and supplications, bespeak the conduct of Heaven; and then, if you don't find this aversion in the object you are so fond of, speedily and perfectly vanish, conclude *God has meant it unto good.* Let your pious wisdom come into its operation. Withdraw your misplaced affection. In due time, let it be placed on one that will better affect you, and count herself happy in your kind aspect upon her, and study with continual raptures of love to make you happy in everything wherein a good wife can make him so, that finds a good thing, and obtains favor of the Lord. The angel that befriended Isaac in his affair can bring you to the view of such a one. And be sure to maintain such a grandeur of mind, that nothing that looks like a disappointment unto you in this affair (and may for a minute or two be an occasion of some various talk among the tattlers), so discompose you as to indispose you for any of the services which God and man are continually expecting from you, and that your most affectionate brother may not be overwhelmed with any perplexities on the account of your uneasiness.'

I do for many reasons presume to offer you, I hope, not improper sentiments as coming from the most cogent adviser that can be thought of. . . . [Close]

Your most sincere and affectionate friend and servant,

To Judge Paul Dudley

U/AAS draft   October 19, 1720

Sir,

Pity, pity to a poor Joseph in the pit! One whose affliction I know you have the goodness to be grieved for!

No man in the world but you can deliver me. And I know your goodness to be equal with your power.

Your Honor is perfectly apprised of the condition (the justified and almost finished condition) which my foolishly-undertaken administration is brought unto. My release from the bonds of it has been once and again promised by one who has declared that he can grant it me, one who would no doubt gladly see (as Your Honor would) a poor servant of Christ at liberty to carry on services for the Kingdom of God, which are fearfully encumbered (many wonder that they are no more so) by the troubles these bonds give unto me. The repeated vexation which one troublesome Irish attorney of a French molester keeps me in daily, hourly danger of, is a very sensible article of my distresses. But I must for all that lie languishing in them if Your Honor do not go to the judge and see him do what he must do for my relief, even (*Intra hunc,* as Popilius expressed it) before you stir out of the room. No words can express the anguish (and I hope for a proportionable success) with which this petition comes to you. . . . [Close]

Your Honor's distressed friend and obliged servant,

To JOHN FRIZZEL

U/AAS draft [fall, 1720]

Sir,

As our good GOD is continually putting into your hand the wealth which enables you to do abundance of good, so He does that for you which He does for very few in the world, by putting into your heart the wisdom to consider that you are but a steward of your wealth, and to abound in those expenses on pious uses that will enable you shortly to give up your account with joy.

The people of GOD know of many good works done by you, wherein your light shines before men, and they glorify your father which is in Heaven. But we have reason to believe that you do many more which are known only to your Heavenly Father, and ascertain for you a recompense in the world to come.

This emboldens me, who am one that never spoke to my remembrance one word to you in all my life, to write unto you a proposal which, I hope, will not be unwelcome to you.

Would you not rejoice in being the happy instrument of doing a service for the Kingdom of God beyond what any man that is now living has ever done! A comprehensive service, whereof whole nations will quickly reap the advantage! I am sure you would.

I have the honor of some acquaintance with Dr. Mather, the younger, a person whom you as well as I have a high value for. Among his other favors, he communicated unto me a composure of his entitled *The Work of the Day*, which he tells me your Mr. White has at this time in his hands. The composure, if I have any judgment, is a most illustrious and uncommon performance: 'tis filled with rich and rare thoughts, and among the entertainments which eminent men have given us, I have not seen the thing that equals it. Let me peruse it never so often, every paragraph still appeared new to me, and I still discovered new treasures and beauties in it. It is admirably calculated for the time, and will answer a thousand good intentions; and if it were brought into the world, it would soon have a blessed operation upon hundreds of thousands of people. I have guessed from some words let fall by the Doctor, that the work was undertaken, and has been carried on, with more than ordinary methods of obtaining the direction and assistance of Heaven for it, and that it is reserved for an engine of great things to be shortly done in the world.

Now, Sir, what I propose is that you would please to take it into your consideration whether your liberal and generous allowance of little more than a quarter of what you have lately done for a people that you have not much satisfaction in, would not bring this noble work of the Doctor's into the world, and would not prove a hundred times more useful to those glorious interests, to which your godly soul would consecrate no small revenues! Will you please to confer with dear Mr. White about it, and pardon the liberty thus taken by, Sir,

Your unknown friend and servant,

Unaddressed

U/AAS draft   November 14, 1720

Reverend Sir,

[Regrets not having written.]

I wrote unto you very largely (yea, more letters than one) the beginning of the last July, and at the same time addressed unto you a large packet of American fruits, by an honest neighbor (called Mr. Lawler) who promised me to deliver them with his own hand. But on this day I am informed that there is great apprehension of this my neighbor's having miscarried, and being foundered in the ocean. By which many other of my costly remittances for London are also destroyed. These are some of the instances wherein *My God will humble me.* [But he must acquiesce in God's wisdom.]

This renews to me an experience which I rarely miss of, that I am hardly ever admitted unto any services, or any enjoyments, but what have a sentence of death first written on them.

[Sends along *Victorina*.]

Your most affectionate brother and servant,

[PROBABLY TO GOVERNOR SHUTE]

U/AAS draft   November 16, 1720

Sir,

Tho' I have the greatest aversion imaginable to the doing or speaking of anything that may give the least uneasiness to Your Excellency, yet it seems a piece of duty in me to inform that a while ago, I wrote a short letter to Lieutenant Governor Wentworth under (perhaps too quick) resentments of the scurrilities in the last of our party-pamphlets, wherein I represented the unhappy state of this town, which was now governed by *idiots* and *fuddle-caps* and *men that love and make a lie*, and so poisoned by *American* (worse than *African*) monsters, that I was weary of my station in it. And I also expressed my apprehension that more justice ought to be done unto the character of Judge Dudley, than whom we had not now a more faithful counsellor, or righteous magistrate. And more of the like stuff.

Mr. Wentworth has done Your Excellency and your servant the kindness of helping Mr. Cooke to a copy of this letter, an action of which I forbear to make any constructions, as I also do to make any report of the following operations.

No man alive knows better than Your Excellency what may be proper to be said of, or to, Mr. Wentworth on such a monstrous occasion. Perhaps the less noise of the matter, the better. [Close]

Your Honor's most hearty and humble servant,

My dear John Briggs has not laid aside his hopes that when Your Excellency shall see cause to make Mr. Lothrop a justice, you will please to make him a sheriff of Plymouth county, or divide it between Mr. Barker and him.

Your Excellency will pardon the freedom of something so like a memorandum.

Unaddressed

U/AAS draft   [Probably November 21, 1720]

Sir,

The favor which you with the Corporation of the College have shown in the allowance ordered for the grandson of your aged predecessor, I ought always to acknowledge with all possible gratitude.

And it augments my solicitous wishes and studies, that the merits of the lad may answer [the?] obligations.

I add my humble request, that what Mr. Hollis (as well as what his grandfather) has been so good as to propose for him, may be for a while continued.

You cannot but be sensible (tho' perhaps less than I) that the difficulties of the times render us glad of assistances for the education of the children whom we would present unto the world.

Which also causes me to pray for your order unto the Treasurer of the College, for the advancing of what your goodness assigned, I suppose, a year and a half ago.

I am, with great respect, Sir, Your most obliged friend and servant,

The enclosed is but a very little of what is due for your paternal cares in the tuition of your hopeful pupil, for the year which expired half a year ago. . . .

I am, with great respect, Sir, Your most obedient friend and servant,

To Peter Pratt

U/AAS draft   November 28, 1720

Sir,

[Thanks him for his account of a "horrible tempest."]

. . . I now do upon much deliberation, earnestly advise you to go on with your pious purpose of muzzling a wolf, out of whose mouth you have been rescued; but some are still in danger of becoming a prey unto it. The execution of what you have purposed will be an excellent expression of your gratitude unto God your Saviour.

I extremely approve of the method that you propose. First of all state the question, relating to some error held by your seducer, and let the answer be a text that shall directly refute the error. 'Tis a short and a sure way, and a few pages will suffice for it. In a small book entitled *Supplies from the Tower of David,* I have seen this method actually taken for the arming of our people against all the errors known to threaten any parts of our country. But then, what you have in view of an historical aspect relating to the strange creature who goes about seeking whom he may devour, or to your own circumstances under and after his fascinations, I believe it will be so entertaining as to make all sell and spread well, and obtain the end of your undertaking. [Close]

Your hearty friend and servant,

TO JOHN WINTHROP

IV Coll 8/MHS   December 26, 1720

My dear Friend,

It is but just now that the post-boy brings me your kind (but short) letter, which was dated five weeks ago. And, as in duty always bound, I set myself *immediately* to answer your desires. But it is hardly any otherwise than by telling you that *I cannot yet answer them.*

All the return I have yet had of the remittances I made the last February to the Royal Society is an obliging letter of Mr. Chamberlain, August 31, whose words are, 'I thank you for your noble entertainment, with which so many of my friends were regaled before I could get a snap for myself, who hungered and thirsted for it, that I had not the pleasure thereof till very lately, and indeed too late to communicate the same pleasure to your illustrious brethren, the gentlemen of the Royal Society, who have always a long recess at this time of the year. As soon as I had perused your learned letters, I immediately communicated them unto Sir Isaac Newton, our excellent president; and he has referred them to the most learned mathematician and great traveller, Dr. Halley, whose report I expect with no small impatience. But as I believe you expect to be informed of their destiny, with respect to their coming to my hands, I was resolved not to skip the opportunity of telling you, they are safe arrived.'

And verily, I had reason to wish for some information, for I was made sensible that the captain to whom I committed my packets proved a base, false, ungenteel fellow (a sorry rake, ycleped Brown) who returning to New England confessed that he had not thought fit to answer my desire, but had however put my packets into the post-office. I gave 'em over for lost. The advice of their being received was good news from a far country to us, and enough to content me for the present.

[Reports that the *Christian Philosopher* has been printed in England.]

I am at this time at work upon an essay which I shall entitle *The Angel of Bethesda*. Pliny was not the first who observed, *Nos optimos esse cum infirmi sumus.* Excited by this observation, I do upon most of the distempers commonly afflicting the children of men, offer the sentiments of piety which the distempered are thereby the most naturally, and rationally and religiously, to be led unto. But then, upon each article, I subjoin such powerful and parable specifics as in my reading or otherwise I have met withal for the cure of these maladies, with proper cautions upon occasions. I am not without hopes that it may prove a very serviceable and acceptable essay.

When I have thought on the circumstances wherein your grandfather and father (and now yourself, and anon, I hope, your Ascanius) have come to any place in their travels, I still have had in view *The Angel of Bethesda* appearing there. I don't know but I have somewhere in print used the expression concerning them. If this little book should ever come abroad, I flatter myself something of the same title may belong unto it.

The book will be more than a dozen sheets, and the publication will be expensive. But my dear Franckius has taught me to go on with useful undertakings, and believe in a glorious Christ for the carrying of them through. . . . [Close]   Your affectionate friend and servant,

To Jeremiah Dummer

U/AAS draft   January 14, 1721

Sir,

[Will ask a favor of the always-obliging Dummer.]

There is a murmur among us that there may be somebody designing, if they can, to get Mr. Secretary Willard removed from his place, and get themselves into his commission. If there should be so, I would in the first place observe to you, that the attempt itself is of so (I will not say uncharitable and ungenerous, but) villainous a nature, that there needs no more to give the character of him that shall make it, and utterly disqualify him. For 'tis a post that none but a gentleman can be worthy of. [Praises Willard.]

. . . I earnestly entreat it of you, Sir, to be inquisitive after what may be a-doing. And if you find such a plot against our common friend carrying on, obviate it in all proper ways. While we enjoy the best of governors, let us also enjoy the best of secretaries. [Close]

Your perpetual friend and servant,

To Thomas Prince

DII/MHS   February 12, 1721

My dear Friend,

Upon trial this day, I find my *locks are cut*. I performed so pitifully that my courage for the lecture utterly fails me, especially considering that the Lord's-day (and table) will follow presently upon it. This last bout has been the most shocking that I have had this twenty years. My return back to this loathsome world is unspeakably less pleasant unto me than the view I had three weeks ago of taking wing for that Glorious World, whereof, oh! could I tell you something of the glories which I am now certain are to be there bestowed upon them who have nothing but a CHRIST left alive unto them!

I durst not ask for the continuance of my poor life one day longer, but purely with the aim and for the sake of doing services for the Kingdom of God, while the ordinary course of nature supposes a capacity for them.

For which cause I would gladly have served the lecture (and vexed the dragon) this week. But I can't—I can't. Wherefore, if you will be so very kind as to do it, I will entertain some hope that by the Thursday after, I may be able to take your turn, and pay a little of what I shall owe you.

But if you really can't, then, I pray, comply with another task which I shall impose upon you. Step in the morning on my behalf as far as my dear Cooper's. Give my service to him. Say not one word that he owes me anything. I utterly decline all such claims, or terms. But join your request with mine, that he would step this week into the lecture, and allow me to take his turn, if I live to the time, and am found able to do it. [Tells him to thank Cooper for the favor.]

And now I reckon myself safe, that between (you) two, I shall not fall to the ground. [Close]

Your poor, weary, tired brother and servant,

To William Hutchinson
U/AAS draft   February 24, 1721

Sir,

[Sends along a recent treatise.]

On the Lord's-day after the flight of your excellent mother, I thought it my duty to make a public mention in her in the great congregation. I paid some dues to the memory of my dear friend, and an honorable mother in Israel.

Upon my second thoughts (or perhaps on my two and twentieth) I was willing to give you a sight of the short sermon, yea, to confess that if you (with your valuable sisters, for all of whom I have therein briefly expressed my regards) may judge it proper to help into the view of the public the testimony here borne to the character of your excellent father as well as mother (to whose memory we are all, and I very singularly, indebted), I should be proud of appearing in such a service. To the memory of those who formerly assisted the publication of so many things written by me, my pen ought very much to be devoted. And in our piety towards our deceased parents, our dutiful carriage towards them when living will have its perfect work. But if any publication may be thought unnecessary (which I entirely leave to your judgment) yet I have the pleasure of giving you that of seeing my sentiments of your honorable relatives, and have only this further to ask: that the notes may not be lost, but in your own time returned (with this book, which is almost borrowed) for to take that fate with my other scribbled papers. [Close]

As I have been to your memorable father and mother, Your most affectionate friend and servant,

To John Winthrop
IV Coll 8 (as 1722)/MHS   March 13, 1721

My dear Friend,

Wondering that I have not enjoyed the satisfaction of one word from you since my last and large answer to yours, many weeks ago, the wonder ceases upon the sorrow which is given me by the advice of your having been under the arrest of an unhappy sickness. [Glad to hear he is recovering.]

I have been myself also confined for three weeks about the latter end of January and beginning of February, by a very ill turn (which had a fever in it) whereof I am not yet wholly recovered. But I am again in the public service. And returning to the use of my pen I could no longer forbear using it in my old way of telling you how much I love you, and love and long to hear from you.

[No intelligence to report.]

A letter of mine to Piscataqua, said that *idiots* and *fuddlecaps* and *men that love and make a lie* now govern us, and *American* (worse than *African*) monsters were bringing the city into a *snare*. To gratify one whom I ought never to contradict, I unawares and unjustly confessed that the expressions were too keen, and I asked pardon of the men (our Representatives) to whom the wife ('tis said) of the gentleman to whom I wrote it, sent my original letter, and who took me on the sudden at a disadvantage in their clamorous way, wherein I own myself not a match for them. I soon had cause given me to repent of my repentance; and our best men will demonstrate and justify the characters I have bestowed on those evil men.

But patience must have its perfect work. I pray, my dear, let it have so in you, as well as in,

Your most hearty (tho' feeble) friend and servant,

[Encloses a publication.]

To John Winthrop

IV Coll 8/MHS   April 17, 1721

Sir,

Our *Christian Philosopher* (blown off the last winter to Antigua) is newly arrived. And tho' I am not myself made owner of more than one, yet our bookseller has one hundred, from which, to detach one at the small expense of a little, dirty, ragged ten shilling bill, is but a very small acknowledgment unto an invaluable friend, unto whose generosity I have been indebted for more than as many pounds.

It afflicts me very much that I cannot hear from a friend so dear to me. But if want of health be the reason (I am sure, it cannot be want of love) I should be glad that the *Christian Philosopher* may do as much for my friend, as Livy and Curtius, they say, did for the persons of quality who recovered their lost health by reading of them.

A spiteful town, and a poisoned country, can't extinguish my poor studies to do good in the world (tho' they unavoidably hinder my doing of the good unto them which they might have had); and therefore, as I can get any time for it, I am slowly proceeding with my *Angel of Bethesda*, whereof, I think, I formerly gave you some account.

But, alas, what will become of it, after all? The booksellers, I believe, must see forty or fifty pounds engaged, before they'll venture on the impression. ["Despairing of my *Angel's* becoming visible," he sends a chapter of it to Winthrop.]   Yours as ever,

[To Robert Ashurst?]

DII (as addressed to   April 28, 1721
Sir William Ashurst)/AAS draft

Sir,

[Has learned that *India Christiana* has reached Ashurst.]

I must . . . confess myself so discouraged by some occurrences as to apprehend it most proper for me to propose a secession from the board of your commissioners for the propagation of the Gospel among our Indians. I am not fond of mentioning what the things are that have discouraged me. But you may be sure, that if I had enjoyed the prospect of doing any of the good my soul has been travailing for, I should have been afraid of declining my opportunities. Instead thereof, I will enclose a copy of a letter which not long since I addressed unto Lt. Governor Dummer, as president of that board; since which, I have received nothing from the board that intimates to me what notice the gentlemen please to take of it. I do it, that so you may see something of what I have wished for, and may give such directions as in your wisdom you shall judge most convenient. The copy of the memorial that accompanies it, is not in the least [offered?] upon any design to obtain from you the grant of the petition in it, or to complain that it was not granted here. I am entirely satisfied, and yet for some reasons let you know another thing that I once also wished for. [Close]

Your Honor's most affectionate friend and obedient servant,

To Thomas Foxcroft

U/UVL   May [day torn], 1721

My dear Friend,

Tho' I am a man of sorrows, and acquainted with griefs, yet I have learned living on a CHRIST so far, that I should not feel the weight of a *grain of sand*, or the light dust of the balance, or any one of all my afflictions, if I could see the bearer of this letter evidently living unto God. Until I see this, my *grief will be heavier than the sand*.

I know that when you see him, you will certainly love him. You will find in him a singular sweetness of temper (which, alas, has been a snare unto him), a ripe wit, a sharp sense, the ornaments of a gentlemanly education; *Diabolus cupit ab illo ornari*.

Serious PIETY would render him—what would be inexpressible.

He longs to be brought into some acquaintance with you (which looks like a hopeful tendency) and I long for his having it, and so does his excellent grandfather—as much as *he* can do.

If you may be a happy instrument of persuading him to, and confirming him in, a perfect work of piety, with a lively and steady adherence to his business, and a hatred and horror of all evil company, I know your joy will be wonderful!

To intermix discourses on other matters of polite and public, or any agreeable, conversation, and favor me and him so far as to let him know that he shall be (as I am sure he will be) welcome to you for future visits, may notably spread the nets of salvation for him. Seize him, and make him CHRIST'S, and make him yours. Take any way for it, only do but seize him.

I need say no more. I am, Sir,   Your brother and servant,

III

On May 26, 1721, Cotton Mather recorded solemnly in his diary: "The grievous calamity of the smallpox is now entered the town." Next day the *Boston News-Letter* reported eight cases of the disease. Mather decided to call together the physicians of Boston and ask them whether the new method of inoculation might be used to save some lives. His question shortly made him probably the most hated man in America.

How Mather came upon the idea of inoculation is uncertain. In an earlier letter he mentions learning about it from his slave. But the idea was well-publicized in England, for instance by Lady Mary Wortley Montagu, who had seen inoculation performed in Turkey. Also, a Greek physician and Fellow of the Royal Society named Dr. Emanuel Timonius, living in Turkey, described the inoculation to John Woodward of the society, who then printed an account of it in the *Transactions*. This account appeared in the same issue with the nine-page summary of Mather's *Curiosa*, and Mather may have become impressed with the method from seeing it juxtaposed with his own name. We know that he read the article, for he discussed it with Dr. Zabdiel Boylston who, like himself, had heard of the method from slaves in Boston and had made some experiments in his own family.

However Mather came upon the practise he had been concerned over the disease since adolescence and had resolved as early as 1716 to introduce inoculation should the smallpox break out again in Boston. He sought at once to inoculate the city. Month after month until the epidemic abated in the winter, he devoted himself to comforting the afflicted personally, dressing their sores and gathering wood for them, and in his diaries compared himself implicity and explicitly to Christ the mercy-giver and healer. He spent June writing essays and letters defending the inoculation and prepared an address to the Boston doctors in which he included letters from Timonius and from Jacob Pylarinus, a Venetian practising in Smyrna. Two of his very important, lengthy letters to the Society are included here. In July, together with Increase Sr., Thomas Prince, John Webb (or Web), Benjamin Colman, and others, he published a letter in the *Gazette* championing Dr. Boylston's attempts at inoculation. In August he desired to inoculate his son Samuel, but feared that if he failed because Samuel took the disease in some other way, the people of Boston would be confirmed in their distrust of him and the method. Increase advised him to inoculate Samuel secretly, which he did; by late August he began seeing the success of the method in his own son. But in September his daughters became ill; one of them died; by September 16 all of his children were ill, and he moaned, "Alas, my afflictions multiply upon me. I cannot number them."

The reaction to Mather's efforts was violent. Terrified of catching the disease, most Bostonians felt that he and his allies were not halting but spreading it by inoculation. On November 4 the freeholders voted to forbid any inoculated person to come to Boston. Mather's letter in the *Gazette* begot a furious verbal assault on the ministry led by the physician Dr. William Douglass and by John

Checkley, speaking through the Franklins' *Courant*. (When another epidemic threatened Boston in 1730, Douglass was the first to urge inoculation.) They revived Oldmixon's criticisms of the *Magnalia* and made Mather's erudition a laughing stock. Cressy somehow got into the furor by his "violent and passionate resentment of an indignity which a wicked fellow [Checkley?] offered unto me," Mather wrote, adding with some pride that for his sake Cressy had exposed himself to danger. On their side the inoculators jeered at the Couranteers' ignorance and lower-class origins. Mather usually regarded his opponents as lower-class ignoramuses—"Leather Apron Men"—just as he regarded all scientists as gentlemen.*

Feeling himself crucified by the people of Boston, Mather this time gave them back not love but the traditional and ferocious invective of the jeremiad. His diary for the period of the epidemic sputters with wrathful curses against this "barbarous people," the "crying wickedness of this town," "dismal picture and emblem of Hell," "this abominable town," "this miserable and detestable town," "Hell upon earth, a city full of lies and murders and blasphemies." To be thus maligned for the most merciful acts he could conceive, was to him an overwhelming discouragement to any further acts of mercy. At a meeting of ministers in January, 1722, he announced that not only had his desire to Do Good been exhausted, but also that his opportunities were "almost entirely extinguished as to this country." His own health failing, he had to ask other ministers repeatedly to take over his duties. In the winter of 1721 he began to talk of his "approaching martyrdom" and feared that he would be assassinated.

Mather's fear was not unrealistic. He had inoculated his nephew

* One byproduct of the heated feud between the *Courant* and Mather may have been the "Silence Dogood" of Benjamin Franklin's essays. The surname clearly seems aimed at Mather's well-known Doing Good. The first name may have arisen from Mather's sermon "Silentiarius," subtitled "The Silent Sufferer," which begins: "If I may not only Get Good but also Do Good. . . ." The dates are suggestively close. "Silentiarius" was Mather's Boston lecture for September 28, 1721, and was published shortly after; "Silence Dogood" first appeared in the *Courant* on April 2, 1722. Mather's lecture is an attack on the Couranteers and the ignorant abusiveness of Boston for having martyred him; Franklin's dour widow is an ironic counterthrust at Puritan solemnity and orthodoxy. If Franklin did derive "Silence Dogood" from Mather's lecture it was a bad, indeed a sick, joke. Mather wrote the lecture to memorialize the death of his daughter Abigail and her infant during the epidemic. This would not be the only time, however, that the *Courant* made sport of New England's ceremonious attention to funeral elegies and sermons.

Thomas Walter, a minister at Roxbury. At three in the morning on November 14, 1721, someone, he wrote, threw a "granado" into the room where the ill and recently inoculated Walter lay. Customarily it was Mather's own bedroom. As Mather described it, the grenade had been filled with turpentine and powder, which spilled out when the grenade was thrown. (The historian and royal governor of Massachusetts Thomas Hutchinson, said that he saw the shell and that it was filled with "a mixture of brimstone and bituminous matter.") Mather recorded that around the grenade was a message which read, "Cotton Mather, You dog, damn you: I'll inoculate you with this, with a pox to you." But in the account published in the *Boston News-Letter* he changed the message to imply that he knew the assassin's identity: "Cotton Mather, I was once one of your meeting, but the cursed lie you told of ———— [Elisha Cooke?] you know who, made me leave you, you dog."

Mather's part in the smallpox crisis only brought to a critically low point the long-waning authority of the old-line Massachusetts clergy. The hatreds he uncovered were not buried in his lifetime. Even after the epidemic the Franklins continued to label him the "Detractor General over the whole Province," who ruled by rumor-mongering. (The House declared that the *Courant* mocked religion and prohibited James Franklin to publish anything without prior approval from the secretary; in February, 1723, Benjamin Franklin took over the paper.) One already mentioned charge levelled against the inoculation was that it rested on "negroish evidence." The blacks of Boston seem to have suffered from the backlash against the inoculators, and after the epidemic Mather seems to have feared a slave revolt, as suggested by the interesting memo attached to his letter to Thomas Prince. The *News-Letter* on July 11, 1723, reported that a slave had set fire at night to a house in Boston. Mather's enemies fought him through the Royal Society as well, hoping to question his scientific credentials and to discredit his name. The Society had appointed a new secretary, DR. JAMES JURIN (1684–1750), a learned physician and student of Newton's. Jurin himself wrote many pamphlets in support of the inoculation, to one of which he appended some of Mather's writings on the subject. Some Bostonians, noticing that Mather did not appear on the printed list of the Society's members, charged him with imposture for affixing to his name "F.R.S."—Fellow of the Royal Society. ("F.R.S." and "D.D." appeared regularly on his published works.) In 1723 they wrote to the Society to ask whether he was in fact a member.

Because of this inquiry several later historians have questioned Mather's standing in the society. There is not the slightest doubt that Mather believed, in all good faith, that he was a member. When the society received the query from Boston, it discovered that Mather's election had not been recorded in the minutes; apparently no vote had been taken on it. Waller and other correspondents at the Society, however, had led Mather unquestioningly to believe that he was a member. The confusion was wholly owing to the Society's unclear qualifications for membership and procedures for electing Fellows. Englishmen abroad, and colonials, were exempt from formal subscription and from ceremonial admission to the Society, since these required their attendance in London. The printed list of members on which Mather's name did not appear, had been prepared for Fellows resident in England who participated in the annual elections. The responsibility for nominating members rested with a Council, which had indeed nominated Mather. When the Society discovered, as a result of the letter from Massachusetts, that no formal vote had been taken on Mather's election, they formally elected him. Today they list his election as of July, 1713, when he was nominated. The procedural confusions dramatized by Mather's case led to a change of the Society's rules under the presidency of Sir Hans Sloane. Characteristically, at the time of this crisis Mather hastily prepared a few *Curiosa* not in series (included here) and quickly dispatched them to Dr. Jurin, presumably hoping to reinforce his claims to membership.

Mather's activities during the smallpox epidemic, like his part in the witchcraft proceedings, have become a touchstone for evaluating his personality. Perry Miller found him to be "again the victim of his old neurosis," his faith in the inoculation amounting to a "shot in the dark" authorized only by his sanctimoniousness. Miller himself would have appreciated the difficulty of treating his findings without either filiopiety or longings of parricide. Yet the reader of Mather's letters is compelled to say that here Miller was wholly wrong. Mather had in fact the reports of Pylarinus and Timonius, the testimony of slaves in Boston, and the writings of many Fellows of the Society. He had as much evidence as anyone had in the eighteenth century. He was as well informed as any man alive in his time. One can hardly read his letters during the small-pox furor without feeling that he was courageously the agent of one of those impressively Promethean moments that the history of medicine provides for the stock of western mythology, made more impressive by the religious passion that drove it on. For this time Mather's passion for Doing Good lost its self-aggrandizing taint and took on all the fervor of the older Puritan piety. It became Doing Good for the sake of God and man, His creature.

This is not to say that the episode lacked paranoid touches. Mather did sometimes take the animosity against him to be purely political or personal, when, really, many of those who scorned the inoculation simply feared for their lives. On the other hand, he can hardly be blamed for having felt pursued. The climate of Boston at the time was much as he experienced and described it. If it was not quite the place he called "a city full of lies and murders and blasphemies," and if he was not quite the wanderer in Dante's Malebolge, descending into a world where no man's word counted and where trickery, betrayal, and connivance had corrupted the media and, to that degree, the possibility of human society, yet he had to deal with real slanders, real corruption in high places, real meanness and suspiciousness, and real attempts to assassinate him. The fact remains that during the smallpox crisis most of Boston was wrong and Cotton Mather was right.

However devastating, the epidemic did not obscure in Mather's mind the urgency of other, ever-present problems. It did prevent him from selling some goods to pay off a demand on the Howell estate brought by JOSEPH BAXTER (1676–1745), businessman, land speculator, and minister at Medfield. New successes of the Church of England confirmed his forebodings of a failing Reformation. Typical of these successes was the apostasy of James McSparran, the minister at Bristol, who had been sent by his flock to England for ordination in the Presbyterian manner. While in England he converted to Anglicanism and became an outspoken enemy to the Massachusetts orthodoxy. NATHANIEL COTTON (1698–1729), the acting minister at Bristol, and a friend of Thomas Prince, wrote to Boston hoping to have the crew of sailors who brought McSparran over questioned about his alleged drinking and gaming. But by 1722 there were so many Church of England people in Boston that a second church was formed under Timothy Cutler (another convert), with a third to follow in 1729. In these threatening circumstances Mather again looked to the prophetic books for signs that God would quickly crush the Catholic church if the New England ministry proved unable to, and he started an informal club in Boston to discuss prophecy. The Indian fighting had also revived, as Mather informed Robert Wodrow, or really had never stopped, for raids and border clashes were frequent despite the official peace. Some of the bloodiest fighting raged around the Abenaki Indian village Norridgewock, on the Kennebec river in Maine. There lived the French missionary Sebastian Rale, who inflamed the Abenakis against English settlers coming up the river. Mather's correspondent Joseph Baxter owned a good deal of land in Maine and tried to hinder Rale's mission. In July, 1722, Governor Shute declared war on the Abenakis; Massachusetts unsuccessfully sent three hundred men to seize Rale. Two years later an English expedition at Norridgewock killed him.

The smallpox epidemic provided an interlude in the struggle between the House and Governor Shute. The epidemic over, Shute was again beleaguered by his political enemies. In December, 1722, he left the government in the hands of the moderate William Dummer and slipped away to England to present his grievances to the Privy Council. The *Courant* blasted his secretive departure, but might have kept silent. While Shute was in London, the King died, Shute's commission was vacated, and he failed to be reappointed for the governorship. Alarmed and almost mournful, Mather never saw his close friend and favorite governor again.

To Nathaniel Cotton

U/BPL

July 10, 1721

My dear Kinsman,

[Congratulates him fervently on his courage in becoming minister at Bristol.]

The deliverance of the church at Bristol from that very grievous wolf who was just on the point of having it fall as a prey unto him, was a conspicuous and an illustrious work of our ascended Saviour. The glorious Head of the church wondrously stepped in with a marvellous interposition of His providence to answer the prayers of some, who day and night cried unto Him. [And God will finish the work.]

That very wicked man, whose infatuated followers have been so bewitched by him—*O foolish Bristolians, who has bewitched them!*—he will find, that he has to do with a God that will not be mocked. He ripens apace! The Holy Son of God has begun to scourge the miserable man out of His temple; yea, the scandalous and infamous apostate has already run himself into the outer court. But, my friend, *Rest in the Lord, and wait patiently for Him, for yet a little while,* and thou shalt see what will become of the wicked man, and what will be the tremendous dispensations of a GOD who will be terrible in His Holy Places.

The poor people of Bristol, who still obstinately follow this deceiver, after he had unto all his other complicated impiety added that of a perfidious apostasy from the scriptural way of worship, which he had been a high and hot pretender for, and which they hired him at great expense to get himself qualified for; and when the people that now came over in the vessel with him can tell how he behaved himself aboard— these poor people are such as the churches in the country do with horror and amazement look upon. 'Tis a marvellous judgment of God that they are no more tender of their own reputation, and so unconcerned about the story which they will afford unto the people of God that are at a distance from them. At the same time, you do what will render your name as precious to all the churches.

One cannot but be surprised when we see how ready the Church of England is to do the office of the scavenger for us. Most certainly, 'tis of God, and He intends the establishment of His people here, in the faith and order of the Gospel, and the religion of their pious ancestors, that such missionaries as McSparran, and some others, must be the men employed for the seducing of our people from it. Surely, such apostles will among a people of our illumination have no successes to be boasted of. [Close]   Your affectionate kinsman and brother,

To Joseph Baxter

U/Duxbury   October 4, 1721

Sir,

Among the other uncomfortable consequences of the smallpox raging in the town, one has been the unfinished condition of my wretched administration, which we were all in hopes that by your presence and counsel, would have been brought ere this unto a happy period.

Tho' the court granted a power to sell something (on Mr. Faneuil's obtaining an execution), there is through the difficulty of the time, nothing yet sold.

I have not one penny of money belonging to that estate; but it owes me great sums.

Nor is it possible for me to do anything at this instant but lodge your letter (and just demands) in the hands of the attorneys, and press their utmost endeavors for your satisfaction. [Close]

Your brother and servant,

To John Winthrop

IV Coll 8/MHS   November 27, 1721

My dear Friend,

Shall I never hear from you again!

I pray, let my sufferings from a barbarous and bloody people help to make you patient under yours.

But look off to an infinitely greater pattern of patience.

Your Governor will exhibit unto you my letter to Dr. Woodward, which after you have perused, let it in a month's time return to me again (but by a safe hand!)

I present unto your Lady a little treatise or two, lately published.

After the miraculous defeat of the late attempt upon my life (which I daily expect a repetition of) I could not but preach a sermon on those words, *This night there stood by me the Angel of the God whose*

I am, and whom I serve. I have had some thoughts to give it the public, but I don't know yet whether I shall (or can) or no.

God grant unto you and yours the benefit of the angelical ministry. I am, Sir, Yours forever,

We have an army at this time under the inoculation. Several preachers of the Gospel, old Mr. Walter and his family, intend to it in a day or two.

To Peter Thacher and John Web

U/HCL   January 10, 1722

The Corporation of the College going so far in settling the affair of the Hollisian Professor, without asking more advice of the Overseers in general, and of some elder divines among us who might have been thought good advisers, in particular, seem to have gone too far, and to have done what may be for no very good precedent; and it may not be amiss to declare some dissatisfaction at it.

But inasmuch as our very great obligations to Mr. Hollis for his goodness in this, and his other bounties, are always to be acknowledged, and utmost care is to be taken that we give him not the least umbrage to count us insensible of his favorable aspect;

Inasmuch also, as a Professor of Theology may prove a blessing to the College;

And abundance of good work is provided for him;

And there is provision made that for the future the designation of the person fall under the cognizance of the Overseers;

And inasmuch as the matter is yet capable of a further deliberation and cultivation;

Why may we not so far acquiesce in what is proposed, as only to desire that there be from time to time a committee at least, of the Overseers and Corporation, to examine the qualifications of the candidate for the professorship, as well those prescribed by Mr. Hollis, as what may also be further judged necessary to recommend him unto the service of religion in our churches.

Sic censeo:

Rerf academicarum alioquin prorsus ignarus, et academia extorris.

To John Winthrop

IV Coll 8/MHS   February 12, 1722
                                              Boston, or, The Tents of Kedar.

My dear Friend,

Entering this day into the sixtieth year of my age, I hope you will congratulate my near approach to that world where I shall with a full joy see the reverse of what this base world is filled withal.

Connecticut cannot be more abusive or distasteful to you, than all New England is to me. But both of us must learn to be patient, and rejoice in conformities unto our lovely Saviour.

I am strangely disappointed of my justly expected returns from London. But allow me to say, I find it almost as hard to hear from New London, as from Old, tho' what comes from thence to me is always as cool waters to a thirsty soul.

[Sends along a publication.]

And pray enrich me with as many communications as you can that may go into my *Angel of Bethesda*. Employ your leisure bravely and nobly, and as a philosopher. Tell me also what you think of your *Christian Philosopher*, now you have talked with him. And continue to love, Sir,   Your hearty and constant,

To Hans Sloane

U/Brit Mus (copy, not in   March 10, 1722
Mather's hand)

So considerable a part of mankind fearfully perishing by the smallpox, and many more of us grievously suffering by that miserable distemper, you will allow me to entertain you with a few more communications, and write you (I think it's) a fourth letter upon it.

The distemper has lately visited and ransacked the city of Boston, and in little more than half a year, of more than five thousand persons that have undergone it, near nine hundred have died. But how many lives might have been saved if our unhappy physicians had not poisoned and bewitched our people with a blind rage, that has appeared very like a satanic possession, against the method of relief and safety in the way of the *Smallpox Inoculated*.

I prevailed with one physician (and for it I have had bloody attempts made upon my life by some of our energumens) to introduce the practise. And the experiment has been made upon almost three hundred objects in our neighborhood, young and old (from one year to seventy) weak and strong, male and female, white and black, in midsummer, in autumn, in winter; and it succeeds to admiration.

I cannot learn that anyone has died of it, tho' the experiment has been made under various and marvellous disadvantages. Five or six have died *upon* it, or after it, but from other diseases or accidents, chiefly from having taken the infection in the common way, by inspiration, before it could be given them in this way of transplantation. However, at present I need say no more of this, having already given you some report of our proceedings in it.

To them who are under the inoculation of the smallpox, we commonly give a vomit in the time of their decumbiture, a day or two before the expected eruption. One of our patients, not vomiting so freely as he would have done, thrust a finger or two into his throat, which fetched up what was to be discharged from his uneasy stomach. He had but a few of the smallpox, and the pustules were sufficiently of the distinct sort, as it uses to be where they have the smallpox inoculated. But the fingers that had been thus employed proved as full as they could hold, and of the confluent sort, which he now thought his whole body would have been, if he had not in this way prevented it.

Your Dr. Leigh, in his *Natural History of Lancashire*, counts it an occurrence worth relating, that there were some cats known to catch the smallpox, and pass regularly through the state of it, and then to die. We have had among us the very same occurrence.

It was generally observed, and complained, that the pigeon-houses of the city continued unfruitful, and the pigeons did not hatch or lay as they used to do, all the while that the smallpox was in its epidemical progress. And it is very strongly affirmed, that our dunghill-fowl felt much of the like effect upon them. We have so many among us who have been visited with the plague in other countries many years ago, and who have never been arrested with the [word torn] after it, tho' they have been exposed as much as any other people to it, that it now begins to obtain a belief with us, that they who have had the plague will never have the smallpox after it.

I will add but one thing more. For succor under the smallpox, where life is in danger, after all the methods and medicines that our Sydenham and others rely upon, I can assure you we have yet found nothing so sure as this. Procure for the patient as early as may be, by epispastics, a plentiful discharge at the handwrists or ankles, or both (I say, *as early as may be!*) and keep them running till the danger is over. When the venom of the smallpox makes an evident and violent invasion on the nobler parts, this discharge *does wonderfully*. I am sorry it was so late before we fell into this way; but it has constantly prospered. I know not that it has once miscarried, since we came into it.

To John Winthrop

IV Coll 8/MHS   March 12, 1722

My worthy Friend,

The feeble state of your health (which I take it for granted is all that hinders your making some return to my repeated addresses) is a matter of concern to me. I will not think it enough to say, *Medice, Cura teipsum;* but I will rather look up to the Lord our Healer for you.

And I will humbly move that you be sure to stick unto all the rules of health and cure which our *Nishmath-Chajim* concludes withal, especially that of a mind kept in a perpetual tranquility.

[Asks the return of his two manuscripts, *Nishmath-Chajim* and *The Seventh Son.*]

I have this request also to add; that whereas I hear there is lately discovered a new snake, who commands and governs the rattlesnakes, and upon their not observing order strikes them dead with a bone which he has instead of a rattle, you would please, when your health allows, to obtain and remit a very particular account of this animal.

We are still kept in a strange darkness about our European affairs. Inoculation goes on and prospers; the new uproar, which keeps the King at home and keeps the camp at Hyde Park still going on, is variously talked about. The plague is almost entirely ceased in France, except at Avignon. Our new scene of troubles here, God knows when and how it will terminate.

I long, long to hear from you. I pray let me at last extort from you that satisfaction to, Sir, Your most hearty friend,

I have not yet one line from any of my correspondents in the Royal Society. Only Mr. Chamberlain tells me (and I feel it from other circumstances) that my twelve letters to him have been published. And yet I have never to this hour seen them, nor have they that have published I know not how many other things of mine, ever given me the sight of them (or else they have miscarried).

I have done, I have done, with expectations from this world.

[Wishes Winthrop were in Boston; urges him to write.]

Your loving and constant and cordial friend,

To Thomas Prince

DII/MHS   June [?], 1722

Sir,

Your printer has, I suppose, got ready your *Minister*; and it was in some view of the opportunity which you might have to disperse many of your books on the approaching festival.

Imagining that the generous goodness which has been exerted by you in this publication does intend a dispersion of the books into the hands of all the ministers throughout the country, it seems necessary that there should be some agreement of the brethren to prevent your interfering with one another in your pious communication. Everyone should know what counties (or parts of the country) he will chiefly take for his province in the dispersion.

And if you order your printer to bring me my fifty shillings worth, I will send our *Minister* through the colony of Connecticut, and some of the more southern provinces.

We are thus preparing for employments in the better world. Waiting for which, I am, Sir, your brother and servant,

I am not well! But my poor wife, struck with a consumption, wants and asks your prayers ———

To Thomas Prince

DII/MHS   [Probably June 3, 1722]

[Will be candid with him, as always.]

I have long been of the opinion that there could scarce be a more comprehensive service done, than to lodge in the hands of the ministers throughout the country, a memorial of the methods which may be taken by them to be very serviceable. No men have such opportunities as they to be very serviceable.

Now my two neighbors, Mr. Thacher and Mr. Web, have had such favorable sentiments for the poor sermon that was offered you last Thursday, as to press the publication of it, and provide for part of the charge. Surprised at their motion, I am come anon myself into the opinion that the poor sermon being transcribed and somewhat amended, may answer such ends as I ought humbly and gladly and zealously to devote my all unto. And the rather because my time for doing is drawing very near its period. If now I can get the assistance of but 50s or 3£ subscribed, I can, I suppose, get through the rest of the expense which the desired publication may call for. [Sends along the sermon.]

Your constant friend, brother, and servant,

To Thomas Prince

DII/MHS

June 12, 1722

My invaluable Friend and Brother,

To you I choose to commit my *Minister*. I enclose fifty shillings towards the expense. I have occasionally had some discourse with Mr. Fleet about the work. For that cause, you must make the first offer to him. I leave the whole to your wisdom and goodness. If you, or any of the brethren, would correct any passage in it, I entirely resign it unto your pleasure. I could have embellished it with many ornaments. But I conscientiously decline the ostentation of erudition lest I disoblige that Holy Spirit, on whom alone I depend for the success of the essay. Besides, I have in a considerable number of other books (besides the *Magnalia*) already pretty well exhausted a good stock of flowers, which ought not to be presented over again. Yea, this very week, I have an ordination sermon published, which I tender to your acceptance. We shall reap together the harvest of this action in the First Resurrection.

To Thomas Foxcroft

U/UVL

[Probably August 26, 1722]

Sir,

Everything of mine being always much beyond its deserts acceptable to you, I did not know whether the character this day given of your good father-in-law might not be what you might be willing to cast your eye upon, and the rather because the sermon cultivates a metaphor which perhaps you have never seen (I know I have not) a discourse upon. [Asks him to return the sermon after reading it.]

Your brother and servant,

To Thomas Foxcroft

U/UVL   August 28, 1722

My dear Friend,

A small number of my neighbors have addressed me for instructions about the coming and Kingdom of God our Saviour, and the intention of the holy prophecies.

I know not how to deny them. This evening between six and seven I design my first lecture and conference.

But among my articles of agreement with my little company, one was that Messrs. Thacher, Prince, Web, and Foxcroft should be welcome to us, and all of them, as well as I, say *most highly so.*

I think you *despise not prophesyings,* or a holy, humble (angelical) inquiry into prophesies. But if you will condescend so far as to hear my introduction this evening, you shall then do as you please. However, I cannot but confess my ambition of having such a scholar. It will be the pride of, Sir,   Your brother and servant,

To Thomas Prince

DII/MHS   [Probably September 5, 1722]

Sir,

The excellent spirit of piety which always endears our worthy brother Sewall to all of us as well as to me, and the intimate communion and correspondence of the most inviolate friendship which we always maintain with him, seems to render it suitable that he should be apprised of our combination to begin this evening a *conference on the sacred prophecies concerning the Coming and Kingdom of our Saviour,* and have the offer of a welcome to it.

It is possible that he may have a less degree of relish for those things, than some others; and there is a peculiarity of constitution in these points not easy to be accounted for. But then, his objections to our interpretations may be of use to us, to prevent our going too easily into mistakes; and perhaps to establish what cannot be shaken. It is,

352

however, fit that he should have the liberty of sharing with us (as Mr. Cooper, I perceive, also will). [Close]   Your brother and servant,

When you visit Mr. Daniel Oliver, bestow all (or some) of these *Golden Curbs* upon him, to put upon headstrong fools, at the times when he has occasion to execute the law upon them.

To Benjamin Colman

U/NYHS   September 14, 1722

Sir,

Something you mentioned unto me last night in the street has invited me to send you what you have now before you, written the best part of two years ago.

And I wholly leave it unto your wisdom and candor, to do what you please with it. An entire confidence in your friendship is forever placed by,   Your brother and servant,

Meeting one day in the street, Mr. Yeoman called me aside, and gave me to understand that My Lord Barrington was in very ill terms with me because I had represented him as an Arian, and because I had written to Mr. Bradbury, who was a person that had offended him. I wondered at it, and made my reply, which because I know not whether his hearing might allow exactly to reach him, I did the day following send him in writing, to this effect:

My Lord Barrington's wisdom and goodness will by no means permit any complaint of my revived correspondence with Mr. Bradbury, when his Lordship shall please to consider how I was introduced into it.

Sending over my *Christian Philosopher*, I prefixed unto it a dedication to My Lord Barrington, wherein according to my poor manner I did what justice I could unto his Lordship's excellent character, and renewed therewithal the expressions of my very high respects unto one whom I then did, and still do, take to be a Governor than whom I know not a better in the world. His Lordship, in a letter wherewith [he] honored me, let me know that he took not un[kindly?] my poor American present; but added, that he had committed it into the hands of Mr. Bradbury, as a com[mon] friend unto us.

I took no further care; but long after this, My L[ord] in another letter told me that Mr. Bradbury had much offended him, and that as for my manuscript in his hands, he would never call for it, nor take any

353

further notice of it. It seemed written also with an air that I suppose might be the effect of some resentments which I was a stranger to.

(I'll transcribe only these words relating to the present occasion— *I know not what he* (Mr. Bradbury) *has done with it, nor am I like to know. I never desire to see him again, till—I say this to excuse myself from not saying anything farther to you in relation to that M.SS., and for begging you to give such directions about it to Mr. Bradbury as you shall see fit.*)

What should I now do! Under this direction I wrote unto Mr. Bradbury to send me my mean composure home again, or do what he pleased with it. Tho' the composure may be never so little esteemed of, yet it was most certainly worth my writing a letter about it, unto him that My Lord had left it with.

But Mr. Bradbury laid me under ponderous obligations by publishing the book, and enriching me with extensive opportunities to do my part among the priests of the creation.

While these things were doing, I took the occasion to write unto the gentleman who thus obliged me, a letter which he saw cause to publish for the service of the most glorious cause in the world. This was the more agreeable to me, because it rescued me from a misconstruction [of?] another letter of mine, which had been dispersed over the nation.

I am very much a stranger to the personal provocations between My Lord and Mr. Bradbury. And the only time that ever I since wrote unto Mr. Bradbury in the least relating to My Lord, it was only this: *I should be glad that there may be as little misunderstanding and exasperation as 'tis possible between so valuable persons, and such as have sometimes maintained the kindest friendship.*

My Lord is too just and generous a person to think that my writing to a gentleman who has laid me under great personal obligations will any ways involve me in the blame of everything which My Lord, or anyone else, may apprehend blameable in him. 'Tis no part of my business with him, nor do such things forfeit unto any gentleman the use of his friends, who don't at all concern themselves in their personal controversies.

As for what has been said of my representing My Lord as an Arian, 'tis wrong. I never spoke it, never wrote it, never thought it. Nor do I know that the good people in this country think him so. I don't remember that ever I heard of anyone's calling My Lord an Arian, but in a complaint I heard our invaluable Governor make of one who spoke it; but he was one, on whose account I have been sufficiently outraged for my saying *we were abused by them who love and make a lie.*

If offense be taken at me for my doing the best I can, that while we are for an entire liberty in the civil state, for all good subjects and good neighbors, and for a union in the church upon the pure basis of piety, we may not unawares betray or injure our holy religion by owning as our brethren in Christ all that will *subscribe the express words of the Scripture* (which Socinians and Quakers and Papists, and all the heretics on the face of the earth will do) and lose the *truths* of the Scripture by keeping to the *terms* of it, without a *necessary explanation of sentiments* upon what we take to be the sense of the terms; this is what I must not ask any pardon for. I do not repent of one word I have written upon it. What I have written is right, and every day brings new proofs that there has been infinite occasion for it. In all I have done, I know not that any one man living is indecently reflected on.

Such things as these I covered unto Mr. Yeoman's, with the following letter:

Sir,

That there may be no possibility of misapprehending what I did speak, or would or should have spoke, in our last interview, I take leave now to lay it before you in black and white. I am sorry I happen to be under the displeasure of one, whom in published speeches, which have been dispersed through the whole British dominions, I have celebrated as *an incomparable person,* and one whose brother will forever be to me one of the dearest men in the world, and the perpetual subject of panegyrics, which my tongue has been or shall be concerned in; and one who is uncle to the gentleman, to whom I now subscribe, Sir,

Your hearty friend and humble servant,

What use Mr. Yeoman made of these things, I know not. And being as ignorant what acceptance, or what construction, any more personal applications of mine unto My Lord might have, I have chose to remain in the silence of one who is unconcerning himself as much and as fast as he can with the affairs of this world, and engaging himself in the views of a better, as one at threescore certainly ought to do.

To Robert Wodrow

U/NLS (not in Mather's hand,   January 1, 172 ;
but signed by him)

My most honored Brother,

It has been a sensible grief to me that a vessel should steal away from hence to Glasgow, and I miss the opportunity of paying my duty to some of the most valuable friends I have in the world. And it has been yet more grievous to me to understand that so many of my packets have miscarried, as there must have done if three years have passed, which you intimate, since you have had any from me.

'Tis high time for me to inform you, and I do it with the greatest gratitude that is possible, that I am enriched with both volumes of your *Martyrology*. It is a good and a great work, which our glorious Lord has herein helped you to do for a church of His which is, I believe, of all that He has anywhere under heaven, the dearest unto Him, and which, I am sure, is well worthy of all the services that the most excellent men on the earth can do unto it. [Praises Wodrow's book.]

In our College [at] New Haven, the Rector, with several young [mini]sters, were lately so left of God as to declare [them]selves unsatisfied of the validity of their m[inistry?] for the want of episcopal ordination. This [a word illegible] of theirs gave an inexpressible alarm to all the churches in the country, which express a general abhorrence of the apostasy. The most of the few apostates have reconciled themselves to their offended churches, but the treacherous Rector is gone over to London for orders.

The Indians of the east, under the fascinations of a French priest, and instigations of our French neighbors, have begun a new war upon us, which for the present has put a stop to the fine settlements which our Scotch brethren from Ireland had begun to make in that part of our country. But through a strange restraint of providence upon the savages, we have hitherto suffered little further damage from them.

A little and wretched (but, in our General Court, very potent) party of men, have by their spiteful conduct so tired and soured our good Governor that (having obtained the King's leave) he is privately gone off this week for London. And we must expect miserable changes, and very heavy chains, to be hastened upon [us?], except the embroilments

begun upon the nations divert them. [Sends along some of his publications, and asks that his letter be shown to Stirling and Clark.]

Your most affectionate brother and servant,

[PROBABLY TO JOHN STIRLING]

U/NLS   January 5, 1723

Sir,

[Little newsworthy in "this poor country."]

[New England] is indeed become so distempered and so degenerate,
that I am often under Elias's juniper; yea, often sighing, *woe is me that
I sojourn in* Boston, *and that I dwell in the tents of* New England!

But then, I see, all flesh elsewhere is everywhere corrupting their way,
and no hope of a better till a future state. And, alas, what is the Glorious One going to do with a woeful world! Yea, what a tremendous
earthquake is your island entering apace unto!

[Notes that some of his packets have miscarried; laments the death
of Jameson; repeats standard criticisms of the SPG.]

At the same time, it has been a marvellous grief unto us, that among
our United Brethren who have lately come over from Ireland unto us,
and found all the good reception imaginable here, there have been some
who have most indecently and ingratefully given much disturbance to
the peace of our churches. To arm an indiscreet person of their nation
for the serving of some factious purposes among our own disorderly and
litigious people, some strangers have clandestinely ordained him in a
private house at Boston, without the knowledge of any one of the ministers; and they have gone on to nullify the covenant of God in our
churches, and extinguish all the relation hitherto religiously professed
and maintained between them, and have decried our synods and councils as things of no authority, and cast the utmost contempt upon them.
We tell them that such proceedings will be as displeasing to you as
they are to us, when you come to hear of them. In the meantime, 'tis
incredible how much our common people are hereby become indisposed
unto those whom some of us have loved and prized and multiplied the
testimonies of our affection to, above any in the world.

[Hopes the students at Glasgow will profit from *The Christian Philosopher*.]   Your most hearty servant,

P.S. One of your name, and related unto you, did me the honor of a short visit many months ago. For your sake, I earnestly solicited him to let me see him again, and give me opportunities of serving him to the best of my capacity. But, for what reasons I know not, he has hitherto kept at a total distance from me.

To Dr. James Jurin

U/RS   May 21, 1723

Sir,

You are better known to me than I can be to you, and I congratulate unto myself as well as unto the world the felicity of your succession in the office of Secretary to the Royal Society. But in order to a mutual better knowledge, I owe you, and must now give you, some very short account of myself; more particularly with relation to that illustrious body whereof, I hoped, I had the honor of being esteemed a member.

Having the pleasure of some correspondence with your excellent predecessor, Mr. Waller, I did communicate unto him (and unto my valuable Dr. Woodward) a great number of American and philosophical curiosities, with an intimation of my purpose to continue the communications. These gentlemen put the as unexpected as undeserved respect upon me, of proposing me for a member of the Royal Society, and they both wrote unto me that I was chosen accordingly, both by the council and body of the Society, on the anniversary day for such elections, in the year 1713—adding, that the only reason of my not having my name in the printed list of the Society was because of my being beyond-sea, and yet a natural born subject, and so not capable of being inserted among the gentlemen of other nations. Your secretary also, Dr. Halley, in the *Philosophical Transactions* of 1714, printed my name with an F.R.S. annexed unto it. Mr. Petiver did the like in his *Naturae Collectanea* and in his letter to me he had these words: 'Your election succeeded without opposition, and you was elected after the usual method of balloting. The reason of your being out of the printed list is your not being personally here to subscribe to the orders that should be tendered you.' To which he added congratulations and compliments not proper to be by my pen transcribed.

A distinguished and a diminutive crew of odd people here, when they could find no other darts to throw at me, imagined their not finding my name in the printed list of the Royal Society would enable them to detect me of an imposture, for affixing an F.R.S. unto my name, on some just occasions for it. And an infamous fellow, whose name is John Checkley, a sorry *Toyman* [sic] (that yet had the impudence to write as a *divine*) wrote a letter full of scandalous invectives against me, which was publicly read in the Royal Society. This wretched man, ambitious to do the part of a divine, printed here some rhapsodies to prove *that the God whom King William and the Christians of New England have worshipped, is the D——l.* A young and a bright kinsman of mine bestowed such castigations on the blasphemer, that I became thereupon the object of his implacable revenges. But of this matter, I gave Dr. Woodward a more full account a year and half ago; which, because I know not whether he ever received it, I now repeat a little of, and fly to your justice if any further indignity of this nature should be offered me.

But, that I may not lay aside any of the meek, patient, humble disposition with which I should address you on this occasion, I shall keep such terms as I used unto my Doctor, when he had what he required of me upon it.

I should never have presumed upon affixing an F.R.S. unto my poor unworthy name, had I not thought that my honorable masters would have taxed me as guilty of some ingratitude unto them for their unmerited favors, if I had always declined it.

The many treatises (many more than three hundred) which Heaven has allowed and assisted me to publish (in the midst of many other constant and heavy labors) on various arguments, and in various dead as well as living languages, added unto some other circumstances needless to be mentioned, had procured me from some European universities, without my seeking in the least measure for them, the testimonies of the highest respect that they could show to the meanest of men, and among the rest a diploma for the Doctorate in Theology. Upon this I was under some temptation unto the vanity of thinking that it was possible the Royal Society also might esteem it no disgrace to permit my name among their members, especially when my remittances to their treasury might for number (however, not for value) be equal to what they might receive of some other members whose correspondence they cast a kind aspect upon. For the embellishments wherewith I studied usually (after the manner of the German *Ephemerides*) to make my dry and dull stories a little more palatable to men of erudition, some of your own members, as well as Monsr. [Tournefut?], helped me to some apology.

But if, after all, it be the pleasure of those honorable persons who compose or govern the Royal Society, that I should lay aside my pretensions to be at all related unto that illustrious body, upon the least signification of it by your pen it shall be dutifully complied withal. I will only continue to take the leave of still communicating annually to you (as long as I live) what *Curiosa Americana* I can become the possessor of. For (my Jewish rabbi's having taught me to *love the work,* and have *little regard unto the rabbinate*) it is not the title, but the service that is the height, and indeed the whole, of my ambition. [Close]

Sir, Your most affectionate friend and servant,

TO DR. JAMES JURIN

U/RS (not in Mather's hand, but signed by him,   May 21, 1723
and with his interpolations)

The Case of the Smallpox Inoculated, further cleared
Sir,

It is a thing well known to all who know anything, that the smallpox has from the days that the Saracens brought it into Europe with them, still proved a great plague unto the inhabitants of the earth, and been enough, if there were nothing else, to procure the denomination of a *woe* for those woeful harpies. The numbers of the slain by this tremendous malady have been far more than of those who have perished by the pestilence; and the distemper which has been by way of eminency called *the destroyer* has not been such a besom of destruction as this competitor to it, among them who have had the graves waiting for them. The perpetual (and sometimes very strangely periodical) visits which this destructive malady is ever making to all the commercial parts of the earth, and even unto them that are afar off upon the sea, do hold mankind in a continual bondage, through the fear of being once in their life seized with it, yea, of having their life extinguished by it. And as the leviathan approaches, from whose mouth sparks of fire leap out, and who makes our blood boil as a pot, how are even the mighty, as well as the many, afraid! The apprehensions of dying a very terrible death, after a burning for many days, in as painful, as loathsome a malady, or at best of having many weary nights roll away under the uneasy circumstances of loins filled with a loathsome disease, and recovering with boils, and scars, and wounds, not quickly to be forgotten, hold the children of men in the terrors of death, until the fiery trial be over with them.

[Mentions that previously it has been impossible to cure the disease.]

One would have thought, when the compassion of Heaven had made unto a miserable world a discovery of an *unfailing method,* not only to redeem our lives from the destruction threatened by this common enemy of mankind, but also to prevent the uneasy circumstances which make the most that outlive it profess that thousands of pounds would not hire them again to undergo them, I say, one could not but think that the children of men should have agreed in the most solemn thanksgivings to a gracious God, and most thankfully have accepted the offered favor. But now to find that people should be generally under the energy of an unaccountable aversion from coming into this method of safety; yea, that they should with a rage that reaches up to Heaven, malign and revile those that only propose it unto them, and not only wish the death of those that come into it, but also actually seek the death of the friends that only show them how to save their lives from a formidable adversary! [But goodness always meets with opposition.]

The manner wherein the opposition has been usually carried on has been so satanic, that he must be very blind who sees not the evident original of it. The railing, the lying, the fury, the bloody malice, and even the subordination of perjury, with attempts of assassination, which has distinguished it, have been such as hardly have ever been equalled on any occasion; and one must, after the manner of men, be engaged as in a fight with beasts at Ephesus, who will appear as an intercessor with people, that they would be willing to have their lives reprieved and sweetened.

But, if there be anything of argument that has ever been produced against this method of safety, I pray let us be apprised of it. [All of the objections have been mere superstitions.]

The objection drawn from this party (political or ecclesiastical) approving the practise, and that party not approving it, is too mean to have so much as one thought bestowed on it. It is with the utmost indignation that some have sometimes beheld the practise made a mere party business, and a Jacobite, or High-flying party, counting themselves bound in duty to their party to decry it, or perhaps the party disaffected unto such and such persons of public station and merit, under the obligations of a party to decline it. And yet I foresee that I shall quickly find it in my way to touch upon one party (mentioned in the third chapter of Genesis) from whence one small essay towards an argument for the practise, has been sometimes allowed of.

One sort of objections against the method of managing and governing the smallpox in the way of inoculation, has been fetched from conscience; and it has been the cry of a multitude that they *can't see through it* how one can with a good conscience bring a sickness on himself, until it shall please the God of our life to send it upon him.

Now and then persons of serious piety become the opposers of it from a real scruple of conscience concerning the practise. And as these, for the most part, express their dissent with modesty, sobriety, humility, and without censuring of those that are otherwise minded, so we ought ever to treat them with the respects of brethren. But it has been somewhat remarkable and equally ridiculous that the most fierce opposers of the practise have commonly been such as have most cast off the restraints of conscience in other matters, and in their way of talking upon this also, show that conscience has very little [awe?] upon them. With a mouth full of cursing and the language of fiends, at the moment, they vow *they would not be guilty of such a wickedness for all the world!* I have known some good people that have opposed the practise brought over to it by this, as the first of their motives: they were ashamed of their company. [Many who oppose the inoculation are the worst sort of people.] However, let us hear what may be said in opposition. Verily, nothing but what may be said against all the preventing physic in the world. It is urged that it is unlawful to prevent our falling into a greater, and even a deadly, sickness by using a remedy which will throw us into a lesser, and more gentle turn of illness, and such a one as will not ordinarily endanger the life of him that uses it. This is a thing that must be affirmed by all that hold it unlawful to seek a deliverance from the danger of a deadly smallpox in the gentle way of inoculation. But they who affirm this, understand not what they say, nor whereof they affirm. With such profound casuites, it is not lawful for a man to undergo so much danger for the saving of his life as every sailor does (and often sickness too) to get a little money. Certainly, never till now was that rule contested, of two evils, choose the least. How commonly do people in health use emetics and cathartics to prevent a sickness which they are afraid of? and those emetics and cathartics too, under the operation whereof ten thousand more have lost their lives, than ever there have under the smallpox inoculated?

Yea, how many millions have only in learning to smoke tobacco (and this perhaps only to qualify themselves for the pleasure of an exercise which their health is little enough consulted in) procured unto themselves much more sickness, and of a more dangerous tendency too, than is undergone by the most of them that undergo the smallpox inoculated?

It is a hundred to one but the objector may have been chargeable at some time or other with one or both of these things. But he would be angry if you should charge them as crimes upon him.

Let us yet more exactly inquire into the conduct of the inoculated patient:

He is in hazard of being smitten with the smallpox, and for ought he knows it may be of the confluent sort, which is that which people do mostly die of; of the distinct sort, there are few miscarry. He is in the way of it; reason and therefore duty bids him to look for it. If it be not so, the inoculation is unseasonable and impertinent. If it be so, his is not one of the whole that have no need of a physician. And if it be so, why should he forget a very ancient oracle, *the prudent foresees the evil, and shelters himself; the simple pass on and are punished!*

Well, he is acquainted with a medicine that never was known to fail of preventing the smallpox of the confluent sort, which he is in hazard of. I beseech you, what is there in the Word of the blessed God (which proscribes and limits the whole duty of man) that forbids the use of this medicine any more than an antidote against the plague? It is rather plain that the Sixth Commandment requires him to use it; and I always thought the Word of the blessed God had instructed us that for our physic as well as for our food, every creature of God is good, and nothing to be refused if it be received with thanksgiving.

Certainly our sacred Bible will not be a dispensatory that shall determine anything in the matter of the medicine to be unlawful. What if it were the powder of toads, or the powder that Johannes Anglicus cured agues withal? What if it be a *variolous quittor*, or the galls of rattlesnakes? The sacred Scripture nowhere says, *touch it not, taste it not, handle it not.*

If there be anything unlawful in the medicine it must arise from the way of its operation. But let us examine this. [Argues that it would not be called unlawful if it caused vomiting or raised a sweat.]

But then suppose the medicine work in the way of what we may call a despumation, and raise a ferment with pustules, that we may call a sort of smallpox, and is indeed so much of it as forever to secure from any further arrest from that grievous distemper? Where is the Word of God that forbids this despumation, when it may be made with expectation of safety and success? Tho' the medicine be a *variolous quittor* applied unto an incision, I say again, where is the use of it forbidden unto us, any more than the rest that the *Microcosmus Medicus* advises of? This, at last, is the very case! *Here* is the *medicine!* He takes a medicine that operates with the symptoms of that smallpox that ordinarily kills nobody, and prevents his ever falling into that smallpox that kills us by millions, and prevents also the distresses which many that are not killed yet commonly meet withal. What shall we say? The Word of God has allowed medicines that operate in all other ways except only that of despumation? Profane caviller! *Add not unto His Word, lest He reprove thee, and thou be found a liar.* [It is true that a few die under the inoculation, but some people die from having a tooth drawn.]

In short, I have never seen any Scripture brought against this practise but what has been brought with as foolish and faulty a violation of the Third Commandment, as it would be to bring that Scripture against blood-letting: *He that sheds man's blood, by man shall his blood be shed.*

But I am now drawn to make some remark upon another sort of objections against the method of saving our lives from the horrible pit, and this they pretend is fetched from nature. They allege, *'tis a dangerous practise.*

Now to confute this allegation, there can be no answer comparable to that of constant experience; and by this it is abundantly answered, and so victoriously, that it is amazing there should be heard the least sibilations of it any more.

[Many foolish physicians argue against the inoculation.]

Now this is what I maintain, that constant experience has declared for this practise that it is a safe and sure method of delivering ourselves and our children from going down into the pit by the stroke of a distemper which dispatches mankind thither by millions. Yea, there never did arrive to us (no, not in the boasted *cortex* itself, or any of its rivals) any medicine recommended with such a constant experience of a divine blessing upon it.

The constant experience to which I make my first appeal shall be fetched from foreign countries. [Mentions the success of the inoculation in the Levant and in Africa.]

But then, my own country, if I may call it so, or that where I was born and bred, and in the tents whereof I am a sojourner, shall be what I will with yet more assurance appeal unto.

When I first addressed the physicians of Boston (as the smallpox was entering the city, two years ago) with the account which Timonius and Pylarinus gave of this practise, one word (of the feminine gender!) let fall in that account caused some to foretell that the physicians would never come into it, but would set themselves to decry it with all their might. I will not mention the reason given for this prediction, because I am far from casting a blemish on that honorable profession from the humors of some that are got into it. But this I will say, the prediction was accomplished unto admiration. And how far they can comfort themselves in seeing above a thousand of their neighbors within a few months killed before their eyes, when they knew a method that in ordinary way would have saved them, *they know better than I!*

Two pretenders to instruct people in the art of physic published their pamphlets against the practise, both of them stuffed with gross lies in matters of fact (which indeed are ever used and needful to be so, for the support of the cause) and both of them full of a nonsense and folly which a text in the twenty-sixth of the Proverbs forbids an answer to.

The first of these was a sorry tobacconist who could hardly spell a word of English (even the word *English* from his acute pen was *Engleche*) and could not read his own manuscript, but prayed the printer to find out the meaning, and make English of it. This hideous fellow, who is more known by the name of Mundiangus than that of John Williams, directed his readers to *Bludde sempeti and anthepeti;* and he forbad this *prates* because to *specke for hoomain invenccions in fisecke* is not *allowabel* (this is a specimen of the orthography in his manuscript). But because the sot abusively brought some clauses from the sacred Scriptures (which he spelled *scakered Scripters*) 'tis incredible how much the mob about the country were enchanted by this poor smoky conjurer. The smoke that came out of a tobacco-cellar made a strange impression on them, and this *Hans en kelder* was a mere apostle (when doing the part of an Apollyon) to his wretched votaries.

[Similarly strikes out against the "gross falsities" spread by William Douglass; mentions the success of the inoculation in Boston and nearby towns.]

There are two towns contiguous to Boston. The smallpox entered the town to the northward, where the people were poisoned with outcries against the inoculation. There they died by scores; they died in shoals; the place was an Aceldama. The smallpox entered the town to the southward, and of the first fourteen or fifteen men that were taken with it, about eleven died. But the survivors, after the example of their wiser pastors, coming at once into the inoculation, there died *not one man* after it. One would think here was an experiment enough to instruct a country; yea, to instruct a nation. [Cites some individual cases.]

Upon the whole, one that shall have the effrontery to utter an intimation that it is confessed, as many die under the smallpox inoculated as there do of the smallpox taken in the common way, ought certainly to have the penance of a very long silence imposed on him. Instead of insinuating so vile a falsehood, it may, for ought anything that I have ever yet met withal, be very truly declared, *it yet remains to be proved, that of the many hundreds and thousands that have been under the smallpox inoculated, there was ever any one person who miscarried, that the operation was regularly used upon.* There never was a more successful operation brought into the world! And the reception which it has among those that should be wiser, administers to Heaven too much cause of that complaint, *wherefore is a price put into the hands of the fools, that have no heart unto it?*

If your physicians will discourage the practise, they will do well to examine their hearts, what principles they act upon, and consider how they can answer to God for the loss of so many hundreds of thousands of lives, as would have been saved if *they* had not hindered it! But *meliora speramus.*

As for the other vehement opposers of this practise, if they are not so possessed that all talking to them would be only to argue with a whirlwind! I would ask them whether it be not a bold presumption in them to make that a sin which God, the Judge of all, has never made a sin, but really commanded and enjoined and required as a duty? And I would ask them whether they can count it a trusting in God, and not a tempting of Him, to depend on Him for the prolongation of their lives, while they neglect the duty of doing what they can in the use of means that He has kindly shown them for it.

I would also ask them whether it be not a most criminal ingratitude unto the God of Health, when He has acquainted us with a most invaluable method for the saving of our lives from so great a death, to treat it with neglect, and contempt, and multiply abuses on them who thankfully and in a spirit of obedience to Him, embrace His blessings!

I would finally ask them whether they have no dread at all of being accessory to the innumerable deaths which may be, in part, owing to their boisterous opposition unto the method of safety?

For my part, I cannot lay aside my sentiments that the sense of the fascination with which the great adversary of mankind makes these unhappy men his instruments of helping the curse to devour the earth, and those who dwell therein to be desolate, so that anon, few, few men, to what might have been, shall be left, may call them to walk humbly all their days, that ever they should be *so left of God!*

In the meantime, we that cry with a loud voice to them, *Do yourselves no harm*, and show them how to keep themselves from the paths of the destroyer, are conscious of nothing but of a pity for mankind under the rebukes of God, a concern to see the madness of the people, a desire to have our neighbors *do well*, and a solicitude for a better state of the world. And all the obloquies and outrages we suffer for our charity, we shall entertain as persecutions for a good cause, which will not want its recompenses.

I write unto a person of so much goodness that I am sure he will pardon the fatigue which the perusal of this long epistle may give him upon an affair, the importance whereof will make its apology; and he will with his usual candor accept the intention of, Sir,

Your most hearty friend and servant,

To Dr. James Jurin

U/RS

June 10, 1723

Sir,

[Introduces the bearer, Isaac Greenwood], an ingenious young gentleman and a graduate in our College, who proposes to make some addition to his accomplishments by visiting Europe, and particularly by visiting of Dr. Jurin.

I recommend him to your favor and advice, and he having been one of our inoculates I offer him to your examination, because I have heard the inoculation is an article on which you are very particularly inquisitive. And considering the importance of it for the saving of hundreds of thousands of precious lives, I do not wonder at it if a person of your wisdom and goodness be so. [Close]

Your affectionate friend and servant,

To Thomas Prince

DII/MHS

June 16, 1723

My dear Friend,

Vigilare decet hominem qui vult sua tempore conferre officia.

In the circumstances of the poor creature who is this week to die by the sword of justice, there is a voice of God crying to the city—not only the condition of such slaves is worthy to be considered, but also the threatenings which there have been of laying the town in ashes, are speaking things.

I would humbly propose to you, and entreat of you, to bend your holy studies a little this way for your approaching lecture. [Urges him to do so.]

Pardon the suggestion. 'Tis my way to project services for others, as well as myself. I am, Sir,   Your brother,

Mather apparently wrote the following notes for a sermon or memorial a day or two after the preceding letter.

U/MHS

This place has lately been brought into uncommon distresses by some of a foolish nation.

The voice of the Lord cries to the city.

First, the burning of the town has been threatened, and there have been many fires kindled, in some of which those of this foolish nation, we may suppose, have not been concerned.

[Urges honest-dealing and Sabbath worship to prevent this conflagration.]

And considering by what hands the town has been so endangered, there can be nothing more seasonable and reasonable than for us to consider, whether our conduct with relation to our African slaves be not one thing for which our God may have a controversy with us.

Are they always treated according to the rules of humanity—

And much more, Christianity which is improved and ennobles humanity.

Are they treated as those that are of one blood with us, and those that have immortal souls in them, and are not mere beasts of burden!

Are they instructed, and made to know—such things, which if they knew would restrain them from exorbitancies and enormities which are complained them, and render them notable blessings in the families they belong unto. The common cavil, that they are the worse servants for being taught the knowledge of Christ, is a cursed falsehood; experience confutes it; it is a blasphemy, and it is fitter for the mouth of a devil than of a Christian to utter it.

But then, there is a voice of Heaven to the slaves, in what this poor creature is left with—

To beware of the sins which may provoke the Glorious One to leave them unto the last degrees of wickedness and misery.

To study a dutiful behavior unto their superiors, and that they may be blessings in the family they belong unto.

To be patient in their low and hard condition.

To become the servants of Christ.

Then, what they shall very shortly see at the end of their short servitude—else, a worse thing.

CHAPTER FIVE

1723–1727

Selection of a new president for Harvard; Mather's bankruptcy; Lydia leaves his house; death of Increase Mather, Jr.; renewed interest in prophecy; illness; attempts to publish final works; departure of John Winthrop; earthquake of 1727; death.

I

Wɪᴛʜ Governor Shute's withdrawal to England late in 1722, Mather's friendship with him dissolved. As Mather bemoaned to ᴛʜᴏᴍᴀꜱ ʜᴏʟʟɪꜱ, ᴊʀ. (d. 1735), nephew of the Harvard benefactor, Shute took offense at a report that Mather had failed to justify his departure in the public prayers. His earlier quarrel with Shute's brother, Lord Barrington, aggravated the slight. Imagining that Shute would take revenge on him and on Massachusetts by trying to have the charter revoked, he wrote to Shute and implored him not to punish all of the province for the fractious politics of a few. Although he lost the governorship, Shute continued to influence colonial policy. Indeed, he was allowed to nominate a new governor, and in August, 1723, he submitted to the king a formal complaint of misconduct against the House for invading the crown's prerogatives. After the House prepared a reply to be sent through Jeremiah Dummer, Shute submitted a second memorial, which was upheld by the Privy Council, which in May, 1725, condemned the House. Again Mather foresaw a revocation of the charter and through that the destruction of religion in New England.

Partly to offset such a disaster if it came, Mather turned his attention to Harvard. "Religion is like to be preserved or betrayed in our churches," he wrote in his diary, "as the College is provided for." He solicited for days of prayer to be kept in the College Hall. But an opportunity not simply to recommend pious measures but to wield decisive power presented itself when on May 7, 1724, President John Leverett died. Mather believed that most people wanted him to be the new president of Harvard. He promised upon taking office to obtain a chair of mathematics for his protégé ISAAC GREENWOOD (1702-1745), who defended him vigorously during the inoculation controversy. He had written a letter introducing Greenwood to Dr. James Jurin in London and, while abroad, Greenwood befriended Thomas Hollis, who broached the idea of founding a professorship of science at Harvard. Greenwood's debts and fancy stockings a little rattled Hollis, but in 1727 Greenwood did become the first Hollis professor of mathematics, and probably the only man in America then making his living at science. A gifted and more learned scientist than Mather himself, Greenwood at the end justified Hollis's doubts about him and, taking to drink, was removed from his professorship.

On August 12, 1724, the Harvard Corporation squashed Mather's hopes for the presidency by choosing Joseph Sewall instead. Mather thought the choice foolish and decided he had been by-passed out of envy. Publicly he ignored his disappointment by insisting to Colman and to others that he had no desire to be president. Sewall, however, declined the post; in November the Corporation chose Colman; he also declined because his salary would be determined by the hostile House. Finally, in July, 1725, the presidency was given to Benjamin Wadsworth. By that time Mather, genuinely, no longer cared; his reputation, he felt, had sunk too low for him to be effective at the college, and his appointment could only create more dissension.

Mather was in no position to accept the presidency anyway, as he was barely able to recover from one personal catastrophe before another crashed upon him. On August 23, 1723, his venerable father, Increase Mather, died, stipulating in his will that he had no money to leave to his son Cotton, and adding a request that Cotton look after his grandson, Mather Byles, the later minister, poet, and wit. Mather sent his frail nephew to live with NATHAN PRINCE

(Thomas's brother; 1698–1748), a tutor at Harvard for twenty years who later converted to the Church of England, was dismissed for drinking, and eventually became deranged. Mather could not have looked after his nephew himself, for he was broke. He had to offer his goods to his creditors to satisfy his debts. These goods included the one worldly possession he cherished: "my very library, the darling of my little enjoyments." Immediately at stake was twenty pounds' interest owing on the Howell estate, which he could not pay. The larger stake was his reputation and, as always, the very cause of God's truth. "The design of Satan herein," he wrote, "is utterly to extinguish my services to the Kingdom of God." By early April in 1724 he had to pay his debts or go to jail. (Perhaps a measure of his anxiety is that in February—so his opponents charged—he advised Daniel Willard's creditors to arrest him, but the details of this, and the identities of the parties involved, are unclear.) On April 1 he told Thomas Prince that he must soon "take a step which much more than all New England will ring of." Because of his debts, the plotting of people who sought his ruin, and the aversion of his friends to help him out, he had decided, it seems, to resign his pulpit.

Luckily, as he informed William Dummer, a "little alteration" in his fortunes reprieved him. On the evening of April 2, four members of his congregation visited him, with assurances that they would help pay off his debts. In July his congregation raised an additional two hundred pounds. One irony made this tormenting case maddening. The three to four hundred pounds of his own money which, Mather estimated, the administration of the estate cost him, was money he paid off for debts "whereof I never," he reflected bitterly, "did myself owe a farthing," debts incurred by people he loathed and feared—the family of his wife Lydia. His letters for this period do not explain what he called in his diary her "horrid, froward, malicious" acts; but he believed that she existed for no other end than harming him and his son Samuel, and that she was insane. On August 13 her tantrums culminated in a show "that seemed little short of a proper satanical possession." She cursed her husband, said she would no longer live with him, and with her niece and maid went to live in a neighbor's house.

One week later, on August 20, 1724, Mather learned that the ship from Barbados on which Cressy was returning from another trip to England had sunk, and that Cressy was dead. "My head is waters," he cried, "and my eyes are a fountain of tears!" He could not have been much comforted by the return, three days later, of Lydia, who wanted as always to patch things up. Cressy's rakish antics and rebelliousness never wholly extinguished Mather's hopes for his redemption, admiring reliance on his business sense, or love for his mildness. Filled with grief, he put together some sermons on Cressy's life to be of use to other young people. In one of them, *The Words of Understanding*, he included a sort of confession supposedly left on his study table by Cressy before departing to England, recounting his secret prayers, meditations, and resolutions to steer clear of evil company. This confession, however, sounds much as if Mather had dictated the very formalized sentiments to Cressy himself, or as if Cressy wrote them down with his father's eyes upon him.

With astonishment, his grief still fresh, Mather learned on September 5 that Cressy was alive, that actually the ship had only lost its masts but had made its way to Newfoundland. With his insane wife, his lost presidency, his absent governor, with his chief works unpublished, his large debts upaid, his activities in the small-pox epidemic still reviled, with "all my sad things" Mather was informed two days later that this story concerned a different vessel. Cressy had actually drowned and was dead: "Lord," he wailed, *"Thou hast lifted me up, and cast me down!"*

His likeness to Christ became more clear to Mather than ever, even as he hinted darkly in his diary of suicide. His entry of March 15, 1724, although written before his trials had gathered to an agony, conveys better than any other his sense of his existence. In fourteen separate articles he listed his major efforts to Do Good, showed how each had come to nothing, and summed up their meaning:

> In all my sad things I discover a conformity unto my Saviour, who was a man of sorrows, and acquainted with griefs. And it is with an incomparable satisfaction that I see myself suffering with Him, having a strong persuasion of the blessed consequences.

None of all my sad things discourage me; but I retain the firmest resolutions, and grow stronger and stronger in them, to hold on after the most industrious manner, serving of God, and doing of Good. And I am willing that my crucifixion go on, and that I should see no deliverance, nor enjoy one comfortable hour in this world, and that at the harvest of what I am here sowing in tears, be put off unto the other side of death, and the grave.

Given this pattern, it was natural for Mather to associate what he sensed was his own approaching death with the end of the world. He began to feel that the Second Coming might be looked for any day. Prophecy always interested him in proportion to his sense of his own inadequacy. Now, as he looked to a vengeful Redeemer to justify his life by crushing his enemies, prophecy became his main intellectual concern.

Would Christ, he wondered, return literally, in person? On this point he sounded out WILLIAM BURNET (1688–1729), governor of New York and New Jersey and later governor of Massachusetts, and the son of Gilbert Burnet, bishop of Salisbury. He also wrote to Gurdon Saltonstall to encourage him to read Burnet's works, unaware that Saltonstall had just died.

To Nathan Prince

U/HSP   October 16, 1723

Sir,

There now flies to your tender wing an orphan, the heart of whose excellent grandfather was exceedingly set upon his welfare.

It has been somewhat beside my intention, and I doubt not much to the child's advantage, that he has been so much absent from the College. But if there be any leeward way to be fetched up, none knows better than you how it may be accomplished.

It is a great satisfaction to me that he is to be under your tuition. But I entreat you to be a father as well as a tutor to him. I know something of your goodness, and I am well assured you will be so.

You will not only oblige him to the well-spending of *all his time* with your kind inspection, but also consider the state of his health, for he is of a feeble constitution. [Close]

Your friend, brother, and servant,

To Thomas Hollis, Jr.

DII/AAS draft   November 5, 1723

Sir,

[Mentions having sent along some packets.] In one of them there are also the acknowledgments which your son Samuel (your first born) has made of your goodness to him, and a copy of his commemoratory oration at our commencement, which, I hope, has reached you.

What I am now to do is to render my brethren's thanks, with my own, for what you have done about our memorials, and acquiesce in what has been done by others.

The truth is, if all the remonstrances that we make about a charity so abominably prostituted as that of the *Society*, will only produce a care of our diocesan to send over better missionaries, we are best as we are. For the missionaries they have hitherto sent, have generally been such ignorant wretches, and such debauched and finished villains, that, like the rattlesnakes in our country, they carry with them what warns and arms our people against being poisoned with them.

In the meantime, I am sorry that a country in which you are daily multiplying your benefits affords to you such matter of trouble, in the mischiefs which your charitable and sympathizing mind sees us by our follies bringing on ourselves. Our Governor was a person of an excellent spirit, and I always thought he studied the welfare of the country more than any one person in it. Had we carried well to him, he would have made us an easy, and had we hearkened well to him we had been a happy, people. His enemies, who began to be so upon a rage which was raised in them from a disappointment of certain projections to enrich themselves, which they suffered from his arrival in the government instead of another whom they thought they had made their property, never were many; but being very subtle, as well as very spiteful, they got the knack of perverting and misleading a majority of poor and weak (tho' sometimes honest) countrymen in our House of Representatives; and so they produced *votes* which any Governor must count intolerable, and which are like to overwhelm our whole people, who generally abhor what is done, in ruins that will be irretrievable. *The evil that I feared is come!* How much a man who is no great seer did foresee these things, and forewarn our people of them some years ago, I am willing you should see by casting your eye on a sermon, for which fidelity I have since been an object for the utmost rage of the satanic party, and not only had their printed libels continually darted at me, but had attempts made upon my very life. Nevertheless, after all that I have performed and suffered on the behalf of our good Governor, I am told that he dismisses me from the list of his friends because of a mis-report that was made unto him of my being at a loss how to mention his voyage in our public prayers, immediately upon his very sudden withdraw from us. But alas, who can tell what is good for man? And if our Governor do obtain the destruction of our charter, how uneasy will he find himself in his return unto us? The wretched men that have provoked him will still be in our assemblies, and continue to do so. At the same time, all his friends (and none so much as they) will be rendered miserable, a good country anon put into the hands of rulers disaffected unto all the best interests of it, the religion of the country insulted, ruined, and by degrees extinguished.

But we grow ripe for confusions. A fearful decay of piety among us ripens us for them. One symptom and effect of which decay is a strange inclination to contention discovering itself upon all occasions among us. I'll mention to you an instance which you will wonder at!

A mighty spirit came lately upon abundance of our people to reform their singing, which was degenerated in our assemblies to an irregularity which made a jar in the ears of the more curious and skilful singers. Our ministers generally encouraged the people to accomplish themselves for a regular singing and a more beautiful psalmody. Such numbers of good people (and especially young people) became regular singers that they could carry it in the congregations. But, who would believe it? Tho' in the more polite city of Boston this design met with a general acceptance, in the country, where they have more of the *rustic*, some numbers of elder and angry people bore zealous testimonies against these wicked innovations, and this bringing in of popery. Their zeal transported some of them so far (on the behalf of *Mumpsimus*) that they would not only use the most opprobrious terms, and call the singing of these Christians a worshipping of the devil, but also they would run out of the meeting-house at the beginning of the exercise. The paroxysms have risen to that height as to necessitate the convening of several ecclesiastical councils for the composing of the differences and animosities arisen on this occasion. And if such an improbable occasion produce them, what is to be expected when our Great Adversary gets a permission to start more hazardous controversies? O! *Tell it not in Gath!*

The world is falling into that period whereof one character is *The nations were angry.* A spirit of *anger* is to possess the nations, and boil up and break out, on all, and even on very small, on the very least, occasions. In our country, people take all occasions, and seem even to seek occasions, for the ebullition of their anger against their brethren. I wish it were more otherwise in yours.

Having mentioned the period we are fallen into, I will only add, it is doubtless the period wherein what the Holy Spirit of God has foretold concerning the consuming of ten kingdoms is to be accomplished. [Close]   Your most obliged friend and servant,

To Governor Burnet

U/AAS draft   November 25, 1723

Sir,

The communicative goodness expressed in the large letters wherewith Your Excellency has lately favored me, call for my most grateful acknowledgments.

I am now more than ever convinced that when persons of a superior genius apply themselves to the study of the sacred prophecies, we shall be enriched with uncommon discoveries.

The remarks which Your Excellency has made on our Saviour's cup, and His apostles' [buffeter?], are sweeter to me than Hyblean honey.

It would be a mighty satisfaction to me to know the demonstrations which our perpetual dictator Sir Isaac Newton has upon the Vials, because I have imagined all to belong unto the Seventh Trumpet—like the seven circuitions on the seventh day for the fall of Jericho; and have been suspicious lest the parts of Europe which border on the sea have now the Second in its effusion begun upon it.

Whether the coming of our Saviour at the beginning of the Millennium can be any other than personal and literal, I have had a thousand hesitations. But that which as yet inclines me that way is, that *then* is the *time of the dead, that they shall be judged, and a reward given to the faithful;* and *a power over nations* is then to be given unto the *overcomers,* who must receive it upon a *resurrection from the dead.* [Encloses some treatises.]

Your Excellency's most obliged and most obedient servant,

To Governor Shute

U/AAS draft   December 7, 1723

Sir,

The hand which brings this, desiring that he may bring something, I take the opportunity to give you no more trouble but only that of being informed that I have lately and largely written to Your Excellency, as well as unto my Lord Barrington, all that appeared needful in answer to the letters which I have had the honor of receiving from you.

Your Excellency has from other hands a full account of all that is doing among us, and from such as are much more able to give it, than I can be. For I know very little of what is done, and indeed I do not so much as ask to know it; for here, he that increaseth knowledge increaseth sorrow; and we are ever doing the part of an intoxicated people.

Nevertheless, I cannot wish to Your Excellency the infelicity of ever being the instrument, or so much as the occasion, of bringing any hardships upon a people (be the faults of a small party among them what they will!) whose ancestors deserved and purchased all the liberties their charters have engaged unto them. [Close]

Your Excellency's most sincere and humble servant,

To "Mr. Pain"

U/AAS draft   [c. February, 1724]

Sir,

No man can be more desirous than I have been to have everything loving, and handsomely, and after a gentlemanly manner carried on in the affair of the 300£ on which Captain Oliver's bond has been lately sued.

It would be too long to trouble you with the story of my just and fair conduct about it, and perhaps little to the purpose.

I think I have had once and again assurances, that Mr. O. would immediately pay half the sum in money, if I would accept the other half in goods; and he would count himself easily dealt withal. I have done what he desired, tho' it was what I need not have done; and it has been to my considerable disadvantage.

And indeed, for the whole sum, I am little other than a steward.

The true owner calling for a third of it, and finding Mr. O. treat him indecently, the other two (whereof now, one is not) were willing he should act for them all. So the whole bond was transferred unto him.

I requested you to delay the execution till [you] had heard further from me, and for your delay I thank you.

But Mr. Willard sends word just now that Mr. Oliver would have him to take his course, and prays me to write unto you for a period of the request I made you.

I have therefore no further to ask but that you please to do what Mr. Willard may desire of you, who, I suppose, will desire nothing but what is proper towards one that abuses him, and equity. [Close]

Your hearty friend and servant,

To Thomas Hutchinson
U/AAS draft   March 3, 1724

Sir,

Yesterday, in a retrospection on some affairs of the year past, when I was going over in a way not improper for one of my profession the catalogue of my benefactors, over and above my daily consideration of them, I found the value of what I had actually recorded of your obliging presents for the support of my family, to be according unto my uncertain computation, so near to at least a score of pounds, that I thought a verbal and a transient acknowledgment of your (unequalled) goodness, would be too base ingratitude. All this added unto what other generous things you are continually doing in the application of your talents! But I do here under my hand confess my obligations, and entreat that if there be any other way than that which you know I take, to approve myself what I ought to be unto you and yours, you would please to make me understand it.

[Asks Hutchinson's advice on a forthcoming lecture.]

Your most obliged servant,

To Benjamin Colman
DII (as 1725)/AAS draft   March 6, 1724

Sir,

Nothing that I have met withal (and continue to meet withal) causes me to lay aside my zealous concern for the welfare of the College, which you have under your government.

I think it my duty therefore to inform you, that within these few hours, I am (from one whose time and heart is more with some folks than I wish it were) informed of great machinations and expectations to see the College demanded into the hands of a daughter of Babylon— and notable over-haulings—

On this occasion, let me not be thought an overbusy intermeddler in affairs which I have been sufficiently forbidden from any meddling with, if I humbly offer two things to your consideration.

The College is in a most precarious, uncertain, unsafe condition, for want of an incontestible charter. You know whose maxim it was, and whose it will be, that when the cow was dead, the calf died in the belly of it; and how often and how long our General Assemblies acted, as confessing of it.

Whether this be true and just or no, the men whom you know too well will as soon as they can proceed upon it. Several opportunities, and even invitations, to get a Royal Charter for the College, were in a wretched manner, and on wretched intentions, thrown away. We have now a King on the throne who is not so much in the interests of High Church, and will not be so fond of doing what King James himself (as my *Parentator* will tell you) confessed a most unreasonable thing, but that if the Dissenters at home will so far lay aside their *unbrotherliness* as to join their intercessions, we may hope to obtain a charter. What I wish for, is that Mr. Colman may be prevailed withal to step over the Atlantic, and employ the talents wherewith God has furnished him, to solicit and prosecute this matter, and that the College treasury may (with other assistances) be at the expense of a hook to catch a salmon! I entreat you think of it. And if there be any service that I can do in forwarding the design (tho' 'tis but very little that I can do in this or any other matter) I shall upon your direction do all that I am able.

[Urges days of supplication to be observed in the college.]

'Tis possible, the same indiscretion which attends all my other essays to do good may be discerned in this also. But it is addressed unto one who knows how to forgive, and candidly accept, his brother and servant,

To Lieutenant Governor William Dummer

DII/AAS draft   March 20, 1724

Sir,

Inasmuch as the good providence of God has placed Your Honor at the head of the Commission of the Affairs of the Gospel among our Indians, as well as the whole government of this extended province, I thought it my duty to venture upon one request more, on the behalf of dying religion among those miserable objects. And in so doing I hope to have so done my duty, that I may without offense ask leave to retire in this point also, as I have thought I have not wanted sufficient intimations that it may be judged proper for me to do, from all interest whatsoever in any other matters of public importance.

The work of gospellizing the aboriginal natives of this country is one of New England's peculiar glories. That it labors under grievous difficulties and discouragements is not at all to be wondered at, considering what lies at the bottom of all. But the greater they are, the stronger must be the application of the instruments to surmount them. The conduct of the commissioners has many eyes upon it; yea, Greater Eyes than those of the Governor and Company on the other side of the water.

To retrieve what is wanting, and produce numberless good effects, I would make a humble proposal to Your Honor and the Board: that the commissioners find out a man of discretion, and probity, and activity, and constitute him *A visitor of all the Indian villages.*

This *visitor* may with an exact scrutiny find out what may be found among the Indians that wants to be redressed and reformed, or better provided for. And he may by inquiry of the most prudent and best affected among the English, learn what would be most advisable to be done for the Indians. And he may return from his visitation furnished with proposals which the commissioners may without needless retardations under the notion of writing and waiting for further informations (which may confound the best proposals, and has often, it may be, done so) immediately find ways and means to put in execution.

The visitor may carry instructions from the commissioners, and a copy of all the articles which his inquiries are to proceed upon. The visitation also may be renewed and repeated as often as the commissioners may judge convenient. And if their servant be well-paid, the money may be well-spent.

The commissioners once employed such a visitor, and it was one of the most useful things that ever they did; and if his report had been acted upon, as it might have been, and not thrown by, it had been followed with many very happy consequences.

[Mentions the neglected condition of the Indians at Martha's Vineyard and Punkapoag.]

I would be thankful for what opportunities I have sometimes had of being patiently and favorably heard speaking at the honorable Board of the Commissioners; and would humbly move that since by mortality, or some enfeebling circumstance in the approaches of it, there is now left not so much as one minister among the commissioners, they would please to think on some nomination for a substitution to be commended to, and confirmed by the Governor and Company at home. And if a minister or two should come into the nomination, perhaps there might be some advantage in it, as well as decency; for the commissioners do not look upon the business of the Board as if it were merely or mainly to save money or manage a discreet and frugal merchandise, but principally and perpetually to invent and pursue the best methods of serving the interests of pure and undefiled religion among the Indians. [Close]

Your Honor's most affectionate and most obedient servant,

To Captain John Dean

DII/AAS draft   March 31, 1724

Sir,

[Says he prepared a sermon on Dean's salvation from shipwreck.]

My purpose was to have assembled a good number of pious gentlemen, at either Dr. Boylston's or my own capacious hall, and there to have spent an agreeable portion of time in proper devotions, especially giving thanks and making prayers on your behalf, accompanied with the sermon, which I proposed then to have printed with the story of your affair, as I did the like ten years ago.

As for the price of a sermon, I know none established in this country. Much less would I have looked for any pecuniary acknowledgment of mine, who have preached so many hundreds of sermons without any temporal requitals. Only if something had been advanced for the charge of the impression, I might have allowed of that.

But when our worthy and hearty friend Mr. Borland arrived unto us, he told us he thought my proposal did not in all points quite answer yours. He thought that you supposed the bells might be rung, and a promiscuous congregation come together on this occasion in one of our public churches, as it might be done in England. Upon this view, it was considered that such a practise being altogether unusual in our city, it might meet with some inconvenient misconstructions. And the religion of this country also not encouraging the anniversary celebration of any stated and certain days, anything that looked that way openly done might be misinterpreted. So we agreed the dropping of the matter at this time, and not proceeding until we receive your further directions after the true state of the case, as it is now represented, has been considered with you. [Close] Your hearty friend and servant,

To Thomas Prince

DII/MHS   April 1, 1724

Sir,

'Tis, I confess, a weakness in me to communicate unto you the enclosed papers; for, to be free with you, the ministers of this town appear to me the most *unbrotherly and unsociable tribe* of their profession that I believe is in the whole world.

But I do it because I have some apprehension that I must within a few days, or weeks, take a step which much more than all New England will ring of—and I am willing to distinguish *you* from the rest, with giving you some satisfaction aforehand about the circumstances leading to it.

[Asks for his prayers.]

I will send Ezer in the evening for the return of these papers, and of Gog and Magog. (Only that about *The State of Religion*, which you may keep a few days, and which you *may*, tho' I believe you *will not*, show to Judge Sewall and Col. Fitch. But if you do, yet leave it not in their hands.)

I wish you and yours all the blessings of goodness, and a condition very much the reverse of what is ordered for, Sir,

Your brother and servant,

To Lieutenant Governor William Dummer
DII/AAS draft   April 4, 1724

Sir,

My disobedience to the command which your goodness laid upon me the last Thursday, requires a just apology; and yet it will require the mention of such unmentionable things, that even that may render another apology necessary.

An indisposition then upon me unfitted me for the payment of my duty. But concomitant with it, I labored under several discouragements.

I need not say, that I apprehended my well-known circumstances of prosecution to *restore what I took* not away, rendered it a disgrace unto such a table, as well as unto any pulpit, for me to make my appearance there. These perhaps are since a little altered.

But I must confess also, that I have thought myself directed by the government (for the serving whereof I have exposed myself to sufferings much beyond any man in the country) to look upon it as a piece of proper modesty, to be as little as possible in their presence, ever since they did above a year ago, with sufficient expressions of displeasure, silence my pen, and forbid the printing of any more about *The State of Religion*. I was, according to the best of my capacity, with a better, endeavoring to do a comprehensive service for the country and religion; and surely, if I had not been reckoned a person worthy of the greatest contempt, I had been by some one or other of the Council spoken with before the country (who much expected the continuation of their satisfaction) had been made sensible that the government was offended at me, as publisher of dangerous libels. Being thus treated as an offender, I have, I hope, with all decent patience commanded a silence to my speech equal to that which my superiors commanded for my pen; but I have with a modest recess, for now a twelvemonth, retired from the old familiarities of the table, as well as other freedoms which I had been once used unto, it appearing to me always rude for an offender to do otherwise.

[Says that his suspicion of the government's aversion for him was recently strengthened by the offense taken at some remarks he made against a "vile party" in the Church of England, although such remarks appear openly in the public *News-Letter*.]

To be disheartened into a peaceable withdraw, as far as may be, from all public exhibitions when I see myself under such (I would not presume to say undeserved) marks of dislike from those to whom I ought always to pay all due deference, may be smiled at as *vapor*; yet this *vapor* will appear to be *reason* unto one under the power of it, having at the same time a thousand other more heavy loads upon him.

There is yet another thing wherein I should reconcile myself unto Your Honor before I can have the courage to do as I have used heretofore to do.

A man for whom *honor is not seemly* has been so gentlemanly as to show here and there a letter with which your invaluable brother had obliged me. Now, tho' I would much sooner have died than have been guilty of so vile an action as to betray a friend, and expose to his enemies what he writes unto me, yet this disaster befalling me, has entirely and eternally shut me out of his friendship, and Your Honor may well judge, you have cause to shut me out of your favor also. Now, I can give no account of the disaster but this. The villains, I mean especially *three*, have certainly employed one of their brethren to do an abominable thing. One of their tools riffled Mr. Penhallow's closet, and conveyed unto them from thence a letter of mine to him, which gave to four their true character. But so meanly was I then deserted, by those who owed me more protection, that I was drawn into the iniquity of asking their pardon. And I must now say, my study has been knavishly and c-kishly [cockishly, boldly] riffled. But about the same time that this letter of him that was once my friend was in this rascally manner seized upon, I had six pounds of money also stolen, which was enough to bear the expense of several tankards. If they would please to tell how they got the letter into their hands, 'tis possible I might guess how my bills of credit were disposed of. This is my case. And tho' the person more immediately injured accepts not my vindication, yet it may be his honorable brother may upon a calm view think me rather unhappy than culpable, and use a lenity in the censures to which I am obnoxious.

I have now declared some of my discouragements, under which yet I hope neither Your Honor nor the Board will ever find me any other than an easy, honest, well-meaning man, one who will not, cannot, strive; one who will forever study to be quiet, and lead a peaceable life under your equal government, and one who at the worst will study to make no other than a humble, and a decent use of all the frowns he meets withal. [Sends along *Parentator*.]

Your Honor's most obedient servant,

To Isaac Watts

U/AAS draft   April 20, 1724

Sir,

Among my poor acknowledgments of your favors, I now present you with a *Parentator* wherein I have taken the leave to make a little mention of you.

I do not suppose that *it*, or anything of *mine*, will find any very kind reception on your side of the water. But I must also say that tho' I must always think very meanly of anything performed by so mean a hand as mine, yet I see that in its exaltation among your people, which forbids my thinking at all the worse of it, for the perverse humors of the critics, who when they can cavil at nothing else, bestow their censures on a *diction*, forsooth, about the rules whereof they are no more agreed among themselves than the builders of Babel.

[Expresses his happiness at Watts's continued longevity.]

We have been much concerned at the (what his best friends judge to have been too impatient and unadvised) step of our good Governor, in suddenly and secretly leaving of us, and presenting a memorial which threatens [to stop?] our (too wantonly abused) liberties. But we are praying and waiting and hoping for a good issue of what has a dark aspect upon us.

The raging attempts of your High Church to hurt our churches, meet with such a clog and blast from Heaven upon them, as will anon be a wonderful story.

But I will no longer detain my father from talking with you. [Close]

Your brother and servant,

To Thomas Hollis

U/AAS draft   April 21, 1724

Sir,

[Sends along *Parentator*, which he expects will be poorly received in England.]

That poor orphan Mather Byles will be an object for your lenity and compassion, if his absence from the College be a matter of complaint about him, when I have informed you that the true reason of his being so little there for more than the last half year, has been constant sickness upon him, with great hazards and symptoms of a consumption, which make us very apprehensive that his death may defeat the hopes and aims we had in proposing his academical education. But in this, the providence of the Holy One must be submitted to, and you will not think your charity towards the son of a poor widow descended from your ancient friend, and intended for the best of services, is thrown away. [Close]

Your most obliged friend and servant,

To Thomas Bradbury

DII/AAS draft   April 22, 1724

Sir,

[Mentions sending along his *Parentator*.]

I have no expectation that anything performed by my mean hand should find any great reception on your side of the water, especially since the prodigious depravation of gust among you, which renders everything unpalatable but what shall have qualities which I will never be reconciled unto. [Tells him to note especially page 241.]

It is an insupportable grief unto us, that so many of our brethren should so openly declare that they look not on the faith of our Saviour's Eternal Godhead as essential to Christianity and salvation, and that they can receive to the regards of brethren in Christ those idolaters who acknowledge no Christ but one that is infinitely inferior and posterior to the Eternal Father. We behold it, and are grieved, that your pretended *Irenicums* do purposely and perpetually leave out the faith of our Lord's Eternal Deity, when they pretend unto an enumeration of our fundamental articles. Tho' they themselves are not gone over to the Arian infidelity, yet by these perfidious pretensions and overtures for peace, they take a fearful step toward the sacrificing of the most Glorious Truth, and the delivering up of the Holy City into the hands of infidels. We are afraid, we are afraid, lest our brethren hereby procure to themselves a sad share in the consuming blows which I cannot but again and again tell you are hastening on a sinful nation, a people laden with iniquity.

[Mentions that in a few parts of the country "little parcels of ignorant, vicious, contemptible people" are declaring for the Church of England.]

Very lately, a little crew at a town ten miles from the city of Boston, were so set upon their old *howling* in the public psalmody, that being rebuked for the disturbance they made by the more numerous regular singers, they declared they would be for the Church of England and would form a little assembly for that purpose, and subscribed for the building of a chapel, and expect a missionary to be sent and supported from your society (aforesaid) for the encouragement of half a score such ridiculous proselytes. But we suppose it will come to nothing.

Our late apostates make no hand on't. And Cutler, for whom they have built a new church in Boston, has by his high flights rendered himself so odious unto the body of our people, and rendered the more temperate and moderate part of his own congregation so disaffected unto him, that he has no very encouraging auditory, and his arrival here is as much a disservice to the Church of England as almost anything that could have happened. The vile High-flying Leslaean pamphlets they disperse among us, meet with such victorious answers as tend greatly to the establishment of our churches.

[Complains that Thomas Reinolds, embroiled in a pamphlet controversy, neglects him.]

To Isaac Greenwood

DII/AAS draft   July 16, 1724

My dear Child,

It is as cool waters unto a thirsty soul, that I hear what I do of you and from you. But it is above all a singular satisfaction unto me to understand that in the midst of the pleasant studies which do at an uncommon rate accomplish you, you still retain your disposition to serve your glorious end, in the work of the evangelical ministry. It is most certain that notwithstanding the many discouragements and humiliations which that work may be attended withal, 'tis the best that a short life can be devoted to; and the consequences of it being well followed will be of all the most comfortable in the Day that is daily to be looked for. I hope you will be a grateful spectacle to Heaven in it, and that the field of your actions will be your own country, which, tho' it be not in all points what you would have it, yet all things considered, the only better country to be desired is the heavenly. The sooner you return to us, the better; for that which is more precious than money, spends apace; and we long to be reaping the fruits of your excellent and exemplary industry.

Whatever lies within my reach to promote your acceptance and usefulness among us, you may depend upon. And if something should happen that some foretell, and many desire, but I don't care to mention, you may be sure I shall consider you as my son, and appear with more zeal to get your proposals answered, than if you were by nature so. But, child, you know 'tis early days in our little country, and merit is very little regarded here; and the most useful erudition is not what we are fondest of. Tho' the College has a revenue to encourage the profession of the mathematical sciences, yet I durst not promise that a sufficient number of scholars will show themselves, whose payment of a proper premium, joined unto that, will be a suitable subsistence for a professor of that, and of experimental philosophy, or not be content with what their ordinary tutors may do for them. So that if you cannot return to us with a mind equilibrious on that point, I am so much under the power of the *hypo* as to say, Then let the scale turn for a dismission of that expectation and of the great expense that must accompany it. But, return, return, O Novanglian, return, return.

[Asks his help in having *Boanerges* published in England.]

Your cordial and constant friend,

[PROBABLY TO GOVERNOR SALTONSTALL]
DII/AAS draft   [c. August, 1724]

I look upon Colonel Burnet's late *Essay on the Scripture Prophecies* as the most penetrating, judicious, decisive essay that has ever yet been made upon that noble subject. He does not expatiate into copious and verbose amplifications, but in a concise way, wherein every word has its weight, he gives those explications which carry demonstrations with them. He has instructed us and obliged us with some illustrations which we never enjoyed before; but such as have in them an evidence which compels us to give a good reception to them. What that excellent person who led him to these happy studies (our late President, Sir Isaac Newton) has been to the world in philosophy, this must his honorable scholar now be in prophecy, and be acknowledged as a dictator above all contradiction. There is indeed no little proof of our being arrived unto the *Time of the End* (and that he has calculated right) in our having Daniel so admirably opened unto us.

I know you will study (in modest, humble, prudent ways) to do good wherever you come. Let one of your essays in your journey be to commend this late performance unto the serious perusal of the gentlemen where you come, and let my character of it be known, and how much it may be wished, that by studies of the prophecies wisely managed (which have been so foolishly neglected, and so profanely derided) we may be rescued from a share in the epidemical sleep wherein the world is to be surprised by the terrible Day of the Lord. The 1260 years being certainly up, there are most certainly those terrible things to be every day expected, which I doubt we are but poorly prepared for.

I am sure, if the 1260 years be up, High Church must go down. Accordingly, I have two things to inform you of, and you may particularly exhibit unto my honored brethren, the Trustees of Yale College, the information which I now give you. That miserable apostate Cutler, experimentally finds the frowns of our glorious Lord upon his apostasy. First, a lady of High Church whom you know, the last week declared unto me, that she had been at Cutler's church, and it was amazing to see how few were there, and what a sort of shabby people they were, and what a shame it was that such a man should be under such contempt among us. Others of the auditory did this day sennight, speak to the same effect unto my worthy colleague. Secondly, this day sennight I read in letters from London, that our Cutler's High principles were strangely going down the wind in the Church of England and growing out of fashion.

Unaddressed

U/AAS draft   August 1, 1724

My honored Brethren,

Is it not pity that any occasion of discord should arise in the General Assembly, where some think every little occasion is too easily laid hold on?

It was the whole General Assembly which directed that a person recommended by four (named) ministers should be offered unto the station and reward of chaplain at the garrison above Northfield.

I am told that the Lieutenant Governor and Council has accepted another recommendation.

Was not this done, since we were in actual prosecution of another, and had it in immediate view.

If it were since yesterday was sennight, it was after I had actually told several of the Council that we had engaged another.

And this person, for ought I know, is better qualified (at least in point of standing) than the other.

We have also much abused him, in putting him to travel to and fro as we have done.

I am not concerned for the slight put upon the ministers, being (more than) a little used unto such things.

But there is a slight put on the House of Representatives, who will infallibly resent it, and it may be never advance a penny of the proposed encouragement when they know that their direction has been superseded. [Close]   Your brother and servant,

To Governor Saltonstall

DII/AAS draft   August 31, 1724

Sir,

[Repeats his anecdote of the crow, as in the July 31, 1719 letter to John Leverett.]

A young man who counts it well worth his travel and expense to visit New London only to come under notice with Your Honor, is also ambitious of riding in your guards to the commencement at New Haven. His having spent so much time not altogether unprofitably in the studies which he has followed so close as to deserve a play-day, causes me to countenance his proposal; but much more, the benefit of waiting on Your Honor, which it will be impossible for him to do without some improvement. It is proper for me to give Your Honor some account of him, tho' how to do it without incurring the censure of *the crow thinks so*, is not very easy. He has been unawares drawn two or three times into public performances; but tho' he has met with uncommon acceptance, yet he resolves to stop, and not by any means appear frequently in public till more months of qualifying study have passed over him. All I shall add is that I am told he is esteemed for an early piety, for a manly discretion, for some erudition, and none of the worst tempers; or, at least, the *crow thinks so*. He wishes that he had been of a year or two longer standing; and then he would have humbly supplicated for leave to have stood as a candidate and competent for a degree, in a College which his father has been sometimes a small actor for, and where the memory of his ancestors would bespeak some easy terms for his admission to so much honor, tho' his learning should not be equal to that of many others. But it must be enough unto him to be admitted as a spectator, among them who wish well to Yale College and would lay hold on all opportunities to put all possible respects upon it. So I leave Ascanius under Your Honor's favorable patronage.

[Foresees the collapse of the Roman church.]

Your Honor's most obedient servant,

To Nathaniel Cotton

U/AAS draft   September 3, 1724

Sir,

There was communicated a letter from you desiring the sense of our brethren upon the case of such as have withdrawn from the covenant and communion of the church with you, to that society among you which say they are the Church of England.

I have taken the liberty to say upon it, that the church-state should so represent the Kingdom of Heaven to the world as to pass a sentence of excommunication only for such offenses as, according to the Word of God, are to be thought what will exclude from the Heavenly Kingdom if impenitently persisted in.

We cannot say that a conscientious transition (whereof indeed there appears little reason or color for a pretense at Bristol) from us to the Church of England is to be reckoned among such offenses.

Nevertheless, the conduct of your withdrawers appears to have at least so much of a fault as to render it proper for you, and your church therein concurring with you, to make them sensible that you do not approve of their disorderly walking.

And if this admonition, after due waiting for the good effect of it, make no impression upon them, none can justly complain of you if you proceed according to that article in the *Heads of Agreement* among the united ministers in London: *It may sometimes come to pass, that a church-member, not otherwise scandalous, may sinfully withdraw and divide himself from the communion of the church to which he belongeth. In which case, when all due means for the reducing him prove ineffectual, he having thereby cut himself off from that church's communion, the church may justly esteem and declare itself discharged of any other inspection over him.*

Indeed, such separatists do *sin condemned of themselves,* and there is no other censure passed upon them than what they do in the nature and language of their own sin pass upon themselves. They have already been aforehand with the church, and have *cut themselves off from the communion* of it, and *esteem and declare themselves discharged from its inspection.* [The Boston ministers agree in this.]

Your brother and servant,

To "H. [enry?] DEERING"

U/AAS draft   September 9, 1724

Sir,

A favor as unexpected as undeserved, which I lately received from you, commands me to the best expressions I can (which at best are very poor ones) of my gratitude.

It has been my infelicity to be hard censured for many things which have been well-intended, and be drawn into sentiments different from those of some that I have yet retained a due value for.

But, without any retrospection upon any occurrences in some days of temptation that have passed (and, I hope, are passed) over us, and crooked things which cannot be made straight, but must be thrown into the proper grave of oblivion, I certainly know myself to be *an honest man.*

And whoever goes to hurt my country must lose my friendship; nor shall I think any man culpably changeable who upon the view of a change in any of his friends, to the prejudice of a good and great interest which must be invariably adhered unto, does change the regards he has once had unto them.

Your sympathy with my exercises calls for my sensible acknowledgments.

To be a man of sorrows and acquainted with griefs, has been the thing appointed for me. But I have an abundant compensation and consolation in the fruits which have been produced by them, not only to myself, but also to the people of God.

I have long had my spirit sweetly reconciled unto them, and particularly unto that remarkable article of them, to be despised and rejected of men. So that I always wonder at it, if I meet with but common civilities. But much more if I am treated with anything like what you have lately shown unto me.

[Thanks him for contributing to the publication of one of his recent works, which he sends along.]

Your obliged friend and servant,

To Dr. James Jurin

U/RS (not in Mather's hand, but   September 22, 1724
signed by him; draft at MHS)
(An unusual vomit)

Sir,

Since my letter is not like to be read until after you have risen from the table, and perhaps have your stomach well-settled with the liquids of the afternoon, I will venture to make strange vomits the matter of your entertainment.

The strange vomits of nails, and pins, and coals, and balls of hair, and other such unaccountable stuff, which have been seen in poor energumens, we will say nothing of, because they seem not any otherwise than from the operations of prestigious demons to be accounted for. What our philosophy may presume to inquire after is all that my pen ventures now to meddle with.

And here I was going to tack the names of my authors to the relations of strange vomits which I was thinking with all possible brevity to bring as an introduction to the story which I am now to add unto them. I was going to remind you that Forestus mentions one who vomited a caterpillar, another who vomited a beetle; Schonfelder, one who vomited those which we call cankerworms; Borellus, one who vomited spiders. To bring vomited animals from another element, I was going to remind you how Cornelius Gemma mentions one who vomited an eel; Segerus, one who vomited a gudgeon; Rhodius, one who vomited a crab. I was going with a *Paulo majora canamus*, and besides those who have affirmed cats and weasels to have been vomited, to have reminded you of the two puppies vomited by the tailor of Hanover mentioned by Paulinius in his *Cynographia*. But fearing lest my quotations be already *ad nauseam*, surfeiting, I laid aside all thoughts of quoting my authors, for the strange vomits of serpents, and leeches, and toads, and frogs, and finally several sorts of lizards, and only observe that I find them generally agree in suspicions that the vomiters had either drunk unawares the sperm of these animals, or swallowed them with their drink when they were very little ones, or that the animals grown larger had stolen down the open throats of the patients while they were asleep.

[Quotes a letter from a physician at Newbury about a man who vomited a lizard.]

Having thus contributed a little evet [a small lizard] unto the stores in your more curious collections, I take leave only to add that the blessings of a good and sound stomach, that shall have nothing in it but what shall agree with it, and answer its offices, tho' they are truly great blessings, yet they are among the least that are wished you by, Sir,

Your most hearty servant,

To Dr. John Woodward

U/RS (not in Mather's hand, but   September 28, 1724
signed by him; draft at MHS)

(A Rare Discharge of Bullets)

Sir,

[Will relate a matter of fact.]

It is astonishing to behold the provision made in the body of man to stave off the evils which may threaten it. Among the instances of this provision we may reckon the successful methods and efforts of nature in uncommon and very surprising ways to bring all to rights and expel and eject an enemy when something is got where it should not be within us. Hippocrates in his book *Of Aliments* is not the only gentleman who has admired the sagacity of nature in the finding out unknown passages (more improbable than the northwest one your navigators talk of) to discharge things that are offensive to the body. 'Tis an article well worthy to have the pen of *The Christian Philosopher* insist upon it; and they who see nothing admirable in it may be worthy to have the Hippocratical fetters assigned unto them.

[Cites various authorities.]

The wife of Joseph Meader, belonging to our Dover, had long been afflicted with that miserable distemper which they call *the twisting of the guts*. Her physician advised her to swallow a couple of leaden bullets, upon which, after some time, her pain was abated, and the use of her limbs returned unto her. A year after this, one day walking in a room, she observed a bullet fall from her on the floor. It gave her an extreme surprise, for she had no symptom or suspicion of any such matter, nor did any pain ensue, any more than there did precede it. But she perceived an orifice a little below her navel, from whence it issued, which yet presently closed and healed without any further trouble. A little while after, the other bullet also dropped out, much as the former did. But that was at an orifice a little above the navel, and it was attended with more uneasy circumstances both before and after its coming away. Yet these also were quickly over, and all is well. I am informed the woman has had something of a hernious malady, by which 'tis thought the discharge might be somewhat facilitated. [Other anecdotes of swallowed bullets.]

I wish my friend may be always out of the way of all bullets that may hurt him. The brace of them which this letter is charged will do him no hurt. They only come with the *report* of my being, Sir,

Your servant, always full of the best wishes for you,

To Dr. James Jurin

U/RS (not in Mather's hand but   September 29, 1724
signed and captioned by him)
(Nature at work with a Needle And some reports of the
Emplastrum Magneticum)

Sir,

Perhaps it may appear a little preposterous, but I will now first entertain you with what shall be no other than a long thread, only to draw on a needle.

Many years ago it was one of my simple speculations that suppose all the morbific matter of our maladies (whereof we find so many relieved by steel-medicines,) were a mass of steel particles, then a magnet applied unto proper emunctories of the body might give a wonderful relief, and wondrously fetch them off. While I was in the midst of my silly speculations, I stumbled on Angelus Sala, and that chapter in him which describes the *Emplastrum Magneticum Arsenicale*, and reports the astonishing effects of it in the pestilence. I took occasion to inform a certain practitioner how to prepare this magnetic plaster, and advise him how and where and when to apply it. The venturesome spark paid little regard unto my cautions, but used it almost at hap-hazard, and made a polychreston of it, and got more than a little money by it. I do not remember all the cures he wrought by it; but this I do well remember, that he cured obstinate heart-burns, and pains in the stomach, by laying it upon the stomach. And one of his ventures I may not forget. He protested vehemently unto me that he not only found it forever harmless, but also in very malignant fevers, when the patients have been in their last agonies, he has clapped the magnetic plaster on their breasts, and within a few hours the plaster would attract all the malignity of the distemper, and fall off with an intolerable stench, and the patients have to admiration recovered.

A more cautious physician than he, having at my desire furnished himself with this remedy to be used upon occasion, was called unto a gentlewoman, who had been long tortured and languishing under the miseries of an arm sorely inflamed and greatly tumified. Many means had by many hands been used in vain; but my physician being entirely at a loss what else to do, clapped on the magnetic plaster. And when he came a few hours after to take off the plaster, behold, it fetched out a small needle with it, and the gentlewoman, would could give no account how the needle came into her arm, yet now being thus delivered from it, her pain was all over, and all came to rights immediately. [Other curiosities about needles.]

One always glad and proud of serving you,

To Dr. John Woodward and Dr. James Jurin
U/RS (not in Mather's hand, but   October 1, 1724
signed by him; draft at MHS)
(Climatical Influences)

Sirs,

It shall not be for your instruction (I am not so impertinent as to imagine myself capable of doing anything for that) but for the use of it which I shall make in the conclusion, that I shall presume to remind you of the strange influence that climates appear to have on the humors and manners and actions of the people that inhabit them. What should be the meaning of it, I beseech you, that tho' the nations of some climates have undergone such revolutions, yea, quite another people have come in the room of the old inhabitants, yet the people remarkably retain the same qualities by which their predecessors were distinguished some hundreds above a thousand years ago?

Everybody knows what it was, *Graecari*, a great while ago, and that the ancient Greeks began with small cups at their merry meetings (in which they would be *as merry as Greeks*) and then call for large ones when they were half seas over. But the modern travellers tell us that their posterity are noted for keeping up their old fashion to this very day.

[Cites similar examples for the Germans and Gauls.]

Nearer home! You need not be told who made that remark upon

the Britons more than sixteen centuries ago, *Dum singuli pugnant, universi vincuntur.* Now what is become of the Britons? And how many nations have their blood running in the veins of a True Born Englishman? But then how remarkably have the English lost everywhere and undone themselves by intestine divisions? There cannot be a juster or a more lasting brand upon us than this, *Dum singuli pugnant*—They are a divided people. Their intestine quarrels and factions exceed what is ordinarily to be found in other nations.

I know not whether the observation be too superficial for you to think it worthy of your bestowing any speculation upon it, or whether the incomparable Sir Richard Blackmore will count his noble poem on *The Nature of Man* confirmed in it. But it will serve to introduce what I have observed in the country from whence you are now written to.

One very observable quality of our Indians has always been this, that they have no family government among them; all family discipline is a stranger to them. Their children are the most humored, cockered, indulged things in the world. One that has given us a narrative of what he found among them relates that in one of their wigwams, beholding a boy behave himself refractorily towards his father, he showed the man the way to employ a switch upon him, and the man was almost scared out of his wits to see what an operation the switch had upon the boy, and unto what good order the little tool in such a hand soon reduced him.

Now 'tis as observable that tho' the first English planters of this country had usually a government and a discipline in their families that had a sufficient severity in it, yet, as if the climate had taught us to Indianize, the relaxation of it is now such that it seems almost wholly laid aside, and a foolish indulgence to children is become an epidemical miscarriage of the country, and like to be attended with many evil consequences.

Another very observable quality of our Indians is this, that they are intolerably lazy; they hate work. To keep them at work would be a more grievous punishment unto them than to scourge them; death would be more eligible to them than slavery.

Now I will not complain of my country as if they were not generally a sober, honest, industrious people; yet I must say I wish we did in this matter less answer our climate and Indianize.

I am sure more industry would not be any harm unto us, yea, more industry would make this quickly become one of the finest regions in the world. It is noted that a laborious English husbandman, coming over hither and laboring as they do in England, presently grows rich and outstrips the natives.

But for the proof of the article I am now upon, I will rather excuse the rest of my countrymen and exhibit myself unto you as an object for your censures. For if I had not been inexcusably lazy, my letters this year to you would not have come short of the number which in some former years they have arisen to. My friends indeed flatter me as a man of numerous and ponderous employments, and some too wonder at my being able to apply myself unto so many correspondences and other intentions. But you will do me more justice if you censure me as a tame Indian, tainted with the vice of the climate, and rebuke me for my idleness. However, the question will be, whether such climatical distempers be not incurable? And so you will be favorable to one who tho' he do little for your entertainment, yet is glad and proud that he can do something, and hopes to do more, if you please to animate him with such a kind reception of what he does, as he has formerly met withal. He is, at least, Sirs,

Your sincere and well meaning servant,

To Mrs. Gurdon Saltonstall

DII/AAS draft   October 2, 1724

Madam,

All these regions unite their tears with yours. The brightest man that shone in these regions has left us. We mourn with you; and we mourn for you. Our sorrows have a tincture of sympathy with yours, upon whom (as well as upon us) the breach is like one of the sea, which cannot be healed. Nothing but a glorious CHRIST can make up your loss; 'tis your happiness that you have long been acquainted with Him, long been espoused unto that glorious Lord.

[Sends along a funeral sermon on her husband.] The hearers all said there was not a word too much; you and I shall both of us think 'tis all much too little. But the time would allow no more, and I endeavored much in a little. I am not so vain as to think that it is worthy of the press, or that one so mean as I am can add any luster to so good and so great a man. It will be honor enough to it, that it be lodged in your scrutoir. But, if it be your pleasure that it should go abroad, instead of what may come to you from a better and a neater hand, your neighbor Green is used unto my copies. But I should earnestly desire my very valuable brother Mr. Adams to preface it with an agreeable dedication to the Lady whose merits ought to be acknowledged in conjunction with those of the deceased. [Close]

Your disconsolate and almost inconsolable kinsman and servant,
The very great civilities which my son has received from you, Madam, as well as from the dear Governor, will never be forgotten with us.

To Dr. James Jurin

U/RS (draft at AAS)   October 5, 1724

Sir,

You have so encouraged me by the kind reception which my former communications have had with you, and by your means with my illustrious masters, that I cannot but in my poor way continue them. I wish that they had been more valuable for curiosity or erudition. But they are what I have. And you will have the goodness to consider me as a man exceeding full of employments, able but now and then after a mean manner to express my zeal for your noble design. 'Tis indeed nothing but that well-meaning zeal that can bespeak for me the room you are pleased to allow me in a Society which I esteem as one of the most illustrious in the world.

Tho' my studies and labors mostly run in a theological channel, and among the effects thereof I have lying by me some very considerable preparations for the public (and much more valuable ones than any of those many more than three hundred which have been on various arguments and in various languages drawn into the public from the mean hand that has prepared these), yet now and then I know not how to deny myself the satisfaction of some visits to philosophy. And these have enabled me to get ready for the press a work of above twenty sheets, whereof this is the title page: [Quotes the title page of *The Angel of Bethesda*.]

I may shortly attempt the publication of this treatise in this country; and I hope I shall have your good wishes to it. I mention this that so you may see I am at work for you, tho' I don't remit my *Curiosa Americana* so fast as I could wish to do. And yet, pray tell me: Have you many correspondents whose remittances are more than your poor American's?

[Hopes to see his letter on the smallpox inoculation published.]

As soon as I can find any capable undertakers, I will prosecute your *invitatio* with all possible vivacity. But it is not easy for you to imagine how destitute we are, partly of well-framed instruments, but very much more of agreeable minds and hands to use them. [Close]

Sir, Your feeble and yet hearty friend and servant,

To Benjamin Colman

Proceedings XLIV/MHS   November 6, 1724

Sir,

Your Saurin, on whom I could not until very lately fall to pillaging, returns with my hearty thanks for the loan.

When I fell upon the pillage I found a very considerable part of his most valuable treasures already lodged in our *Biblia Americana*.

Some he has afforded me.

But you shall allow me the vanity to declare that if you do not find entered on the one book of Genesis alone, in that amassment, more than ten times the rich entertainments there are in Saurin on the whole pentateuch, I will, yea, I will venture to declare (suffer such a fool!) the Church of God has never yet seen such an amassment of the finer illustrations on the sacred oracles. Thus has a sovereign and gracious God favored the meanest of men.

To be pouring in upon the scholars at your College those treasures (not once a month, or a week, but) with a profusion of more than six hundred exercises in a year, would be a thing so worthy of your president, that if I should live to see the man, I should with pleasure offer him the stock to subsist upon.

Especially, if it should be the person whom I wrote a letter to Judge Davenport once to get the post assigned unto, and who needs them the least of any among us.

However qualified you might think me, on the account of these treasures (for I know you can't on any other account) for to be the man, I do with the greatest acquiescence and gratitude approve the declaration of your sentiments to all the country, that I am on other accounts utterly disqualified. Yea, for erudition too, as well as capacity and activity for management (tho' whether for the third qualification, which with the two former, you conscientiously go by, that is, fidelity to the interests of religion and the churches, I should own myself inferior to any, I cannot say so well) you have already met with one superior to me, and may easily light on many more.

And tho' I am aware of the talk about the country on this occasion sufficiently to my disadvantage (whereof I should be more stupid than even they who have the most diminutive thoughts of me can imagine me, if I were not sensible!) yet I do with all possible sincerity thank you for the inexpressible ease you have given to, Sir, Your obliged brother and servant,

To Dr. James Jurin

U/RS   December 15, 1724

Sir,

Having lately addressed you with even some number of letters, I have just now nothing to add but that I have an agreeable occasion of introducing to your knowledge and kindness a friend that has been to me as the golden wedge of Ophir.

'Tis Mr. Zabdiel Boylston, the sight of whom will doubtless be the more welcome to you because his name has already reached you.

He is a gentleman whose performances as a chirurgeon (and very particularly in lithotomy) have hitherto been equalled by no person in these parts of the world. And as a physician he has been to an uncommon degree successful, and so beloved and esteemed that his absence for a few months from us, on his present voyage, is a matter of uneasy apprehension to a multitude.

But that which will more particularly recommend him to your notice is that *this* is the gentleman who first brought the way of saving lives by the inoculation of the smallpox into the American world. When the rest of our doctors did rather the part of butchers or tools for the destroyer to our perishing people, and with envious and horrid insinuations infuriated the world against him, this worthy man had the courage and conscience to enter upon the practise; and (generously beginning with his own family) he alone, with the blessing of Heaven, saved the lives of I think several hundreds; yea, at one time he saved a whole town from a fearful desolation, after the smallpox had begun to do the execution of a great plague upon it. With an admirable patience he slighted the allatrations of a self-destroying people, and the satisfaction of having done good unto mankind made him a noble compensation for all the trouble he met withal.

You having done so much to oblige the public in your candid essays to procure a just reputation for a practise, which if mankind were not obstinately bent upon self-destruction, would soon save the lives of millions, it cannot be unacceptable unto you to have an opportunity for inquiring of this gentleman what has occurred in his own experiments, and particularly, how far he can justify the account I have given you of those few who died after the inoculation.

Yea, perhaps the Prince and Princess themselves, if informed of such

402

a one coming to London, may not be unwilling to take some cognizance of a person so distinguished by an operation of so much consequence. [Close]   Your most hearty servant,

II

THE record for the last three years of Cotton Mather's life is very fragmentary. The major source is his diary, which shows that in 1725 his health seriously declined: in January he felt very feeble, in February suffered coughs and a fever, in November coughs, fever, and asthma. To his horror, his surviving son Samuel now decided to go to England. He feared that Samuel, like Cressy, would drown, and pleaded with him to delay a year. He considered it a providence that Samuel was somehow prevented from making the voyage. Like a Puritan Lear he prayed for patience, and then for deliverance. At the same time his final letters, in a crowded, trembling hand, depict him at the point of exhaustion, straining to finish some of his most important works and to have them quickly published and widely distributed: *Ratio Disciplinae, Manuductio, Agricola*, the never-published *Tri-Paradisus*. But as he surveyed the life of Massachusetts he felt that these and his other tremendous efforts had changed nothing. The currency was still depreciated, Arianism and Anglicanism flourished, the churches of New England still squabbled, the Indians still attacked and were still unconverted.

The fortunes of his friend John Winthrop had changed, but for the worse. In 1724 the ambiguous land-titles of Winthrop's estate brought him into Probate Court proceedings that became a celebrated case in colonial law, Winthrop v. Lechmere. In May, 1726, Winthrop was arrested. Leaving his wife in Connecticut, he later went to England to plead before the king in Council. The Council found for Winthrop and repealed the Connecticut law in question. While in London Winthrop vengefully submitted twenty-nine articles accusing Connecticut of acts of independence. Jeremiah Dummer was called before the Privy Council to answer the charges, which again jeopardized the always insecure charter. The decision in Winthrop's favor invalidated many land titles in Connecticut, and together with his accusations made him widely hated at home. Rather than face his neighbors, and desiring to keep the good company that favored him in London, Winthrop stayed in England, like Mather's other friend Shute, for the rest of his life. He died in Kent in 1747 after exchanging letters with his wife in Connecticut for twenty-one years.

To John Winthrop

M;IV Coll 8 (as May 1)/MHS   May 16, 1725

Sir,

Having passed through a winter of much feebleness (and some employment) it appears high time for me to renew my acquaintance with a friend who would have been in my debt for I know not how many letters, if his vast civilities to my son had not much more than cancelled it.

He would have joined with me in the acknowledgments I am now making, if he had not been at this time at seventy miles distance from me.

Such is my penury that I have nothing to send you but, first, a few of our latest publications. And then, my humble request and advice that you would not let your mind be disturbed, much less your health impaired, by the base usages you may be maltreated withal.

I know not how better to address you on this occasion than by letting you see how one whom you love well is used. And if the best man in Connecticut government will use a poor minister as I have been used, you will not wonder if inferior people treat you as I have heard they do. [In the margin: I could wish Mr. T. Woodbridge knew it; but I don't care to tell him.] With the help of Heaven I concoct all with patience. And I shall find the God of patience to be the God of consolation.

I know not how better—yes, I do. Set before yourself the example of the glorious Lord, who was as the sheep is before the shearers.

We have no intelligence worth a straw. I was going to say, no intellect. We are like to continue one year longer as we are, inexpressibly happy in the Lieutenant Governor's wise and good administration.

You know what I wish you, and that I am, Sir, Your most cordial friend and servant,

To Robert Millar

U/NLS (not in Mather's hand)   May 28, 1725

Sir,

You have exceedingly enriched me and obliged me with your excellent *History of the Propagation of Religion,* and I embrace it as a sweet opportunity to exercise that great article of our holy religion, *The communion of saints,* with rejoicing in the talents wherewith our glorious Redeemer furnishes his faithful servants, and the use which it pleases Him to make of them.

I do without the least adulation freely report my sentiments on the performance, with which (not you but) the grace of God with you has entertained us. It is a composure full of erudition, and a well-disposed amassment of what lies dispersed in an army of writers, on a subject than which few are more worthy to be treated on. And it is managed with the spirit of genuine and generous piety and catholic charity, with which the noble design that is treated on ought forever, but is not always, presented.

Your History has been communicated by me to as many as the time has allowed for, having been in my hands very little since my own first perusal of it. [Praises the work.]

[Describes the self-defeating activities of the SPG.]

And yet let my learned and godly brother allow me to lay before him in a word, some of my sentiments, and some of my suspicions. It appears plain to me, that the Second Coming of our Lord will be at and for the destruction of the Man of Sin, whose period of two hundred and sixty years is now expiring. It appears plain to me, that at the Second Coming of the Lord, there will be the terrible conflagration which the inspired Peter has described, and all the prophets with open mouth, and with one mouth, have warned us of, and from which none shall escape except the elect, that by the angels are caught up to meet the Lord. It appears plain to me, that the promised rest for the Church of God on earth, and the good things of the Latter Days (particularly that Reign of Universal Righteousness which the excellent spirit of my Millar is laboring for) will be in that New Earth which is to take place after the coming of the Lord, and the burning of the world. I despair of the things hoped for, before.

I cannot find any inhabitants for the New Earth except those faithful ones who shall be caught up at the descent of our Saviour, and changed like Enoch and Elias and made sinless, and be made like Adam and Eve in the New Paradise, and have all the circumstances in the sixty-fifth chapter of Isaiah's prophecies compatible to them, and be in some circumstances different from the raised, who marry not nor are given in marriage in the New Heavens hovering over the New Earth, and affording teachers and rulers to the (soon greatly multiplied) kingdoms of it, whereto these changed ones will be in His time and way translated.

You may look upon me as very paradoxical, but after long trials to make other schemes agree with the sacred oracles, I am compelled unto these paradoxes. However, I should be thankful if you will bestow better instructions upon me. And I do not think that these apprehensions are at all to supersede or discourage such struggles for the Kingdom of a Lord ruling in the midst of His enemies, as Mr. Millar has done so much to animate. I again say, let us be found so doing. And if we do not gain our point, our God from the Machine of Heaven will shortly do more than we have looked for. [Close]

Your most affectionate brother and servant,

To Robert Wodrow

U/NLS June 15, 1725

My dear Brother,

[Sends along his *Palm-Bearers*; regrets the lack of interesting intelligence.]

You will pardon me that I am so vain as to wish that the *Parentator* may also find a second edition among you, for which my reason is because an unhappy pen at London has with a base disingenuity made a most injurious extract from it, and stripped it of the most valuable things in it (and particularly of all the regards paid unto the Church of Scotland), and rendered it a useless performance.

Among the rest of the enclosed you will find a small French essay, upon which how glad should I be if you could find out some conveyance for it, that it may penetrate into France, where I have some apprehensions it may prove seasonable and serviceable, and the glorious Appointer of Times will make it operative.

[Describes the condition of the churches in New England. They have no Arians among them, yet share in the general decay of "real and vital piety." Self-defeating attempts of the Church of England.]

The country is in distress by a war which a French priest (whose wicked scalp has now paid for it) stirred up his eastern Indian proselytes to make upon us. We are much distressed by our frequent alarms from such an inaccessible enemy. But our gracious God, by the sword of His injured people, ever now and then gives mortifying strokes unto them, and we are in a hopeful way of utterly destroying them.

One of our great calamities is, that no silver coin passing among us, our bills of credit have, by a coincidence of several unhappy circumstances, been so depreciated that silver is now valued at sixteen shillings an ounce.

This raises the price of European goods proportionably, and grievous oppressions are from hence felt more or less by all sorts of people; but most of all by ministers, and those who subsist on salaries and cannot make reprisals, as others can.

[Mentions the departure of Governor Shute.]

I heartily thank you for introducing me unto some acquaintance with good Mr. Millar, to whom I have written what I judged proper for my first letter to him. I doubt he will count me little short of a heretic— but I hope he will admonish me before he reject me. [Close]

Your most affectionate friend, brother, and servant,

To Thomas Prince

U/MHS December 15, 1725

Sir,

If you will be so good as to peruse this rhapsody, and at your own time return it with your castigations upon it, it will (what you have done a thousand times, and never did anything else) oblige me.

'Tis the preface to the *Manuductio*, your perusal whereof was a great service to it.

I must complain to you, as my father Higginson did once to me, *Latinitas mea contraxit quandam rubiginem.* I pray, rub off what you find, and so do likewise at all times, to the author,

Your brother and servant,

Should not I do well to add, *the private academies of the Dissenters* in the dedication?

To Thomas Prince

DII (as 1727)/MHS   January 24, 1726

Sir,

Having first expressed my satisfaction in what you have written to Mr. Watts, I will freely, and in the most open-hearted manner, offer you a little of my opinion about the [crossed out, but legible and meant to be read: foolish] *Disquisitions* which that man has lately published.

I take him to be a very disqualified person for the managing of the vast subject he has undertaken.

He is not only too shallow for it, but also led away with a spurious and criminal charity for those abominable *Idolaters*, the Arians, and ready to embrace as brethren in Christ those ancient and perpetual enemies of Christ, whom to treat, as a great part of the Dissenters are *wickedly* come to do, is a high treason of a greater and blacker consequence than ever an Atterbury was charged withal.

His compliments to that execrable crew of traitors (I mean, the Arians) are unchristian, and scandalous, and have a plain tendency to destroy the religion of God.

His attempts, to compound with them, on these two anathematizable terms:

First, that there is no Eternal Son of God (well-fare, poor *Assemblies'* Catechism!) and that there is no filiation in the Godhead, but this, that God (*Sabellianically!*) created a super-angelical Spirit a good while ago, and intimately possessed him;

Secondly, that a Holy Spirit in the Godhead may be called a *Person*, as the grace of Love, and some other things, are *Personalized* in the Scriptures.

These attempts will be detestable to all that think *The faith once delivered unto the Saints* worth contending for.

Could his predecessor once again take his pen into his hand, he would charge him with nothing less than grievous *heresies*. His answer to Biddle, for that!

For my own part, I look on the part which our brethren (I will not now say, *United Brethren*) have taken in countenancing the conspiracy to dethrone and degrade and ungod the Eternal Son of God, as having a deep share in preparing the world for that *catastrophe* which my *Diluvium Ignis* warns you of (you have not yet read the two last leaves of it).

As for you, *my son*, (if not my *age*, yet allow my *love* to call you so!) I will say one thing to *you*. *Take heed unto your spirit.* The candor, or humor, in the spirit of our friend on the other side the water, has betrayed him into a most mischievous treachery to the faith of the Gospel, and unhappy disservice to the best cause in the world. I highly approve and admire the goodness of your spirit, and the equanimity with which you look upon displeasing things. But yet, watch over it, lest you admit of an *indolence,* where a holy zeal shall be called for, and where a John himself would be a Boanerges, with zealous testimonies: and lest you unawares at some time or other hurt a glorious cause, by an air that may carry too much complaisance, where warm expressions of the greatest abhorrence are what our glorious Lord would be most pleased withal. [Close, in Latin and Greek]

Sir, Your most affectionate brother,

(Mr. Henchman has the *Agricola;* you will give the enclosed unto him, when 'tis filled as far as you think fit. And ask him to carry it, with the *Agricola,* to Mr. Checkley, if he purposes to do any thing about it.)

To John Stirling and Robert Wodrow

U/NLS   January 28, 1726

Most honored Sirs,

The unaccountable usage, and Ammonitish abuse, which our *Parentator* has undergone in London under the influence of Dr. Calamy, and seems to have been designed for some indignity, or discovery of disaffection, to the Church of Scotland, has rendered me very desirous that a new edition of it might be produced with you.

That which above all gives life to this desire, is that there may be a living and a lasting testimony of the esteem which this country has for Glorious Church, as also that my deceased parent may not cease to do good on earth, as diffusively as may be, after he is gone to Heaven. [Encloses a copy of the work.]

Your most affectionate friend and servant,

To Robert Wodrow

U/NLS   January 28, 1726

Sir,

[The vessel for Glasgow is about to sail.]

Our eastern savages finding themselves under a necessity of suing for peace, it is restored.

The clouds which threatened our liberties from the Court, are happily blown over.

Our churches enjoy much tranquillity, and the builders of Babel fall into repeated confusions.

The result of my most inquisitive thoughts on the *Things to be Looked For,* you have in my *Diluvium Ignis,* which I should not be unwilling to see transmitted into every part of sleeping Europe.

If the *Parentator* should be reprinted with you, let the last line of the Epitaphium be left out. I cannot forbear wishing that my parent may live in the Church of Scotland, and have his history made one medium of our union with it. [Close]

Your cordial and constant friend, brother, and servant,

To Thomas Prince

DII/MHS   January 31, 1726

My dear Friend, and one of my dearest: Madding Day

[In margin: *Si vales, benè est; ego* (a word illegible) *non valeo.*]

If you ask, *How I do?* I can scarce allow myself air enough to give you an account in the terms of the letter the poor soldier at Casco wrote unto my brother Walter at Roxbury. Yet for part of it, I may.

If you ask, *What I do?* Alas, methinks my name is *Do Little,* tho' in deed and in worth much inferior to him that wore that name.

I am hastening into the work of my *Triparadisus,* but perhaps making more haste unto the *Paradise* of God.

The less I *do* myself, I think, I must contrive the more for *others* to do. [Asks him to direct the publication of *Agricola.*] I leave it with you to direct him [Henchman] and advise him, very particularly about the method of sending the *Proposals for Subscriptions* (which he has in his hands) into the country towns. Mr. T. Green will, I suppose, be so kind as to help us all over Connecticut. Perhaps, I may add, *excite* him too against loss of time, and against living at the *sign of the snail.* You see how I set you to *ploughing,* even under the *cold,* yea, *because* of the *cold.* The *Harvest!* The *Harvest!* It is near; Lord come quickly. The rest (I want strength; my side aches for this!) I reserve to another time. I am your brother*, *as merry as one bound for heaven.*
*Mrs. Askew's subscription. [The handwriting slants off the page.] Let

no *vulture's eye* see the enclosed. But let it, at your own time, return safely to me. The fair copy met with a strange deliverance, which at another time I may tell you of.

To Thomas Prince

DII/MHS   April 5, 1726

Sir,

[Thanks him for his favor to the *Ratio Disciplinae*.]

That work will certainly prove one of the usefullest things that ever were offered unto the churches. Their perpetual confirmation and establishment in the *faith and order of the Gospel*, and their vindication to the (Court and) world, will be but some of the consequences that will be found upon its publication.

Our great adversary thinks so. Hence he obtained a permission t'other day to scatter two thirds of the copy unto the four winds of Heaven, in loose leaves, whereof some were taken up by strangers, others were found in a garden, others in a wood-pile; when, if it had been to save my life, or one worth ten thousand of mine, I could not have recovered it. But the Angel of the Lord looked after it. Not a leaf, nor a line of it, is missing!

The work proceeds. Nine sheets are now printed off.

But lo, now, our good bookseller does declare the work shall stop; not a sheet more shall be done.

He'll tell you *his* reason, if you ask him. And I have told you *mine*!

I don't wonder that such a work must be brought forward with a *struggle*. 'Tis a sign 'tis for the Kingdom of God. [Asks him to visit Mrs. Saltonstall, who may wish to subscribe.]

Your brother (and servant) in the labor and service and patience of the Kingdom,

To [Thomas?] Hollis

U/Hunt (HM 22325)   October 27, 1726

Sir,

The subject upon which I now address you is *the relation of what the grace of our God has done on one island of our Christianized Indians.*

411

One reason why your servants the commissioners here did no more to bear the expense of publishing it in this country, was not only because it would be very great, much beyond what it would be in London, but also because it would be much better done, and (which may appear a little surprising!) much *sooner* at London than at Boston.

'Tis at length undertaken by a bookseller here, and by such a bookseller as the brothers of the trade on your side the water (so far as I and many others have had experience) must pardon me if I say, I wish were less of a rarity among them; a bookseller who is a person of real piety, and exact honesty, and one that is a perpetual stranger to trick, and to everything that is mean and base and sordid. His name is Mr. Samuel Gerrish.

On this occasion he desires of me nothing but that I would represent him to the honorable corporation whereof you are a member, as not intending any presumption in his offering to meddle in such a matter without their order, but requesting that you may be informed of it, and that he may be allowed in it.

[Asks the corporation to encourage Gerrish by taking off two or three hundred of his copies.]

I make this proposal with the more of solicitation because the disposition of our people obliges me to believe that if our good bookseller be not assisted by you, he will be a loser by his pious and forward generosity in running the risk of so bulky an impression. [Close]

Your most obedient servant,

To John Stirling

U/NLS   November 30, 1726

Most honored Sir,

Some apprehension whether my dear friend Mr. Wodrow may be living (in this *land of the dying*) moves me to enclose unto you my letter and packet for him, open. [And this way Stirling can read the letter also.]

But the principal intention of this note is to impose upon you the trouble, which your goodness will readily allow me to do, of dispensing to each of your four universities, two or three apiece, as you may judge proper to proportion them, of the *Manuductios* . . . as also to request that after you have communicated the *Ratio Disciplinae* to as many as you please of our brethren, you would allow it a standing in your College library. . . .   Yours under never-forgotten obligations,

To Robert Wodrow

WIII/NLS   November 30, 1726

My invaluable Friend,

The arrival of some vessels from Glasgow, without bringing me a line from you, or a word of you, raises in me some uneasy apprehensions. But I will not let slip the opportunity which now offers, to let you know that I still am what I hope you also are.

The vast benefits of commerce are what mankind in general now feel and own and celebrate. We cannot sit at our tables, but the instances of the benefits are sensible, and afford a copious theme unto us. But you will allow me that the *epistolary commerce* is a sort not the least beneficial. And, of what I enjoy in this way, that which you favor me withal gives me not the smallest entertainment and satisfaction.

In the XXVII chapter of Leviticus, I observe that the estimation for a head between twenty and sixty years old was fifty shekels; but after sixty, the estimation presently sunk to fifteen shekels, not a third part of what it was before. Tho' according to this estimation, your friend should not be a third part worth so much as he was a little above three years ago, yet he is of the persuasion that in old age we must labor to be as useful as we can. The Orientals have an unhappy maxim that *old age is to be reckoned no part of life*. But I have read of *still bringing forth fruit in old age*; and certainly, so to do is to *live*. I have cause to lie down in much confusion, from a just reflection on my great and long unfruitfulness; but yet after I have had opportunities to bring forth some little fruit, particularly by the way of the press, in my younger years, the glorious Lord allows me still in my old age to bear something that may be of some little use among His people. I say, my *old age*, because I have now outlived that which they foolishly call *The Grand Climacteric.*

I had once a simple fancy that if I should arrive to see *three hundred and sixty-five* publications of poor treatises, which my shallow pen should have elaborated, this number would be the period of my life, and finish all that I have to do. But lately look on my catalogue, I found the number were arisen to *three hundred sixty-nine*, tho' the preparations which the sovereign wisdom of Heaven orders to lie by unpublished are much more bulky and weighty and wealthy than any of those that have been yet exhibited. It remains, then, that I know not the death of my death; but I would keep working, and waiting, and hoping, and rejoicing, and looking for the mercy of our Lord Jesus Christ in Eternal Life. [Sends along some of his recent works.]

But because you asked me about our Tranquebarian brethren, and expect from the West Indies an account of what is done in the East Indies, I have enclosed a short extract of the last letters I have received from the excellent missionaries.

I pray, make my remembrances acceptable to our never-to-be-forgotten Lord of Pollock. The world (I say not, *our* world!) ripens apace for the *Diluvium Ignis*, my short essay upon which you have seen. But I don't expect any other effect of that essay in the world, than what would add materials for the continuation of Petrus Licetus's book, *De hujusce seculi coecitate.*

May our glorious Lord continue you still many years a useful servant of His Kingdom, while it appears as yet but in the condition of a *little stone*, and give you a recompensing *lot* when it shall appear in the condition of a *great mountain*. Lord JESUS, come quickly! I am, in Him, Sir   Your affectionate brother and servant,

To Thomas Prince

DII/MHS   January 13, 1727

Sir,

With many thanks for the liberty you have indulged me, I return your laborious *Many-Reader*.

About the *illustration* extracted from him, which I now send you, some time or other (if we live) we may change a word or two.

I am this morning in a querulous humor.

Very many months ago, a number of ministers who once were fathers to Mr. Clap addressed him with their tenderest and most obliging admonitions, and exhortations, and persuasions to reform a great and public scandal that he had long persisted in. He took no notice of them. And yet, the ministers of this town appear afraid of so much as telling him that they dislike his conduct.

At the same time, the state, and at last the pen, of the scattering flock makes a loud cry unto us, and gives us the fairest opportunity and introduction for our advice to them that can be. All delay carries destruction in it; and yet all we do is to let them know that we shall delay giving them the advice their difficulties call for, till we have some direction from Mr. Clap to do it.

The two letters you ordered yesterday (tho' I, who would ever submit unto your better judgments, have signed them) I verily fear are only to harden a melancholy man in a gross iniquity. And only to lengthen out the time for the Great Adversary to accomplish the scattering of the holy people, and ruining a valuable interest.

I would not abound in my own sense; and I [am] very sensible of my being more liable to mistakes than my brethren. However, I must confess I don't understand our conduct.

But I *very well understand* the meaning of the indecency and indignity I am treated withal. To order me to draw up letters, and make me lose my time, which grows more and more precious to me, and own that I have exactly followed my orders, and then turn 'em upon me again and substitute instead of them, that which can be of no *other use* but only to render *them useless*—I say, *I very well understand it*. However, you'll find me very patient and easy, and under no other impression from it but only a resolution to look on myself as excused for the time to come from the labors of your clerkship. [Close]

Your affectionate brother and servant,

To Thomas Prince

U/MHS
February 11, 1727
Finishing sixty-four

Sir,

You have here a paragraph of our *Triparadisus*. Perhaps it may be so distasteful to you for its contradiction to an opinion wherein you have had the prejudices of your education to settle you, that I may call it *a glass of bitter*. But then, it may serve to whet your appetite for the further entertainment.

I pray that it may return in about a week, because I know not how soon the transcriber may want it.

But I much more pray that you would advertise me of any weaknesses you may discover in it. Mr. Baxter desired Adoni Avi to confute him if he saw any error in his writings. He did it in this point; that is, made an essay to do it. But at the same time, was in the wrong. Mr. Baxter was in the right; and my father in the close of his essay irrefragably proved that which, as I take it, entirely confuted himself. With me, you see, *Magis amica veritas*. But I make Mr. Baxter's request unto Mr. Prince—with the same success, will it be?

415

I pray one thing more: let nobody, no not so much as your good neighbor and colleague, see what I send you. My hour for it is not yet come. I am, Sir, Your brother and servant,

III

In the winter of 1727 Cotton Mather's health deteriorated until on January 28, 1728, his church appointed a day of prayer for him, directed by Colman, Thacher, and Sewall. Mather died on February 13, 1728, a day past his birthday, his estate amounting to 245 pounds. He was succeeded in his ministry by his son Samuel Mather. Many sermons observed his death, some by his longtime correspondents, who interpreted what Mather's piety and good works, his curiosity, learning, and international celebrity, said about the ongoing Reformation and about the New World civilization emerging from the wilderness:

> When the physicians intimated to him that there was now no prospect of his life, he lifted up his hands and eyes, and with a particular pathos said, *Thy will be done on earth, as it is done in . . Heaven.* When he was informed how much the people of God prayed for him, he seemed greatly pleased with a thought arising from that, *The prayer of the upright is His delight.* He thought it worth being sick, only that the infinite God might have the delight of the prayers preferred by such numbers of upright ones.
> —Joshua Gee, *Israel's Mourning for Aaron's Death*

> He was a wonderful Improver of Time, and 'tis almost amazing how much he read and studied, how much he wrote and published, how much he corresponded abroad, not only with the several provinces in the British America, but also with England, Scotland, Ireland, Holland, Germany, and even the Eastern as well as the Western Indies. And yet how much he conversed, visited, contrived, and acted at home! How many languages, histories, arts and sciences, both ancient and modern, he was familiarly versed in. What a vast amassment of learning he had grasped in his mind, from all sorts of writings, of which he had one of the largest and richest collections that ever was in these ends of the earth, and which he was at all times ready to use in the most sudden and *extempore* manner.
> —Thomas Prince, *The Departure of Elijah*

God has this week taken up from us one whom he enabled by His grace in a singular manner to walk with Him. We mourn the decease from us (not his ascension to God) of the first minister in the town, the first in age, in gifts, and in grace, as all his brethren very readily own. I might add (it may be without offense to any) the first in the whole province and provinces of New England, for universal literature and extensive services. Yea, it may be among all the fathers in these churches from the beginning of the country to this day, of whom many have done worthily and greatly; yet none of them amassed together so vast a treasure of learning, and made so much use of it, to a variety of pious intentions, as this our reverend brother and father, Dr. Cotton Mather.

—Benjamin Colman, *The Holy Walk*

Besides his charity, his humility and patience distinguished him. For although he alone was able to support the character of this country abroad, and was had in great esteem through many nations in Europe, as well as many other places, which he could not but know, and which others could not but observe, though they beheld his reputation with envy and would sometimes speak of it with indifference; I say, although he was thus honored by those who ride upon the high places of learning and good sense, yet how patient was he to see himself slighted, how willing to be laid aside and how even glad to see other men exalted above him?

—Samuel Mather, *The Departure and Character of Elijah*

Three months before his death Mather composed his last extant letter, to William Dummer, requesting a day of public fasting. The occasion was an earthquake that shook New England at around ten o'clock on the night of October 29, 1727, mightily enough to be felt as far as New York and Pennsylvania. The florid calligraphic devices, loosely reproduced here, make it an atypical letter, but emphasize the meaning, at once personal and universal, that Mather read out of the event, how once again it testified to the power of the covenant, how once again it bespoke a God who would thunder vengeance upon a land that would sacrifice His son and servant.

To Lieutenant Governor William Dummer
U/UVL   December 9, 1727

Sir,

'Inasmuch as our Glorious GOD and SAVIOUR after several other awful appearances of His Holy Providence for our awakening, has terrified His people with a tremendous and far extended EARTHQUAKE, the roars and shocks whereof have continued sensibly to affect many parts of the province for now many weeks together; tho' the most of the churches in the province may have had their *particular days* for the proper exercise of religion, with *fasting*, on this extraordinary occasion, yet it may be judged a most agreeable and seasonable action, for the GOVERNMENT also to proclaim a GENERAL FAST throughout the province upon it.

'The whole people on the view of the Almighty GOD *coming forth to shake terribly the earth* are to be called upon, that there be kept a DAY OF HUMILIATION and of SUPPLICATION, in all the worshipping assemblies of the province—To confess with a due and a deep contrition before our God our many miscarriages, the contempt of His Gospel, and the many trespasses against the rules of a *godly* and a *sober* and a *righteous* life therein given unto us, whereby we have provoked Him in so formidable a manner to threaten us, and for which He might justly destroy us. And therewithal to lift up our prayers and cry mightily unto Him:

'That the crying sins of the land may be pardoned for the sake of the atonement made by the Great Sacrifice, which is to be pleaded for the congregation;

'That the *voice of the LORD crying* to the country in the *earthquake* may be well understood, and attended, and suitably complied withal;

'That the *good impressions* produced by the *earthquake* on a multitude of people may be effectual and abiding;

'That through the *Holy Spirit* of our GOD and SAVIOUR accompanying of it with His influences, the *earthquake*, instead of being a forerunner to a more *fearful desolation* than what we have yet seen, may prove a more useful dispensation than any that we have yet met withal;

'And, *That* being admonished by the *signs of the times*, we may be found religiously preparing for the things which may be coming *as a snare upon all them who dwell on the face of the whole earth.*

'At the same time, there is to be a *thank-offering of praise* to our Glorious *Preserver*, in that in an *earthquake* reaching so far, and holding so long, we yet know not of one life lost, or one house entirely fallen; with our fervent *prayer* to HIM that in this day of His *long-suffering to us-ward, all may come unto repentance.*

'For which purpose also, all persons in their several places and stations are to look upon themselves as called by a loud voice of Heaven, both to reform whatever they may find amiss in themselves, and exert themselves for the reforming of the like in all about them, and suppressing those irregularities which may have a tendency to enkindle the Divine displeasure, and procure a progress and increase in the dreadful testimonies of it.'

May it please Your Honor,

In what I have hitherto been writing, I have (upon an intention easy to be discerned) comprised and expressed, as well as I can, the sentiments wherein I have of my brethren concurring with me (and bespoke an action which a multitude unite in wishing for). And having some allowance for it, I humbly lay them in a sort of a memorial before Your Honor, being well-assured that whether the form of it be so or no, the matter and the design of it will be highly acceptable.

In the days of Queen *Elizabeth*, 1580, *England* felt an *earthquake*, which did no considerable hurt; but this good was done by it: the government by a proclamation called upon all the subjects throughout the kingdom to be earnest in prayer, that the wrath of God might be averted from the land; yea, it called upon every householder to offer such prayer every day in his family, and more particular directions were given what should be prayed for.

The excellent piety which Your Honor expressed on the thirtieth of October had a precious effect on the city, and so on all the country.

What is now humbly proposed, is but such a continuation of it as is, I think, very much asked for, and hoped for.

In former times also, our General Assemblies now and then set the whole people an example of piety in keeping such days by themselves, in the times of their sessions.

May our glorious LORD prepare us for all that may be coming, and may He grant us long to enjoy your benign and happy influences,

'Tis the prayer of Your Honor's
Most obedient servant,
Co. Mather

419

Glossary of Correspondents

The relevant facts about most of the following entrants are given fully in the introductory essays. The interested reader should consult the index for the appropriate page numbers. Mather's correspondents are brought together here for the sake of handy reference and, in a few cases, to add some information about them. The glossary also includes several correspondents not sketched in the introductions. These are denoted below by an asterisk. "HC" means Harvard College.

ANDREWS, JEDEDIAH (1674–1717; HC 1695). First Presbyterian minister in Philadelphia.

ASHURST, SIR HENRY (1645–1711). London merchant and alderman, treasurer of the New England Company.

ASHURST, ROBERT (d. 1726). A wealthy sugar refiner in London, the son of Sir William Ashurst, below. In 1720 he succeeded his father as governor of the New England Company, whose affairs he managed diligently until his death.

ASHURST, SIR WILLIAM (1647–1720). Sir Henry's younger brother, governor of the New England Company from 1696 to 1720. Mather dedicated *Bonifacius* to him.

BARNARD, JOHN (1681–1770; HC 1700). Minister of Marblehead, born in Boston, author of some excellent sermons. According to one story, when Boston rose against Andros and took the fort, Barnard, age seven, was among the first to enter it. In 1701 he wrote a pamphlet defending the Mathers against Calef. Cotton Mather's enemies saw Barnard as Mather's tool. In 1716 Mather gave the charge at Barnard's ordination in Marblehead.

BAXTER, JOSEPH (1676–1745; HC 1693). Minister at Medfield.

*BELCHER, JONATHAN (1682–1757; HC 1699). Prosperous, cultured, and vituperative merchant who spent much time at the courts of England and Europe and was the subject of an adulatory poem by Isaac Watts. By bribery and shady dealing he rose high in Massachusetts politics and served on the Council from 1718 to 1720, 1722 to 1723 and 1726 to 1727. By 1728 he had reversed his allegiances and become intimate with Elisha Cooke and other "popular" leaders. Becoming governor after the death of Burnet in 1729, however, he once again proclaimed his love for prerogative. Later, as governor of New Jersey, he helped to build Princeton University. He was appointed by Connecticut to try to reverse the decision in Winthrop v. Lechmere.

*BISHOP, SAMUEL. Lydia George's nephew. He apparently lived in England.

BOEHM, ANTHONY WILLIAM (1673–1722). German chaplain at the English court who sent letters and packets for Mather to August Francke in Germany and to Bartholomew Ziegenbalgh in southern India.

*BOWMAN, CAPTAIN. Perhaps Noah Bowman of Charlestown. Mather sent his son Samuel, a student at Harvard, to board with Bowman.

BRADBURY, THOMAS (1677–1759). Congregational minister in London who delivered a noted series of lectures on the duty of psalm singing.

*BRIGGS, JOHN (fl. 1700–1720). One of Cotton Mather's lawyers in the Howell administration, "a great blessing unto me." Mather presented him with a silver-headed walking stick for his efforts. Briggs seems to have been related to Mather, and was a neighbor of Samuel Sewall.

*BROWN, JAMES (d. 1714). Dean of the faculty of the University of Glasgow (1704–1713) and minister of the church of Glasgow.

BROWNE, SIMON (1680–1732). English divine and writer. In the Salters Hall conference he would not subscribe to the imposition of a trinitarian test, leading him into a later controversy with Thomas Reinolds, below. Around 1723 he seems to have become mentally unbalanced, gave up his ministry, wrote children's books, compiled a dictionary, and opposed the deists from a rationalistic point of view.

BURNET, WILLIAM (1688–1729). Colonial governor, godson of William and Mary. Appointed governor of New York and New Jersey in 1720, transferred to Massachusetts as governor in 1728. While in New York he established a favorable trade policy for the English with the Indians, which brought him into conflict with the powerful New York merchants.

CALAMY, EDMUND (1671–1732). Rather courtly English historian of Nonconformity and lecturer at Salters Hall. He studied at Utrecht and at Oxford. In his histories he explained and justified Nonconformist separation, and emphasized liberty of conscience as the key to Nonconformity.

CALEF, ROBERT (1648–1719). Probably born in England, Calef settled in Boston by 1688 as a cloth merchant. In 1693 he accused Mather of trying to stir up in Boston a witchcraft crisis like that in Salem.

*CHISWELL, RICHARD (fl. 1660–1680). Bookseller in St. Paul's churchyard, London, and publisher of *Weekly Memorials for the Ingeniose*, a review, which Mather read, of recently published books. His son was a member of the New England Company.

*CLARK, ELIZABETH (MRS. JOHN) (d. 1722). In 1718 she became the second wife of John Clark, below. After her death Clark married the widow of President Leverett.

*CLARK, JAMES (d. 1723). Minister in Glasgow.

CLARK, JOHN (1667–1728; HC 1687). Boston physician, member of Elisha Cooke's "popular" party, brother of Cotton Mather's second wife.

COLMAN, BENJAMIN (1673–1747; HC 1692). Minister of the Brattle Street Church, ordained by the London Presbytery in 1699. A prolific writer and correspondent himself.

*CORWIN (or CORWYN), GEORGE (1683–1717; HC 1701). Minister at Salem, son of one of the witchcraft judges, owner of a large library. He was ordained by Cotton Mather, who felt that the Salem people disregarded religion.

COTTON, JOANNA (1642–1702). Wife of John Cotton, below.

COTTON, JOHN (1639–1698; HC 1657). Cotton Mather's uncle, an important adolescent influence. His mother married Richard Mather of Dorchester after the theologian John Cotton's death. He married Joanna in 1660 and had eleven children by her. Cotton Mather later wrote a life of him.

COTTON, NATHANIEL (1698–1729; HC 1717). Somewhat hot-tempered minister of the faction-ridden congregation at Bristol, son of Rowland Cotton of Sandwich. He subscribed to seven copies of Samuel Mather's biography of Cotton.

CRAIGHEAD, THOMAS (d. 1739). Minister and physician from Ireland, a relative of Lydia George and instrumental in bringing her and Mather together.

DANFORTH, SAMUEL (1666–1727; HC 1683). Minister at Taunton who worked at Christianizing the Indians and prepared an Indian dictionary. At Taunton he set up a society to reform disorders, similar to Mather's in Boston.

*DEAN (or DEANE), JOHN (or JASPER) (1679–1761). Captain of a ship bound from Ireland to New England with fourteen men in 1710. After the ship struck a rock off the New Hampshire coast, his crew stayed for three weeks on a tiny island, half-frozen, and were forced to eat the corpse of a crew-member. Mather wrote to Samuel Penhallow for an account of the episode, preached on it, and later published the sermon (*Compassions Called For*, 1711) in which he included Dean's narrative of the events. After appearing in Mather's sermon it went through seven or eight separate editions in Boston and London.

*DEERING, H[enry?] (d. 1717). Probably the Boston shopkeeper, outspoken opponent of prerogative and defender of the "popular" party, noted for his slogan, "liberty and property."

DUDLEY, JOSEPH (1647–1720; HC 1665). Governor of Massachusetts from 1702 to 1715.

DUDLEY, PAUL (1675–1751; HC 1690). Student at the Middle Temple, F.R.S., chief justice of Massachusetts, and son of the governor, who made him attorney-general during his administration. Dudley speculated in frontier lands and clashed with Elisha Cooke. His brother-in-law was John Winthrop, who felt that Dudley betrayed him in the Lechmere case and was even responsible for bringing it on.

*DUDLEY, WILLIAM (1686–1743; HC 1704). Youngest son of the governor, brother of Paul Dudley. In 1705 he was sent to Canada by his father to spy out French fortifications, but ostensibly to exchange prisoners; he returned with several prisoners. His father's enemies declared that the purpose of the mission was to trade privately with the enemy, and that other prisoners had been left behind as an excuse for further smuggling trips. In 1706 he was sent back to Canada and effected the release of more prisoners. It was later charged that his father gave him all the plunder from the Port Royal expedition. Dudley lived in Roxbury, where he served for ten years in the House and was Speaker from 1724–1728. A vigorous man, he trekked through the woods on twenty-one intercolonial boundary commissions. He also tried, unsuccessfully, to court Samuel Sewall's daughter Judith.

DUMMER, JEREMIAH (c. 1679–1739; HC 1699). Colonial agent and author, born in Boston, died in Plaistow, England. In 1715, when Parliament was attacking the charter again, he wrote a *Defence of the New England Charter*, from which John Adams and James Otis later drew arguments for independence.

DUMMER, WILLIAM (1679–1761). Brother of Jeremiah, chief judge during the pirate trials, commander-in-chief and lieutenant governor of Massachusetts. In 1725 Mather asked his help in convening a synod of churches by the civil government; the Episcopal ministers and the Bishop of London succeeded in stopping it.

EDWARDS, JOHN (1637–1716). English divine in Cambridge, called by his admirers the Calvin of his age; wrote more than forty theological works.

FOSTER, JOHN (d. 1711). Boston merchant, very active in the overthrow of Andros. A prominent member of Mather's church who apparently published and to whom Mather dedicated his *Monitory Letter* (1700).

FOXCROFT, THOMAS (1697–1769; HC 1714). Minister of the First Church in Boston. His father was an Anglican, and he himself felt that he could subscribe to the Articles of the Church of England. His funeral sermon on John Coney was published in a single pamphlet with Mather's *The Soul Upon the Wings* (1722). Foxcroft was a close friend of Mather's nephew, Thomas Walter.

FRIZZEL (or FRIZZELL), JOHN (d. 1723). Very well-to-do Boston merchant who with his wife paid for the printing of several of Mather's works and seemingly did business favors for Cressy.

GEORGE, LYDIA (LEE) (d. 1734). Cotton Mather's third wife, the daughter of the Reverend Samuel Lee (Mather owned a number of Lee's manuscripts). His sister Rebecca was the third wife of John Saffin, below.

GERRISH, JOSEPH (1650–1720; HC 1669). Minister at Wenham.

GREENWOOD, ISAAC (1702–1745; HC 1721). First Hollis professor of mathematics at Harvard, one of Mather's proteges.

HACKSHAW, ROBERT (d. 1738?). Apparently a printer's paper merchant in London. Having a lot of paper on his hands he took the manuscript of Mather's *Magnalia* from the Reverend John Quick and helped to get it published, selling off his paper in the bargain. A Robert Hackshaw, a London merchant with some ties to New England, died in England in 1738.

HALLEY, EDMUND (1656–1742). Noted astronomer, assistant secretary of the Royal Society, and for a time editor of its *Transactions*.

HINCKLEY, THOMAS (c. 1618–1706). Governor of the Plymouth colony (1681–1692).

HOBBY, SIR CHARLES (d. 1715). Mather's friend and candidate to replace Joseph Dudley as governor of Massachusetts.

HOLLIS, THOMAS (1659–1731). London Baptist merchant, benefactor of Harvard.

HOLLIS, THOMAS, JR. (d. 1735). Nephew of the above, a Londoner, sent a microscope to Harvard. A third Thomas Hollis (1720–1774) was also a benefactor to Harvard.

*HUNTER, ROBERT (d. 1734). Versatile royal governor of New York and New Jersey who fought in the battle of Blenheim and compiled a distinguished military record. As governor of New York he managed to heal a number of feuds inherited from the Leisler administration. With Joseph Dudley he set up a postal express system between Boston and Albany. A writer as well, he befriended Swift, contributed to the *Tatler*, and wrote the farce *Androborus*, sometimes called the first American play.

*HUTCHINSON, THOMAS (1675–1739). Boston merchant and councillor, Cotton Mather's landlord. He owned the house in Ship Street that was rented for Mather at the charge of the North Church in 1715. Mather called him a "gracious and generous landlord" and requited him by looking after his son, the future governor, at Harvard.

*HUTCHINSON, WILLIAM (1683–1721; HC 1702). Selectman, Justice of the Peace in Boston, friend of the Sewalls. He succeeded Oliver Noyes in the House of Representatives and died during the smallpox crisis, shortly after Mather's letter to him.

JAMESON, WILLIAM (fl. 1689–1720). Blind and learned Presbyterian controversialist, lecturer on history at the University of Glasgow.

JURIN, JAMES (1684–1750). Wealthy London physician who studied at Leyden. F.R.S., secretary of the Society (1721–1727), and editor of volumes 31 to 34 of the *Transactions*. A Latin scholar and one of the most learned men of his day, he experimented with motion, the system of fluxions, and the specific gravity of the blood, and also wrote on optics.

KING, SIR PETER (1669–1734). A mainstay of the Whig party in parliament. He defended William Whiston during his heresy trials and wrote histories of the primitive church and of the Apostles Creed.

LACY, JOHN (b. 1664). English pseudo-prophet, wealthy member of Calamy's congregation at Westminster.

*LEVERETT, JOHN (1662–1724; HC 1680). Speaker of the House, member of the Council, judge of the probate court, president of Harvard, F.R.S., a favorite of Governor Dudley's. A religious liberal, Leverett supported the Brattle Street Church. In 1707 he was unanimously chosen president of Harvard by a corporation made up largely of his friends, to Cotton Mather's dismay. As president he introduced the first college club and periodical. Mather considered him the "pretended president" but called upon him for favors. Toward the end of his life he came under public attack and died in considerable debt.

MATHER, ATHERTON (1663–1734). Mather's cousin in Suffield, Connecticut.

*MATHER, INCREASE (1639–1723; HC 1656). Cotton Mather's father, born in Dorchester, Massachusetts. After taking his M.A. at Trinity College, Dublin, he preached in England and, upon returning home, at the Second Church in Boston. His first wife, who was also his stepsister, was Mary (or Maria) Cotton, the daughter of John Cotton of Boston.

When Randolph tried to arrest him, Increase hid in the Charlestown house of Col. Philips, whose daughter became Cotton Mather's second wife. Once in London he preached, met eminent English divines, promoted a union between Presbyterians and Congregationalists, and became friendly with Robert Boyle and with Richard Baxter, who dedicated a work to him. He had several interviews with King James and with William and Mary. When it became obvious that the old charter would not be restored, he tried to obtain concessions in the new charter: he prevented Plymouth from being annexed to New York and got the privilege of nominating the new governor. Impoverished by having had to pay much of his own expenses, he returned to New England in 1692 with the new governor, Sir William Phips. During his absence his son Cotton, who had been settled as his colleague in May, 1684, took over most of his duties.

Increase shared his son's enemies—supporters of the old charter, the Brattle group, and the Dudleys. These made it impossible for him to continue as president of Harvard unless he neglected his church and went to live in Cambridge. He also shared his son's interests, temperament, and theology: he championed the inoculation, leaned toward Presbyterianism, reputedly spent sixteen hours a day in his study, and wrote about one hundred and thirty books and pamphlets, plus dozens of prefaces and contributions to other books.

*MATHER, INCREASE, JR. (1699–1724). Cotton Mather's scapegrace son, drowned at sea. Several of Mather's sermons deal with him, notably *The Words of Understanding* (1724) and *Tela Praevisa*

(1724). Mather Byles's daughter said that she read the latter forty-four times.

MATHER, MRS. SAMUEL (nee Townsend). The wife of Samuel Mather, below. She belonged to an old Oxfordshire family. Sir Henry Ashurst wrote to Increase Mather that by marrying her "your son hath a handsome good woman, and a considerable fortune." She and Samuel had seven daughters.

MATHER, SAMUEL (1674–1733; HC 1690). Cotton Mather's brother, the first Congregational minister in Witney, near Oxford, England.

MAYHEW, ZACHEUS. One of several members of the Mayhew family who acted as legal counsellors to the Indians on Martha's Vineyard. He also acted as an intermediary between the Indians and the Commissioners of the New England Company, of which Mather was one. Mayhew served in these capacities at least from 1717 to 1724.

MICO, JOHN (d. 1718). Prominent Boston merchant. In 1700 an anonymous tract, *Gospel Order Revived* (perhaps by Benjamin Colman), was published in New York in response to Increase Mather's *Order of the Gospel* (1700). The author charged that he was forced to publish in New York because Increase controlled the Boston presses. In a rebuttal issued by the Boston printer Bartholomew Green, Cotton Mather denied the charge. A further document issued by some Boston merchants again insisted that the Mathers prevented the printing. Mico was among the signers of this document.

*MILLAR, ROBERT (1672–1752). Theologian and minister in Paisley, Scotland. His collected works, in eight volumes, appeared in 1789.

NEIL (or NEAL), DANIEL (1678–1743). English historian and minister, a schoolmate of Isaac Watts. In 1720 he published a *History of New England.*

NEWMAN, HENRY (1670–1743). Secretary of the S.P.C.K. from 1708–1743, agent in England for New Hampshire and for Harvard.

NICOLS (or NICHOLS), JOHN. A minister named John Nichols is mentioned a few times in Sewall's diary.

NOTTINGHAM, DANIEL FINCH, SECOND EARL OF (1647–1730). Tory, later Whig, leader in Parliament, very popular with the clergy, F.R.S., author of a widely read attack on Whistonian Arianism. In 1714 he was made president of the King's Council, with a seat in the cabinet.

NOYES, OLIVER (1675–1721; HC 1695). Physician, politician, real estate speculator, leader in the forming of the Brattle Street Church.

After his first wife died he married the daughter of Sewall's Madam Winthrop.

*"PAIN, MR." Possibly Thomas Paine (1694–1757; HC 1717), father of Robert Treat Paine and minister at Weymouth.

PARKER, DANIEL. Like Zacheus Mayhew, above, an intermediary between the commissioners for the New England Company and the Indians on Martha's Vineyard.

PARSONS, JOSEPH (1671–1740; HC 1697). Preached at Farmington and New Lebanon, Connecticut, but created trouble in both places by his talebearing and slander.

PENHALLOW, SAMUEL (1665–1726). Merchant, judge, and historian who came to Charlestown, Mass., in 1686 with Charles Morton. He desired to enter the ministry and preach to the Indians, but gave it up and moved to Portsmouth, New Hampshire. One of Cotton Mather's closest friends.

PETIVER (or PETTIVER), JAMES (1663–1718). English botanist, entomologist, and apothecary, F.R.S.

POLLOCK, SIR JOHN MAXWELL, LORD (1648–1732). Strict Scottish Presbyterian. Robert Wodrow, a distant relative, lived with him in his youth and preached in Pollock's parish of Eastwood.

*PRAT (or PRATT), PETER. Perhaps the son of Peter Pratt of Lyme, Connecticut. Sewall a number of times mentions going to "Pratt's chamber."

PRINCE, NATHAN (1698–1748; HC 1718). Grandson of Governor Thomas Hinckley, brother-in-law of Peter Thacher. Prince was a schoolmaster at Bristol, then at Plymouth, then (1722) minister at Nantucket and Yarmouth. In 1723 he was recalled to Cambridge and, something of a mathematician and scientist, appointed a tutor at Harvard. One of his pupils was Mather Byles.

PRINCE, THOMAS (1687–1758). Theologian, scholar, and bibliophile, who was very close to the Mathers. He wrote A Chronological History of New England (1736) and was very active during the Great Awakening.

REINOLDS (or REYNOLDS), THOMAS (1667?–1727). Presbyterian minister in Little Eastcheap, England, studied in Geneva and under Herman Witsius in Utrecht. He published a funeral sermon on Mrs. Clissold that the Mathers particularly liked and gave to their children to read. It was reprinted in Boston with an introduction by Increase Mather.

RICHARDS, JOHN (1641?–1694). Judge of the Supreme Court, member of Mather's church, and one of the witchcraft trial judges.

*RUCK, JOHN (b. before 1662). Merchant, member of Mather's congregation, related to the Hutchinsons. He owned a warehouse in Boston, where he was a selectman and an overseer for the poor.

SAFFIN, JOHN (1626–1710). Merchant, lawyer, poet, assistant judge, councillor in Boston and later in Bristol, Rhode Island.

SALTONSTALL, GURDON (1666–1724; HC 1684). Minister at New London and a celebrated preacher until in December, 1707, he was chosen to succeed Fitz-John Winthrop as governor of Connecticut. He was annually re-elected for as long as he lived. Mather wrote a funeral sermon on him, *Decus ac Tumen* (1724).

SALTONSTALL, MARY (MRS. GURDON) (c. 1665–1730). Third wife of the governor of Connecticut, patron of Cotton Mather's.

*SEWALL, SAMUEL (1652–1730; HC 1671). Merchant, judge, diarist. Born in England, Sewall came to Boston at nine, was a classmate of Edward Taylor's at Harvard, and was chosen tutor at Harvard in 1673. From 1681 to 1684 he managed the colony's printing press. He served on the Council from 1686 to 1725, when he declined reelection. In 1692 Governor Phips appointed him one of the special commissioners to try the cases of witchcraft. Later he publicly regretted his role at the trials and, a fairly liberal jurist, took stands against capital punishment for counterfeiting and other harsh laws. In 1718 he succeeded Wait-Still Winthrop as chief justice of the Superior Court. Sewall wrote on slavery, prophecy, and other subjects, and recorded the life of Boston between 1674 and 1729 in his informative but intimate *Diary*.

SEWALL, STEPHEN (1657–1725). Samuel Sewall's brother, clerk of the special court of oyer and terminer at Salem.

SHUTE, SAMUEL (1662–1742). Colonial governor of Massachusetts, appointed in 1716 and succeeded by William Burnet; Mather's favorite governor.

*SLOANE, SIR HANS (1660–1753). British physician and naturalist, president of the Royal Society from 1727 to 1740. His collection of plant specimens, books, and manuscripts became the basis of the British Museum.

SQUIRE (or SQUIRES), JOHN (c. 1685–1758). Minister of Forres, Scotland, who visited America in 1715 and reported his distaste for the country to Robert Wodrow.

STIRLING, JOHN (1654–1727). Scottish preacher and principal of the College of Glasgow, intimate friend of Robert Wodrow, with whom he conducted services at Eastwood.

STOUGHTON, WILLIAM (c. 1631–1701; HC 1650). After taking his M.A. at Oxford, Stoughton returned to New England in 1662 as a commissioner for the United Colonies. He was a close friend of Joseph Dudley, who in July, 1686, appointed him head of the courts, where he remained during Dudley's presidency. When the courts were reorganized in March, 1687, Dudley was made chief justice, Stoughton judge-assistant. Governor Phips made him chief justice of the witchcraft trials in 1692.

*THACHER, PETER (1677–1739; HC 1696). Minister at Weymouth who in 1719 was approached about becoming minister of the New North Church in Boston. Bitterly divided on Thacher, the New North ratified his selection by a majority of one vote, apparently that of John Webb, below. A quarrel developed between the stricter Congregationalists and Mather and his quasi-Presbyterians. The Mathers repudiated Thacher, tried to obstruct his election, and stayed away from his installment ceremony held at Webb's house in January, 1720. The ceremony itself, one spectator wrote, was like a "bear garden": the opposition tried to forcibly prevent Thacher's installment, but Webb led him out a back gate. Pamphlets appeared for and against him, and the opposition minority withdrew to form their own church, the New Brick.

*VAUGHAN, GEORGE (1676–1724; HC 1696). Businessman, born in Portsmouth, New Hampshire. In 1707 Vaughan was appointed a judge of the Court of Common Pleas. He supported Dudley and opposed the Mason claims to New Hampshire lands, which in July, 1708, he was sent to England to fight. In 1715 he was appointed lieutenant-governor of New Hampshire but was unable to get along with Shute, who in 1717, with the Council's consent, suspended him.

WALLER, RICHARD (d. 1714). Secretary of the Royal Society from 1687 to 1709 and 1710 to 1714.

WALROND, HENRY (fl. 1715). English divine who tried to help Mather publish the Biblia Americana in England.

WATTS, ISAAC (1674–1748). Liberal Calvinist, one of the most popular writers of the day.

*WEBB (or WEB), JOHN (1687–1750; HC 1708). Senior pastor for eighteen years at the New North Church with Peter Thacher, above. Cotton Mather's relation with him ran to extremes. He was ordained by Mather, whom he joined against Dudley. He supported Mather on the inoculation. Yet when Mather entrusted to him his nasty letter to Joseph Parsons, Webb read it to a friend. (By the next year Mather had forgiven the indiscretion.) Again in 1721 Webb (and Thacher) displeased the Mathers by ordaining ruling elders in their church.

*"WENDEL, MR." Probably Jacob Wendell (1691–c.1761). A Dutch merchant, born in Albany. As a youth he entered the counting house of John Mico, above, who trained him in business. A friend of Samuel Sewall, one of the governor's council, and a colonel in the Boston regiment. One of his descendants is Oliver Wendell Holmes.

*WIGGLESWORTH, MICHAEL (1631–1705; HC 1651). Minister and poet, born in England, who came to New England in 1638. He was a fellow and tutor at Harvard, and later settled as minister at Malden, where he studied and practised medicine, in continually feeble health. Mather characterized Wigglesworth as a "little, feeble, shadow of a man," although in the *Magnalia* he paid tribute to him as a great preacher. Increase Mather wrote to Wigglesworth to try to dissuade him from marrying his second wife, a serving maid.

WILLIAMS, DANIEL (1643?–1716). English divine, founder of the famous Dr. Williams' Library in London. Mather used his life as an example of remarkable youthful piety in *Token for the Children of New-England* (1700).

WHITTINGHAM, RICHARD (c. 1663–1730; HC 1689). In his diary Mather mentions that this "hopeful young gentleman" prayed with him in his study before going to England. He was the brother of Mrs. Saltonstall, above; apparently he died in Boston, England.

WINTHROP, JOHN (1681–1747; HC 1700). Cotton Mather's very close friend, born in Boston of an extremely distinguished family, the only son of Wait-Still Winthrop. His grandfather was a governor of Connecticut; his great-grandfather was Governor Winthrop of Massachusetts.

WINTHROP, WAIT-STILL (1642–1717). Father of the above, chief justice of Massachusetts, major-general, brother of a governor of Connecticut, son of John Winthrop (1606–1676), grandson of the first governor of Massachusetts. He was a close friend of Sir Henry Ashurst. Mather dedicated *Memorable Providences* (1689) to him and composed a verse epitaph and a funeral sermon upon his death.

WODROW, ROBERT (1679–1734). Learned Scottish minister and ecclesiastical historian, a sort of Scottish Mather. At Mather's death Wodrow noted in his *Analecta* that "he and his father kept life in the Independent interest in New England," although he considered Cotton's style "peculiar."

WOODBRIDGE, TIMOTHY (1656–1732; HC 1675). Member of the Synod at Saybrook in 1708 from which came the Saybrook Platform. Minister in Hartford, Connecticut, and for a time rector of Yale. He strenuously opposed moving the school to New Haven.

*WOODSIDE, JAMES (fl. 1720). Irish minister who preached to the Indians in Maine. Sewall mentions that Woodside and Mather dined with the governor. Woodside was released from his commission in June, 1720, when his health failed.

WOODWARD, JOHN (1665–1728). English geologist and physician, professor of physic (i.e. medicine) at Gresham College, F.R.S.

YALE, ELIHU (1649–1721). Official of the East India Company and philanthropist who gave his name and money to Yale College.

Index